THE PATRIOTS' REVOLUTION

The Patriots' Revolution

HOW EASTERN EUROPE
TOPPLED COMMUNISM
AND WON ITS FREEDOM

Mark Frankland

Ivan R. Dee
Chicago

Library of Congress Cataloging-in-Publication Data:
Frankland, Mark, 1934–
    The patriots' revolution : how Eastern Europe toppled communism and won its freedom / Mark Frankland.
        p.   cm.
    Includes index.
    ISBN 0-929587-80-4 (alk. paper)
    1. Europe, Eastern—History—1945–1989.   2. Communism—Europe, Eastern.   I. Title.
DJK50.F73   1992
947.085—dc20   91-26403

Contents

Acknowledgements

Most of the material for this book was gathered while living in or travelling through East Europe, although it has been supplemented from the press both Eastern and Western. I have also depended on the BBC Monitoring Service's invaluable Summary of World Broadcasts; and often referred to the research papers of Radio Free Europe. Illona Gazdag, *The Observer*'s assistant in Budapest, was irreplaceable, and a tireless and resourceful guide to Hungarian mysteries. Isolated by its language, Hungary nevertheless has in the *New Hungarian Quarterly* a unique publication which fought to keep up high standards under Communist restraints and, now free of them, deserves the widest audience.

I am very grateful to Donald Trelford, the Editor of *The Observer*, who has made it possible for me to travel widely over many years and to take the time to write this book. I owe much to colleagues and friends who have both deep knowledge and affection for the region, among them Neal Ascherson, David Binder, Eric Bourne, Judy Dempsey, Timothy Garton Ash, Disa Hastad, Henry Kamm, Richard Swartz and Michael Simmons.

I shall always be grateful to two friends in particular. In Warsaw Gustaw Gottesman has been a wise and patient mentor. He has helped many British people come to understand and appreciate Poland. In my case he was ready to put up with a great deal of ignorance; my debt to him is enormous. Dessa Trevisan, long the East Europe correspondent of *The Times*, having taken a suspicious look at me when I was very raw, decided to persevere in my education for which I am immensely thankful. She has a rare combination of knowledge, passion and insight; and limitless generosity in sharing them with others.

I am also grateful to various publishers for permission to quote extracts from:

'Lament for Smederevo' from *The Slavs Beneath Parnassus* by Miodrag Pavlovic. Selected poems translated by Bernard Johnson (Angel Books, London, and New Rivers Press, St Paul, Minnesota, 1985).

If Not Now, When? by Primo Levi, translated by William Weaver (Simon and Schuster Inc., 1985).

'A Short Fairy Tale' by Stanislaw Grochowiak in *Postwar Polish Poetry*, edited by Czeslaw Milosz (Doubleday and Company Inc., 1965).

'The Wonder Castle' by Gyula Illyes in *Modern Hungarian Poetry*, edited by Miklos Vajda, (Corvina Press, Budapest, with Columbia University Press, 1977).

'Song of the Balkan Peninsula' from *High Albania* by Edith Durham (Virago, 1985).

A Note on Spelling and Definitions

Most of the languages of East Europe use systems of diacritical marks that have little in common between them. Crucial both for meaning and pronunciation they are nevertheless an additional stumbling block for those who are neither linguists nor native speakers, and for that reason I have chosen the imperfect solution of leaving them out in the spelling of proper names. Accents are used, however, in quotations of phrases or sentences in any of the languages, as is the familiar *Umlaut* whenever appropriate in German names. Perhaps the divide between East and West Europe will be truly overcome when we can pronounce Poland's Łódź and Hungary's Kiskőrös with as little trouble as Lübeck or the Rhone.

Not the least mischievous achievement of the old regimes of East Europe was to muddle language and imprison words in their own self-serving definitions. In this book 'socialism' is used to mean what it meant in the old Soviet bloc, a system under which the state owns all or most of the means of production and there is a one-party dictatorship. That others did and do not think this is 'socialism' was beside the point for those who lived in East Europe. Similarly 'Communist' is used to describe the ruling parties and their members, even though the Poles (Polish United Workers' Party), East Germans (Socialist Unity Party) and Hungarians (Hungarian United Socialist Workers' Party) avoided the word. The people under their rule called them 'Communist', which is what they were, and it is pedantic to use official names that were chiefly meant to fool the unwary.

INTRODUCTION

The Ghosts Return

They are like characters from one's distant youth, or from a play seen long ago and barely remembered. There is the Pole, devout in the defence of national honour; the moody Hungarian, preoccupied with the survival of his culture and his race; the Czech democrat, straightforward yet with a knack for slyness. The traveller in East Europe rubs his eyes. How can such figures from the past reappear in countries that half a century ago were mangled in Hitler's war, then swamped by the Soviet flood? How did it happen that the new Communist world about which so many boastful words were spoken could vanish so quickly to reveal this new but apparently familiar cast of characters?

Communism was supposed to have produced a new breed of East European; an industrial proletariat swollen by peasants from the land; peasants that remained cured of the age-old desire for private ownership of land by assignment to state or collective farms; a progressive intelligentsia loyal to socialism. Most important among these new types were the leaders, who not only talked but often looked like their Soviet patrons, which was not surprising for frequently enough many of them were peasants propelled to power by supposedly proletarian revolutions. More often than not these men did their best to rule their countries in the Soviet manner. In the early years, while Stalin was still alive, they conducted purges and show trials, and backed them up when necessary with prison camps and executions. They used the same violent language of public debate, and observed the same tedious but menacing public rituals. Inheriting societies many of whose structural bones had been broken by war, they themselves broke the remaining sound limbs and shoved the lot into Soviet splints. Polish men still kissed the hands of women. East Germans retained their native diligence.

But as social beings they were categorised and organised in ways that had little to do with their respective national pasts, and everything to do with Stalin's tested system of social and political control. Priests were transformed into propagandists for 'peace'. Boy scouts and girl guides became the Komsomol in toggles but without Baden-Powell hats. Old political parties with honourable and not so honourable traditions were applied as make-up to the grim features of one-party rule. Trade unionists doubled as factory cops.

This new world in the East seemed frighteningly different to people in the West – the Iron Curtain helped see to that. Inhabitants of the British Isles, accustomed to living behind a strip of water, were least likely of all Europeans to appreciate the violence that this new frontier had done to the Continent. For Britons in the first years after the war to cross the Channel to France was achievement enough. There can have been few people in London or Edinburgh who greatly missed not having easy passage to Budapest and Warsaw. Wrong about Hitler he may have been, but Neville Chamberlain was probably right in the eyes of many of his fellow countrymen about Czechoslovakia being a faraway place. After the war, and until very recently, a Briton driving through West Germany and Austria could feel that the Iron Curtain that prevented him going further east was as natural a barrier as the Channel. And so in time it came to seem to many young West Europeans, too, though not to their elders, or to any young person with a scrap of historical knowledge.

That ingenious line of posts, watchtowers and wire was in fact as savage a blow to the natural order as the diversion of a river or the amputation of a leg. It challenged geography, history and economics, and at first seemed to challenge them successfully. The border between East and West acquired the inevitability of a natural phenomenon. It was as though a new mountain range had been thrown up which, together with the Alps, Carpathians and Pyrenees, would finally pin the restless peoples of Europe into their allotted space. This new frontier erased previous history. To the east of it, men put red stars on top of ancient buildings and by this simple act seemed to turn stone witnesses to a European past into props for a future scripted in Moscow. Behind this new border traditional economic links, plain from a glance at any map of Europe's railways, roads and rivers, were broken off with the wilfulness of a little boy re-routing the track for his toy trains.

The Soviet undertaking in East Europe was so audacious that it persuaded many people that it would succeed. And in time the division of the Continent became almost convenient to the Western half because, in the end, it brought security. Once the worst of the Cold War was over, and arms talks between the superpowers had reduced the likelihood of any but accidental nuclear war, the West could appreciate that the Iron Curtain and the *Pax Sovietica* that reigned behind it had calmed a once dangerously unstable continent. The incorporation of East Europe into the Soviet empire had obliged the West to maintain its own unity which in turn fostered the conditions for unimagined prosperity. The Iron Curtain had also cut the West free of the poorest, most disputatious and disputed part of the Continent. The Germans had at last been tamed: tied down in two different alliances, they could no longer move anywhere or grow overwhelmingly powerful. National conflicts that for generations tempted the peoples of East Europe to seek advantage in every international crisis had been frozen. For the first time in two centuries Poland looked secure within its borders and therefore was, in this sense at least, no cause of worry to its friends. Passionate, insoluble disputes – the problem of Transylvania, the Macedonian question – appeared to have become exotic chapters in history books that few bothered to read any more.

There were others in the West who had always welcomed this new East Europe as an antidote to what they disliked in their own societies. Industrial Europe had long dreamed of socialism, without being entirely sure what it would be like. Many people had soaked up enough Marx to suppose socialism was inevitable. They had wanted to believe Moscow when it claimed in 1917 to be bringing it to the Soviet Union, and a good many continued to believe it in spite of evidence, from the 1930s on, of Stalin's crimes. The Soviet domination of East Europe after 1945 served to strengthen such people's belief. Was it not progress, albeit heavily disguised as the Soviet army, that was moving inexorably westwards? Far from being a break in East Europe's history the Soviet occupation was seen as the start of a new wave of history that grew organically out of its past. This wave that had started in the East was moving towards the West and could not be stopped. The language of socialism made the belief easier to sustain. However you defined it socialism was usually taken to mean the public ownership of the means of production. Had not the people of East Europe claimed their nations' wealth for their own? Mills and factories had been nationalised, stock exchanges turned into museums. The aristocrats and the church had lost their great estates. Money, instead of dominating men, had become the docile creature of central planners who themselves surely symbolised the most rational government mankind had yet known. There were blemishes, of course, but wasn't it enough to be going on with? If this wasn't socialism, what on earth was?

What came to be called socialism's mistakes were excused by these Western admirers as the errors of a late-born child, all the more easily indulged because so long waited for. As time passed, though, believers dropped away. Some who applauded the crushing of the Hungarian uprising in 1956 (why should the Esterhazys get their land back?) could not stomach the 1968 Soviet invasion of Czechoslovakia. But even as late as 1980 part of the West European Left could not understand why socialist Poland needed this rebel trade union called Solidarity. The visitors' books of trade-union guesthouses throughout the Soviet bloc continued to fill up with the names of well-known brothers from the West.

In truth East Europe was a confusing place, like one of those puzzle pictures in which faces are hidden in a landscape of trees and flowers. The more you studied it the more these unexpected faces – survivors from the pre-socialist landscape – stared back at you. There is, of course, an element of illusion in all revolutions. Read an account of the Russian Revolution of 1917 or what Hungarians may now call their revolution of 1956 and you find, in spite of their very different purposes, the same belief that everyone and everything can change, or be changed, overnight. Revolutions deny the stubbornness of men and things, which is why men dare to make them, and also why they often come to grief. But in spite of their illusions the Communist revolutionaries in East Europe were as thorough as could be. They brought about the required transfer of power and pulverised the old ruling groups so that they could no longer present a coherent challenge to the new order. And yet there were things the Communists could not capture and could not destroy. On the one hand there was the new rulers' immense and ruthlessly applied power; on the other recalcitrant human beings strengthened in their stubbornness by national memories and traditions. How the latter held out and eventually triumphed is part of the story of this book. How great that victory was can only be judged if one remembers what overwhelming power the Communists possessed in the first years after their victory in East Europe.

I belong to the generation that grew up when the Soviet empire seemed at its most threatening. News of the outbreak of the Korean War – Stalin's work, one had no doubt – came during a school break and made us pause in our usual fight to get at the tray of Chelsea buns, as though we understood that some of us would grow up to fight in it. Arriving in 1952 at Victoria Barracks, Portsmouth, for national service in the navy our group of Temporary Probationary Coders (Special) was lectured by the commanding officer on the imminence of war with the Soviet Union. We were about to learn Russian so we, linguistically at least, would be in its front line. Stalin's death we learned of one afternoon after classes at the School of Slavonic Studies in London. A newspaperman at Tottenham Court Road station sung out the news and held up the evening paper for us to read the stark headline. No one supposed it made our conquest of Russian grammar less necessary. Two years later I found myself in East Europe.

It was the summer of 1955. A group of students at Cambridge, wondering how to spend the long vacation, heard there was to be something called a World Youth Festival in Warsaw. None of us knew what a youth festival was, which was not surprising for this was one in a series of ersatz events designed by Moscow to show that it was loved by young people all the world over. But it was terribly cheap and that, in the days before charter flights and package tours, was enough. Of Poland we knew little too, though I had come across émigré Poles. That was the striking thing about them; they were émigrés. Poland had tossed them aside, as a bolting horse throws off its rider, and they seemed to have given up all hope of remounting. One of these Poles was a count who that summer was wooing a divorcee friend of my family. He showed not the slightest interest in our Polish travel plans. We might have been going to a country he had scarcely heard of. There was another Pole we knew, a fellow undergraduate, who had the same famous name as my family's acquaintance. He spoke English with a drawl, and had once been spotted wearing a bowler hat on King's Parade. As far as we could tell he had completely freed himself from Poland to pursue other passions. Extremely good-looking, he liked to invite girls to tea in his rooms and appear before them dressed only in a jock-strap.

I had come across a third Pole while learning Russian at the

School of Slavonic Studies. Teacher of grammar to our class of Midshipmen (Special) – we had been promoted on leaving Portsmouth – he had been badly wounded flying alongside the Royal Air Force in the war, and survived thanks to skin grafts and an artificial arm. Later I began to wonder whether he did this tedious job in the hope that one day we might use our skill in a battle to free Poland. Perhaps he imagined us monitoring Soviet radio messages while the British navy released landing craft onto the white beaches of Poland's Baltic coast, in which case one could understand his insistence that we correctly distinguish between the perfective and imperfective forms of Russian verbs. But these thoughts only came later; at that time he was just another émigré. Straight-backed in spite of his wounds, brown hair *en brosse*, scratching a scarred cheek with the leather-covered fingers of his artificial hand, he seemed a man without a country and with precious little future.

It was hard to connect these men with the Warsaw we woke up in one Sunday morning after a slow train journey across Europe in a wooden-seated third-class carriage. The city was being rebuilt on ruins so complete that there had been talk of abandoning it and starting a new capital elsewhere, and it seemed to us as much a triumph of Communist will as the Festival itself. Large parts of old Warsaw had already been reconstructed from the rubble. By rebuilding Nowy Swiat, Krakowskie Przedmiesce and the Old Town the Communists gave the appearance of having claimed possession of the city's past and tamed it. These old-new streets and squares were museums in which history was safely locked up for display. Communist will-power achieved another, more modest, miracle with our incohesive group. Aside from a party of young British Communists we were only inquisitive young people, and yet before long we had been turned into a progressive British delegation. Together with more genuine delegations from other countries we marched up and down the Warsaw streets and across the Poniatowski Bridge to attend rallies in the sports stadium on the other Praga side of the Vistula. What we did there was mostly chant 'Peace and Friendship', the motto of this and all succeeding World Youth Festivals. To the unsuspecting onlooker we were peace-loving youth, flesh and blood evidence that in the West, too, life was developing as Marx and Lenin had predicted.

These goings-on amused rather than annoyed us. But there was also something awesome about them, as there was about the newly built Russo-Gothic skyscraper, a present from Stalin to Poland, in whose shadow the Festival's activities took place. Later one would see this so-called Palace of Culture for what it was – a gift of incomparable malice. At that time it impressed as a barbarian act of will, standing like a great Soviet boot in the heart of Warsaw to proclaim the durability of the new order. No one who saw it could doubt that the Communists had come to stay.

Over the years this impression of a Poland taken firmly in hand by Communism began to change. It was as though the mind had snapped a photograph that needed time to develop. The Festival with its marching and slogans, its Communist organisers and the unpardonable skyscraper, faded in the memory while other events and people came into sharper focus. There was the morning of our first day in Warsaw. After the shock of an East European breakfast of bread, cheese and pickled cucumber we went outside the school we had been billeted in to find a crowd of young Poles waiting for us. Without asking what we wanted to do they led us to the centre of the city and to our surprise and the young British Communists' horror brought us to a church. It stood at the end of a broad, dog-legged street of reconstructed palaces and churches, echoes of a neo-classical past washed in pale northern light. The young Poles led us up steps to a porch before the church door where a large statue of Christ carrying the Cross leant out into the street below. We went inside. Priests were celebrating mass. The church was full. Men and women unable to find a seat knelt on the stone floor as easily as if it were a pillow of velvet.

The Polish Communists were at that time still trying to cut the Catholic Church out of Poland as a surgeon removes a tumour. In 1950 the Government had confiscated all Church property. Now, five years later, it was still throwing priests into prison. For the last three years even the Primate of Poland, Cardinal Stefan Wyszynski, had been confined to a monastery in the distant Bieszczady Mountains. By bringing us to this church only recently risen from the ruins our new Polish friends were showing us that even the Communists with their phenomenal will-power had not yet succeeded in tugging out Poland's Catholic roots. The world outside Poland might be impressed by the appearance of 'progressive' priests who were ready to cooperate with the Communists, or by the fellow-travelling Catholic organisation called Pax, for which the Soviet

NKVD had picked a Polish ex-Fascist as leader. It was less easy to mislead the Poles themselves with such tricks.

Another image that came only later into focus was that of a bronze medal that lies today on my bookshelves. Its reverse side bears two dates: 19.10.1813 and 19.10.1913. The front depicts a handsome, melancholy-looking man wearing a uniform that buttons at the neck. His nose is aquiline. A long cleft chin rests on the edge of the tall collar. He has brushed his hair forward over the brow in the Napoleonic manner.

'Prince Jozef Poniatowski', says the inscription, and the letters continue like a halo round his head: '*Bóg mi powierzył honor Polaków. Bogu co oddam.*' 'God entrusted me with the honour of the Poles. To God I give it back.' I cannot remember who gave me the medal, though there may be a connection with an evening spent drinking vodka mixed with cherry brandy out of tumblers. Neither at school nor at Cambridge were we taught to search British history for lessons practical or inspirational for the present day. People had favourite periods. Some preferred Cavaliers, others Roundheads. There was a natural division between enthusiasts for Burke and for Tom Paine. But to look in the past for a map to the present would have seemed ridiculous, making as little sense as retreating down a hill when you are already approaching the top. Being English was poor preparation for understanding that few nations, and certainly not a single one in East Europe, see their history as a gradual ascent to ever sunnier plateaux. It needed time to read the medal's message in the way its unremembered giver surely hoped it one day would be.

Jozef Poniatowski, nephew to Stanislaw Augustus, the last king of Poland, like many other Poles threw in his lot with Napoleon in the hope of liberating his own country after it had been swallowed up by Russia, Austria and Prussia at the end of the eighteenth century. He was a great general, leading the advance guard of Napoleon's army in the march on Moscow, and commanding its rear throughout the perilous retreat. Trapped and wounded at the Battle of the Nations at Leipzig, Poniatowski realised that the Polish cavalry under his command was doomed and chose honourable defeat. He rode his horse into the middle of the river Elster and drowned. He died on 19 October 1813. Poland still did not exist as an independent country when the bronze medal was struck a hundred years later. It was meant as both memorial and inspiration.

Most East Europeans see history as unfinished business. It is as though the centuries have bequeathed them a pile of examination papers that have been failed – albeit often, as in Poniatowski's case, heroically – by previous generations. Each new generation must take another shot at the old problems in the hope of conquering them one day. Seen in this light the history of East Europe since 1945 is less of an aberration. The struggle for independence that developed throughout the nineteenth century and was won, briefly, between the two World Wars, had to be taken up again in the second half of the twentieth, long before the old exam papers had been forgotten. When in 1989 Hungarians were free again to take to the streets of Budapest to celebrate the anniversary of the Revolution of 1848 their demands echoed point for point those drawn up then by the poet Sandor Petoefi.

Determination to continue the struggle of ancestors was the hidden message in our visit to the Church of the Holy Cross and in the gift of the bronze medal. Had I understood it at the time it would have seemed a desperate boast. What Pole, even, could have then foreseen that a mere thirty-two years later another plaque would go up on the same church's walls to rival the one that marks the urn containing Chopin's heart? This new plaque is on the western wall, by the Christ bent beneath the Cross. It records a meeting in the church in 1987 between Pope John Paul II and the Polish intelligentsia which took place during Karol Wojtyla's third papal visit to his country. His first visit, a Polish writer suggested, had been 'Poland's second baptism', proof more powerful than even Poles can have dared hope for of the durability of Poland's marriage to the Catholic Church. The legacy of Jozef Poniatowski and others like him would also emerge in a thousand different ways. Some candidates at the elections in June 1989 used a three-word motto in their campaign propaganda – *Bóg, Honor, Ojczyzna*. That was Poniatowski's motto. After four decades of Communism Poles were again being asked to respond publicly to the cry of 'God, Honour, Fatherland'.

The journey to Poland ended with another omen that we also needed Polish help to understand. We left the country on a train that would go south into Czechoslovakia and re-enter the West in Bavaria. Before crossing the first border we stopped at the Silesian city of Stalinogrod to be given lunch by local young people. It was meant to be the final celebration of the Youth Festival, but when we had eaten together and the train began to pull out of the station the young Poles lined up on the platform and chanted in unison 'Ka-to-wi-ce! Ka-to-wi-ce!'

Katowice was the town's old Polish name. To shout it aloud in public in 1955 bordered on treason against socialist Poland. Stalin might have been dead for two years but his successor Nikita Khrushchev had yet to make the secret speech that set off the first explosions under the dictator's granite reputation. The first of Poland's anti-Communist revolts, the Poznan riots in which seventy-four workers and policemen would die, was still a year away. There was only one person on the train who could properly appreciate the scene at the station of Stalinogrod-Katowice. Stash, a Pole still in his teens, had joined us in Warsaw with the intention of smuggling himself to the the West.

We had come across his elder brother Alex first. Alex was an early specimen of Soviet-bloc dissident. There was something of the wideboy in him and a great deal of what Stash, years later, would call the 'shit-raiser'. Alex regarded the Youth Festival as a marvellous harvest sent his way unwittingly by stupid Communists, and we were part of his catch. The brothers' father, a well-known journalist and diplomat, had died in a car crash which the family suspected might have been arranged by the Communist secret police. Their mother was convinced that their family background robbed the boys of any hope of a decent future in Poland and supported Stash's plan to escape.

Taller and easier-going than his brother, Stash was just as casually dismissive of the brave new world he was supposed to be living in. The first idea was that one of our group, of Stash's height but with only very approximately the same features, would give him his passport, engineer an invitation to stay behind when the rest of us left, and later declare his passport lost. This unoriginal plan was dropped, but not before Stash had dyed his hair black and made a large burn on his hand with a cigarette to imitate the passport owner's birthmark. Instead he just got on the train in Warsaw as though refusing to accept that he was locked up in Poland like the rest of his fellow countrymen. It was dangerous enough for him to stay on the train while we were in Poland, for his English was poor and there was the risk that one of the young Communists might turn him in. He was still in our carriage that evening as the train approached the Czech frontier. There are not many places to hide in a railway carriage. In some there is space under the seat cushions, but we were in third class again and sitting on wood. There are spaces, too, above the ceiling panels in train corridors but there was no way Stash could climb into one of those unobserved, and the border guards were anyhow equipped with little step-ladders which they mounted in order to poke around behind the panels. But the trains of forty years ago had luggage racks made of net which on long journeys could be turned into tolerable hammocks. A rug on top of the netting, then Stash (luckily as slim as he was tall), another covering over him and then a plucky girl pretending to be tired and ill – with such simple tricks, we discovered, was it possible to cross the frontiers of Stalin's empire.

The Polish frontier guard asked the girl to come down. We said she was not feeling well. Perhaps it was Polish gallantry; more likely we were saved by the illusion created by the sinister Festival we had attended. We were not potential body smugglers. We were progressive youth, friends of People's Poland. The guard, who was no older than us, hesitated and moved on. Our magical identity from the Festival and a little juggling with passports got us over the second border with almost as little trouble. As the train crossed into Germany Stash went into the corridor and danced.

It seemed a rare adventure, but it was nothing of the kind. Stash was an early link in a long, sad chain of escapees from Communist East Europe. In the following year, 1956, tens of thousands of Hungarians would leave their country after the failure of their uprising. Twelve years later it would be the turn of Czechoslovaks and also most of Poland's remaining Jews. This stream of refugees was at first taken as evidence of the victory of the new order. People like Stash left because there was no place for them and apparently never would be. The Communist rulers were pleased to see them go for it seemed safer to dump this human rubbish in the West than to store it at home. Nevertheless the new regimes still feared that the émigrés might be dangerous. Not for nothing did the Polish Government put a ban on the works of Joseph Conrad whose championing of fidelity even to a lost cause was seen as encouragement to anti-Communist resistance. The East European regimes kept close watch through their embassies in the West on émigré communities, and, in the case of Bulgaria, were prepared to kill outstanding or troublesome personalities among them as late as the 1980s. Czeslaw Kiszczak, a young officer in Polish military

intelligence sent to observe Britain's large Polish community after
the war, was to become a general and the mastermind of the martial
law imposed on Poland at the end of 1981. Eight years later, as
Minister of the Interior, Kiszczak would negotiate the return of
Solidarity to legality and so unwittingly prepare the way for the
final defeat of Communism in Poland. The paranoia over Conrad
had proved justified; a lost cause can become a winning one if
enough people remain faithful to it.

Ever since the Russian Revolution people had argued about
whether it was better to leave a Communist country or to stay.
There seemed greater strength in the argument of those who stayed
because so many of those who left continued to wonder whether
they had done the right thing. Pride in staying, whatever the price,
and scorn for those who left, was expressed by the Russian poet
Anna Akhmatova when, as an elderly woman, she looked back on
her life in the Soviet Union she had determined never to leave.

No, not under foreign skies,
Or under foreign wings' protection.
I was together with my people,
Where they, to their misfortune, were.

But as time passed it turned out – just as the Communists feared
– that many of the émigrés had not really gone away. Their faces
and the faces of an earlier type of Pole, Hungarian and Czech that
was also supposed to have vanished became plainer and plainer to
see in the puzzle picture of the supposedly new East Europe. The
Polish historian Adam Michnik was one of the first to understand
why. In Poland, too, where many educated men and women were
brought up by their families in a tradition of resistance, it was
natural to suppose that those intellectuals and artists who left Poland
were little better than traitors to the national cause. But Michnik
discovered that this emigration performed an important function.
It acted, he said, as the lungs through which Poland and the rest of
East Europe could draw in badly needed fresh, free air from the
outside world. Identities and values under assault from the Communists at home could be protected and developed abroad. In this way
East Europe lived two lives, one confined within its geographic
frontiers, the other spreading out over the great web of emigration
in West Europe and North America. Little magazines and struggling

printing presses developed so fast that by the 1980s no one doubted that the most important publishing houses of Czech literature were in Canada, not Prague. Even those exiles who seemed to have no use, or to be lost forever in the past, probably served a purpose because the ecology of an emigration, like that of a forest, is a complicated matter; a necessary mixture, perhaps, of the living and the dying. The Polish Government-in-exile in its 'castle' in London governed nothing at all; but its existence, however artificial and even comic, reminded people that the Communists had taken power unconstitutionally. The maimed pilot who taught us Russian grammar was part of this tangled émigré forest and so too were the pair of counts, the old one and the young, obscure though their function in it was to others and themselves.

Beginning in the 1970s a different sort of East European began to turn up in the West. Some stayed; others came to work for a while and then went home; the luckiest just popped across for the shopping. The governments of East Europe were less sure about the desirability of letting them go than they had been about losing the post-war refugees, but they had little choice. The regimes of East Europe were beginning to have intimations of the economic disaster that would eventually contribute so powerfully to driving them out of power. Over-awed by the continuing world revolution in economics and technology, and falling deeper into debt with the West, they knew that the Iron Curtain no longer performed the function they had expected of it. Far from being a protective wall around their socialist paradise it was becoming a shaming divide between decline and prosperity, with the East Europeans on the wrong side of it. Previously despised émigrés were transformed into desirable partners by the magic of hard currency. George Soros, a successful Hungarian-American financier, was allowed to set up a foundation in Budapest to repair in many ingenious ways the damage forty years' isolation had done to the country he abandoned as a young man. Polish businessmen returned to Warsaw from the West and, though hobbled by restrictions, were given a chance to show off the skills they had learned abroad.

Stash, too, went back. He was given a visa in the summer of 1979 for the Polish Pope's first visit home. We stood together one warm evening in Krakow outside the archbishop's palace while thousands of young Poles sang songs for the Pope who listened to them from a balcony, he as reluctant to go to bed as they to end their serenade.

Eleven years later Stash was married (for the second time) in the church of the Holy Visitation on Krakowskie Przedmiescie, close to where he met the British students who, without giving the matter much thought, helped him to leave Warsaw in 1955. Thirty-five years – forty-five if you count from the war's end – is the best part of a man or woman's life. They cannot be recovered any more than the wheel of history can be made to turn full circle. The familiar characters who have returned to East Europe are therefore not entirely familiar. It is an illusion to suppose that Poles, Hungarians or Romanians have thrown off their socialist masks to become exactly the people they were fifty years ago, as though nothing had happened in their countries. They may, like their ancestors, be patriots but they cannot be patriots in an identical mould. They can sing the same old songs but they will hear a different meaning in them. They have undergone a searing experience. Victims of the most ambitious and terrible revolution man has yet known, they are the proof that this revolution and the heavy bundle of ideas and hopes that fuelled it were flawed, that the devil's work emerged from what once had seemed a gift from heaven. No one knows what lasting effects this experience will have on the survivors and their countries. All we know is that they have fought free of that malign revolution with something like a revolution of their own. This revolution developed slowly and there is much that remains unclear about its many slow and spontaneous processes. Only the final dash for freedom in the remarkable year of 1989 took place entirely in the light. In this book I have tried to evoke moments in those earlier stages as well as the final dash itself, for the latter cannot be properly seen for what it was without remembering the former.

THE PATRIOTS' REVOLUTION

1

Flood

THE OLD WORLD

One summer shortly before the outbreak of the Second World War a young Hungarian poet called Gyula Illyes took a ride on the cogwheel railway that climbs up nearly eight hundred feet from Budapest's Varosmajor Park to the top of Szerchenyi Hill. Born the son of a poor farmhand on an estate in Western Hungary (Transdanubia, the Latin-loving Hungarians call it), talent and the support of an unusual family had won him an education that ended in several years of writing and study in Paris. Success, though, had not made him forget the poverty that he – and most Hungarian peasants – had grown up in, and it was with their judging eyes that he looked through the window of the train as it ground up the hillside that was thick with fine trees and handsome villas.

It was an ordinary working afternoon, yet people here were at their leisure. Two young women sunbathed on a flat roof. Cards were being dealt in the shadow of a walnut tree. As the train climbed higher the air became cooler and free of the dust that haunted the summer-tired city below.

It was as if, from the hell of the plain below us,
We were borne up from circle to circle
Into some present-day Turkish heaven.

Tennis balls flew over hedges. Girls laughed. A paunchy man in pyjamas and smoking a cigar looked the very figure of 'Property' as depicted by cartoonists in the Budapest left-wing newspapers of the day. Outdoor restaurants for which the hill was famous were getting ready to serve suppers that would cost an ordinary working man a week's wages.

The poet regrets that he sees no shepherd 'nonchalantly sipping iced pineapple'. There is no miner or baker, though they might have liked to discover what their 'creations are up to in the world'. The poet's only consolation is that he may survive to see this unjust world vanish. He imagines the day when

the marsh rises . . . to topple
the myriad towers and huge axle
of this glittering miracle
all coming to pass as in the old tale,
that 'grass grow not, nor stone remain on stone'.

Illyes vows to be an observer so that one day he can make a calm, impartial record 'of how life was before the flood'.

And the flood came. First there was the war. People died in huge numbers and cities were turned into ruins, but this was not the real flood. Dead soldiers leave behind wives and children, while ruins are made of stones and bricks that can be salvaged to put up something new or even recreate what was destroyed as the Poles did their capital Warsaw. The real flood, the flood that Illyes was expecting, came after the war, when the Communists imposed their power on Hungary and throughout East Europe. This flood swept away men and women like those the young poet saw that pre-war summer afternoon, but it carried off much more besides. Its waters threatened to swallow up the invisible landscape that every country must inhabit to survive: its image of itself, its moral traditions and those customs that, even when uncomprehendingly followed, pass on to new generations wisdom acquired over centuries by those that went before.

There were some people who from the very beginning understood the extent of this damage, but many did not, not least because of East Europe's recent past. East Europe before the flood had been colourful and struggling, brilliant and brutal. None of the countries that composed it had known independence for more than a hundred years, and some for very much less. All were born or recast in the reordering of the Continent at the end of the First World War. Poland emerged from one hundred and fifty years' partitioning among its three great neighbours, Austria, Prussia and Russia. Hungary, though it lost two-thirds of its territory in the process, was at last separated from the Austrian empire which also gave unwilling birth to Czechoslovakia. Bulgaria and Romania had escaped from the declining empire of the Turks only in the previous century. The very existence of these countries was taken to mark the end of European empires. As for the Soviet irruption into East Europe, optimists saw this as bringing a new life as purposeful and controlled as the waters of a giant reservoir that would cover up unjust and struggling societies. How much of what was now hidden beneath the waters of socialism deserved to be regretted? Not much was these people's answer, and they could call writers like Illyes in evidence.

Gyula Illyes was one of a group of Hungarian writers who before the war had concerned themselves with the troubles of their still predominantly peasant nation. In 1936 he published a book called *People of the Puszta* in which he used his own experiences to evoke and comment on a peasant world locked into a poverty that often came close to slavery. Two-thirds of the population of the Hungary that emerged from the First World War lived in the countryside. Peasants made up all but a percentage point of the landowners but their holdings came to little more than half of all the land that was cultivable. The rest was split between 7,500 large estates. Because most peasant farms were smaller than the ten acres needed to provide a living at the lowest level the most familiar figure in the countryside was the rural proletarian, condemned to live in the worst of both worlds. Illyes recalled that even the dirt-poor farm servants among whom he had been brought up pitied the seasonal labourers who had to sleep in the cowsheds when they came to work on the estate. And he told the story of how they kept their right to this wretched life by going on strike, at the beginning of the century, against the introduction of harvesting machines that would have destroyed their living completely.

Illyes saw this world through the eyes of a peculiarly gifted child, and for that reason was able to recreate the moments of beauty and warmth in its impoverished life. The peasant societies of East Europe had always known harshness from man or nature, and usually from both, but they possessed cultures that attempted to make sense out of that harshness. What the rulers of pre-war Hungary, including its great landowners who successfully fought off attempts at significant land reform, did not understand was that this rural life, and the social order that rested on it, could not survive in the modern world. Most of East Europe was in this same position of trying to catch up with the better-established nations of Central and West Europe without wanting or knowing how to create the conditions to make that possible. Poland, particularly its eastern part, mirrored the conditions of Hungary. Great Polish aristocrats like the Potockis and Radziwills had estates that matched the 160,000 acres owned on the eve of the Second World War by the Hungarian Prince Paul Esterhazy. In Romania and Bulgaria peasants made up four-fifths of the population, a greater proportion even than in Poland or Hungary. In some places there had been land reform but in general the East European peasant had one thing in common: he seldom ate meat except on the great religious holidays or when the law of hospitality obliged him to slaughter an animal to offer to a guest.

After this hard rural world had been washed away by the flood one of the greatest marvels revealed by the new world that took its place was, simply, pork. The butcher's shop became the barometer of East European contentment. In Poland failure to maintain a supply of cheap pork to the newly urbanised peasantry could bring rioters into the street and governments to their knees. The stability of the Communist regimes in Hungary, East Germany and Czechoslovakia eventually came to be most convincingly demonstrated by their butchers' shops where in good times cuts from the pig were piled into Renoir-pink altars, and sausages hung along the tiled walls, as neat and regular as organ pipes. At the beginning of the 1980s the man who was Janos Kadar's unofficial apologist asked a British visitor if in his country it was usual for a family of five to buy as many pounds of pork each weekend. It was in Hungary. 'This population, for the first time in its history, is consuming, not just existing. Our people were used to being hungry. Now they are happy they can eat. As for the peasants, they go crazy eating, and their wedding feasts can last as long as three days.' And before the flood? It will pay, when trying to puzzle through the twists in East Europe's fortunes, to remember a story written in 1933 by Zsigmond Moricz, another Hungarian writer who, like Illyes, observed the wretched of his country with a steady eye.

Farm labourers are hoeing a field somewhere on the great Hungarian plain, among them Janos Kis, John Little. 'He has the shortest name and the longest record of poverty.' The estate owner, a good-looking young count, has noticed Kis's pretty wife and flirts with her. She resists but extracts a promise from him to throw a supper for the labourers when they finish work on the three hundred acre field where that midday she had brought her husband his usual meal of soup, a 'kind of brown liquid' with spots of congealed fat floating on the top. The count agrees on condition that the wife dance with him, for he also promises to provide a gypsy band.

He keeps his word. Cooks set up a big cauldron on the *puszta* and throw in fourteen sheep. They have brought wine and also made soup, and this is real soup, 'like oil, rich and thick'. At the smell of it Janos Kis's 'whole body trembled with hunger, yet after the tenth spoonful he felt he could not eat any more'.

The dancing starts. Some policemen arrive, apparently by chance. Two of them sit down next to Janos Kis. The count asks Kis's wife to dance. 'Go on eating, just eat,' one of the policemen says to the peasant. Kis grasps his knife tightly, muttering 'a man hasn't got two stomachs to take everything in . . . a poor man hasn't even got a belly.' He watches the count kiss his wife. Janos Kis's hand 'stiffened on the knife, and he plunged it into the policeman up to its handle'. The story is called *To Eat One's Fill for Once*.

Memories of the sort of poverty and injustice described by writers like Moricz help explain why the flood waters hit the societies of East Europe with such force. The post-war East European revolutions would never have taken place without the Soviet armies and the regiments of commissars and NKVD men they brought behind them. But the failures of the pre-war regimes helped persuade many that this Soviet force, far from being a damaging diversion, represented a legitimate new chapter in the half-continent's history. Memories of pre-war wretchedness would continue to burn like candles before private altars even in the minds of some of the Communist apparatchiks who forty years later were stubbornly guiding their countries towards disaster. An elderly woman, widow of one of Poland's first post-war Communist leaders, after listening to criticism of socialism's failures from a young Solidarity journalist, hit back with a question of her own.

> Do you have any idea how humiliating it is not to be able to find any work? I remember what it was like before the war: Poland in 1933 was full of unemployed lining up for their free rations of soup. The soup was full of added soda to make it expand in the stomach and calm people down.

In the East Europe of the 1970s and 80s there was scarcely anyone to rival the reputation of the Czechoslovak Politburo member Vasil Bilak as a pro-Soviet hardliner. One of the small number of Czechoslovak officials who in 1968 asked the Soviet Union to invade their country to save it from the supposed horrors of Dubcek and the Prague Spring, Bilak appeared to accept unpopularity as his Communist duty. When he did agree to meet foreigners he invariably appeared cheerful and self-confident with, it was said, 'a sparkle or a glint in his eye, depending on your point of view'. And yet there were moments when he talked of his young days, and the poverty and unemployment that drove the poor to emigrate from Czechoslovakia, even though it was the only country in pre-war East Europe that proved itself as a democracy. Such memories provided a good deal of the cement that kept the Communist house standing as long as it did.

Czechoslovakia apart, the region's pre-war politics had offered small hope of progress. Poland's complicated but enduring hero Marshal Pilsudski finally put an end to democracy in 1930 when he locked up troublesome opposition leaders in the military prison at Brzesc. Like many authoritarian regimes before and after, the Polish Government then declared it was intent on a moral cleansing of the nation. The result, writes the British historian Norman Davies, was that 'by the end of the 1930s, the radicalisation of the Polish masses was already well-advanced'. If Poland had not been done to death in 1939 by Soviet Russia and Nazi Germany 'it would soon have sickened from internal causes'.

Hungary was no better placed. On the eve of the Second World War its economic and social conditions were as bad as anywhere in East Europe. The electoral system disenfranchised a large part of the countryside, but to make doubly sure the gendarmerie prevented opposition parties from working in the villages upon whose obedience Hungary's social and political order depended. Admiral Horthy, the Regent of Hungary, was scarcely an evil man: like many successful Hungarians, he was something of a charmer. An American writer whom Horthy invited out shooting was bowled off his feet by him. He admired the old man's bright brown eyes, his black hair that had 'the sheen of great health', the 'clean-cut, square face, with nutcracker chin' whose effect was 'singularly merry'. The American (who was in other matters no fool) had no doubt that this was a leader possessing 'the divine fire'. The Admiral, a 'spare, well-knit figure' reeking of 'the quarter-deck' had first received his visitor wearing his blue-and-gold sailor's uniform. This, at least, might have struck a warning note. Hungarian sailors had lost their profession with the collapse of the Austro-Hungarian empire and yet here was a man who still gloried in the title of admiral, unaware that a leader who wears naval uniform in a land-locked country risks appearing absurd in the eyes of the rest of the world.

Horthy's fondness for looking back was not peculiar to Hungarians. Most of the countries of East Europe lived under the shadow of great but distant empires that they had once created and ruled over. Serbs and Bulgarians warmed themselves in the embers of medieval glory. Romanian nostalgia stretched across millennia to Dacian ancestors whose bravery in war, Romanians liked to recall, had earned them the admiration of the Romans by whom they were eventually conquered. Polish memories were more recent and therefore served as a more precise source of inspiration. They could fix on the end of the eighteenth century when the Polish Commonwealth, just before its dismemberment, produced the Constitution of 3 May, 'the only act of freedom', Karl Marx called it, 'which Eastern Europe has undertaken in the midst of Prussian, Russian and Austrian barbarism'. But nowhere was this obsession with a glorious past stronger than in Hungary because that past was, for Hungarians, only yesterday. The 1920 Treaty of Trianon stripped Hungary, as a defeated nation of the First World War, of two-thirds of the old kingdom's territory and almost the same proportion of its inhabitants. That most of the lost inhabitants were not Hungarian was no consolation. What Budapest remembered was that three million Hungarians were left outside the borders of a motherland whose own population numbered only seven and a half million.

Most Hungarians did not pause to think that their country had, since the middle of the nineteenth century, been a semi-imperial power, co-ruler with Austria over lesser peoples (the Hungarian, rather than the more enlightened Austrian, interpretation of the imperial mission). Like someone who has suffered a fearful accident, Hungary's instinct was to deny the reality of the loss brought by the Trianon Treaty; obsession with redressing it came later. At school Magyar boys and girls learned a mournful song about how once great Hungary had shrunk to a little land, at which point they were taught to mime with their hands a pathetic little shape the size of a snowball. Children played with wooden jigsaw puzzles that, when assembled, showed the outline of the pre-war kingdom, uncannily like that of a human brain, that stretched from the county of Modrus-Fiume on the Adriatic coast in the West (an outlet for Admiral Horthy's ships) to Brasso and Haromszek deep inside what in 1920 became, and remains today, Romania. 'Such a handsome shape,' a Hungarian acquaintance whose parents had given him one of these puzzles recalled fondly. 'It was the shape you could never forget.'

The more the pity because, eyes turned on a past it would not admit was lost, Hungary could only stumble into the future. Its rulers were often not very wise – a minute written in the British Foreign Office at the end of the Second World War suggests matter-of-factly that Horthy was simply not bright enough to be considered a war criminal. The other countries of East Europe that shared the Hungarian preoccupation with the past also gave signs of finding the present an unsatisfactory substitute. National narcissism helped make up for the centuries that had been lost under the rule of foreigners. New national identities seemed most solidly grounded in conservatism. In such an atmosphere it was natural that Hungary, although it had lost its Royal Family with the abdication of the Habsburgs, should still call itself a kingdom and be ruled (only temporarily, it was understood) by a Regent, the Admiral who had no navy. Conservatism supported those classes whose interest lay in opposing the trends of the century, for example the minor gentry of Poland and Hungary who made up in pretension what they lacked in substance. As for the Balkans, they were even less prepared for the tests of the new age. In Romania, with its mass of peasants conditioned by centuries of Turkish rule, and a middle class that was small, sometimes brilliant but politically immature, it only needed one clever, unscrupulous king to throw the country into a political and social pit.

Ask an educated Romanian today about King Carol II and he will quite likely exclaim 'Carol? He was the most corrupt man in all Romania!' Carol's grandfather, Carol I, was a German prince chosen by the great powers of Europe from the Catholic branch of the Hohenzollerns in the hope that he would maintain the newly independent Romania of the nineteenth century as a buffer between Russia and Turkey. Carol II ruled from 1930 – 40. Clever, tireless and quite without scruples he was exactly the king Romania did not need, for his own bad qualities matched and then magnified those of his country. In private life he had a passion for the cinema about which he probably knew more than anyone in Bucharest, liking to watch a film each night in his private theatre. He liked poker too, on condition his partners let him win. And even in a country whose ruling class was strikingly unpuritan he was notorious for his sexual appetite. His choice as mistress of the Romanian commoner Magda Lupescu, a woman of apparently immense sexual endurance, sparked off major political battles that Carol usually won. As to public life, the King summed up his philosophy of government with the remark that 'here the ministers do what I tell them'. Nevertheless in 1940 he was forced out of the country by Romania's new Fascist leaders for whose rise he himself was partly responsible. Escaping by train to Yugoslavia he and Magda Lupescu had to lie on the floor of their carriage to avoid the bullets of the Fascist Iron Guard who harassed them all the way to the border.

Few of East Europe's inter-war leaders have earned epitaphs as damning. In his book *Eastern Europe Between the Wars*, the British scholar Hugh Seton-Watson summed up Carol in words almost harsh enough for a later Romanian tyrant.

> Superficially brilliant and basically ignorant, gifted with enormous energy and unlimited lust for power, a lover of demagogy and bombastic speeches . . . [and] determined to be a Great Man, the Saviour and Regenerator of his country . . . For a decade the history of Romania consisted of this man's flamboyant gestures and cunning manoeuvres, set against a drab background of peasant misery and police oppression.

RUSSIA'S SHADOW

Nothing better demonstrates the force of the flood that swept into Europe after 1945 than that two countries as different as Romania and Czechoslovakia should within a few years appear to have become passable twins. Pre-war Romania had only a tiny Communist Party. Most of its leaders were not even native Romanians, but Jews or members of national minorities who believed Communism would bring the freedom and equality denied them under the old regime. In industrial Czechoslovakia, where the working-class movement was incomparably stronger than in Romania, the Communist Party had performed respectably in pre-war elections. And yet these differences soon seemed to count for nothing. Communism, like armies, appeared to have the power to turn individuals or, as in this case, countries into identical warriors. It was an illusion, but many people at first believed it because they wanted to and because it was the mood of the historical moment. The poet Gyula Illyes's premonition of impending change was probably even shared by some of the privileged people he saw enjoying themselves in the Buda Hills. East Europe, on the edge of the Second World War, was a troubled place, waiting for disaster. The war intensified the belief that change, when it came, would be thorough, unlike anything known before. Judaeo-Christian messianism combined with confidence in modern science to convince people that the new society must be entirely new. That the blueprint for this new world had already been tested in the Soviet Union did not, in those days, look the disastrous flaw it came to seem later. For the Communists it was of course an advantage. The doubts of East European Party members about the bloody events in the Soviet Union of the 1930s, not least Stalin's culling of their own comrades who had sought refuge in Moscow, were largely blown away by the war. Both the Soviet Union's ruthless might and ruthless example were now essential to their own survival. Silviu Brucan was a gifted young intellectual in the tiny Romanian Communist Party who spent the war editing the Party's clandestine newspaper *Scinteia*, hiding in Bucharest because it was the only place a printing press was to be found. For Brucan and his comrades in the wartime underground there was no choice: 'Stalin was our only hope.' Even the Yugoslav Communists, more masters of their fate than any other Party in East Europe and of proven toughness in battle, were at first swept off their feet by a girlish adulation of Stalin and everything they thought he stood for. They even imagined that when they got to Moscow they, though speaking Serbo-Croat, would inevitably understand the Russians because as Slavs and Communists both had to be of one mind.

Milovan Djilas was a member of the first Yugoslav military mission that went to Moscow in 1944. Years later he recalled the emotion with which he set off for the Soviet capital.

> I was trembling with excitement at the thought that I was going to see the Soviet Union, the land that was first in history – I believed, with a belief more adamant than stone – to give meaning to the dream of visionaries, the resolve of warriors, and the suffering of martyrs.

After the necessarily roundabout wartime journey a Soviet plane at last carried the Yugoslavs across Stalin's frontier. It was for the young Djilas

the realisation of our dreams and our hopes. The deeper we penetrated into its grey-green expanse, the more I was gripped by a new, hitherto hardly expected emotion. It was as though I was returning to a primeval homeland, unknown but mine.

Djilas eventually came to understand what a few clear-minded observers had grasped much earlier – that Communism, the supposed science of the future, was a new belief, not just a new political programme. Others had known it all along. The Polish writer Gustav Herling would observe, after years in Stalin's Gulag, that 'one only has to see old Communists in Soviet prisons to become convinced that Communism is a religion'.

What Communists saw as dream becoming reality presented itself scarcely less powerfully to the ordinary citizens of East Europe as yet another twist, never predictable but always expected, in a fate they did not presume to determine. How do you resist a future that strikes like a tidal wave? One can only try to imagine what it was like to watch the awesome German Reich, possessor of the most powerful army Europe had ever seen, first crumble and then fall back before the soldiers of Russia. Victory on the battlefield has beatified far less worthy conquerors than the Red Army. Psychologically, too, much of the half-continent was poorly prepared to resist this wave, because the war and German occupation had left such broad deposits of guilt. This was most obvious in what was to become East Germany, where almost total complicity with Hitler destroyed the political immune system of the entire country. In Romania, Hungary and Bulgaria there was the guilt of wartime alliance with Nazism. In Czechoslovakia collaboration remained an individual affair, though it was still widespread. Many bets had been hedged, not least by Czechs who could claim some faint German origins. And throughout East Europe there was guilt, albeit often suppressed, over passive and sometimes approving connivance at the slaughter of Jews, gypsies and others whom the Nazis judged to be subhuman.

It took several years before old East European grudges and antipathies towards Russia became common currency again, but then it was discovered that there was a rich hoard of judgements stored at the back of collective national minds. Nowhere were these judgements more gloomy than among Poles who for so long had had to puzzle out why fate had made them Russia's neighbours. Joseph Conrad's dislike and fear of Russia and Russians once again appeared entirely relevant. Writing before the 1917 Revolution in an introduction to *Under Western Eyes* he had warned that Russia might settle on an

> imbecile and atrocious answer of a purely Utopian revolutionism encompassing destruction by the first means to hand, in the strange conviction that a fundamental change of heart must follow the downfall of any given human institutions.

The blackness that Conrad believed was buried in the Russian heart was felt by many other Poles, Gustav Herling among them. When at last about to leave the Soviet Union to join the Polish army that was being formed in the West he pronounced it a place where 'it is possible to cease to believe in man, and in the purpose of the struggle to improve his lot on earth'.

By 1979 it seemed quite natural for the writer Kazimierz Brandys to exclaim in his *Warsaw Diary* that 'Russia's fate is not part of our consciousness. It is alien to us; we feel no kinship with it or responsibility for it.' Brandys even feared Russian literature, particularly the grotesque stories of Gogol and Saltykov-Shchedrin: 'I would prefer not to know their literature exists. One has to be a Frenchman [i.e. not a Pole, who must live next door] to feel safe with that literature.' As for Dostoyevsky, the modern Polish writer disliked him as much as Conrad, who had abhorred the Russian as a 'grimacing, haunted creature' whose work sounded like 'fierce mouthings from prehistoric ages'.

Non-Slavs like the Magyars and Romanians had a less envenomed relationship with Russia. They disliked and feared it as smaller animals fear the king of the beasts whom in this instance they had just had the misfortune to fight against in a war. When the Soviet Red Army put down the Hungarian uprising in 1956, Hungarians recognised it as a repeat of Russia's crushing of the Hungarian bid for independence of 1848. The moral was to keep as far away from Moscow as possible. Only in East Germany, Czechoslovakia and Bulgaria, the former with its unique burden of guilt towards

Moscow, the latter two with the strongest Russophile tradition, was anti-Russianism kept in check. Where else but East Germany could the slogan 'To learn from the Soviet Union is to learn to win' have survived into the 1980s? Where else but Prague could one have seen – still glowing above the heads of the demonstrators in Wenceslas Square in November 1989 – the neon-depicted words *With the Soviet Union for ever*? Ordinary Czechs, though, had had enough after 1968. It was no longer surprising that a Czechoslovak writer, Josef Skvorecky, should put a savage anti-Soviet gloss on the Polish Conrad's *The Heart of Darkness*. The émigré Czech university teacher in Skvorecky's novel *The Engineer of Human Souls* tries to explain to his puzzled, innocent Canadian students why Conrad's book is a 'prophecy about the Russians and Russia'. Kurtz crying out 'The horror of it!' was none other than an appalled Lenin looking back over his life's work from his deathbed. Nor was it surprising that when Mikhail Gorbachev appeared in the Soviet Union some Czechs refused to be impressed. 'Again they think they're better than us,' a well-known contributor to the Prague underground press grumbled.

Communist East Europe's thinking about Russia came to differ in one important respect from reflections that might have been offered before 1945. To the instinctive shudder at the mention of the Russian name was added the realisation that Communism, far from being the gospel of the future, was a remarkably complete political articulation of all they feared most about Russia itself. Here, too, the premonition of Gyula Illyes as he looked at the luxurious life on the hills above Budapest and dreamed of a cleansing flood proved remarkably accurate. The flood with its sister images of great hydroprojects and dams that destroy with one hand and give life with the other went to the heart of the Russian system in which East Europe, to its horror, found itself trapped. Some twenty years after the end of the war the Polish novelist Tadeusz Konwicki imagined in *A Dreambook of Our Time* a confused, unhappy community somewhere in Poland soon to be submerged beneath a water reservoir. 'The water will flood everything, the town will be covered for ever and only the legend of a town at the bottom of the lake will remain.' This unease was not so different from the centuries' old fears of East Europeans that their towns and cities would survive only as legends after wars waged by foreign invaders. The Russians were in this respect successors to the Turks who had terrorised the region for centuries and of whom memories persisted. Until a few years ago, at least, it was possible to buy in the markets of southern Poland brightly painted wooden figures of Janissaries on horseback. The toy Turks had great pointed helmets and in the right hand a wooden club that swung up and down ferociously when they were pulled along the ground. Appropriately it was a Russian writer who most vividly developed the flood as a metaphor for the sickness of the Soviet system that had become the political and economic system of East Europe too. East Europeans reading Valentin Rasputin's *Farewell to Matyora* would have understood that the old cry of 'barbarians at the gates' no longer held good. The barbarian was now within. Written in the mid-1970s when Soviet censorship precluded frontal criticism, the story describes the last days of an island village on the Angara river in Siberia before it is submerged under the waters of a dam built to feed a new hydroelectric station. The village of Matyora and its soon to be displaced inhabitants represent a way of life that cannot defend itself, and a past that will soon be forgotten. The old village woman at the story's centre says, 'There is truth in memory. He who has no memory has no life.' The words were a coded epitaph not just for the Russian countryside but for Russia itself. A world had sunk beneath the waters. Russia was in danger of becoming, in some respects already had become, a second Atlantis. After Mikhail Gorbachev came to power the Russians were able to talk about this openly. They could discuss the twenty-eight million acres of forest and meadow submerged beneath water reservoirs, and the consequent damage both to the environment and the natural food supply. But the point that was increasingly made was that the most destructive flood had nothing to do with water. 'The first dam was Stalin's collectivisation.'

The perception went to the heart of the tragedy of the Communist experiment: the involvement of idealism in great enterprises that both in conception and realisation were inhuman. The paradox was at first too great – indeed, too evil – for many European Communists to penetrate, because they had been brought up to think in modern, sunnier categories. Alexander Dubcek, the East European Communist leader who better than any other personified decency as well as socialist conviction, demonstrated this in an interview he gave only seven months before the November 1989 revolution in Prague. Dubcek, who went to school in the Soviet industrial town of Gorky where his father worked in a car factory, insisted he never was and

never could be 'an anti-Soviet person'. Yes, he had lived through
Stalin's collectivisation. 'I was aware of the poverty . . . the hunger,
I have seen people dying of hunger, I have seen a lot.' But he still
felt 'wholeheartedly' for the Soviet nation. 'Why? Because I have
experienced the joy aroused by the completion of a hydroelectric
power station.'

THE MONUMENTS OF DESPOTISM

Dubcek's remark evokes images from the early Soviet cinema
that celebrate the marriage of scientific planning with collective
labour. Like those distant film-makers, but with less excuse, he still
did not grasp the connection between the suffering brought by
collectivisation and the power station that he worked with such
innocent happiness to complete. Yet they were intimately connected; on the one hand the destruction of a human landscape, on the
other the construction of great machines to impose on the shapeless
land a pattern convenient only to its new rulers.

If Dubcek did not understand this there was a Czech who did –
the man whom he embraced on the stage of Prague's Magic Lantern
Theatre on the November evening when the Czechoslovak Communist leadership resigned, signalling that the old system was at last
giving ground. In his essay *Politics and Conscience*, written in 1984,
Havel called for modernisation to be carried out with humility. It
'must not be simply an arrogant, megolomaniac, brutal invasion by
an impersonally objective science, represented by a newly graduated
agronomist or a bureaucrat in the service of the "scientific world
view."' This was precisely what had happened in Czechoslovakia in
the 1950s.

> Our word for it was 'collectivisation'. Like a tornado, it raged through
> the Czechoslovak countryside . . . leaving not a stone in place. Among
> its consequences were, on the one hand, tens of thousands of lives
> devastated by prison, sacrificed on the altar of a scientific Utopia about
> brighter tomorrows. On the other hand, the level of social conflict
> and the amount of drudgery did in truth decrease while agricultural
> production rose.

But while the Prague butchers' shops were able to present a
charming picture of plenty, great damage, indeed the greatest, had
been done unseen.

Thirty years after the tornado swept the traditional family farm off the face of the earth, scientists are amazed to discover what even a semi-literate farmer previously knew – that human beings must pay a heavy price for every attempt to abolish, radically, once and for all, that humbly respected boundary of the natural world . . . They must pay for the attempt to seize nature, to leave not a remnant of it in human hands, to ridicule its mystery; they must pay for the attempt to abolish God and to play at being God.

Havel's analysis could have been a great deal gloomier, though in this passage he did spell out the connection between the scientific Utopianism that ignored natural limits and the political system that depended on and grew out of this method of directing human society. The post-war governments of East Europe, following the example of Stalin's Soviet Union, were drawn towards massive projects that called for massive inputs of manpower and resources. The hydroelectric power station was the most glamorous (and later the most feared) symbol of this approach, for was not electricity plus the 'power of the Soviets' Lenin's formula for Communism? The Soviet Union early embarked on great hydraulic projects, conveniently supplied with armies of prison labour directed by the secret police, and the obsession continued until the demise of neo-Stalinism in 1985. It was not by chance that one of the most controversial projects of the 1980s was a plan to divert the rivers of Siberia to provide irrigation for the Ukraine and Central Asia. Such a massive tampering with nature could only be undertaken by an all-powerful state and, like previous projects, would serve both as monument to that state and justification for its existence. By this time East Europe, too, was covered with giant industrial projects that were causing a second flood – pollution. Massive steel mills had to be fed with Soviet iron ore. Open-cast brown coalfields fed sulphur-breathing power stations. Chemical complexes wrapped the countryside in a malign haze. The key to all these projects was that the more gigantic the undertakings the greater the need for a powerful Communist state to plan, finance and carry them out. Only such a state, the East Germans believed, would allow them to carry out the plan of their leader Erich Honecker to turn their small country into a world giant of microelectronics. It appeared to be a perfect symbiosis, a political perpetual motion machine such as the Western world had never known.

The Orient, though, had long had knowledge of such things. Asian civilisations depending on irrigated agriculture had over centuries demonstrated the interdependence of massive agro-industrial projects and absolute state power. Who could maintain the vast system of dikes on which the survival of China depended? Only the Emperor. In such a world the kingdom's survival depended on the safe hands of a totalitarian bureaucracy. A population for the most part living in villages that were self-sufficient, isolated and dispersed provided the natural foundation for its rule. The accusation that the Russian Revolution brought tested Asiatic methods to the Soviet Union (and later to East Europe) had been made by Karl Wittfogel in his *Oriental Despotism*. Published shorly after Stalin's death, the book revived the old Marxist debate, long taboo in the Soviet Union itself, about whether there was such a thing as the 'Asiatic mode of production'. Marx declared Tsarist Russia to be semi-Asiatic. Wittfogel argued that Lenin had indeed been close to exclaiming 'The horror of it!' on his deathbed, for he had come to understand that his Revolution must inevitably end in a 'new type of Oriental despotism'.

Gyula Illyes was granted his wish of a flood, but he also had to accept the immense, crushing machinery that would be necessary to pump the purifying waters, the machinery of an Oriental despotism on European soil. The chapter headings Wittfogel provided for his description of ancient Asian despotisms would have sounded familiar to any East European who reflected on the nature of the Communist world he or she lived in: 'A State Stronger than Society'; 'Despotic Power – Total and Not Benevolent'; 'Total Terror – Total Submission – Total Loneliness'.

East Europe, of course, had stronger internal defences against despotism than medieval China or ancient Egypt. Attempts to granulate its societies into manageable, disconnected morsels like the villages of old Asia never entirely succeeded. Churches; local patriotism; the glue of a common culture; the brake of memory, not least memory of the European tradition, ensured the process was never complete. In one country, though, it went further than most, and it was there that the most flamboyant symptoms of an Oriental despotism on European soil were displayed.

The Polish writer Ryszard Kapuscinski in his account of the fall of Haile Selassie, *The Emperor*, records a courtier's description of the Ethiopian ruler's last attempt to save his empire by building dams across the Nile.

> Many years hence, everyone who could get to the Imperial Dams would cry out, 'Behold all ye! Who but the Emperor could have caused such things to be done, such extraordinary wonderful things, whole mountains flung across the river!'

Only the emperor could do such things. The emperor was therefore indispensable. This was Nicolae Ceausescu's logic, too. While the rest of East Europe fell into the hands of committees of 'totalitarian bureaucrats', Ceausescu's style was as imperial as it was Oriental. He was the only East European leader known to have been influenced by the new despotisms of the Far East. In 1971 Ceausescu and his wife Elena travelled to Peking. It was the time of the Cultural Revolution. Mao's wife Chiang Ching was in the ascendant. The Ceausescus appear to have admired everything the Chinese showed them. Returning home via Pyongyang the couple met Kim Il Sung of North Korea, a modern Oriental despot with a passion for asserting his power through massive buildings. Here, too, Ceausescu and his wife seem to have been fascinated by what they saw.

Like the rest of the Soviet Bloc Romania had adopted the Stalinist practice of using forced labour for the great construction projects which alone seemed worthy of the new Communist world. By the early 1950s forty thousand prisoners were at work on the Danube-Black Sea canal, and many more on hydroelectric stations and industrial installations in other parts of the country (ironically this apparently loyal mimicking of Soviet methods would later infuriate the Moscow leadership, for the Russians came to believe that their interests would be better served by an agricultural Romania). Ceausescu kept his passion for great hydraulic schemes till the very end. One of the first acts of the revolutionary government that replaced him was to cancel all work connected with the still unfinished canal linking Bucharest and the Danube, as well as other hydroelectric stations, water diversion projects, and plans to drain the marshes and forests of the Danube delta, rich in wildlife, and convert them to farmland. Also abandoned were yet more giant chemical plants, as surely intended as monuments to the *Conducator*, the Leader, as any portrait painting or sculpture.

Ceausescu came to believe, as other despots before him, that great power, if it is to awe the present and echo through the future, must be expressed in great buildings. When the Communist regimes of East Europe eventually collapsed there was inevitable curiosity about how their leaders had lived. Had luxury been another of their crimes? Had they lived like princes in what they told everyone else was the age of the proletariat? The truth was not as sensational as many had anticipated. The Communist leaders did, of course, lead privileged lives. Even in the ruins of post-war Poland the leadership had lived comfortably enough on an estate at Konstancin outside Warsaw, where they had at their disposal a restaurant and cinema, maids and cooks. Their clothes were made by private tailors selected by the security service, and other habits of the privileged were acquired: it was not done, one of them recalled many years later, to talk in front of the servants. But none of this, it could be argued, went beyond functional comfort, the support necessary for people who spent most of their lives very hard at work. The ghetto at Wandlitz, in wooded countryside north of Berlin, in which the East German Politburo lived up till the very end, was also well equipped but its comforts, though certainly beyond the reach of most East Germans, would have been familiar enough to middle-class West Germans. This was not luxury on the royal scale.

It was also a stealthy life, lived behind walls that were in turn protected by guards. For this reason alone it was singularly unroyal, for real kings have a duty to be ostentatious. What angered East Germans most was not so much the discovery that Erich Honecker and his colleagues had enjoyed large private hunting grounds, but that this privilege had been enjoyed in secret. In the end it was the hypocrisy and deception, more than the level of luxury, that infuriated.

Ceausescu, too, remained bound by the convention that Communist leaders should lead a private life so discreet as to be almost clandestine. Primavera, the house he had built for himself in Bucharest, was certainly grander and, on the outside, much more handsome than the villa of his patron and predecessor Gheorghiu-Dej (the latter would have fitted unremarked into any moderately successful West European suburb). It was said that Ceausescu also had some eighty palaces, residential villas and hunting lodges – several of which had belonged to the old Royal Family – at his disposal throughout the country. Many of these buildings, like the villas reserved for him in each county, he never used. But though they had a certain value as shrines to his invisible presence the streets and areas surrounding them were usually barred to ordinary citizens, and even Romanians could not be awed by what they could not see. What Ceausescu needed were big buildings, bigger even than the biggest surviving royal palace, something against which the Romanian citizen could measure himself and be humbled. He needed vast public buildings and for this East Europe had scarcely any precedents. There was the Palast der Republik that Honecker had built in East Berlin in 1976 but it was puny by Ceausescu's Asian standards and, worse still, let itself be outshone by the heavy-domed classical cathedral which stood opposite it on the other side of the Karl-Liebknecht-Strasse. The only true rival to Ceausescu's House of the Republic was the Palace of Culture in Warsaw, Stalin's wicked gift to the Poles. The Polish comrades seem to have been well aware what Stalin was up to when he told them of the gift he had in mind, for they tried to persuade him to give a housing estate instead. It would, the Poles assured the Soviet leader, be named after him. Stalin would have none of it. Anyone could put up housing estates, and he knew better than most that what was named one day could be renamed the next. What he wanted, and got, was a building that dwarfed everything and could be seen all over the city. No one else could have put it there but him. It alone could symbolise the concentration of power that was the essence of the system he had built.

That was what Ceausescu wanted too. Not long after his return from the Far East he began to consider rebuilding the centre of Bucharest. The earthquake that did considerable damage to the city in 1977 served to justify the first demolition orders. Ceausescu intended to put up several monster buildings, including an opera house with seats for three thousand and a museum of national history with twenty-two halls of 10,000 square feet each. But the biggest building, and the only one that was almost finished when he died, was the most important, the House of the Republic. In this palace were to be gathered the offices of the President and his consort together with all the other great bodies of state, while the ministries that served them would be in the new quarter, also largely completed, that surrounded them. The House of the Republic, standing at the top of the two-miles-long Boulevard of the Victory of Socialism, would demonstrate that Ceausescu's power was immeasurably greater than that of any Romanian who had gone before.

In the bitterly cold days after his death on Christmas Day 1989 a heavy mist often hung over Bucharest. Sometimes it would veil the monstrous building, as though the nation's memory was already trying to blot out the man and his works. Later the mist parted and the palace emerged like an iceberg in the Atlantic, a warning that Ceausescu would haunt the country for generations to come. It is a singularly ugly construction; unpleasantly sited in a large open space; and out of scale even with the massive new government and residential buildings around it. Ceausescu used some of Romania's best architects to build the latter but he chose for this palace a little known architect who, the consistently uncharitable gossips of the city said, had never built so much as a chicken coop in her life. Several alternative designs had been suggested including one with towers like those on London Bridge and almost-Mansard roofs that recalled a Paris railway station. This post-modern design, size apart, might have suited a city much of which had been built under the influence of the French *fin-de-siècle*. The design that Ceausescu settled on was certainly the worst; even as an expression of power it is constipated. The façade is made of white rectangular block piled on rectangular block, and crowned by a foolishly puny pylon, as though at that point the *Conducator*'s imagination had been exhausted.

17,000 men – almost half as many as built the Danube–Black Sea canal – toiled in shifts twenty-four hours a day, each worker under the eyes of a pair of guards from the *Securitate*. The entrance to the Ceausescus' wing was to the right of the façade. The immense steel doors that guarded this wing opened onto halls of white marble from which staircases, also marble, led up to the first floor and the Ceausescus' offices. These rooms, separated by an anteroom, were large – a nice suburban house would have fitted into either of them – and richly and expertly decorated (Romanians have long been fine stone masons and carvers of wood). Ceausescu's room had an inlaid parquet floor that was partly covered by handsome carpets worked in subdued colours. The walls were panelled in mahogany and rosewood; the marble fireplace was baroque. The room's three huge chandeliers would have burned throughout the day because the windows were partly covered by heavy, swagged curtains. Elena Ceausescu's office had a light wood panelling. Unable to imagine what her chosen designs would look like she had ordered a full-scale

mock-up carpet and specimen chairs. These gilt Louis XVI imi-
tations, upholstered in gold silk, clustered like frightened courtiers
in a corner of the room, the only objects, when the revolution came,
in an otherwise still empty palace.

No one apart from Ceausescu, his wife, the architect Anca Petre-
scu and the craftsmen who built it had seen his office. It was said
this was because he was frightened for its security, but was it the
only reason? The palace seemed to baffle those Romanians who
guarded or visited it. The soldiers showing round visitors concentrated on statistics. The Hall of Romania was 260 feet long by 130
feet wide by 65 feet high. The biggest chandeliers (twenty-two of
them in the Hall of Union alone) cost one million Lei each. Squads
of apprehensive conscripts, ropes over their shoulders and flashlights
in hand, were sent to explore the building's nether regions, for
rumour (incorrect) had it that there were as many floors under
ground as above, as though the answer to why the palace had been
built might be there. Educated young Romanians who walked
through the empty marble halls refused to believe it made any sense:
'but it's totally useless!' No one would admit that the building had
a purpose because that purpose was so humiliating to Romanian
self-esteem. Ceausescu's office could not be seen by profane eyes
because it was the inner sanctum of the cult. The cult was the key
to the palace's layout: the trek through empty halls and up staircases
to reach the *Conducator*'s office; the massive door in the Hall of
Union that was to be used by the Ceausescus alone. As a cult object
it did not need to be convenient and Ceausescu had ordered that
lavatories be built only at each of the palace's four corners. Small
wonder he would not allow any other temple to be visible from the
windows of the House of the Republic. The monastery of Mihai
Voda was moved six hundred feet out of sight, its walls razed to the
ground, and the hill on which it had stood levelled. The pretty little
Antim church was spared a similar fate only because buildings on
the Boulevard of the Victory of Socialism were re-aligned to hide it
from Ceausescu's gaze.

A man born into a poor peasant family had come closer to setting
up an Oriental despotism in Europe than anyone before him (Stalin
ruled over an Eurasian land). The Turks who had long dominated
Romania were no rivals, for unlike the empires of ancient Asia
theirs had been remarkably loose-jointed. In less than three decades
Ceausescu had sketched a violently speeded-up version of the rise

and fall of the Khmer empire of Angkor, but without the religious myths that gave beauty, and appeared to give meaning, to the Khmer rulers' equally unintended self-destruction. Ceausescu's palace and other projects had, like Angkor's great buildings, plundered the resources of an overstrained economy. The marble mines of Romania were obliged to send all their production to the palace; the people could no longer have even the smallest marble tombstone. Romanians were allowed to burn only forty-watt bulbs while crystal chandeliers were hung in all the palace's major rooms.

It is not suprising that Romanians preferred to say that their dead ruler's work made no sense. As for other East Europeans, they professed to despise Ceausescu's Romania but it scared them, too, for they could recognise in it a fate they had barely escaped themselves. That point was not lost on the Hungarians when uproar over a great hydroelectric scheme helped speed the demise of their own Communist regime. In the mid-1970s the governments of Czechoslovakia and Hungary decided, with typical lack of any public discussion, to build two dams across the Danube between Bratislava and Budapest, re-route part of the river, and build a hydroelectric power station; the whole project an undertaking almost on the scale of the Suez Canal. When the Budapest Government did later ask the opinion of the Hungarian Academy of Sciences and received a negative report it promptly pigeon-holed it. By the mid-1980s Hungarians were attacking every aspect of Gabcikovo-Nagymaros, as the project was called. The complex flow of the Danube downstream from Bratislava, with its network of marshes, tributaries and islands would be destroyed. It would threaten one of the Continent's largest natural underground reservoirs of drinking water. There was horror at the arrogant destruction of natural and historical landscapes. Had not Schubert, someone remembered, written the Trout Quintet on a tributary, albeit Austrian, of the Danube? The proposed dam also revived fears that the order imposed on East Europe after the war was threatening the survival of the Hungarian nation itself, for the towns and villages that would be destroyed on the Czechoslovak side of the Danube were largely inhabited by the Hungarian minority that since 1945 had been cut off from the motherland.

After Hungary's long-time leader Janos Kadar was eased out of office in the spring of 1988 the Gabcikovo-Nagymaros affair acquired the simplicity of a morality play. On one side were those who supported the old system: the heirs of collectivisation, acolytes more or less eager of the hierarchical, centralised application of power that Kadar had made somewhat more humane but certainly not abandoned. In this camp were the true-red Communist leaders of Prague, determined to keep Hungary up to its obligations, and those Hungarian Communist leaders, Kadar's successor Karoly Grosz among them, who could not imagine life outside the system. They defended the dam project with talk of international agreements already undertaken, the impossibility of wasting work already done, and the horrendous cost of fines in the event of cancellation. At heart, though, they seem to have realised that their own survival depended on winning this battle. Their opponents, who included reform-minded Communists and most of the by then rapidly developing Hungarian opposition, certainly understood this. Miklos Nemeth, Hungary's last Communist Prime Minister, a reformer, called Gabcikovo-Nagymaros 'the symbol of a model that must be superseded'. It was the fall of the Communist government in Prague that finally killed the project. Within weeks of taking office, Czechoslovakia's new President, Vaclav Havel, pronounced it a 'monstrosity'.

Speaking to the Hungarian Parliament in September 1989 Nemeth used the expression 'national resurgence'. Some people, he said, were annoyed when they heard it but he begged for understanding. Hungarians should remember the time of the Tatar invasions when

> Our ancestors fled into the swamps, and only the reed through which they breathed in air showed above the surface . . . We, too, have been submerged, and threatening forces have pushed us under the water – the joint strength of a tyranny, a bureaucracy, which deformed a beautiful philosophical promise into a freak.

How East Europe managed to put its head above the waters is the story of the rest of this book. It was a complex process, which began as soon as the Communist flood had arrived, and was well-advanced some years before the Communists had an inkling of the coming revolutions of 1989. Szerchenyi Hill in Buda, which inspired Gyula Illyes to write his poem invoking the flood, is only a few miles downstream from Nagymaros. Anyone who in recent summers rode up it in the broad carriages of the cogwheel railway was likely to make the journey in the company of quite ordinary families, some squabbling, some merry, but mostly intent, in the Hungarian manner, on the enjoyment of the moment. But if the atmosphere in the train was as egalitarian as befitted a socialist state, the views through the windows were less so. Some of the old villas that Illyes saw remained, but what caught the eye were the new houses and blocks of comfortable apartments of a kind to be seen in Austria or southern Germany. Privately built, they were little more accessible to the ordinary miner, baker and shepherd than the houses that stood on the hill fifty years before.

2

The Cities

BATTLE FOR THE STREETS

The flood that swept across East Europe changed the face of
the countryside. Poland apart, the Communists found it infinitely
more malleable than the cities that fell into their hands. Collectivisation altered, probably beyond repair, villages, customs and
landscape. The state treated the countryside like a patient on an
operating table. Villages were picked up and re-assembled elsewhere. Old habits that did not fit into the new pattern of socialist
organisation were done away with. When the Hungarian Government gathered in a new settlement farmers used to living in isolated
homesteads, some of the men and women committed suicide. Memories contained in the manor houses of the greater or lesser gentry
were rendered harmless by letting them fall into disrepair or turning
them into schools or hospitals. Memory was erased from the land,
too. The large open fields of Hungary or East Germany where the
trees and hedgerows have been removed are as unfamiliar as a face
from which the eyebrows have been shaved. The countryside would
play little part in the revolutions of 1989, for the peasants were not
inclined to take risks. They had known too much turmoil in the
past forty-five years, and learned time and again how defenceless
they were in the face of Communist authority. Memories of the
campaigns against the *kulaks*, the mischievous word borrowed from
Russia to describe often only slightly better-off farmers, remained
vivid. When the first real elections did take place in Hungary in
March 1990 much of the impetus to revive village politics came
from old men who had joined the Smallholders' Party before or
immediately after the war. Coming from families that had owned
small amounts of land, some of them might have taken part in the
limited Hungarian resistance to the Germans during the war; after

it, considerably more would have been imprisoned or sent to forced labour building Soviet airfields or barracks. There was hatred of the Communists in the villages, and the satisfaction was great when they were at last seen to be losing power. 'Those gentleman,' said old Hungarian peasants who had suffered at their hands 'they used to be such a puff-chested lot, but now we've buttoned up their waistcoats for them.' But they nevertheless respected 'those gentlemen's' power to inflict pain, and remained quiet until the battle had been won in Budapest.

There was another reason for the passivity of the countryside. Take the case of a farmer in Tolna County, south of the capital. His father had been a landless labourer on one of the many Esterhazy estates. Given some acres in the first post-war land reform, he was forced within a couple of years to take his land into a collective farm where he lost all control over it. To all intents and purposes it had become the state's. Come the 1956 uprising the collective collapsed. Like other farmers he took his acres back, but as soon as the Communist government re-established itself it made his life so unbearable with taxes that again, like the others, he returned with his land to the collective. Owning land had only brought this family trouble. The son, with a good job on a state farm, wanted nothing more to do with it. He had a small house with a garden, and in addition to that a separate plot for growing maize to feed his twenty pigs and a hundred and fifty chickens. Food price rises that might plague the Hungarian town-dweller scarcely affected him, for he and his family were almost self-sufficient. Over large parts of East Europe the Communists did manage to give farmers a better life. The surplus labour that had been at the root of the countryside's troubles before the war had moved to the new industries in towns. The heavy agricultural machinery available to collective and state farms took away much of the drudgery of labour for the peasants who remained. That these farms were subsidised and inefficient by world standards made them all the more attractive to those who lived and worked, often not very hard, on them. If the collective farmers of East Germany and Czechoslovakia poured into the cities to take part in the national protest demonstrations in the autumn of 1989 it was and remains a well-kept secret.

Once the pain of the first years of collectivisation was over it almost paid the peasants of East Europe to go along with the Communists. There were over twenty million acres of arable land in Hungary of which only slightly more than one eighth belonged to peasants as gardens and private plots. Yet on this small share of the land they grew over a third of Hungary's food. The Hungarian villages of 1989 had little in common with that impoverished world Gyula Illyes grew up in and which had existed up to the outbreak of the Second World War, when Admiral Horthy's kingdom was still known as 'the land of three million beggars'. It was one of East Europe's best known paradoxes that the only country where collectivisation was abandoned in the face of peasant opposition suffered the most miserably from both food shortages and discontented farmers. Only in Poland did peasants still live in a countryside much of whose landscape of small fields, copses and hedges remained familiar. Only in Poland were peasants comforted and supported by an independent institution, the Roman Catholic Church. Throughout the rest of the bloc, with the partial exception of similarly Catholic Slovakia, the churches were too weak in numbers or resolve to match those Polish parish priests who marched at the head of their flocks at festivals and demonstrations like officers leading regiments into battle. The Polish Communists punished their peasants for their victory by withholding the means they needed to develop their farms, and by tyrannising them with state monopolies through which they were forced to buy and sell. The result was known to anyone who had ever heard a Polish joke about butchers' shops. Poland, not for the first time, ended up with the worst of both worlds.

The cities proved immeasurably more recalcitrant. It was in the cities that the Communists' troubles began with the East Berlin workers' revolt in 1953 and the bloody Poznan riots three years later. It was in the capitals of East Europe that the fate of Communism was finally settled. And for that the cities themselves, their layout, their architecture, and the uncensorable memories and messages contained in them were partly responsible. The Communists could and did, as we shall see, alter the human life that flowed through the cities. They could only marginally change the city's face which looked down so quizzically on the new regimes.

The capital cities of East Europe were so full of potent ghosts that a hundred years of Communism would scarcely have been enough to exorcise them. Bucharest and Budapest, as they survived in 1945, were evidence of the brilliant rebirth of Romania and Hungary that began in the second half of the nineteenth century.

Once liberated from Turkish rule the Romanians turned their city into an appealing Balkan echo of Paris. In those days, too, ambition got the better of Romanians as it later would their Communist *Conducator*. When the new Savings and Deposit Bank went up on the Calea Victoriei (named in 1878 to mark the humbling of the Turks) there were protests in Parliament that it had cost the equivalent of the country's annual output. A lie, the indignant Prime Minister of the day replied, the true amount was only half that much. As for Budapest, there was scarcely a city in Europe that conveyed so powerfully the memory of a national renaissance concentrated into only a few decades. Though Hungarians complained that they were still tied to the Habsburgs, the so-called Compromise of 1867 had made them virtual co-rulers of the empire, and they built and rebuilt their capital as real kings and emperors might have done. The city's architecture reached a peak of self-congratulation in the monument erected on the thousandth anniversary in 1896 of the Hungarian settlement on the plains enclosed within the horseshoe of the Carpathian mountains. In Heroes' Square the Archangel Gabriel who gave the crown to Stephen, Hungary's first king, stands on top of an 118-foot column at whose base gather seven giant horsemen – Arpad and the other tribal chiefs who led the Magyars out of Asia into Europe. The Square and most of the other creations of the Hungarian nineteenth-century renaissance never fitted comfortably into the new Communist city. Subversive by reason of their past and original purpose, they awaited the events of the late 1980s like a stage prepared for a play whose script was not yet written.

East Berlin was no more amenable to its new rulers. The capital of the German Communist state had to live with a bricks-and-mortar *Doppelgänger* across the wall that mocked every attempt to turn East Berlin into a socialist city. And Warsaw? It was perhaps the worst of all the urban inheritances that passed to the Communists even though in one gruesome respect it should have been the best. Old Warsaw scarcely existed when the war ended in 1945. After the uprising in the summer of 1944 Hitler had ordered the city to be levelled. Nine out of ten of its houses were destroyed or damaged beyond repair. To complete their work the Germans drove away all the 600,000 remaining inhabitants into concentration camps or forced labour in Germany. The Soviet Red Army in January 1945 reclaimed an empty, ruined city.

The Hungarian novelist Gyorgy Konrad wrote of the city's staying power:

> The city is a sensuous and constant reality, the state is more arbitrary and abstract. The city is a work of art that creates itself. It is human society's work of imagination. States come unwound and topple over, but the city remains. The city comes to new life again even after it has been bombed and has sunk into rubble and ashes. It survives occupying powers, empires and dictators that have won power over it.

Cities are subversive, too rich and complex to be moulded to the will of any one ruler. And of all the cities of East Europe none was to prove more stubborn than ruined Warsaw, whose first victory over its new rulers was to impel them to rebuild so much of it as it had always been. Consider this scene that was acted out many times during the summers of the 1980s in Warsaw's Ogrod Saski, a small park that is almost all that remains of an eighteenth-century royal palace in the city's heart. Visitors on fine afternoons would be startled by the sound of a shrill 'BRRRR' as though a coachman was signalling to his horse to pull up. Investigation revealed a gammy-legged old man, perhaps once a cavalry soldier but now wearing a worker's cap over thick white hair, who was pulling a child in circles on a wheeled rocking horse. Made of scrap metal covered with black cloth, the unusual animal drew behind it a carriage big enough for a child, but more often containing a couple of dolls and perhaps a toy rabbit. The children who were the old man's clients usually preferred to ride on the horse itself. A child mounted; with a wave of the whip that lightly struck the horse on the neck the old man drew the contraption round and round at the end of a leather rein. A Polish flag always flew at the horse's head. On special days like 9 May, the anniversary of the defeat of Nazi Germany, the animal bore an appropriate cardboard sign. 'BRRRR' cried the old man, and the ride was over.

A walk through Warsaw in the autumn of 1988 with G., a Polish friend who had lived much of his life in the city, was another lesson in its vitality. No sooner had the war ended than the streets came to life again, G. recalled as we set off along a wooded path between the Vistula and the Sejm, the Polish parliament. When Marszalkowska, one of the main thoroughfares, was still no more than a shaky line of first floors among the rubble it already had all kinds of shops including bakers making marvellous bread, and more restaurants than in all of modern Warsaw put together. Restaurants the Communists had managed to spoil, but luckily not everything else. G. walked slowly, stopping first to light a cigarette, then to catch his breath or to contemplate a building that caught his attention. The Ujazdowski Palace, an eighteenth-century structure of limited appeal apart from its pepper pot towers, had been the residence of Moscow's Governor when Tsarist Russia ruled over Warsaw and the eastern part of Poland. The Russians had not moved far away. The Soviet embassy, only a little smaller than the Ujzazdowski Palace, was close by, opposite the Belvedere, the white neo-classical manor house built for a Russian Grand Duke and today (in 1990) Poland's Presidential Palace. It had been a national shrine since Marshal Pilsudski lived there when he was President in all but name, playing patience as he got older, or sitting looking down the sloping garden to the park created by King Stanislaw Augustus. It was bad enough that Boleslaw Bierut, Poland's first Communist President after the rigged elections of 1947, should have taken up residence there. Worse still was the man's total lack of decency – G. stopped, so indignant he had to catch his breath. Imagine what Bierut had done. He had kept the Belvedere even when he relinquished the Presidency and lived there till he died. There was Communist shamelessness for you.

Many Poles did not like it any better when General Jaruzelski, who had imposed martial law in 1981, became President and set up his offices in the Belvedere. But Jaruzelski was driven by opportunism or residual conviction to move slowly with the tide of the city's mood and memories. It was after imposing martial law that he gave the army back their *rogatywka*, the four-cornered cap recalling a peaked mortarboard that Polish soldiers had worn until the Communists took it away. The gesture infuriated the opposition intellectual Adam Michnik who declared it had turned the proud cap into the 'clown's hat of a Soviet lackey'. Poles had seen Moscow's Polish collaborators use these tricks before. It was the young Pilsudski who argued that the putting up of a statue to Mickiewicz in 1898, when the Tsar ruled Warsaw, was no more than an attempt to reconcile 'Polish patriotism with Muscovite captivity'. In the same vein G. was reminded, on reaching Ujazdowskie Avenue, that Jaruzelski had had the army parade soldiers along it dressed in the uniforms of Pilsudski's Legions (formed in 1914 when there was still no

independent Poland) while bands played the Legions' march 'We
of the First Brigade':

> The Legions stand for a soldier's slog
> The Legions stand for a martyr's fate.

Such things were not trivial to Poles. G. remembered how as a
boy he would stiffen to attention if he heard the national anthem
while lying in bed. He grinned, wondering if Jaruzelski might one
day even revive the Polish cavalry. It did not seem far-fetched. The
General's staff was already speaking of him as a man loyal at heart
to the old Polish traditions. Had not the General's grandfather taken
part in the anti-Russian uprising of 1863? And was his family not
among the oldest of the Polish middle nobility, and its coat-of-arms
to be found in the oldest surviving book of heraldic record that
dated back to 1420? As for the General's dark glasses that people
found so off-putting, his apologists insisted that far from using them
to hide behind he had no choice but to wear them. His eyes had
been irreparably damaged by the glare of the Siberian snows when
he was deported to the Soviet Union along with one and a half
million other Poles in 1939. This was too much for G. It wasn't
amusing any more. They were trying to turn the man who had done
Moscow's dirty work over martial law into a victim of the Russians.

His mood improved as the Sejm came once more in sight. It
made him think of the pre-war senators, who had taken themselves
so seriously. They had always dressed formally and hung large oil
portraits of themselves behind their office desks. If possible they
also displayed a photograph showing them together with that
miracle-worker, the old Marshal. *Plus ça change* – in Poland above
all. When a few months later Solidarity announced its candidates for
the June 1989 elections that would finally destroy the Communists'
credibility, the chosen men and women were called to Gdansk by
Lech Walesa. There they were photographed together and separately
with the man in whom some Poles saw the makings of a proletarian
Pilsudski. These photos, displayed during the candidates' election
campaigns, were to prove as miraculous as any of the old Marshal's,
for scarcely a single Solidarity nominee lost.

G. and the other citizens of Warsaw had over a number of years
been able to watch, and sometimes take part in, a sort of guerrilla
warfare in which the Government on the one side, and the Roman

Catholic Church and/or opposition on the other, fought symbolic battles for the control of the city and its potent memories. Poles had realised earlier than other East European nations that victory would go to the side that took possession of the national past. It was the Polish Communists' misfortune that most Poles believed that during the war the Communists had been guilty of treachery, the worst of Polish sins. An insignificant political party before the war, the Communists were brought to power by the Soviet Red Army, although the wartime resistance within the country was led by the non-Communist *Armia Krajowa* (the Home Army, usually known by its initials AK), the largest resistance force in the whole of occupied Europe. The Communists' contribution to the resistance, the *Armia Ludowa* (People's Army), had been puny by comparison. For many Poles the Communists were usurpers who could never be forgiven, and the bitterness scarcely faded over the years as was shown in early 1989 when Poland's last Communist Prime Minister, Mieczyslaw Rakowski, invited a ninety-eight-year-old hero, General Stanislaw Maczek, to return to Poland from exile in Britain to attend ceremonies marking the fiftieth anniversary of the war's outbreak. Maczek and others like him who had fought on the Western side in the war had been pronounced traitors by the post-war Polish Government. The General had been wronged, Rakowski now wrote in his letter, but he himself had always considered Maczek 'a paragon of a patriot and a soldier'. If he came back he would be greeted 'with all due reverence, as a national hero'. The old soldier's family declined politely. 'What did Rakowski expect? A general fraternisation? It's impossible,' was the comment of Jozef Czapski, who as a survivor and then researcher of the long-denied Soviet massacre of Polish officers at Katyn was an authority on truth that is told too late.

There were some great set pieces in this war without guns between regime and people, notably the three visits of John Paul II, who until his election as Pope was Karol Wojtyla, Archbishop of Krakow. The first papal visit in 1979 removed fears, never far beneath the surface, that the Church in pursuit of its eternal interests might one day do a deal with the regime behind the people's back. The dissident Jacek Kuron noted that the visit left behind 'a feeling of general triumph and strength'. It was, he thought, a 'sign that the Government cannot separate Polish society from the Church'. The visit also made it possible to identify the sides in the coming struggle.

'Before the Pope's visit,' people said, 'we knew who *they*, the regime, were. After it we knew who *we* were.'

Each papal journey home reclaimed more of the city for the insurgents. In 1979 the Pope celebrated open-air mass on Victory Square, the empty space bounded by the Ogrod Saski, the Opera, and Warsaw's new Inter-Continental Hotel, a showy child of the false boom of the 1970s. Occupied until 1918 by an overbearing Russian Orthodox Church, tsarist predecessor of Stalin's Palace of Culture, the square was used for military parades, for the Tomb of the Unknown Soldier lay on its west side. The papal service on Victory Square overshadowed all succeeding Communist ceremonies there, and was matched only by the funeral mass celebrated on the same spot for Cardinal Wyszysnki in the spring of 1981. Early identified by the Communist secret police as exceptionally able and dangerous, Wyszynski remained a troublemaker in death, repossessing the city just when the Communists thought they were rid of him, for after the funeral people kept marking the spot where his coffin had lain during the mass with flowers arranged in the shape of a giant cross. Whenever the police cleared them away more flowers and little candles took their place. The battle seemed lost when martial law was declared in 1981, but the visitor who walks across Victory Square today will find a plaque let into the spot in its concrete surface where the Pope preached and the Cardinal lay among his people for the last time. In a nearby square in front of the little Wyzitek Church on Krakowskie Przedmiescie sits a bronze Wyszynski, mitred head resting in long-fingered hand. Although the Communists gave permission for the statue, was it not a monument to the man who had been the country's only genuine leader in the post-war years? Warsaw had no statues to the regime's own patriarchs.

On his last visit to Communist Poland Karol Wojtyla stormed the Palace of Culture itself. The Polish Church turned this symbol of everything they detested into a giant reredos and altar, from where the Pope blessed young Polish missionary priests about to set off to recruit new soldiers for the holy army Stalin so badly underestimated. By that time (the year was 1987) few found anything remarkable in a Polish Pope saying mass against such a background. The struggle for Warsaw was almost won.

The most persistent battle, waged throughout the city and at all times of the year, was for possession of the memory of the Resistance and the Warsaw Uprising. Hard as the regime tried, it never managed to persuade people that it was a credible celebrant of this most powerful of modern Polish patriotic cults. The Uprising was a particular embarrassment to the Communists because when it began the Soviet army was sitting on the other side of the Vistula but did not stir itself in any way to help. Only some of the Polish units that had been formed under Communist control in the Soviet Union tried to cross the river, as though they understood that to have taken part in this battle would be essential credentials for any political force in post-war Poland.

Throughout the Communist years memory of the Resistance and Uprising were kept alive in the capital's churches. Many had plaques to the Uprising's fallen soldiers. The cult of the Uprising reached a peak in churches like the Holy Mother of God of Czestochowa on Zagorna Street, for which Wyszynski laid the foundation stone in 1979. There cannot be many churches in the world that have a machine gun set prominently in one of their walls: this one was found when the foundations were being dug. The façade is covered with the names of the units and fighters that perished in the hopeless battle. 'Patroness of the Home Army, pray for us,' says a memorial to guerrillas from the sweetly code-named Pheasant District. Another lists the *noms-de-guerre* of a unit called Kryska – there is Maciek, Marlena, Ewa, Trojan and Eagle. None of them were over twenty when they died and one, a boy called Bet, was only fifteen. Under the familiar heading 'God, Honour and Fatherland' a bronze inscription reads 'May they remember only this about us so that freedom shall be the law.'

Was it surprising that the Polish Communists so often seemed to get everything wrong? People have bad days when nothing goes right. Jinxed from the start, this regime had bad years. It set off on hopeless schemes – like the 1987 referendum on economic reform, which finally scuppered the Communists' chance to put the economy to rights – and yet was surprised and even hurt when they failed. Typically disastrous (and not un-Polish, it must be said, in their defiance of the odds) was the Government's decision to put up its own monument to the Warsaw Uprising, more precisely to the 'Heroes of the Warsaw Uprising', a dedication at once taken by Poles to imply that in the regime's opinion not everyone who had died in the capital in August 1944 had been a hero and that the Communists were once more trying to write history to suit themselves. This monument, its larger-than-life figures disagreeably reminiscent of official war memorials throughout the Soviet bloc, was not unveiled until August 1989, when the last Communist Government had only a few more days to live. But the battle for this particular bit of the past was pressed till the last minute. On the eve of the official unveiling several thousand people gathered in the Powazki Cemetery for the consecration of an alternative memorial to Generals Bor-Komorowski, Tokarzewski and the other seven leaders of the Uprising. This monument was simple, filling barely five feet across the cemetery's brick catacomb wall. On one side little brass crosses climbed to the top of the wall while on the other the names of the nine were carved in brick. The Resistance fighters had painted their messages on the brick walls of Warsaw; let plain brick be their memorial now. Most people had brought flowers, usually no more than two or three stems of red, white, or orange gladioli, which they put at the foot of the wall. There was such a crush that little could be glimpsed of the bishop doing the consecrating except for the tip of the brush with which he flicked holy water on the bricks. Clear, though, for all to see were the silver-crowned Polish eagles tipping the end of faded partisan flags carried by old men in black berets, and the feathers in the four-cornered caps of a quartet who had come in uniform. Poland, their Poland, had all but won the long war without guns but they still needed to affirm their right to inhabit the past for which it had been fought. Hands went up in the victory salute as they joined in *God Protect Poland*, the hymn sung a thousand times in churches during martial law: 'God save us with your protection . . . Let us return to a free Poland . . . Crush the sword that hangs over our country.' The incorrigibly buoyant national anthem followed, and then the *Rota*, whose promise to shed the last drop of blood to defend the motherland had first been heard in the days of the German Partition. At the end people went up to greet Agathon, Bor-Komorowski's last ADC and one of the memorial's designers. For once the bearer of a *nom-de-guerre* had lived beyond youth. Agathon, a lively old man who wore his white hair *en brosse*, was delighted with the occasion. 'Everyone who should have come did.' Indeed they had. When to alleviate the crush during the ceremony people had moved away from the wall to stand among the tombstones it was as though Poland itself was rising from the dead.

Visitors to Warsaw who attended ceremonies like this could not fail to be moved. Yet there was in them something that left the stranger uneasy, something that seemed to contain disagreeable echoes from the past and also, perhaps, threats for the future. In Poland, as in the rest of East Europe, the sense of having suffered more than others, more than any nation deserved to suffer, could lead to self-dramatisation and self-pity. The evening after the ceremony at Powazki Cemetery a service commemorating the Uprising was held in St John's Cathedral in the presence of Poland's new Primate, Cardinal Glemp. Many more people had come than the Cathedral could accommodate and several hundred stood in the narrow street outside listening to the mass over loudspeakers. It was a scene to rival the vast canvases with which the nineteenth-century painter Jan Matejko recreated great moments of the Polish past. When the bread and wine were blessed the street fell to its knees. A grey-bearded man in a filthy raincoat and shoes worn almost through knelt beside a long-skirted girl guide with an aquiline nose, her beret worn at the most fetching possible angle. Next to them a scout grasped his cap, peak to the front, in his left hand which he supported with the right, as though he were holding a prince's crown. When vergers came onto the street with bags for the collection a beggar who had been sitting on the steps of the church next door leaned across his crutches towards them, a banknote trembling in his hand.

At the end of the service some two thousand people set off in procession for the Tomb of the Unknown Soldier in Victory Square. It began with a *coup-de-théâtre* to make a Communist weep with envy. Three small children holding tommy-guns, a tiny girl in the middle, marched at the column's head. Wrapped in khaki capes, their faces were scarcely visible beneath adult steel helmets. Thirty-six battle standards of units that fought in the Uprising followed, some embroidered with pictures of the Black Madonna of Czestochowa, others depicting the Resistance fighters themselves. Friends from Powazki reappeared. The uniformed four with plumes all carried sabres. One wore boots and spurs. Order was kept by guides and scouts (who had had their own formation in the Uprising). The scouts had ironed their floppy version of the incipient *rogatywka* to accentuate the caps' four corners. With long staves in their hands and capes thrown carelessly over the right shoulder the old Polish cavalry could scarcely have looked more dashing.

In the Cathedral they had listened to a sermon with a familiar theme. All Poles knew who was responsible for the failure of the Uprising. Once again Poland and Warsaw had experienced suffering unknown to other nations in the service of those three imperishables God, Honour and Fatherland. Who could deny the genuineness of the feeling? Yet how long would this cult of Polish martyrdom last?

In Primo Levi's novel about the fortunes of a group of Jewish partisans *If Not Now, When?* a Polish commander in the *Armia Krajowa* recites some poetry to the Jewish soldiers, most of whom come from Russia.

> Mary, don't give birth in Poland,
> Unless you want to see your son
> Nailed to a cross the moment he's born.

The Jews' leader asks when the lines were written. 'I don't know,' the Pole answers, 'but for my country any century would have done.' The belief that Poland was the Christ among nations, crucified yet left to suffer in spite of its cries of pain, had won a firm hold over Poles in the nineteenth century, not least because it had been elaborated by some of their best writers, Adam Mickiewicz among them. Pilsudski's Legions awaited the 'martyr's fate' because faithfulness until death, even if the cause seemed lost, was the ultimate test of both Polish nation and Polish patriot. When the Communists came to power they tried to drive these cloudy passions from Polish heads but with little success. How could it have been otherwise since the very presence of these 'foreign' Communists challenged the Poles to keep the old faith? During martial law Warsaw acquired another exceptionally powerful shrine to Polish martyrdom. When officers of the secret police killed the young priest Jerzy Popieluszko his church, St Stanislaw Kostka in the well-to-do suburb of Zoliborz, became overnight a new patriotic bridgehead in the capital. If, as Catholic laymen said, half of the junior priesthood was already dreaming of becoming Karol Wojtyla, the other half now saw their model in Father Popieluszko, the perfect modern Polish martyr.

The condition of Poland, of which the endless battle fought out in Warsaw was a microcosm, encouraged Poles to look for the cause of their troubles outside both themselves and their country's borders. G., on another walk through the capital, talked about the Poles' belief that they were spotless in a wicked world. 'The Poles think they are without sin. They blame everything on the Communists.' Communism was certainly not Polish; it was a Russian invention or a Jewish plot (Polish innocence still sometimes seemed to shine more brightly when set against supposed Jewish guilt). Warsaw was an innocent city, constantly sinned against but never sinning. The message was there on every street, in the fresh bunches of flowers under the little plaques that marked each death in the German-occupied city; in the posters and leaflets with the dancing logo of Solidarity, as much a banner of innocence as any church standard bearing the image of the Virgin Mary, Queen of Poland. Like Warsaw the other capitals of East Europe would also claim that nothing was their fault. Soviet occupation had washed away their sins too, even removing the uneasiness of Budapest and Buchar-est about having taken Hitler's side in the war. Hungarian and Romanian Communists tried hard to pin guilt for this on the 'class enemies'. For the most part, though, Soviet occupation proved a detergent strong enough to remove most guilty stains even if no one matched the immaculacy of Polish innocence that shone in Polish eyes as white as the walls of Pilsudski's Belvedere.

By the late 1970s Warsaw had come to epitomise active resistance to a regime considered to be foreign. The Czechoslovak capital Prague had in one respect suffered a similar fate. Raped by Hitler, then taken into Stalin's empire, Czechoslovakia was with Poland the only other country in the Soviet bloc that could correctly claim always to have numbered among the century's injured innocent. Yet Prague's resistance was of a quite different kind. Warsaw opposed to the point of self-destruction. Prague opposed by making sure it survived and not taking the occupier too seriously.

TIME AND TRANSFORMATIONS

Where Warsaw was passionate and impatient Prague was sceptical and ready to take its time. An explanation lay in its extraordinary buildings. Apart from a few painful losses most came out of the war intact, and since that moment there had been a battle between the message of their architecture and the ambitions of their new masters. Drab dressers themselves, the Communists managed to bring superficial drabness even to this glorious city. Socialist surrealism became the order of the day. It was not thought the least bit odd that a restaurant should have in its window a large photograph of a potato field and the announcement 'quality potatoes for your table'. In clothes shops women's dresses hung diagonally, some from left to right, others from right to left, as though the city's window-dressers were taught by a master who had once seen the floating bodies of a Chagall painting. Mixer taps were displayed with pride in shops on Wenceslas Square, supposedly the grandest place in the city. As for the shopping arcades in the palaces of commerce put up at the turn of the century, like the Art Nouveau-style Lucerna built by Vaclav Havel's father, they felt like caves in which some prehistoric activity now hard to understand had once been carried on. Displays in backstreet shops might not change for years. Plastic key rings and old-fashioned safety razors were put on view in confidence that no new competitive product would enter the Prague market (perhaps this was the reason that hotels still provided guests at the end of the 1980s with little slips of paper on which to wipe their razor blades). The regime's propaganda had a similar dream-like unreality. The notorious neon sign in Wenceslas Square that cried *With the Soviet Union for ever* still came alight each night even after Mikhail Gorbachev had begun to take his country where no Czech leader wished to follow. An *agitpunkt* of the Communist Party's front organisation near Old Town Square was still offering in November 1989 the same display of dried flowers, Lenin bust, and landscape painting placed upside down that had graced its window for several years past. Western news-papers were nowhere to be bought but second-hand shops were allowed to sell old magazines giving a strange view of life abroad such as *Le Nouveau Pif, Femme Actuelle* and *STOP* ('Caroline distressed! Risks losing her baby').

Prague was being slowly starved, in ways both visible and invis-ible, by a regime that feared it could not control the city if it ever came to life. It lay gathering dust like an exquisite violin that no one had the courage to pick up and play. The neglect created a beauty of its own. Stone figures holding up classical pediments acquired new drama when they turned black as Africans in the sooty air. The remains of an old orchard were allowed to survive close to the Prime Minister's office by the Manesuv bridge although its trees produced cherries that never ripened and apples that were the size of golf balls and tasted no better. It was charming that the beech hedges were never tidily clipped in the gardens of the Palace of Wallenstein, named after the commander of the Thirty Years War whom the Habsburg emperor had assassinated for having designs on the Czech throne. A fistful of Gothic spires seemed even more glorious when glimpsed above façades stained with damp, or framed between skirts of wooden scaffolding wrapped round buildings to stop decrepit masonry tumbling onto pavements below. But as years went by the feeling grew that this regime, after promising so much, had proved its unworthiness by its inability even to maintain the patrimony it had taken over.

The Communists' problem was that Prague had been through so much before. To some the city spoke of good times that the Communists could never hope to match. In the museum that was once Wallenstein's riding school an old woman attendant would take visitors by the arm and point to the glories around her. *'Damals waren wir sehr reich, damals'* – 'In those days we were very rich' – she would mutter, repeating the words 'in those days' to make sure her point was not missed. To others, Prague's message was durability through adaptation. Many of the old buildings were turncoats that several times in their existence had changed their style, colour and purpose. The river Vltava on whose banks the city lies was prone to flooding until an embankment was built in the last century and the land level raised. Present-day basements are old ground floors with the result that quite a few Prague cellars go back to Romanesque times. In the seventeenth century new fire laws required that wooden ceilings be plastered over. A house that today boasts baroque mouldings may in fact be hiding a handsome Renaissance ceiling in painted wood. When the city restorers wanted to paint a building in its original colour they would find themselves having to choose from as many as twenty different paints preserved on layers of old plaster. Monuments that everyone had supposed to be baroque, like the Bell House in Old Town Square, were suddenly revealed to be several hundred years older, going back to Gothic times. Churches from whose Gothic altars Hussite sermons had been pronounced had been transformed into fortresses of the Counter-Reformation by the addition of melodramatic shrines and altars in the baroque manner.

These transformations suited a city some of whose famous citizens, from Faust to Wallenstein, had dabbled in magic and alchemy. The Communist alchemy looked feeble in such company, and nowhere was this brought more forcefully home than at the Clementinum. This large unwelcoming complex that covers almost as much ground as the castle of Prague itself served the Jesuits as their college for two hundred years until the Order's abolition in 1773. Its Baroque Hall houses the Jesuits' collection of theological books. Here, beneath a ceiling fresco depicting an allegory of human knowledge, eminent members of the Order look out from their portraits with the assurance of men who know that not all knowledge is fit for humans. Prominent among the bookshelves is a locked cupboard above which are the words *Libri Prohibiti* – forbidden books.

The Clementinum was evidence of the success of a campaign of indoctrination or brainwashing (the modern words seem quite appropriate) that began after 1620 when the Habsburgs routed the Protestant nobility of Bohemia in a battle on a hill outside Prague known as the White Mountain. When the Jesuits had come to Prague the previous century they urged the Emperor Rudolf II to kill the Protestant followers of the Czech Jan Hus by sword, wheel, water, rope and fire. They got their chance after White Mountain. Historians explain the decrees issued then by the Emperor Ferdinand under Jesuit prompting as having 'the double aim of transforming the existing social and political order in Bohemia and extirpating the religious faith upon which it had been built'. The Jesuits, believing that two-thirds of the population was tainted with heresy, made bonfires out of books written in the Czech language that the Hussites used and, in the spirit of *Libri Prohibiti*, exercised such a harsh censorship over others that almost nothing of literary worth could be published. They also prevented the teaching of Czech history in schools. 'The Jesuits', the nineteenth-century Czech historian Vaclav Tomek wrote, 'had imprisoned the Czech national spirit in a centuries-old tomb.'

If this sounded familiar enough to inhabitants of Communist Prague so too did another Jesuit ploy. Determined to destroy Czech reverence for Jan Hus, the father of the Czech Reformation, they recovered from obscurity a fourteenth-century vicar-general of Prague called Jan Nepomuk. The latter's only claim on memory was that he had crossed the irascible King Wenceslas IV over some monastic appointment and been tortured and tossed from Charles Bridge to drown in the Vltava. This unfortunate but otherwise unremarkable cleric was the Jesuits' candidate to replace Jan Hus as the hero of good Czech Christians. An altar was erected to him in Prague's St Vitus Cathedral in 1621, the year after White Mountain. All sorts of wonders were claimed for him, not least that his tongue was found pink and firm when his coffin was opened three hundred years after his death.

Similar techniques of intellectual control and terror were remarkably less successful in Communist hands. When in 1648 the Protestant Swedes stormed through Bohemia to seize Prague they met sturdy resistance from the first generation of Czechs to have been educated in the new manner by the Jesuits. Twenty years of Communist censorship, education and the manufacture of new heroes failed to bring Czechs onto the streets to greet the Soviet tanks when they arrived at the gates of Prague in 1968.

In difficult times Czechs would say that the city's beauty was their only consolation and sometimes their only reason for not seeking to go abroad, but the city also presented them with a not always comforting truth. The Prague they loved was dominated by baroque buildings, perhaps the finest examples of the style anywhere, and all these palaces and churches were propaganda for the Counter-Reformation. It was Kilian Ignaz Dienzenhofer, the city's greatest baroque architect, who built the pilgrimage church at Jan Nepomuk's birthplace outside Plzen, and it was entirely appropriate that the first church Dienzenhofer built in Prague should end up being dedicated to Nepomuk when he at last achieved canonisation. If these monuments were tolerable in spite of what they stood for it was because the Czechs had, finally, come out on top. At the end of the Thirty Years War, when the Jesuits were already engaged with full fury on remodelling both the city's buildings and the minds of its inhabitants, there were perhaps no more than 800,000 inhabitants left in all Bohemia. Thirty years earlier the population may have been as large as three million. Most of the old Czech nobility and gentry were decimated by the war and the reprisals that followed, and never recovered. But over the next 150 years the Czech peasant consolidated, and then slowly pushed his way back into the towns. Prague, dominated by a German elite until the middle of the nineteenth century, was once more a Czech town in 1900. Even then Czechoslovakia, like much of East Europe, remained a kaleidoscope of a country. It only needed a gentle shake for things to take on a different appearance. Was the river that ran through Prague the Czech Vltava or the German Moldau? Bratislava was the capital of Slovakia from 1918 but it was the same place that the Austrians called Pressburg and Hungarians Pozsony. The Hungarian writer Paul Ignotus marvelled at how the mongrel city of Budapest had managed by the end of the last century to become a real Hungarian capital:

> It had sprung from the resolve of the Magyar gentry to become middle class; of the German-speaking middle classes to become Magyar; and the Jews to become both.

These shifting identities, the result of living under empires for which class and religion counted for much but nationality almost nothing, were to be found throughout the region. The Romanian town of Brasov, at the southern entrance to Transylvania, sometimes appeared disguised as Hungarian Brasso, at others as the German Kronstadt. Readers of modern German newspapers still come across reports from Breslau, Brunn and Hermannstadt, towns that do not exist on their respective Polish, Czechoslovak and Romanian maps. The countries of East Europe were composed of as many layers as the buildings of Prague, and there were moments when a layer or detail no one paid great attention to was suddenly restored and blazed forth in startling colours. In the last war the old German communities in Hungary and Romania came alive to provide Hitler with volunteers for the SS. The war also gave the German minority in Czechoslovakia a chance to recover ground lost to the Czechs over the preceding hundred years.

The Czechs established themselves as a modern nation by patience, growing numbers and sly disrespect for their Austrian masters. They had no gloriously disastrous uprisings such as entranced the Hungarians and Poles when they looked back on their history of the previous two centuries. The First World War exploits of the Czechoslovak legions, made up of prisoners from the Austrian army who fought for the Western Allies in Russia, strengthened Czech claims for independence, but they did not alter many Czechs' self-deprecating picture of themselves as people who only moved when they had history breathing down their necks. 'We are too used to being given things. We didn't really fight for independence. We didn't have a proper national liberation movement in the Second World War.' Czechs, in this case a member of Charter 77, offered such judgements as though they were facts too stubborn to change. A Communist, a man whose job it was in the 1980s to persuade the Party leadership at least to glance at new ideas, used the same matter-of-fact tone when explaining that enforced collaboration with foreign powers over the centuries had taught the Czechs to be opportunistic. Wait things out – that was Prague's message, and all the more convincing because the Communists, unlike earlier conquerors, managed to build so little that was entirely their own in the city.

What did they leave behind? There was an ugly monument to their first Stalinist leader Klement Gottwald; and a pretentious congress hall, put up after 1968, where Moscow's trusty Gustaw Husak imagined the Party holding untroubled meetings ever after, but which ended up seeing the first panicky Communist gatherings called after the November revolution. The comrades in the rest of East Europe did little better as remodellers of their capitals. The Hungarian Party built a new headquarters for itself in Budapest. Close to the Parliament on the bank of the Danube it could not have had a more excellent site. But it was a relatively unobtrusive modern building in white stone, no match for the architectural egos on display in the rest of the city. The Hungarians mostly contented themselves with putting red stars on public buildings, or having the city's gardeners arrange plants in the pattern of stars in municipal flower beds. Only when it came to the Soviet war memorial was flamboyance worthy of Magyars achieved, for the bronze figure of a woman holding a palm branch to the sky stood on the peak of Gellert Hill overlooking the Danube where it could be seen by almost the whole city. In the end even this achievement was undermined by the story that the Russian generals had chosen the statue from the studio of a well-known Budapest sculptor who had intended it for the grave of Admiral Horthy's airman son. In the original version, the gossips said, the lady held up not a branch of palm but an airplane propeller.

Why was it that East Europe had to wait thirty-five years for a Communist leader determined to leave an unmistakable mark on his capital? Did lack of confidence, doubt in their national credentials – neither of which troubled the Romanian Ceausescu – hold them back? Were they over-awed by what they had inherited or did they secretly admire it? It is striking that the Polish regime, quite apart from its decision to rebuild so much of the old city as it was before the war, never managed to pull off any grand and convincingly Communist vista. They had an opportunity with Marszalkowska, the street on which Stalin's Palace of Culture stood, but if by the end of the 1980s this ensemble stood for anything it was the collapse of an ill-thought-out Utopia. Soon after the war grey stone buildings that might have been transported from Stalin's Moscow were put up at Marszalkowska's southern end round Constitution Square. Their impact would have been greater had the planners managed to remove the nineteenth-century Church of the Holy Saviour whose spires easily out-topped the new buildings. They wanted to, but their nerve and public support failed them. In the sixties a row of steel and glass department stores, flats and office buildings marking the age of socialist consumerism was sited opposite the Palace of Culture. The seventies' boom engineered on money borrowed from gullible Western banks and governments brought a beige skyscraper hotel built by Scandinavians. The eighties brought nothing, except that the socialist department stores had to open hard currency sections in order to have something to sell, and street traders of a kind not seen since before the war re-appeared on Marszalkowska's pavements.

The East Germans started off with greater confidence. Urged by the Russians to build something grand for East Berlin they came up with the Stalinallee, later renamed Karl-Marx-Allee. Even Moscow's Chief Architect found its disciplined mile of apartments and shops too rigid an interpretation of Stalinist style. 'Typically German,' he called it. 'To the left a company at attention, to the right a company at attention.' Its East German designer, a pre-war student of the *Bauhaus*, said the street would give the working class courage, but when Stalin died the Party newspaper *Neues Deutschland* accused him of having been taken in by the Soviet leader's personality cult. After that unhappy experience the East Berlin leadership little by little gave in to the Prussian past, of which there was already a trace in the Stalinallee. Erich Honecker not only let his showy Palast der Republik be overshadowed by the old Berlin Dom but also had a façade from the demolished Hohenzollern palace stuck on the front of the building of the State Council. The East German Party never put up its own offices, preferring to remain in the ugly but voluminous building that had formerly housed Hitler's Reichsbank.

HUMAN TIDES

East Europe's Communists could have said that their memorial would be new factories and the housing estates for the workers who manned them. As for the old cities, they would pursue a policy of functional metamorphosis and make use of them as they were. This produced edifying results. The Budapest stock exchange, built at the turn of the century to be the biggest in Europe, became the headquarters of Hungarian State Television; the stock exchange in Warsaw a museum of working-class achievements. At the same time the Communist flood drove a fresh tide into the quiet rockpools of the cities, carrying in new varieties of life and sweeping out the old. The metaphor is apt for the process was often as pitiless as nature. The twenty years after the Communists tightened their grip on power in 1948 saw about a million well-to-do Hungarians (civil servants, businessmen, farmers and professional people) suffer what sociologists described calmingly as 'loss of status', while the same number of peasants and workers moved up the social scale to take their place. While in 1948 few members of the professions had working-class origins, by 1984 almost two-thirds of professionals were the children of manual workers. Much the same happened throughout East Europe. The Polish dissident Adam Michnik later reflected on the difference between Nazi and Soviet occupation. The Germans hoped to turn the Poles into slaves but otherwise left them alone and promised them nothing. The Russians, working through the Polish Communists, killed the recalcitrant but offered the hope of conversion to a new faith, encouraged the poor to plunder the wealthy. This 'deadly mixture of terror and social promise . . . ennobled common robbery by endowing it with ideological meaning, and so destroyed the traditional structures of social organisation.'

The cities recorded these changes in shifts of property, in loss of home as well as loss of factory and farms. In Bucharest many middle-class households were given twenty-four hours to collect their belongings and clear out of their pleasant villas near Herastrau Park. Fortunes differed. Bourgeois families like the Havels in Prague might be allowed to keep a flat in houses they had built, while a once famous Hungarian actress, a friend of the Horthy family, lived out the end of her life in a broken-down railway carriage on a Budapest station siding. The war had done some of the Communist bailiffs' work for them. Forty per cent of the pre-war population of Warsaw was Jewish. Many belonged to the middle class and would have been ripe for expropriation had they survived the Nazis. Prominent among those who gained from this process were the writers, painters and other artists who supported the new regimes.

Throughout East Europe writers' and other creative arts' unions took over grand houses in the capitals while in the countryside they were given castles and palaces for their members to relax in. 'There are flowers in the park,' the Hungarian dissident Miklos Haraszti wrote mockingly, 'a lake for the poet, a glade for the novelist, picturesque peasant houses in the village – nor is the capital too far away either.' Even this was not always enough. A Bucharest woman was rung up by an acquaintance who had an important job in the new cultural bureaucracy. He told her he wanted to take his family to stay for a few days in her villa in the hills and would call round for her in his car. He arrived in a chauffeur-driven black Zis with his wife and two small sons, and held a pistol to the woman's side throughout the journey to make sure she understood what 'staying a few days' meant. The flood did not always carry off what most people would have said were the dirtiest inhabitants of the old cities, those who had collaborated with the Nazis. Members of Hungary's Fascist Arrow Cross movement who served the Germans in subaltern capacities provided most of the NCOs for the AVO, the new Communist security police, even though among the latter's leaders were Jews who had survived Hitler's camps. ('Jews and Nazis idyllically united,' the Budapest joke ran, an accurate comment on the difficulty of achieving purity even in a revolution.) As was to be expected the members of the new forces of law and order also did well out of the redivision of real estate. Employees of the Hungarian interior ministry had put at their disposal a turn-of-the-century neo-classical palace, conveniently next door to the ministry, where they could watch films and other entertainments in a pretty private theatre lit by *putti* holding electric candelabra. If many did not mourn for the vanishing old elite, the delight of the newly powerful in their privileges was neither forgiven nor forgotten. Milovan Djilas, the brilliant young Montenegrin who was Tito's right hand, liked to drive slowly down Belgrade's Terazije in the open Mercedes-Benz that he boasted was the best car in Yugoslavia, better even than any of the Marshal's. Memories of such things was one reason why, as the anti-Communist opposition grew in East Europe over the years, there would always be tension between those who had joined the Party and left, and those who had never been members at all.

Punitive expropriation reached its height of brutality in the prison camps set up for those of the dispossessed thought to be particularly dangerous. The NKVD deported 30,000 East Germans to the Soviet Union, and between 1945–50 held 122,000 in Hitler's old concentration camps. There were certainly Nazis among them, but the middle-class elite of businessmen and professionals was also an important target. A third of these camp inmates died. Czechoslovak Communists made a violent assault against the Catholic Church. All its bishops were interned or imprisoned. The monastic orders were broken up and two-thirds of their members also imprisoned or interned. Tens of thousands of priests and Catholic laymen, including most Catholic intellectuals, spent many years in jail. In Hungary, too, there were deportations to the Soviet Union while other 'undesirables' were put to forced labour inside the country. The regime sent those it feared most to a prison camp at Recsk on the slopes of the Matra Hills in northern Hungary. Recsk's existence was for many years denied, probably because none of its inmates were supposed to survive. The security police automatically put the file of anyone sent there into the cabinet marked 'deceased'. The camp held over 1,200 prisoners. They included members of the pre-war political parties (mainly Social Democrats although they had in theory merged voluntarily with the Communists); *kulaks*; students; young peasants; army officers; aristocrats; and Jews who had only just been let out of Dachau and Buchenwald. The latter were the toughest of the prisoners and never tried suicide, the most common method of escaping from the camp.

In the end it proved impossible to strip the cities of their power to subvert. New functions and new inhabitants were not enough to rob buildings of the memories and examples they preserved merely by still standing on the streets. It was hard for young people with a little knowledge of history to walk through Budapest or Warsaw and accept that they should always obey regimes held in place by 'backward' Moscow. Prague's message to young Czechs was more muffled: artful, mocking patience rather than head-on resistance was its recipe for dealing with alien rulers. And in spite of the savage changes brought by the end of the war and the Communists' coming to power human lines could remain unbroken even in the cities. In one of the pleasantly green Bucharest streets near Herastrau Park there is a house built in the 1920s by a First World War hero for his young family. The hero, the first Romanian aviator to shoot down a German plane, died prematurely and his widow and children were living there when the Communists came to power. A shrewd woman, the widow guessed what might be in store and before the order came to pack up and leave she let the ground floor to a Western diplomat. This gave her the right to remain when her neighbours were driven out. The diplomat left in a couple of years but she kept the right to stay by taking in tenants. Stuffing the family possessions in the attic and withdrawing to her bedroom, she let the rest of the house to families of peasants who had come to the capital to work in the newly formed army, police and security service. When a family took possession of a room they knocked holes in the wall for their cooking and heating stoves but since most of the men carried guns there was no point complaining. Whenever it seemed favourable the widow came out of her bedroom to show the uneducated peasant wives how to improve their cooking and to cope with city life. Then the flood began to turn. Her tenants got flats in new prefabricated blocks. As they moved out she won the house back room by room. In 1974 a law was passed allowing expropriated owners to reclaim their houses if they had paid the annual tax on them which most, not surprisingly, had not done. The widow had, selling an heirloom from the attic each time the tax man called.

She was still in her house when Ceausescu was overthrown, surrounded by the surviving ikons and family portraits, and by solid nineteenth-century *objets* and furniture made by men who did not dream of revolutions. When heavy fighting broke out in the street her neighbours panicked and moved away. The widow, aged eighty-nine, refused to budge. Her strategy had always been survival – in this case, another word for victory – by staying put, and it worked once more. Bullets cracked through the walls of her bedroom but she had moved to the ground floor where no harm came to her.

Victory by staying put: it was an appropriate motto for those cities on whose streets the final acts of East Europe's revolutions were to take place.

3

Urban Guerrillas

PARTISANS OF NON-VIOLENCE

If the cities were the battlefields on which the first skirmishes in the undeclared war for democracy were fought, who were the soldiers? The cities themselves offered an ancient arsenal of non-violent weapons, and the inhabitant of Budapest Gyorgy Konrad listed some of them: 'cleverness, discussion, slyness, money, temptation, bribery and enchantment'. These were the tools with which city life had always chipped at the power of conquerors and tyrants, and they had their effect on the Communists of East Europe too, but the men and women who first set out to reconnoitre on behalf of civil liberties and human rights selected different weapons. They were clever, certainly. They also knew how to be sly and greatly relished discussion. But faced with regimes whose survival depended on the citizen surrendering his self-respect, on saying what he did not believe in order to have an unimpeded life, the most devastating weapon at their disposal was truth. To begin with it was a matter of denying the official lie by speaking the truth among themselves, which in turn opened the door to the world of *samizdat*, books copied at first by multiple carbons and typewriters, later by word processors and up-to-date printing machines. Here was the age-old resourcefulness of the city devising new ways to confound tyrannical masters, but it was more than that too. Those who wrote and produced *samizdat* were by that act living truthfully. The chief message of the struggling democrats of East Europe became: do not wait for the end of Communist rule and the coming of democracy, for that lies far in the future, if at all; act now. Acting now meant, in an expression favoured by the members of Czechoslovakia's Charter 77, 'living within the truth'. It would be enough, as a first step, if something could be done to counter what the Polish historian

Adam Michnik, writing in 1979, called the 'tragedy and perfidy' of the Communist system: that it 'pushed people whose honesty could not be questioned into behaving in morally ambiguous ways'. The strike at the Lenin Shipyards that led to the creation of Solidarity in August 1980 was often said to have begun over the sacking of a worker called Anna Waletyowicz. She never thought so: the chief reason was 'the cheating and lying. Truth isn't told to the people.'

The dissidents – a word most East Europeans disliked, Vaclav Havel always putting it between quotation marks – began to find their feet as a group after the Communists had shown that they could not reform themselves. This was finally proved by the failure of the 1968 Prague Spring and the Polish events of the same year, when elements within the Polish Communist Party used anti-Semitism to get rid of those members who believed change was necessary. With Brezhnev in power in the Soviet Union the whole Communist world appeared set in cement. After these miserable events it was obvious that if there was to be change, it would have to come from outside the Communist Parties. Ex-Party members, both those who resigned in disgust and those who were expelled, came to form an important group within the new opposition.

The dissenting world developed in an extremely uneven pattern throughout East Europe. The East German Government was able to get rid of trouble-makers by dumping them in West Germany. This was always the fate of anyone who seemed likely to develop into a figure of authority. Romanians passed from being too enthusiastic about Ceausescu (he had become a national hero by attacking the Soviet invasion of Czechoslovakia) to feel the need for dissidents, to being too terrorised by him for opposition to survive in any organised form. The Hungarians, ruled as well as rulers, handled matters with more suppleness and greater cynicism. The regime of Janos Kadar had its critics, prominent among them people with Communist backgrounds like the philosopher Janos Kis and the ex-Maoist but permanently radical Miklos Haraszti. But it took care to construct for the intellectual world, from which most dissent could be expected, what Haraszti contemptuously called a 'velvet prison'. Hungarians joked that if Solzhenitsyn had lived in Kadar's Hungary he would, given time, have become president of the Writers' Union; therefore no one would have written the *Gulag Archipelago*; and if he had, Solzhenitsyn would have voted to drive him from the Union. As an insight into the Russian writer the joke was questionable; as a judgement of the Hungarian intellectual community it was uncomfortably accurate.

'Living within the truth' sounded to some Western ears an unrealistically moral approach to politics. But in the 1970s and for most of the 1980s the purpose of conventional politics – obtaining power – was beyond the imagination of any serious opposition group in East Europe. Michnik, in an essay called 'A New Evolutionism' published in *samizdat* in 1976, made a typically Polish comparison with the problems facing the opposition's ancestors in nineteenth-century Poland to show that no one should put his hope in violent change.

> The dilemma of nineteenth-century leftist movements – 'reform or revolution' – is not the dilemma of the Polish opposition [today]. To believe in overthrowing the dictatorship of the Party by revolution and consciously to organise actions in pursuit of this goal is both unrealistic and dangerous. As the political structure of the USSR remains unchanged, it is unrealistic to count on subverting the Party in Poland. It is dangerous to plan conspiratorial activities.

Revolutionary violence was excluded for practical reasons but on even more compelling moral grounds. The East European oppositions were the first 'freedom movements' to draw warning lessons from Europe's modern revolutions. Looking back over a dark century they found the spirit to re-affirm belief in reason and humanity, and the courage to live by what they said. Had they done no more than this they would have won an honoured place in the history of Europe. Starting with the Russian Revolution and ending in the Russian-controlled Communist takeovers in East Europe violence had been used self-righteously as a political weapon directed against old friends as much as enemies. As a historian who knew his French Revolution, Michnik argued that no one should forget the possible consequences of revolutionary violence. 'The experience of being corrupted by terror must be imprinted on the consciousness of everyone who belongs to a freedom movement.' The alternative was that 'freedom will again become a refugee from the camp of the victors'. Michnik argued that it was particularly important for Poles to understand this well, because the familiar 'cult of martyrdom, of heroic sacrifice' that continued to be celebrated had 'created in the Polish tradition a beautiful but dangerous ethos'. Prepared to suffer any evil in the national cause, ready 'at all times to die heroically', the Polish conspirator ended up by idealising himself as an angel and seeing only slaves in the passive population around him. His world split into good and evil. Such Manicheanism took away 'the brakes' on human behaviour and had, Michnik commented, 'been the faith of saints and inquisitors . . . Manicheanism has also been the curse of captive peoples.'

Nothing impressed the foreign observer in East Europe so much as this reasoned defence of non-violence in lands where governments only remained in power by the threat of violence, and where captive peoples were all too often given evidence of their masters' evil. These Polish thoughts were of particular relevance to Hungary where there was also a powerful myth of martyrdom in the national cause, and where the 1956 uprising against the Communists had brought reprisals and lynchings. Yet men like Kis, Haraszti and their group round the *samizdat* journal *Beszelo* were no less firm than Michnik in pointing out the dangers of violence. The young Czechoslovaks who took to the streets of Prague in November 1989 were as committed to non-violence as their elders in Charter 77, although most of them had certainly never seen a single Charter publication. By chance the Prague National Theatre put on in 1989 a production of *Danton's Death*. A student who saw it that summer came away horrified by St Just's speech in which he argues the need for the revolution to kill its enemies. The same young man took part in the student march on 17 November that sparked the revolution. He could not believe that even the regime he despised so much would use such unmeasured violence against peaceful protesters. It increased his scorn for the Communists but not his readiness to reply with similar methods, 'We don't want violence,' was one of the commonest slogans to be seen on the walls of Prague during the tense November days. It was not a coincidence that Romania, the only country where the old regime was violently destroyed, was never able to develop an opposition movement that could prepare the Romanian people, and perhaps even some officials inside the Ceausescu machine, for a different kind of change.

The opposition said no violence, but it also taught people not to hope for a change of the system through conventional political means. Even when the Solidarity movement born out of the strikes on the Polish Baltic coast in the summer of 1980 had grown to carry almost the whole nation with it, its leaders never supposed that they should try to take power. Michnik at that time talked only of reaching a 'compromise between a non-sovereign government and a sovereign society'. Solidarity's goal was declared to be a 'self-limiting revolution'. The compromise was necessary because it was every-one's first article of faith that the Soviet Union would never allow the Polish Party, or any other Communist Party in East Europe for that matter, to lose power. The opposition activist Jacek Kuron (later Minister of Labour in Poland's first non-Communist govern-ment) would tell anyone who visited him in the late 1970s that 'for everyone in Poland the crucial limit is when the Soviet tanks start moving. Everyone has to keep this in mind. And one of the factors that could provoke the tanks is a threat to the leading role of the Communist Party.' It was evidence of the extreme caution, born of a sense of responsibility sharpened by years helping keep Poland at peace, that even when it came to holding partly free elections in the summer of 1989 the Polish opposition agreed to a formula for allocating seats that they expected would still allow the Communists to form the Government. It was central to Vaclav Havel's teaching that 'far-reaching political change is utterly unforeseeable', and that Czechoslovaks, if they wished to live in as dignified a way as possible under the Communists, should not get trapped in 'political tactics' or 'entertaining fantasies about the future.'

Mikhail Gorbachev's succession to the Kremlim leadership in 1985 gave rise to hopes. It was not only men like Michnik who began to study the Soviet media for hints about what the new policies of *perestroika* and *glasnost* might mean for East Europe. In Prague people who had never bothered to have a television set bought one so they could watch the Soviet programmes that had become so astonishingly interesting. But Gorbachev still chose his words carefully when he spoke about East Europe. His visits to Prague and Warsaw began in excitement but ended in disillusion, for he would say nothing publicly that might shake the old men out of the offices they had so long occupied. The logic of Gorbachev's policies was plain quite early on; the Soviet Union would use no more force in East Europe. But uncertainty that he would abide by his own logic, or be allowed to by others in the Kremlin, would remain until the very end.

Nowhere was the world of these urban guerrillas committed to non-violence less comfortable than in Prague. The regime kept up almost permanent pressure on the thousand or so people who eventually signed Charter 77 and who represented a coming together of all who refused to knuckle under to the 'normalisation' that followed the Soviet invasion of 1968. Far more painful than loss of their own jobs was the discrimination against their children that prevented them getting a full education. The police sometimes beat people up, but they usually kept such methods for the young and the unknown, especially those living outside Prague where even Charter 77's own diligent Committee for the Defence of the Unjustly Prosecuted (VONS) was not able to monitor all incidents. It was understood that no one could expect a fair hearing if he or she were brought before a court. Those who over-estimated their own strength were the most likely to be defeated and to leave the country. The writer Ludvik Vaculik considered his refusal to give in to the pressure put on him to emigrate to be his final act of resistance.

Frequent interrogations, described by the police as 'prophylactic', were the favourite weapon against the dissenters. In the summer of 1980 the writer Jan Vladislav, responsible for the *samizdat* Quarto Publications, remarked that his interrogators' most startling quality was their air of knowing everything. 'They are self-righteous and omniscient because they know they have power on their side. I don't think they believe in the ideology. It's the feeling of omniscience and omnipotence that counts for them.' Vaculik, who had played an active part in the Prague Spring and ran another *samizdat* house called Padlock Publications wrote regular *feuilletons* for the underground press. At one of his interrogations Colonel Noga, his personal interrogator, said he supposed Vaculik would one day publish an essay about their meetings. 'And you'll call it *A Cup of Coffee with my Interrogator*,' Noga added – a statement, not a question. 'I almost fell off the chair,' Vaculik wrote in the *feuilleton* he did indeed publish under that title. 'It was no use – they knew everything.'

In the end Vaculik would show Noga his latest work, while another regular attendant at interrogations acquired from his questioner a passion for tropical fish, which gave them something else to talk about when they met. The humour of it was at best macabre, for these relationships revealed what Vladislav had guessed – policemen who delighted in holding powerless creatures in their hand. The helplessness was all the greater because the Chartists knew that the Czechoslovak people would do little to support them. Jiri Hajek, Foreign Minister in Dubcek's Government, put a good face on it by saying that 'people sometimes criticise us and sometimes applaud us. It's as if we were a soccer team of which they're not committed fans.' Four years later, in 1986, Vaculik's essay *Words* was far less forgiving. It was not the Government that was the problem, he wrote, but the people.

It is the so-called nation . . . which has for fifteen years now seemed to me like a heavy immovable boulder. The people! The football crowd. Our consumer, that large, futile mass that swears at 'the conditions' but does nothing. It is at them that The Word should be aimed, but what right have we to do that? In any case we cannot possibly reach them with the means we have at our disposal today, while they, in their ignorance or apathy, make no effort to reach us.

Zdena Tominova, one of those who was eventually forced to emigrate, had a couple of workmen round to do some repairs at her flat. They knew she was in trouble with the authorities, but far from sympathising they laughed at her for it. They thought she was stupid to be seen to resist and then be made to pay for it. 'Piss on their slogans when their backs are turned,' was their advice. If anything made leaving Czechoslovakia easier it was the knowledge that she would not have to bring up children in this atmosphere of sour subservience.

The Chartists were never united in their political attitudes. In his little house on the edge of the city Hajek, a bird-faced old Communist whose thick-lensed spectacles suited his careful judgements, would try against the odds to see signs of hope in Moscow. At the other end of Prague the eminent translator from English Zdenek Urbanek had had no time for Communists since their newspaper *Rude Pravo* ignored Hitler's march into Bohemia and Moravia in March 1939 and printed instead a front-page story on irrigation in Soviet Kazakhstan. Urbanek, born the year before the creation of the Czechoslovak Republic in 1918, talked affectionately of the pre-war Czech democracy. 'It worked, you know. It worked.' A keen motorist (before the war he had driven his father's Skoda to London) Urbanek assumed the job of chauffeuring for his friend Havel who had a car but did not like driving. Not surprisingly this shrewdly benevolent man of letters found a policeman on his tail almost whenever he went out. Rudolf Slansky Jr., son of the most famous victim of Czechoslovakia's Stalinist purges, had a tiny study in a modern tower block in the direction of the airport where he would analyse with patience the latest snail-like movements within the Communist Party, or explain the disastrous effect on the Czech economy of its forced ties to Moscow (where Havel was to send him as Czechoslovak ambassador in 1990).

This diversity was not enough to prevent some Chartists feeling they were becoming trapped in a ghetto. Petr Pithart, a stocky man who personified the evolution of the Czech peasant into intellectual, believed it vital for Chartists to 'build bridges' to those who more or less unwillingly worked for the regime. *Samizdat*, in particular its specialist publications for economists and other professionals, should aim to be read by and to print contributions (anonymous if need be) from people outside the dissenting community. Perhaps the only one of the Charter's prominent members who was a natural revolutionary was the left-wing Petr Uhl, organiser with his equally determined wife Anna Sabatova of the vital flow of information about the opposition and its fortunes both within the country and to the world outside. To their own eventual undoing the Czech security service misread Vaclav Havel as a man who would bend under pressure. No policeman could have misread the tough-looking, handsome Uhl, and it was not surprising that he spent more time in jail than most other Chartists. The Uhls' flat just off Wenceslas Square – worn, utilitarian furniture; untidy bookshelves; clothes on the chairs; ashtrays that were seldom empty – proclaimed a family dedicated to a cause, and was the sort of home more often found in Warsaw than in Prague. Turning forty at the beginning of the 1980s Uhl had immense energy and could keep the details of innumerable police and court actions against dissidents in his head. He admitted to retaining enough Marxist teaching to make him doubt that anything would change in Czechoslovakia until the working class turned against the regime. 'What counts,' he was still arguing in 1988, 'is the balance of forces, not what Mr Vaclav Havel says.'

In the early 1980s Adam Michnik commented that the Czech dissenting world resembled 'the first Christian communities hiding in the catacombs more than . . . an illegal political opposition movement'. The Chartists themselves often worried about what they had achieved when so little had changed in the life of the country. Not much, the philosopher Ladislav Hejdanek thought just two years before the 1989 revolution. 'Charter 77 only expressed something that was already commonly known. It said the emperor has no clothes, but no more than that. It was important to us because we at least feel free. And it may have improved the atmosphere because people know that somewhere someone dares to speak openly.' The mess in Czechoslvakia, he would also say, had two culprits: 'the stupidity of the Communist leaders and our weakness'. A Protestant who despaired of the feebleness of the Protestant churches, Hejdanek was a leading organiser of the unofficial seminars whose purpose was to preserve, for a small minority at least, traditional Czech academic standards. Towards the end of the 1980s he was not sure how effective even this assiduously pursued activity had been. Although there were at least thirty seminars meeting secretly in Prague by then he believed that police pressure had affected the quality of the students, and that it was the bravest, but not the brightest, who attended. It was typical of the world of Charter 77 that the chronically ill Hejdanek, who kept a little picture of Don Quixote in his living room, should worry about falling intellectual standards. It was significant, too, because what the Charter came to represent above all else was individuals who had chosen to lead their own lives decently regardless of what was going on in the country around them.

HOW TO BE A GOOD GREENGROCER
The Chartists were sometimes visited by representatives of Western peace groups. These meetings could be difficult, because the Czechs sometimes found the Westerners unable or unwilling to appreciate the difference between the Soviet bloc's foreign propaganda and how Communist governments behaved at home. Hejdanek, grinning kindly, would reproach the Westerners for lacking what Spinoza called *fortitudo animae* in their attitude to the Soviet Union. *Fortitudo animae* was exactly what the Chartists had, though Hejdanek was too modest to claim it. They were men with strength of spirit who were sure of their moral ground: *that* they would never surrender, though in all else they would keep an open mind. There was no danger of these men and women turning into the self-righteous angels that Michnik had felt it necessary to warn the Poles against. It had happened that the Charter's first role was – not by the signatories' conscious choice, for they were neither immodest nor prigs – to set an example of principled behaviour to the rest of Czechoslovak society. Uncertain when, if ever, political change would come their second role was to explain to Czechoslovaks

how they, too, could lead decent lives even as subjects of a corrupting political system. The Catholic layman Vaclav Benda who was imprisoned together with Havel in 1979 put this in Christian terms. Since the heaviness of the state penetrated even to the inside of its citizens 'every genuine struggle for one's own soul becomes an openly political act'.

The Charter did not call people to the barricades. It did not expect acts of reckless heroism. In an essay published in *samizdat* in 1978, the year after the Charter's publication, Ludvik Vaculik tried to explain why, as a connoisseur of his own people, he believed no good would come of trying to turn them into heroes. Most people were aware of their limits, and knew that heroic deeds were 'alien to everyday life'. A distinction had to be made between heroism and the 'integrity of the ordinary man' because in one way life was worse than it had been in the Stalinist 1950s. Then there had been revolutionary cruelty but there had also been selfless enthusiasm among some of the Communists (Vaculik himself had been a Party member and his first sucessful novel, published in 1966, told of a farmer who took an enthusiastic part in collectivisation even though it destroyed his own family). There was no enthusiasm any more but, with a few exceptions, not much cruelty either. 'Violence has become humanised. The total surveillance of the entire population has been spread more gently over everyone and every thing . . . It is an attack on the very concept of normal life.' Paradoxically this led to a danger far greater than any that had existed in the 1950s precisely because it was easier to live a quiet life under such conditions. For this reason Vaculik argued that

> every bit of honest work, every expression of incorruptibility, every gesture of good will, every deviation from cold routine, and every step or glance without a mask has the worth of a heroic deed.

This, then, was the world to which the playwright Vaclav Havel began to offer his philosophy of dissent. It was a world that spread beyond Czechoslovakia to include all East Europe, regardless of whether Havel was read there or not. The Czech who only wanted to write plays found himself addressing people in societies where living conditions were for the most part no longer cripplingly bad and where, at least until the start of the 1980s, people continued to see proof of gradual material improvement in their lives. At the same time these societies were controlled by a self-selecting ruling caste whose power depended ultimately on violence, and which to protect its self-esteem and long-term survival was obliged to crush independent thought. The consequence was that all members of society were drawn into daily rituals of deceit which either anaesthetised their moral (one could not talk of civic) sense, or continuously affronted it. With the exception of Czechoslovakia East Europe had had little enough time in the twentieth century to enjoy democracy. Its post-war experience was, however, different from anything it had known under the pre-war dictatorships. Havel spotted five essential novelties that distinguished the system from the regimes of the 1920s and 1930s. The Communist system covered many countries to form a vast geopolitical bloc. Unlike the old dictatorships it had a still resonant lineage in the nineteenth-century social and political movements that were thrown up by industrialisation. Communism had an ideology that covered all aspects of life and whose outlines could be grasped even by quite simple people. It possessed techniques of social, political and intellectual control undreamed of by earlier dictators. Here the Tsarist inheritance of absolutism was brought to perfection by modern technology, and further powerfully concentrated by the fact that the Communist state was the sole significant owner of property. There was, therefore, almost no corner of life into which the citizen (a word that in fact had lost its meaning) could escape in the hope of hiding from the state. The fifth and final element in what Havel called this 'post-totalitarian system' was the injection of some of the values of the modern consumer societies of the West. These, he argued, all too often delivered the final blow to the few ghosts of civic virtues that remained, for they served to strengthen the selfishness that Communism itself so powerfully promoted.

Havel offered those who had no choice but to live in the Communist world a philosophy of the old-fashioned kind – a teaching that made sense of life and suggested moral guidelines by which to live. If the urban guerrillas of East Europe had a secret weapon, this was it. Havel was not a trained philosopher, or a trained anything else come to that because his bourgeois background had cost him the right to a formal higher education in the new Czechoslovak Communist state. As a young man he had been overawed by the philosopher Jan Patocka, continuer of the Czech tradition of Comenius and Jan

Masaryk, and a godfather of Charter 77. When Patocka spoke several times in the early 1960s at the Theatre on the Balustrade where Havel was starting his career 'listening to him was bliss'. But it was not long before Havel had shown trained philosophers like Hejdanek that he was 'enormously clever in discussing philosophy . . . a natural philosopher whose writings are a challenge to the professionals'.

The point of making plain Havel's unusual intellectual credentials is to be able to dismiss them. Brilliance would have counted for nothing had it not been for the strength of character he developed, to the surprise of some of his friends and perhaps also himself, and that enabled him to live what he taught. The essays in which he outlined his thinking were published in *samizdat* and read by very few Czechoslovaks. Even had they been more easily available it is unlikely that many more people would have studied them, for they were not written in a popular style. Indeed throughout the 1980s the majority of Czechoslovaks had probably not heard his name. He was not even the formal head of Charter 77 – it had no formal leaders – merely one of its best-known members. When he appeared to speak for the first time to the crowds in the decisive week in November 1989 most of the country still had only a hazy idea who he was. He certainly was not yet the national hero he became a few weeks later. None of this diminished his achievement. On the contrary, his rise to leadership could only happen so quickly because of the price he had already paid in years of intellectual effort and personal sacrifice. The Czechs say they do not like people who take themselves too seriously, but when Havel was eventually brought into full public light even they could admit he was a man who, in Patocka's words, had proved 'there are some things worth suffering for'.

Havel tried to explain the mechanism of the Communist system; to show how it humiliated its subjects, but also how the rulers were bound by it as much as the ruled; and how, though no hope could be offered of the system's collapse, it was still possible for the ordinary man and woman to re-establish for themselves a world in which 'values like trust, openness, responsibility, solidarity and love' had a place. Anyone who followed Havel through his arguments was brought to a surprising conclusion: that they should not wait for a better life, but act as if it had already arrived:

For the real question is whether the 'brighter future' is really always so distant. What if, on the contrary, it has been here for a long time already, and only our own blindness and weakness have prevented us from seeing it around and within us, and kept us from developing it?

Havel had religious faith of an unspecific kind. Writing from prison in the years between 1979 and 1983 he often referred to an 'absolute horizon' against which man could only make his mark by accepting responsibility for himself. In this spiritual sense, waiting for a better world to come was irresponsible, but it was also bad practical politics. People did not believe in the possibility of over-turning the system; if they were not to collapse into apathy they needed to be told what they could do now. It was Havel's strength that he offered something to work on at once.

Under the Communist system everyone had something to lose, so everyone had something to be afraid of. Bribery was the name of the game. Social conformity was induced by graded awards, all the more seductive since what was demanded was only outward adaptation. To illustrate the dilemma facing the East European man and woman Havel thought up a character who might have come from one of his own plays, a greengrocer who places among the carrots and onions in his shop window a poster with the slogan 'Workers of the world, unite!' Why did the greengrocer put it there? Because that is what he ardently wanted, and therefore hoped to infect others with his idealism? Very unlikely. Because he thought he knew how this proletarian unification might take place? Obviously not. The poster was delivered to the shop by the state wholesalers together with the fruit and vegetables. The greengrocer put it in the window because 'these things must be done if one is to get along in life'. What he was signalling with the slogan had nothing to do with the future of the world proletariat. It was a coded bid for personal survival: 'I am obedient, and therefore have the right to be left in peace.' This was just the signal that the state wanted him to give, but what would have happened if the matter had been handled more openly; if the greengrocer had been instructed to place in the window a sign that read 'I am afraid and therefore unquestionably obedient'? In that case there was a risk that even the most tractable greengrocer might refuse to display this proof of his humiliation. Ideology was the way round the difficulty. The greengrocer was only asked to display a slogan that he might have believed in, and which therefore allowed him not to dwell on the real and uncomfortable reasons for his conformity. Ideology, commented Havel, 'offers human beings the illusion of an identity, of dignity, and of morality while making it easier for them to *part* with them'. The system and its ideology were effective not simply because they were wicked and brutal, but because many people did not much mind 'divesting themselves of their innermost identity' if there were rewards to be had in exchange.

What would happen if the greengrocer refused to put the propaganda poster in his window? He would certainly lose hopes of promotion to a career in the bureaucratic heights; he might lose his job; there could be trouble for his kids at school; his wife might not get the holiday voucher to the Black Sea coast resort that she had been counting on. But he would have begun to live in truth, and would have joined the real opposition to the system that was made up of all those people who threatened it just by refusing to conform to its customs. One day he might even try to organise his fellow greengrocers into an independent association to protect their interests. At that moment he would have become a fully-fledged member of what some Chartists liked to call the 'parallel *polis*'. This other world or second culture was home for any group activity that took place independently of activities devised or permitted by the state. *Samizdat* obviously belonged there and so did the unofficial seminars conducted by Professor Hejdanek and others. Performances such as those the banned actress Vlasta Chramostova put on in her Prague apartment of *Macbeth* (the guilt of the powerful was a relevant theme to Czechs) belonged in this second world, and so did unofficial rock groups that the authorities refused to recognise (it was the persecution of a rock group called the Plastic People of the Universe that gave the impetus to the creation of Charter 77). It seemed likely that the more such independent activities there were, the more umbrella organisations of a human rights character would be born. These activities would have a chance to survive by exploiting the system's need to preserve the appearance of legality. The regime wanted laws that looked respectable by international standards, Havel explained, as a 'bridge of excuses' to make it easier for people to serve it. But by appealing to and exploiting these laws the alternative society had a chance to keep a space for itself. And by living within that space people might be able to experience that the 'brighter future' had already arrived.

How many greengrocers, or other Czechoslovaks for that matter, knowingly or unknowingly followed the precepts that Havel set out in this essay with the vibrant title *The Power of the Powerless*? Perhaps not many, one was inclined to think, after attending a typical ceremony at which successful greengrocers and their like had a chance to display their achievement to each other and the public at large. Each year, for example, the annual celebration of victory over Nazi Germany was held in a hall in Prague's Fucik Park and it was well attended by middle-aged men in grey or brown suits, the uniform of the upwardly mobile and tractable Czech. Though heavy and scarcely elegant, these men had the instantly recognisable, and to many so enviable, sleek solidity that could only come from a generous diet of beer, pork and power. Their wives were there, in perms and flowered dresses, and some of their schoolgirl daughters whose job was to present bouquets to the Soviet officers and old Communists who were the occasion's honoured guests. The pubescent girls with their little flower-shaped earrings and grown-up stockings beneath the short uniform skirts gave the occasion a pleasant spice of lubricity. Outside in the park the great day would be celebrated, and all its participants rewarded, with a delivery of bananas that were sold direct from the box to children who screamed 'Bananas! Bananas!' as though they had never seen them before, and to old women who poked around the bunches to find the single ripe fruit that was all they could afford to buy.

Unlike Poland, Czechoslovakia never gave the impression of a country on the edge of revolt. Anyone who saw workers from the Skoda factory in the buffet of Plzen railway station emptying a half dozen litre mugs of the rich local beer before their journey home had to suppose that this was a regime with a considerable margin of safety. The Skoda workers' heavy, uneven faces, the same faces that look out of the watching crowds in Czech medieval religious paintings, signalled a readiness to mock, but no great readiness to act. Members of Charter 77 complained about the working class's passivity – 'Marx was so wrong about the workers being the class of the future!' – but there was very little they could do about it. They knew the system allowed many working men to lead a comparatively easy life. Chartists who were not allowed to practise their own professions and were forced to work as stokers or in other menial factory jobs told depressing stories about their experiences. An ex-journalist had the time to translate two dozen books while watching the dials on the boiler entrusted to him. The men who worked with him thought he was crazy. He despaired of them: 'we have become a lazy nation, but then Montesquieu said that being lazy is the slave's only privilege'. The fate of the November Revolution remained undecided until it became clear that the factories were coming out in its support. As late as the middle of the decisive week in November Petr Pithart, who had become the newly created Civic Forum's chief of staff, was apprehensive about what the factories would do. 'We may have to pay for our negligence. It is a bad old tradition, this weakness in links between the intelligentsia and the working class.' Uhl the left-winger had never had any illusions about who would be citizens of the beautiful 'parallel *polis*'. Certainly there were not likely to be trade unions there; and it would remain the affair of a small minority until the real 'revolutionary process' began.

Was the Charter such a threatening urban guerrilla after all? It was troublesome to the Government, causing problems for it not only in the West but also with other regimes in the Soviet bloc which felt that repression and political trials in Czechoslovakia reflected badly on them too. But Charter 77 and the dissenting world around it were always containable. Enjoying some public sympathy, they never reached the overwhelming public support needed to turn them into a real menace. Leading Chartists used to hold occasional secret meetings with Solidarity stars like Michnik and Kuron on the mountainous border between their two countries. Having puffed their way to the heights there was a certain consumption of alcohol and black tobacco, cheerful snapshots were taken, and satisfaction expressed at having outwitted their security police watchdogs, one of whose main jobs was supposed to be stopping dissenters establishing contacts across frontiers. In those days, before Havel became an international superstar, the Polish participants looked much the more substantial and self-confident. The Polish 'parallel *polis*' had been visible since Solidarity's birth in August 1980, when Michnik wrote an essay outlining its limits. He admitted it was unrealistic to try for independence or parliamentary democracy because the Russians would never stand for that. But it was realistic to aim for targets which, if achieved, would substantially alter the daily life of Poles for the better.

These included pluralism in public life; liquidation of preventive censorship; a national reform of the economy; competitive press and television; freedom of learning and university autonomy; public control of prices; and independent courts and police stations 'where people are not beaten up'. No Czech or Hungarian dissenter would have dared entertain such dreams either then or several years later. Even writing in prison in 1982 during martial law, when Solidarity had been crushed as a public organisation, Michnik felt able to ponder a strategy of 'the long march' towards a 'reformist Poland' which, though mindful of Soviet interests, might not necessarily be ruled by the Polish Communists.

THE POLISH ALLIANCE

Poland's opposition intellectuals were the strongest in East Europe because they so often acted as both pathfinders and commandos for two of the most powerful bodies in Polish society – the Roman Catholic Church and the working class. It was the fusion of intelligentsia, Church and working man that made Poland's urban guerrillas such a potent force. The coming together of intelligentsia and Church was well under way by the time Solidarity was born but it was not an automatic process, and in many respects the priest and the professor were far from natural companions. If 200 years of struggle had seemed finally to have melted almost all elements of Polish society into one extraordinarily strong metal, it was not always so. It became convenient to forget that the Polish gentry of the sixteenth century had seen the Reformation as a chance to liberate itself from the Catholic Church's political and spiritual power. The gentry hoped to expropriate its property and set up instead a national Calvinist Church that they could control. Relations between the Church and that supreme Polish hero Pilsudski had never been easy though one would not have guessed it to judge by the masses held each May to mark the anniversary of his death. Cardinal Glemp himself sometimes presided at the mass in St John's Cathedral, blessing the banners that were brought by the Marshal's surviving old soldiers. Outside the churches on these occasions one came across young men selling picture-books of Pilsudski's funeral in the Wawel, the royal castle of Krakow, and there was a minor sensation when Polish television announced in 1989 the discovery of film footage of the occasion. The truth was that the then Archbishop of Krakow, Cardinal-Prince Adam Sapieha, had refused to allow Pilsudski to be buried in the Wawel's crypt where fourteen

Kings and Queens of Poland and other heroes like Prince Jozef Poniatowski lay. In the end the Polish army had to extract the Cardinal's permission almost at gun-point, but he still refused to be present at the funeral mass. To Sapieha's mind Pilsudski was a disloyal son of the Church and therefore had disqualified himself from the supreme honour of burial at the Wawel.

Progressive Poland and Catholic Poland were not natural allies. It remained a matter of wonder that so many Poles could be so punctilious in attending mass yet pay such little attention to the Church's highly orthodox attitude to sexual relations. Communist pugnaciousness towards the Church helped drive these two Polands together. Hard though it is to believe now, as little as three years before John Paul II's first papal tour of Poland the Communist official in charge of religious affairs was writing in confidential Party documents that 'if we cannot destroy the Church, at least let us stop it from causing harm'. The Church itself began to give greater attention to human rights in their entirety, and not just to its own and believers' rights. This encouraged opposition intellectuals to consider what the basis of future cooperation with it might be, and some who had once been agnostics or Communists were eventually themselves baptised. The Church both openly and secretly put immense resources at the opposition's disposal. Much depended on the inclination of individual bishops and priests though the entire clergy was encouraged in this direction by the pronouncements of the Polish Pope. Some of this support, especially under martial law, was secret but a great deal was quite open. Nowhere else in East Europe was there a place like St Stanislaw Kostka, the Warsaw church of the murdered priest Jerzy Popieluszko, which became a mixture of opposition shrine, *agitpunkt* and fortress. The fence around its grounds was hung with Solidarity banners that had been carried at the open-air papal masses. Its memorials recorded saints and martyrs both official and unofficial, including all the Polish officers murdered by the Soviet NKVD at Katyn. An exhibition of photographs showed the place where Popieluszko had been killed with a caption that read 'The end of Father Jerzy's martyr's journey.' An immense bell, inaugurated by the Pope and inscribed 'God and Fatherland', was engraved with a picture of John Paul II on one side and St George (in Polish Jerzy) slaying the dragon on the other. What ordinary Pole could visit this church and fail to come away moved by these tales of a national struggle that was also so obviously

God's? What Solidarity activist, regardless of his relationship to that God, could fail to have his Polish spirits raised by attending a service in such a place?

To a considerable extent Polish Church and Polish working class came in one package. In the last century workers at rallies organised by the Socialists sang the *Red Flag*, but they also waved the red and white Polish colours onto which they had pinned pictures of the Black Madonna of Czestochowa, Poland's holiest image. Lech Walesa, the young electrician who became Solidarity's leader, may not have sported a Black Madonna badge the day he climbed over the wall of the Lenin shipyard to assume command of the August 1980 strikes but he had worn one on his lapel ever since. And it was in the relationship between Walesa and Henryk Jankowski, the parish priest of Gdansk's St Brygida's Church close by the shipyards, that the modern alliance of Polish Church and Polish worker reached one of its most curious peaks. Jankowski turned his church, too, into a patriotic museum. Popieluszko was commemorated there in a life-size bronze figure that showed the priest lying twisted on the ground after being dumped from his killers' car. Jankowski's greatest service, though, was to serve Walesa as his quartermaster. What would Walesa have done without this suave, well-groomed priest? In the most difficult days Jankowski's vicarage provided Walesa and his colleagues with a couple of rooms free of electronic bugs; with meals cooked in a large kitchen, whose equipment was gradually modernised by gifts sent from admirers abroad; with an assistant staff of a half dozen junior priests all of whom, it was said, hated Communism like the Anti-Christ; and even, if need arose, with a squad of little old women who could be relied to carry secret messages under their dresses through any police checkpoint. As times got better Jankowski looked after Walesa's official entertaining. The constantly improving kitchen fed foreign ambassadors and politicians, while Jankowski himself saw to it that the wine was served at the right temperature. People who stayed in the vicarage's guest rooms, each named after a saint, praised their spaciousness; the way that beds were turned down each evening; and heaters and hot water bottles thoughtfully provided in winter.

This was not the natural habitat of the dissident Warsaw intellectual but no more was the factory and the world of the common man. The indifference of the peasant and the 'little man' to the troubles of Poland's patriotic (and quite often aristocratic) rebels was a favourite theme in Polish literature. When in the 1980s a young Pole tried his hand at translating a famous Polish author into English it was natural to pick a story like *Ravens Will Tear Us to Pieces* by the turn-of-the-century novelist Stefan Zeromski. It tells how a Warsaw intellectual turned revolutionary, transporting arms for the anti-Tsarist uprising, is lanced to death by a Russian patrol as he drives his cart across the open field. One of his two horses is shot dead; the other panics and breaks his leg in a wheel of the upturned cart. The peasant on whose land this happens arrives to strip the dead man of his clothes and the horse of its skin. When he is finished he throws them down a well, but leaves the other animal to die. Setting off home he hears the horse neigh and turns to see it raised on its hind legs against the darkening sky. The story's closing words are 'From beyond the world there came night, despair and death.' The two men's attitude to God underlines the unlikeliness of their coming closer. The revolutionary dies reciting the Lord's Prayer, confident that immortality awaits him. The peasant, who 'truly and deeply adored God', thanks Him as he takes home the unexpected gift of harness and clothes.

The young translator had written a story of his own in English. It was about the police breaking up a students' demonstration in Warsaw in 1981, and ended with a taxi driver who picks up the escaping student narrator swearing at the troublemakers. 'It's all those students' fault.' It was a pale reflection of the nineteenth-century tale but an insight nonetheless into abiding fears among the intelligentsia that their ideals were not shared by the rest of the nation. This still was the experience of educated and progressive groups in the rest of East Europe. The isolation of the Czechoslovak Chartists from the working class was fully matched in Hungary, where the opposition's attempts to reach the working class met little success. Only ninety people turned up in May 1989 when Hungary's *Szolidaritas* trade union held its founding meeting in Budapest though its promoters had been to Poland and returned with Lech Walesa's blessing. Another independent Hungarian union that came into being the year before was in fact an association of teachers and assistants in higher education, an under-privileged group throughout the Soviet bloc but scarcely members of the working class.

The fusion of Polish dissent with industrial workers came about in 1976 when a number of dissidents founded the Workers' Defence Committee (KOR) to help employees and their families who had been victimised for taking part in strikes and protests. Not all the dissenting world at first approved of KOR, and the thirty-two original members were sometimes mocked for becoming 'social workers', but it was to a large extent thanks to KOR and its supporters that the unexpected marriage of working class and intelligentsia was eventually arranged. When the first reports began to reach Warsaw in July 1980 of the strikes that were breaking out in various parts of the country in protest against higher meat prices KOR ceased to be merely a group of socially conscious dissidents. That much was plain from a visit of KOR member Jacek Kuron who at that time operated from his flat in Zoliborz, just round the corner from Popieluszko's church. Kept going by three packets of Ekstra cigarettes a day and innumerable glasses of claret-coloured tea Kuron passed on information from the factories to the world's press, and in doing so was transformed. With his cement-mixer voice and prize-fighter looks Kuron had always been a toughie, but his toughness was immeasurably increased by being put at the service of hundreds of thousands of Polish working men and women. On their own the dissidents risked becoming a marginalised, unofficial institution. 'Those dissidents,' a character in Konwicki's *A Minor Apocalypse* sneers. 'They're the same sort of apparatchiks you find working for the state. They're dissidents with life-time appointments.' The bridge offered by KOR changed that. Intellectuals – like Bronislaw Geremek, leader of the Solidarity deputies in the Parliament elected in 1989, and Tadeusz Mazowiecki, Poland's first non-Communist Prime Minister – were transformed by becoming advisers to the new-born trade union. It allowed them to clear at one jump the always threatening walls of the dissident ghetto to find their feet in a world of real politics.

Thanks largely to KOR there were intellectuals in Poland from the late 1970s onwards who knew a great deal about working-class life, and they were to be joined a little later by workers whose experience was in turn expanded by contact with intellectuals. Jan Litynski was a Warsaw activist with the same background as Michnik. Both were born after the war into Jewish families, though Litynski's parents had been loyal to the old Socialist Party while Michnik's were Communists. A member of KOR, Litynski also helped produce *Robotnik*, an underground paper for workers that by August 1980 was printing 45,000 copies (by comparison *Beszelo*, the main dissident journal in Budapest, had reached in 1988 a circulation of only 2,000, the maximum possible, the Hungarians thought, under conditions of illegality). Litynski already knew when the strikes began on the Baltic coast how badly workers needed help not only in organising themselves but also in such simple matters as formulating their demands to the management. He had just been to the textile factories in Zyrardow where the mainly women workers had forgotten to ask for such obvious things as wash basins and lockers for their clothes. Litynski plunged into this work with no great hope of far-reaching results. 'I have to believe in what I am doing, but that is the only sense in which I am optimistic.' A slight man, in the scruffy clothes that were the Polish activist's uniform, he was to be seen that summer handing leaflets to striking workers with all the tentativeness of a child offering a lump of sugar to a very large horse. By the end of the decade he had proved himself a skilled organiser in the mines of Silesian Walbrzych and was elected from there as deputy to the 1989 Parliament.

If there were few Litynskis in the rest of Communist East Europe there were certainly no Zbigniew Bujaks. Bujak was born in 1954, the year after Stalin died. Strong, good-looking, intelligent and Catholic, he was ideal material for a worker's leader. Reading an issue of *Robotnik* led to contacts with the opposition and the start of his education. Chosen to head Solidarity in the Ursus tractor factory in Warsaw in 1980 he led a legendary life under martial law, escaping from a round-up by jumping from the Black Maria that was taking him to the police station. What was striking about him was his readiness to use his new acquaintances among Warsaw's dissenting intellectuals as tutors in his further education. He listened to them talk about politics and world affairs. He borrowed books from them. He was completely at ease in such company, though when an evening broke up and the intellectuals returned to their flats in central Warsaw he had to hurry to the station to catch the last train to his home at the city's edge. These two men represented what the Communist regimes of East Europe feared most – a coming together of the two social groups that had at all costs to be kept apart. That the union took place with the blessing of the Catholic Church made matters that much worse. Bujak had got his first copy of *Robotnik* from his parish priest. *Robotnik*'s editor Litynski was eventually baptised.

But was this new tough blend of Polish metals called Solidarity quite as strong as it seemed? The man who in the eyes of Poland

and the world symbolised Solidarity was Lech Walesa, the electrician with Pilsudski moustaches. Walesa also resembled Pilsudski in that he seemed to have no close friends though he did sometimes acknowledge leading intellectuals as teachers who taught him 'Polishness and patriotism'. He used the brains of the Geremeks and Mazowieckis but avoided the intimacy that came naturally to a man like Bujak. Walesa was like some super-sensitive radar directed towards the mood of ordinary Polish men and women. In public his eyes were always moving as though to catch every hint of change. His sometimes confused and contradictory statements irritated journalists but did not seem to bother the many Poles who themselves had many contradictory thoughts and feelings. An event in March 1990 was revealing of Walesa and significant of the less-than-solid unity that Solidarity represented. In that month an appointment was at last made for Walesa to meet the new Czechoslovak President Vaclav Havel. Although Havel had already once visited Poland since his election as President he had not then made the journey to Gdansk where Walesa was accustomed to being called on by any foreigner of importance. At Havel's suggestion the two men met at the same place on the mountain border between Poland and Czechoslovakia where he and his Charter friends had held their clandestine picnics with Kuron, Michnik, Litynski and other leaders of the Polish opposition. Walesa arrived on Mount Sniezka dressed in suit and tie, Havel wore one of his favourite sloppy sweaters. The two men did not take the chance to go off for a private chat together. They addressed each other throughout the encounter in the formal manner as *Pan*, Mister, a word not to be heard at the earlier gatherings of dissident Poles and Czechs on the mountainside.

It was said that Walesa was put out that the playwright Havel should have become President of his country while he, Walesa, though commanding for a decade an army of millions, occupied neither the Polish presidency nor any other high Government position, but there was more to the uneasiness of the encounter than that. Although supposedly both leaders of popular movements that freed their countries from Communism, the two men had never represented identical forces. There had long been tensions between Walesa and some of the intellectuals in Solidarity. Walesa could be both wilful and secretive. He was an eccentric chairman of committees, and his interpretation of democracy in the conduct of

Solidarity's internal affairs had caused irritation almost from the start. It was also obvious that while many of the best-known Solidarity activists like Michnik and Geremek had social-democratic inclinations, Walesa and the majority of the Solidarity rank-and-file were closer to Christian democracy.

Polish intellectuals had long feared that their country might free itself from Communism only to surrender to an authoritarian nationalist leader in the Pilsudski mould. They could not forget that the most revered Pole throughout the greater part of the Communist period had been Cardinal Wyszynski; and that Wyszynski, who never had much time for intellectuals, had set out to win over ordinary Poles with a populist-patriotic brand of Catholicism in which slogans, banners, festivals and processions counted for more than reasoned argument. One of the reasons for the warm welcome Karol Wojtyla received from the Polish educated class in 1979 was that this first Polish hero since Pilsudski had turned out to be, as a Warsaw writer put it, 'not a nationalist, a fascist, or a demagogue'. A year later Poland acquired another hero in Walesa whose real nature was considerably harder to divine. If one had to look for a Polish equivalent to Havel, John Paul II fitted better than the Solidarity leader. Both Havel and Wojtyla reflected upon the general moral problems of twentieth-century human existence. They went on to draw certain specific recommendations for their native countries from those considerations – no one knew better how to touch the Polish heart than the Polish Pope – but essentially both men spoke to the whole of humanity. Havel's greengrocer was not obviously a Czech or Slovak. He was any modern European man living under conditions of creeping totalitarianism, a character from Kafka, not *The Good Soldier Svejk*.

Similarly the broad stream of intellectual dissent throughout East Europe was democratic in a general sense, not doctrinally to the right or left. 'Solidarity,' Michnik believed, 'never had a vision of an ideal society.' Communism had taught these men of dissent the absolute value of human rights, and obliged them to think of politics not as the search for a paradise on earth, but as the business of creating a democratic society in which these rights could be exercised and defended. It was never a surprise to come across in a flat in Prague, or Warsaw or Budapest a copy of de Tocqueville on democracy in America or that undogmatic handbook of the American founding fathers *The Federalist*. Their presence did not signal unbounded admiration for everything American, merely recognition that early America had tackled some of the same problems before, and in a strikingly anti-Utopian way. If earlier generations of twentieth-century European intellectuals had been guilty of *trahison des clercs* by surrendering to the angelic temptations of Fascism, communism and revolutionary-ism in general, amends of a heroic kind were at last being made in the Continent's long-neglected eastern half.

The greengrocer Havel imagined himself addressing did not have to be Czech, but there was never any doubt that Lech Walesa's audience was Polish, the sort of men and women who before declaring a lengthy strike took care to arrange that a priest should come to say a regular mass for them. The enlightened greengrocer was essentially an inhabitant of the city, whose natural language (or so the inhabitant of Budapest, Gyorgy Konrad, believed) was democracy and where dissent had its natural roots. Walesa's audience was the nation, of which some of East Europe's dissidents were almost as wary as the Communists themselves. The latter were confident they could hold their fortress against attacks launched by the guerrilla-opposition from their bases in the city, but could they crush a nation if it rose up against them?

4

The Party Fortress

OLD MEN REMEMBER

It was often said that the Communist leaders of East Europe were impenetrable. They were hardly known at all in the sense that senior politicians in the West are known within the world of government or even to their electorates. How they lived; what they really thought; even what they did when they went to their offices in the Central Committee – it seemed that no one could answer these questions with any certainty. And yet were these men (there were almost never any women among them) really so mysterious?

Imagine a visitor to West Berlin in the days when the wall dividing the two parts of the city was still standing. The weather is fine. He has never seen a Communist country and, having a few hours free, decides to take the S-Bahn to Friedrichstrasse Station in East Berlin. The short journey proceeds as expected. An East German driver replaces the Western one at the last station before the border crossing, as though special skills were needed to guide the train along the Communist rails ahead. The wall that looked as fragile as icing sugar when seen flying into Tegel airport at last takes on its anticipated brutal air. Friedrichstrasse Station itself might be some mythological junction for souls trapped between two worlds. Ill-lit and unpainted, it is everywhere that people have been forced to wait while fate makes a caesura in their lives. After this unnerving entrance to the East the visitor is agreeably soothed by first acquaintance with the streets of the Communist city. There is none of the louche busy-ness of the Kurfurstendamm in the West. The four-horsed chariot on top of the Brandenburg Gate has been turned about to look East along the Unter den Linden where almost the only signs of commerce are a Soviet bookstore and a shop that sells souvenirs and peasant ware from People's Bulgaria.

After the palaces and museums of the Unter den Linden, the street continues over a bridge across the Spree to a large space landscaped to do honour to a pair of modern statues. No prize for guessing who they are: Karl Marx is the one sitting down, while Friedrich Engels stands at his shoulder. Both are dressed in frock coats, and though their shirts democratically open at the neck they have the stiffness of peasant woodcarvings. The two men gaze towards eight slabs of stainless steel arranged in pairs; on inspection the metal is found to be engraved with photographs. There are pictures of the horrors of war: British Tommies gassed in the trenches of the First World War; Hiroshima after the atom bomb has fallen; an old Vietnamese farmer taken prisoner and blindfolded. Other photos portray poverty: soup kitchens; beggars in India; ragged children at heavy work and Russian peasant women yoked like draught animals to a river barge. They are counterpoised by scenes and heroes of struggle: the Russian Revolution; Fidel Castro; a Soviet cosmonaut; Ho Chi Minh; British workers reading the *Daily Worker*; Lenin; North Vietnamese troops capturing an American pilot. And there are German scenes and heroes, too: workers on strike; Ernst Thälmann, leader of the pre-war German Communist Party who died in Buchenwald in 1944; 1920s Communists dressed in boots, belt and britches ready to take on any Nazi thugs who might try to interrupt their demonstration.

There were also a couple of pictures of Erich Honecker but they were not placed prominently and were easy to miss. If the monument was not an attempt to glorify him, what was it? Something much more revealing – a glance inside his mind. When Honecker looked at the world past and present surely this was what he saw. Who could deny that injustice, poverty and war had been replaced by peace and progress? Revolution was conquering the world, the same revolution that Honecker as a young man had also dressed up in belt and boots to fight for. What it had achieved in East Germany could be seen if the visitor retraced his steps a little down the Unter den Linden to call in at the Museum of German History. Here in the modern section covering the life of the German Democratic Republic one could take another walk through Honecker's mind and memories. The first exhibits were the tools of the Republic's post-war reconstruction from the rubble – shovels, pickaxes and drills, but also a caterpillar tractor given by the Soviet Union in 1949 and a tiny nineteenth-century steam engine on which someone had written in white paint *Bau auf!*, 'Build!' Hammer, pincers and chisel belonging to Wilhelm Pieck, the first President, demonstrated the new state's impeccable class character. Though poor, the state cared about its people. The first consumer goods were made of materials at hand: soldiers' helmets transformed into saucepans, hand grenades into flower vases, sheets into dresses. 1950 saw the birth of the first East German tractor, the following year the first television set. Called the Leningrad its screen was lost in a cabinet as large as a pre-war radiogram. The first washing machine with centrifugal dryer came in 1956, one piece of good news, at least, in the year of the Hungarian uprising.

Not that this was a museum to be put off its stride by counter-revolution. On the contrary, it expected it, and relished the chance to show how it could be crushed, for this was the second theme that sounded through the rooms that traced the growth of proletarian prosperity. The first of the many uniforms on display dated from 1948 and belonged to the *Volkspolizei*, the Vopos, the new People's Police. The exhibition dummy wears a black cap and black uniform, black Sam Browne, dark purple shirt and a red tie to make the politics plain. He is armed with an automatic rifle and wooden truncheon. Other uniforms follow thick and fast: the FDJ (Free German Youth) with light blue shirts and dark blue skirts for the girls; the *Kasernierten Volkspolizei* whose officers' grey greatcoats reveal that these are regular troops in the making; the armband worn by the Vopos' volunteer helpers; the uniform that a battalion commander of the Combat Groups of the Working Class, the workers' militia, wore on 13 August 1961, the day the Berlin Wall went up; and finally, perfection attained, the field-grey tunic worn with britches and tall boots of the Ministry for State Security's Feliks Dzierzynski regiment.

This was a display to keep the people on their toes. The revolution must be defended. The museum does not actually show the building of the Berlin Wall – it does not even directly mention it – but the threat from the West is constantly evoked. A quotation from Honecker, who supervised the wall's construction, reminds visitors that Western 'economic aggression' (meaning chiefly the flight of East Germans to the West before the wall was built) cost the young country 112 billion Marks between 1951 and 1961. There are displays of 'ideological poison' – long-playing records entitled *Ein Volk, ein Reich, ein Führer* that the explanatory notes claim originated in West Germany; paperbacks with lurid covers that glorify Nazi exploits; even a book with its pages hollowed out to conceal a revolver. We have achieved much, ran the message, but we must be ever on guard in the defence of our achievements. The very last words are Erich Honecker's, and typically warn of the need for vigilance in years to come: 'Europe will not survive the Third World War.'

To suppose that displays of this sort were no more than cynical manipulation of the ruled by the rulers is to miss the tragedy that lies at the heart of the Communist experiment in East Europe and of which Honecker, among all the East European leaders who survived till 1989, was the most exact personification. Born in 1912 he reached the age that often sets a man's underlying attitudes for the rest of his life in the years that Hitler came to power. His own experience might have come from the pages of an old Communist textbook.

Honecker's parents, who were poor, working class and Communist, lived in the Saarland. Theirs was a world pretty much as Marx had predicted. Workers in the mines, the main local industry, were impoverished while life around the Honeckers' village of Wiebelskirchen was dominated by one pit owner known as the King of Saarabia. The family was strong, and the conscientious and progressive Honecker parents brought up their children to believe in neither God nor German nationalism. Honecker told the story of how when only eight he heard his father and friends discussing politics. They used words he did not understand. 'What is it, Lenin and Revolution?' he asked, or so he liked to remember. Two years later he joined the Communist youth organisation known as the Young Spartacists, the very name evocative of the militant politics of both German Left and Right at that time. It was this sort of dramatic, angry political activity that took up his spare time in his last years at school and when he became an apprentice roofer, a craft he liked because it demanded alertness, accuracy and dexterity. In 1928 he joined the *Roter Jungsturm*, the youth branch of the combative Red Front Fighters' Union. This was when he acquired his first uniform of windcheater, peaked cap, leather belt and shoulder strap – a get-up remarkably similar to the early uniforms of Communist East Germany preserved in the Museum of German History.

Two years later he travelled to the Comintern school in Moscow with a group of other potential leaders from the German Communist Youth Association, a journey he sometimes became emotional about in later life. He had seen in the Red Army guards at the border 'brothers and comrades' whom he wanted to embrace in the Russian fashion, for were not the badges in their caps the same red star that was the emblem of the German Communists, the star he had begun to love even as a child and which 'lit up the future'? The border the Russian troops watched over made a great impression on him. This was no ordinary frontier, but a model for the one which in years to come would separate East and West Germany, 'a frontier between two worlds, a frontier at which the power of capital ended and the power of workers and peasants began'. Stalin had warned the German Communists against becoming a parliamentary party like the Social Democrats, and Thälmann, the likeable but not very bright German Party leader was never a man to contradict Moscow. The Comintern school accordingly taught the young Germans shooting, riding and other paramilitary skills useful in time of civil war. Honecker got excellent marks throughout. His teachers described him as a 'strong and self-reliant young man' who understood how to 'link theory with the German class struggle'. To make sure that the young Germans went away in a high state of emotion the Comintern school arranged for Honecker's class to make one last procession on horseback through the Soviet capital. Was it surprising if a young and poorly educated German worker thought he had joined the most powerful knightage the world had ever known?

The Germany Honecker went back to was becoming increasingly violent and for the left wing the lines between good and evil were clearly drawn. Though not a streetfighter himself he was a speechmaker who prepared the toughs of the German Communist Party for their frequent punch-ups with the Nazis. After Hitler had come to power Honecker went underground as a youth organiser. He managed to avoid the Gestapo until 1936. Described by the Nazi court as a 'convinced and unbudging' Communist, Honecker was sentenced, aged twenty-four, to ten years' imprisonment. In the harsh conditions of Brandenburg-Görden jail (considered at that time to be the world's most modern and secure) he underwent another period of development and toughening in which the bias of his early years was confirmed. He got something of a schooling from educated Communists who introduced him to the German classics, but on all the issues that divided the Communist prisoners he took the Stalinist line. He supported the Moscow show trials. He helped organise a little early-morning meeting to pronounce the Molotov-Ribbentrop pact a success of Soviet diplomacy. He argued that the Second World War was to be welcomed as imperialists falling at each other's throats. Although Honecker behaved well in prison – it was the Communists' strategy to become prison trusties so they would have more freedom for their own activities – his sentence was never commuted because the authorities suspected that his Communist beliefs remained unshaken. When a Soviet tank appeared at the prison gates at the end of April 1945 the scene was set for a modern *Fidelio* except that these prisoners came out singing *Wacht auf, Verdammte dieser Erde!*, the words of the Internationale. Had a camera recorded it, the moment would have fitted excellently among the other pictures of struggle and triumph engraved on the steel slabs in the Marx-Engels Forum.

The teenager who had his photo taken during his stay in Moscow had full lips, thick hair, quite friendly eyes and an almost chubby face. The man in his early thirties who was appointed to the leadership of the Free German Youth (FDJ) after the war was leaner, with lips more likely to be pursed and the eyes unrelaxed. As the Communists edged towards full power Honecker found it hard to put on the show of tolerance towards non-Communists that the Party demanded until the full takeover of power when pretence could be abandoned. Honecker had told friends he was convinced the Soviet Union was about to become the most powerful country in the world and that as its ally a united socialist Germany would bring socialism to the rest of Europe. Victory was in sight, so why should they delay?

Honecker's idealism (without, to be sure, its sharp revolutionary edges) and his belief that history favoured the Soviet Union were shared to greater or less degree by many East Europeans at the end of the war. 'New, new, new is the star of Communism, and there is no modernity outside it,' a Czech avant-garde writer had proclaimed in the 1920s and much had happened since then to convince less imaginative folk that this was indeed so. There must have been a lot of bright young teenagers in the early post-war years who imagined like the Pole Jacek Kuron that socialism would be 'a big bang followed by eternal happiness'. Conversion could also take place for reasons that were trite, but no less compelling for that. A middle-class schoolgirl in Prague remarked in the classroom that a 'gentleman' had called at the school kitchen door. The teacher rebuked her. She should have said 'man' because gentlemen never came to the doors of kitchens. In post-war Prague joining the Communist Party could be a spirited girl's answer to that sort of minor snobbery. Naivety played a role, too, naivety of a kind not unknown in West Europe at the end of a long war when people wanted to believe that the future must hold something better. In a story called *My Country* the Czech writer Ivan Klima describes a family holiday in the countryside soon after the war has ended. Father, an engineer, tells other guests at the inn about the shining future that awaits them. Princes, landowners and big businessmen will disappear. 'There would only be the working people and they would share out fairly the goods produced by them.' As a result 'for the first time in history everybody would do what he really wanted to do'. All who were capable would get an education and they would then invent 'further technical improvements, so that an ever growing number of ever cheaper articles would be produced' and these would liberate more people from toil. There would be 'marvellous machines' producing ever more goods and

> there would no longer, in a new society governed by the people, be any reason for hankering after property, no envy, hatred or hostility, there'd be no cause for wars because ultimately the fundamental cause of every war had been greed and the attempt to rob the vanquished. There would therefore be peace and trust, an age of comradeship would dawn, and eventually nations would vanish as would the frontiers between them.

This fine prospect does not appeal to a doctor who is among the listeners. 'You're not a bad person, Engineer,' he says. 'I'm sure you believe everything you're saying – but I hope for your sake you won't live to see it.'

The engineer, poor fellow, was too naive to understand what the doctor was getting at. There was also a mixture of ignorant innocence about the Honeckers of East Europe, a dangerous quality in people who are interested in power. They were ignorant about what drives human beings and about the part economic motives play in human behaviour. They were ignorant about the effect of power on people and above all about its likely effect on themselves. Why had the German Communists not drawn some lessons from their encounter with Hitler? Could they not have learned about the danger of unchecked power from him? No, because they were already infected with the angelic disease that magnifies the evil of opponents and blinds revolutionaries to their own failings. They had fought black Fascism and therefore could only be purest white themselves.

THE DEVIL'S BARGAIN

Unaware of the moral perils of the revolutionary profession the Communists pursued power with all the means at hand. When preparing for the Communist takeover in East Germany Walter Ulbricht reminded his colleagues that everything must be done to appear open and tolerant. 'It must look democratic, but we must hold everything in our hand.' Ulbricht was not just being faithful to the methods of Stalin. He was following the logic inherent in Lenin's Bolshevism and whose roots went back to the nineteenth-century Russian revolutionaries recorded by Dostoyevsky in *The Possessed.*

The Honeckers of East Europe were the tools Stalin needed once he decided to extend the Soviet Union's defensive glacis up to the frontiers of the West. He offered them a tempting bargain. He would put them in power; they would then use whatever means were necessary to stay in power as long as his, Stalin's, interests demanded. Until 1985 the Soviet Union would not tolerate any change that would weaken the East European Parties' hold on power. There was a telling moment at the Polish Party congress in July 1981 when the Communists were struggling to keep control of a country that had visibly sided with the insurgent Solidarity movement (and part of the Party too – one in five congress delegates were Solidarity members). Viktor Grishin, the funereally-suited Soviet Politburo member and consummate apparatchik sent to represent Moscow, watched the angry and confused affair with a condescending smile. The smile vanished when the Polish Party leader Stanislaw Kania turned to him to apologise for the length and complexity of the proceedings, explaining it was the result of practising democracy. Practising democracy indeed! For the Grishins of the world Communists had no business practising democracy either inside the Party or out, and the other East European Communists also understood that perfectly. Nothing could have been more misplaced than the editorial that the Polish reformist newspaper *Polityka* had published on the eve of the congress describing the delegates as 'heroes of an impromptu play that is about to begin'. The only heroes a ruling Communist Party needed were dead ones, and as for the impromptu play, it abhorred it utterly.

From revolutionary who fought with force for his ideals to Party boss who used force to translate them into social reality was a short psychological step that most found easy to take. 'The Party always has to have an enemy to consolidate its ranks,' an old Polish Communist remarked and there was no shortage of enemies, above all in the West, whose existence conveniently proved that the world was split between good and evil. In truth the Communists who presided over revolution in East Europe were in a double trap. Stalin would not let them go, and there was no way to escape his punishment if one displeased him. He even saw nothing wrong in telling the Poles to include in one of the new prisons they were building special sections for senior members of the Party leadership. Small wonder that the first Communist President Boleslaw Bierut, for all the pleasure he might have got from living in the Belvedere, abandoned years of support of the Temperance Society and took to drink. The second trap was that having decided to take power and then keep it regardless of the wish of the majority of the population they could only justify themselves with a devious mixture of cynicism and intermittent, and increasingly unconvincing, idealism.

When the post-war Polish leaders turned to self-justification they could at times sound like ordinary intelligent Poles worried about the legacy of the Polish past. The notion that Poland is a dangerous 'Pandora's Box' was offered by a young poet, a Solidarity activist, contemplating the opposition's overwhelming victory in the 1989 elections. He was not sure he was going to like everything that happened now that Poles were becoming free again. Jakub Berman, a member of the post-war Party leadership's inner circle, used exactly the same expression when interviewed as an old man by the journalist Teresa Toranska (this collection of interviews, published under the title *Oni* – 'They' – recreates vividly the world of the first generation of Polish Communist rulers). Asked what evil spirits he thought were hiding in the box Berman answered in words that Adam Michnik might have used: 'dreams of a great Poland, of Poland as a great power, a Christ among nations, and of the Poles as a chosen nation'. But usually the Communists' language was different. There was a revealing moment in Toranska's interview with Berman in which he lost his temper with her because she jibbed at his cynical logic. She had asked him about the rigged referendum of 1946 which was an important step towards the Communists' final capture of power. The Government claimed that sixty-eight per cent had voted in its favour, whereas in the few districts where the real figures were known people had voted more than four to one against. Why, Toranska asked, weren't those figures published?

> My dear lady, you can't, not if you want to stay on. If we'd had an alternative – if we win, we stay, if we lose, we hand over power – then of course you can tell the whole truth. But here we were compelled by the situation: in an election, we can't go by the criterion of a majority, because there isn't anyone we can hand over power to. There wasn't then and there isn't now.

Nettled by the journalist's shake of the head Berman continued with a mixture of scorn and indignation.

> You'll be telling me in a moment it would have been democratic if we had [handed over power]. So what? Who needs that kind of democracy? And we can no more have free elections now than we could ten or twenty years ago, even less so, because we'd lose. There's no doubt of that. So what's the point of such an election? Unless, of course, we wanted to behave like such ultra-democrats, such perfect gentlemen, that we took off our top hats and bowed and said: fine, we're going to get some rest, go ahead and take power.

Berman, who was in his seventies at the time, was quickly reduced to angry shouting. Politics, he said, was not something one did for pleasure or in order to be loved. If the Poles did not understand that their post-war history was inevitable it was because of their 'mental backwardness', their attempt to live by 'nineteenth-century concepts'. Perhaps by now regretting that he had agreed to talk to this young woman who would not let herself be patronised he produced two lines of defence. Stalin had decided to control East Europe and above all Poland, lying as it did on the route of invasion to Moscow from the West. One simply had to make the best one could of that and the truth was – he argued – that 'we, the Polish Communists, rescued Poland from the worst'. It was they who broke the impact of Soviet bullying in whatever way they could, they who had to be in their offices from six pm to midnight because those were Stalin's preferred working hours and he might call them on the special telephone line that linked them all to Moscow.

The second defence was that given time the Poles would come to their senses, give up the old ideas about Poland and accept the Communists. 'The nation must mould itself into its new shape. It must,' said the old man heatedly. A new 'consciousness' would emerge when the advantages of Communism became clear.

> And then we, the Communists, will be able to apply all the democratic principles we would like to apply but can't apply now because they would end in our defeat and elimination. It may happen in fifty years or it may happen in a hundred . . . but I'm sure it will happen one day.

What appeared to men like Berman as the only possible policy of survival was in fact slow suicide. Believing that they could not afford to bother with democracy and the opinions of the people, all the Communists of East Europe to greater or lesser degree lost touch with reality. Attentiveness to local constituencies never made a Party career; attentiveness to the moods of the leadership one notch above did. It was typical that Honecker should have disliked Hans Modrow, who as Party secretary of Dresden was the one East German provincial leader who enjoyed some popular sympathy, and kept him out of the Politburo. It was typical that few of the East European leaders had more than the most formal contacts with ordinary people. When Gorbachev visited Prague the Czechoslovak Party leaders who had to accompany him when he went for a walk through the city could be heard grumbling that such outings were a waste of time.

From the outside, though, the Parties still looked fortresses to be reckoned with, and at the beginning of 1989 they all possessed immense assets. Even in Hungary, where the Party presented a friendlier face than most, about one in six active adults were members, which gave the Party the theoretical possibility to convey its messages and influence to every part of national life. These members, bound by Party discipline, were in theory the Party's hands and also its eyes and ears. The Hungarian United Socialist Workers' Party (the full name, like those of the Czech and East German Parties, intentionally avoided the word 'Communist') was of course no longer a political party in the usual sense of the word. Ostensibly financed by its members' dues, it was by the late 1980s getting a fifty per cent subsidy from the state. It had over four thousand full-time officials, and controlled large amounts of real estate, by some counts perhaps three thousand buildings in all. It also owned at least four holiday resorts and some two dozen newspaper and publishing companies. The world of the Party functionary was self-contained. Controlling the state and the country but not quite of them, their life seemed measured and orderly, as life within a great fortress should be. Those occasions when the public saw that it was not, like the Polish congress of 1981, were considered untypical and their memory suppressed. The mixture of routine and intellectual pretence was summed up by the East German Communists' Higher Party School in East Berlin, which served as a theological finishing school for Party high flyers. On entering the buildings the new arrival's attention was caught by a quotation from Engels, written in large letters on the wall, announcing that 'our theory is a theory that develops, not a dogma that one learns by heart and repeats mechanically'. Advised of the limits set by the school to free enquiry (for it was plain to an East German that the words had to be understood in the opposite sense), he could turn to a smaller notice by the lift door. This laid out with military precision the staggered meal times for staff and students, an exact half hour each for breakfast, lunch and afternoon coffee. If more hours had been spent worrying about those words of Engels and less about students interrupting teachers while still at their noodle soup the Party high command might not have been quite so surprised by the events of 1989. As it was the new revolutionaries of 1989 were able simply to nip round the fortress with as little trouble as Hitler's tanks avoiding the Maginot Line, leaving the garrison to decide for itself on the moment of guilty surrender.

Matters looked differently in the early years. All the Parties needed new recruits, and membership offered self-fulfilment as well as rapid rise to power and privilege. The Soviet-directed revolution had resulted in the elimination of much of the traditional ruling and professional classes, which in the case of Poland and Czechoslovakia had already been singled out for decimation by the Nazis. Those members of the old educated ruling classes who did survive were for the most part not trusted to serve the new state. Communists had to be appointed to run everything with curious results noted by sceptical local inhabitants. A Czech explained what was going on to a young Englishwoman, Rosemary Kavan, who had gone to Prague with her new Czech Communist husband. He called it a sort of general swapover. The highly qualified professional people are laying roads, building bridges and operating machines, and the dumb clots – whose fathers used to dig, sweep or brick-lay – are on top, telling the others where to lay the roads, what to produce and how to spend the country's money . . .

The Party was itself perhaps the most important vehicle of the social revolution that occurred in East Europe after the war, and that it was a revolution in which some went as visibly down as others up made it all the more satisfying for those ascending. Life was at such a low level that the smallest sign of progress and rebuilding seemed to justify Party optimism about the future. People did not find it difficult to believe that they were at last, as a Polish poet put it, on the way

> To the sweetly unknown
> And promised land of statistics.

In spite of the dogmatic cage of Stalinism the Party could also count on the support of genuinely enthusiastic 'progressive' intellectuals and the apparent support of others who wanted simply to survive. The Polish poet Czeslaw Milosz in his book *The Captive Mind*, written after he had escaped from Stalinist Poland, turned to the nineteenth-century Frenchman Gobineau for help in explaining what had happened to the battered intelligentsia of East Europe. Gobineau had for many years served as a French diplomat in Persia where his observation of life in a feudal Islamic society led him to conclude that the thinking man could survive only by practising what was known as *Ketman*. This meant never revealing one's true opinion, though Gobineau warned that there were times when even silence could be dangerous.

> Then one must not hesitate. Not only must one deny one's true opinion, but one is commanded to resort to all ruses in order to deceive one's adversary. One makes all the protestations of faith that can please him, one performs all the rites one recognizes to be the most vain, one falsifies one's own books, one exhausts all possible means of deceit.

How appropriate that this guide to survival for thinking people in the new Communist societies of East Europe should have come from a man who had studied a traditional Oriental despotism, and how familiar the remark a Persian made to Gobineau that there was in reality probably 'not a single true Moslem in Persia'. Milosz identified various sorts of *Ketman* that were practised by Polish Communists. Particularly common, unsurprisingly, was national *Ketman*, hatred of Russia combined with Polish patriotism and which of course was disguised by copious praise of everything Soviet. Professional *Ketman* – doing one's job as best as one could under the circumstances – was also common. There were other varieties of *Ketman* but Milosz believed they had one thing in common. The need to nourish one's convictions in secret, to allude to one's truth by heavily masked signals if at all, turned intellectual life into a constant battle against something, into a permanent test of both mind and will. For those with strength and patience there was satisfaction to be got from practising the art of *Ketman*.

The test of the convinced intellectual Communists and of the Parties, too, came after Stalin's death. There was not much the Party leaderships could do when, at Stalin's command, they had to put their own colleagues on trial, and prepare their own prisons to hold those found guilty by courts guided by the Soviet secret police. The situation changed after Khrushchev delivered his secret speech to the Twentieth Congress of the Soviet Communist Party in 1956 outlining some of the dead dictator's crimes. Some Communists reacted with horror. Even a man like Bierut, perfectly aware that Stalin had murdered many of the Polish Communists living in exile in Moscow in the 1930s, was nevertheless staggered by Khrushchev's revelations. Other East Europeans saw the speech as a chance to put the Party onto a more healthy basis, and it was in fact a senior Polish Party official who leaked the Soviet leader's speech to the world. The most significant attempts at reform were made in Hungary, Poland and Czechoslovakia, where those who had for years been practising a form of revisionist *Ketman* came into the open. Each attempt ended in failure, not to say disaster. These failures were the cause of much anguish at the time but in the end they were to contribute powerfully to the perception of both dissidents and discontented Communists in the 1980s that it was pointless to talk any more of reforming the system; that the only solution was to sweep it away.

All the three main revisionist attempts were ambiguous from beginning to end. Did Imre Nagy, the Hungarian leader who challenged the Soviet Union during the uprising in the autumn of 1956, believe he was doing so in the name of a reformed socialism, or had he ceased to regard himself as a Communist? When he abolished the one-party system on 30 October 1956, did he really accept that this could mean the Party's loss of power? The puzzle remains unsolved to this day, and was the cause of a good deal of heart-searching in Budapest in the summer of 1989 when Nagy was finally given an honourable burial. The drama of the Polish Party intellectuals who failed, in early 1968, to push the leadership into reforms involved no blood but it, too, was suffused with the same ambiguity. The intellectuals launched ideas that were later helpful to the non-Communist opposition but they never represented or tried to create a broad popular movement outside the Party. Having lost their battle they then lost their positions in the Party and were of no more significance within it.

Ambiguity was the name of the Prague Spring from beginning to end. Although the majority of the population supported it, the reform movement was begun by the Party and kept under its control until the very end. There was much naivety in the air. Jiri Hajek, Dubcek's Foreign Minister, later confessed thinking that 'Moscow would understand that our reforms were also essential to them'. The Russians, however, saw one thing much more clearly than the Czechs: once you start claiming popular support, as the Czech Communists did, you must reckon with the day when that support vanishes. What happens then? If you hand over power you destroy the system that is based on Communist Party rule. If you refuse, all your talk about popular support is shown up for what it always was – irrelevant. The only sensible thing is never to raise the subject in the first place. The Czech novelist Josef Skvorecky was still in Prague at that time and gave an amusing account of the cloudy language in which Party officials muffled the awkward edges of this rather vital matter.

> Some resorted to wishful thinking. I heard an important Dubcekist assert that the Communists would retain their leadership because the nation, appreciative of the reintroduction of democracy by the Party that had once destroyed it, would keep the Party in power.
> Foreign Minister Jiri Hajek, at a party Mr Dubcek gave for writers, explained to the playwright Vaclav Havel his own concept of the mystery: the Party would be a sort of Mississippi River, and various other

organisations like streams and whirlpools in it, but Old Man River would carry them safely to the sea.

The Warsaw Pact invasion of Czechoslovakia saved the Czechoslovak Communists from having to face up to the relationship between power and popular will in the Soviet socialist system. Czechoslovaks had immense respect for Dubcek and the other Communist leaders and this gave them extraordinary power through consent. But it was not a solution to the long-term problem of Party power and democracy and about which the Prague leaders had no ideas. It was because Dubcek had never had to face up to it that he was, for all his charm, somewhat suspect when the November revolution of 1989 began; suspect not in his person, for all held him to be a thoroughly decent man, but suspect in his clarity of thinking about the nature of the experience he, his Party and his country had been through since 1945. The point was made at one of the great public meetings that November when Dubcek mentioned the misery of the 'past twenty years'. The crowd, uncannily well-timed as ever with its counterpoint, called back, 'Forty years, Mr Dubcek, forty years'. They would not let him get away with the suggestion that there had been anything right in the whole period of Czechoslovak socialism.

An essay written by Adam Michnik on the tenth anniversary of the Prague Spring summed up the significance for the future of East Europe of these failed attempts by the Party to reform itself. It had to be understood, Michnik wrote, that 'in Soviet semantics the word "socialism" means the total domination of the Communist Party, whereas the word "counter-revolution" denotes all actions that subvert the totality of this domination'. Episodes like the Hungarian uprising and the Prague Spring were partly the work of the first generation of Communists who had joined the Party when membership still called for idealism and was not just a ticket to power. These early East European Communists thought socialism could combine both the Soviet political system and the ideals of the international working-class movement. But since power, and not idealism, was the purpose of the Stalinist Party their 'humanistic slogans' soon came into conflict with 'totalitarian practices' and were inevitably defeated. Revisionism, Michnik declared, was the 'revolt of the flower against its roots'. It never had a chance. And it was the old Czechoslovak revisionists who were themselves best proof that the flower was dead. In the twenty years after 1968 the half million men and women who were expelled from the Party after Dubcek's fall, though supposedly its most sophisticated members, simply vanished as a political force. When some of them did show signs of life in the late 1980s, one group was chiefly concerned with being rehabilitated by the Party. Another which chose the typically hopeful name *Obroda*, 'Renaissance', had dropped Leninism but was still dreaming of Marxist reforms. Neither *Obroda*'s members nor its ideas interested the people who took to the streets of Prague in November 1989.

The collapse of revisionism showed that the Devil's bargain offered by Stalin was still in force. He had given the East Europeans power they never could have won by their own efforts, and they had thought they were right to take it because of what they believed were the good things they would do with it. When the poisoned nature of the agreement became clear it was too late to escape: it was for their own survival as much as for the Soviet Union's that the East European regimes had to defend that power with all means at their disposal. Whenever they were reproached with this East European Communists became either self-righteous ('no one knows how much we have done for this country') or gave a self-pitying nod in the direction of Moscow. But for those Russians, the message was, who knows what splendid changes we would have made. It was an argument of this kind that occupied an important part of the speech of farewell by First Secretary Mieczyslaw Rakowski to the Polish United Workers' Party, the Communists' official name, on the eve of its transformation in January 1990 into the Social Democracy of the Polish Republic. (Since both the idea of social democracy and the pre-war name Polish Republic were abhorrent to the old regime this cumbersome title was supposed to assure the public that the Communists had at last broken free of Stalin's bargain.)

Not surprisingly Rakowski spent a good deal of time justifying the Polish Communists' imposition of martial law in December 1981. He asked for sympathy. The Brezhnev team had been incapable of understanding what was taking place in Poland when Solidarity was born. All the Russians ever wanted to know from Kania and Jaruzelski, respectively the Party leader and Prime Minister of the day, was, 'When will you begin to fight against the counter-revolution?' Senior Soviet officials including Marshal

Kulikov, commander of Warsaw Pact forces, and Foreign Minister Gromyko, had flown frequently to the Polish capital on bullying missions. Rakowski was himself a deputy Prime Minister at the time and he described a meeting he had with Leonid Zamyatin, Brezhnev's media chief. 'He carpeted us,' Rakowski said, 'or rather it is difficult to speak about the carpet, it was bare floor, and for several hours delivered a list of complaints about why we allowed the Polish press to publish counter-revolutionary voices and opinions.' These events were 'most unpleasant' and 'made me often feel help-less'. Rakowski continued in a paragraph sticky with self-pity and self-excuse.

> Brezhev's doctrine [that the Soviet Union had the duty to intervene if an East European Communist government came under threat] hung like an axe over the Polish Party and its leadership teams. It had its political consequences and psychological results. Both were expressed in the appearance, for many years, of the sacred question: what will the Soviet comrades say to this? Neither should one forget the fate of Dubcek, thrown on a plane which was flying in a direction unknown to him and his comrades, which reminded one about the permitted limits for independence.

The embarrassing truth about martial law was that, unlike Dub-cek and his men in Prague, the Polish Party was made to face up to the reality of its situation and do the Russians' work for them; but, even more embarrassing, it was their own work too. Would the Soviet Union really have risked organising a Warsaw Pact invasion of Poland in 1981 or 1982? Could Brezhnev, who may not have been wise but was certainly cautious, have contemplated Soviet troops engaging Polish soldiers, some of whom almost certainly would have fought back? These were not questions that any Polish Communist would wish to discuss in public. As for Rakowski, he was typical of those East European Communists who even after the explosion of the revisionist bubble continued to talk as though the system could be made habitable by reforms. One of the many Polish peasants' sons for whom joining the post-war Party had been a personal revolution, highly gifted and extremely hard-working he had for many years as editor of the Warsaw weekly *Polityka* provided intelligent though loyal criticism of public affairs. Far more cultured than the usual apparatchik he told an acquaintance when first elected to the Party Central Committee in the mid-1960s that he had no desire to reach the very top. He couldn't, he explained, bear the thought of spending all his time with 'those people'. In fact ambition took him in 1988 into the premiership where fate at last trapped him. Within months of declaring, 'Certain things will never change. The Communist Party will continue to lead Poland throughout this period of change,' the Communists were whipped in the June 1989 elections. Rakowski could say in his defence that like many nineteenth-century Polish public figures before him he had co-operated with Moscow to save Poland from the worst. In his case, however, dictatorship was inherent in the nature of the organisation he had made his career in. That he should have tried till the very end to put all the blame on Moscow was one more piece of evidence of the corrupting power of the deal into which Polish Communists had entered forty-five years before.

Others tried to do the same. The Hungarian Communists, on the eve of the Party congress in 1989 at which they, too, attempted to get rid of the *corpus delicti* by renaming the tainted Hungarian Socialist Workers' Party as the Hungarian Socialist Party, published a long document describing the many occasions on which their efforts to do the right thing had been frustrated by Moscow. 'Our fate has always been decisively influenced by external factors,' announced Foreign Minister Gyula Horn, one of the leading Party reformers, in his introduction. Starting with the Soviet intervention in 1956 the document, which had been drawn up by Party historians, listed numerous moments when Moscow prevented the Hungarian comrades from making the right decision: the execution of Nagy and his closest colleagues; arms burdens beyond the capacity of the Hungarian economy; limits placed on East European countries' contacts with the West, which made it impossible to react in time to changes in the world economy; limits placed on Hungary's own economic reforms – these were only some of the obstacles dumped in the way of Hungary's Communists. How much better we would have done had we been left on our own! Few Hungarians paid any attention because by then it was obvious that the Party and Moscow were merely different aspects of the same thing, and that the Party could not survive outside the cage Stalin had built for it. This, surely, was the truth written on the face of Janos Kadar, itself scarred like the buildings of Budapest after the disastrous uprising. When Kadar abandoned Nagy to go over to the Soviet side at the critical moment of the October uprising it was as though to keep a rendezvous with Stalin's ghost. A committed Communist since youth, Kadar understood that if the system was to survive in East Europe the Stalinist bargain had to be accepted in full, and therefore he agreed to let Soviet power install him as Hungary's new and reliable Party leader.

To give Kadar his due, it was hard to imagine him excusing himself or his colleagues by saying it was all the Russians' fault. And if he alone among the bloc leaders gave the impression of a man who had been caught in the Medusa's gaze and only just avoided being turned to stone, innocence was not a quality one expected to find in any of the East European Communists; hypocrisy and self-deception in sometimes vast quantities, yes, but never innocence. Self-deception reached its height in East Germany; the peculiar vulnerability of an East German state condemned to live beside a far bigger and richer German neighbour combined with guilt over the Nazi past to produce not only an ideologically committed Party intelligentsia scarcely to be found elsewhere, but also opposition intellectuals who declared themselves committed socialists. There was an innocence about the place, although it was the disturbing innocence of people who could not or would not understand the artificiality of the little world they lived in, and at what price it was being sustained. It was Honecker's East Germany, after all, that produced in Gregor Gysi the only new Communist Party leader to enjoy some undoubted popularity after the upheavals of 1989.

Gysi, a clever Berlin lawyer of Jewish Communist parents, dashed around the country during the March 1990 elections like a Pied Piper, drawing remarkably young audiences. When he spoke to the pupils at his old school, the Heinrich Hertz special high school just off what was once the Stalinallee, they listened entranced as though he were a pop prophet. Squatting on the floor of the gymnasium converted from a Nissen hut, dressed in clothes of fashionable gloom and sloppiness, the kids threw him not a single difficult question. A short man, prematurely bald, composed though full of energy, Gysi enchanted this audience with the slippery barrister's argument that since both Stalinism and the Western system had 'betrayed mankind' by plunging into an arms race and destroying the environment, a 'third way' had to be found. The pupils, like Gysi himself so-called 'Wandlitz children' from successful Party families, gave him tremendous applause when he insisted that East Germany must take its own special values and achievements into any union with the West. The children's enthusiasm was understandable. Gysi was telling them that their and their parents' lives had not been wasted. It was, however, hard to believe that this shrewd man did not himself understand that East Germany's achievements – cheap food, kindergartens and the like – were no more than coins, and depreciating ones at that, tossed from the window of the tyrant's carriage, and that its only untainted values were those formed resisting that tyranny. Gysi was the last eye-catching revisionist leader, the last deceptive searcher after flowers that might suggest the system's roots were not entirely rotten.

THE WIZARDS OF OZ

At first the East European Parties seemed strengthened by beating off the revisionist challenges of the 1960s but the victory was deceptive and in the long run fatal. The Parties developed even further into two-tier organisations. The *real* Party was the *nomenklatura*, the few hundred thousand men and women whom the Party judged suitable to hold decisive jobs not only in the Party but in government, industry, media, the arts, army and of course police. The ordinary Party members, the majority, were needed as the clothes to make this naked core of power look decent. The two-tier Party had existed in some form from the start. When the Hungarian Social Democrat Anna Kethly urged a senior Communist official to begin reforms some months before the start of the October 1956 uprising he told her it was impossible to 'undo the national network of the regime'. This network, he said, consisted of about two hundred thousand major and minor functionaries including AVO-men (secret policemen) whose lives were 'bound to the regime'. (If the families of these people were included the core was, in fact, quite a big proportion of the Hungarian population which then only numbered just over nine million.) After the 1968 invasion of Czechoslovakia the Soviet Union set about creating a new core for the Czechoslovak Party that had gone so foolishly off the rails. Soviets and trusted Czechs drew up lists of some two to three hundred thousand names from which to appoint a new and reliable Party apparat, a new State Security, and a new leadership structure for the army and government bureaucracy.

One of the most colourful figures of Czechoslovakia's November revolution, the reform economist Valtr Komarek, soon to become Deputy Prime Minister, pointed out that this 'mafia' with its increasingly 'social Fascist tendencies' was the real enemy, not the Party leader Milos Jakes who had played an important part in the mafia's creation after 1968 but was now merely its spokesman. Komarek had recently been in Moscow where Soviet friends remarked it was a pity that the Czechoslovak Party no longer had a reform wing. That these Russians should still be thinking in terms of 1968-style 'reform' was typical of the confusion of Communists throughout the Soviet bloc, and the answer Komarek claimed to have given must have shocked them deeply if they understood it. Czechoslovakia, he said, had something much more important than a reform group within the Party. It had a 'reform *nation* of educated people that has not lost its European thinking and traditions'. When the day came that the nation took matters into its own hands the Party would be irrelevant.

The Communist Parties were rejected as a body rejects a false transplant. This was the same process Ryszard Kapuscinski had noticed as Iran turned against the Westernising system imposed by the Shah. Once the process began it was irreversible. 'All it takes is for society to accept the conviction that the imposed form of existence does more harm than good.' The defeat of the revisionists speeded the process not least because fewer people of intelligence became Party members out of conviction. Joining the Party became increasingly a matter of calculation. 'This isn't a political party,' said a young Hungarian official in 1989, 'it is power. I'm a Communist but it doesn't mean anything. I don't do anything about it. But I am part of power.' 'The quality of the Party decreases year by year,' a Warsaw writer was noting in 1980, and he was convinced even then that it could never be revived. The ambitious and able young might join to further their careers, but they were unlikely any more to want to make a career in the Party apparat itself, which was where all the vital decisions affecting their country's future were made. The Party had become, the writer found, increasingly 'Orwellian'. In the old days there had been 'intellectuals, fanatics, puritans and even ordinary people' among its officials. Today, 'there are only small, round, well-dressed people', chiefly the canny sons of peasants now enjoying the privilege of running a bureaucratic machine kept in place by Moscow. These apparatchiks found themselves under almost permanent ambush from the unexpected.

Edward Gierek, leader when the labour troubles of 1980 began, was 'deeply surprised' when the striking workers paid no heed to his speech urging calm. The description was Mieczyslaw Rakowski's who attacked Gierek after the latter's summary removal for having been 'captivated by his own propaganda' and trapped within a mental prison beyond reality's reach. Gierek's successor Stanislaw Kania did no better. Very much one of the small, round and well-dressed people Kania appeared full of confidence and energy but he did not fool the Poles who observed him. How to account for the man's sunny appearance? 'Lack of imagination,' said a Polish journalist, as good a spontaneous epitaph for the Polish Party as one had right to expect.

There was a notorious collapse of quality in the Czechoslovak Party after the purge of a third of its members following the crushing of the Prague Spring. Conversations with some of those who did join after 1968 out of a mixture of conviction and ambition (they would probably themselves have been unable to say which predominated) could be painful affairs. A young Czech diplomat entertained a visitor to lunch in a Czech embassy in West Europe. The two men sat down to eat in a sombre room to be waited on by an equally sombre maid. The hospitality might have been that of a Czech farmhouse, with tankards of Plzen beer, bottles of good Moravian wine, and pig meat a prominent feature of both the copious *hors d'oeuvres* and main course. Sweating from the alcohol and food, but also moved by them to a moment of intense confession, the young diplomat told the Westerner of his dream. The Czechoslovak people had for too long looked to the West and what had they got from it? The Germans had for centuries dominated them, the Catholics brainwashed them. Finally at Munich the British betrayed them. There was only one solution. Czech heads must, as it were, be turned completely round. The Czechs must look East, to Russia. The young man mopped his forehead. He did not say he was confident of success.

If intelligent people continued to join the rank and file of even the Czechoslovak Party, it was often because they felt they had no choice. At a barbecue in a cottage garden outside Prague in the late 1970s at which Havel, Vaculik, and other leading signatories of the recently published Charter 77 were present a man was to be seen wandering uncertainly round the tables, and occasionally bumping into dancing couples. He was a junior official in the Ministry of

Foreign Trade and had reached the point where, to continue his career, he had to join the Party. He was miserable about it, had therefore got drunk, and was treated with understanding even by these men and women who were already suffering considerably for having stuck to their principles. A similarly agonising choice was made a couple of years later by a theatre designer whose father-in-law was a well-known signatory of Charter 77. He became a Party member in order to be able to continue to work and to protect the future of his children who would within a few years be starting higher education. He made his own rules. He would not sign anything he disagreed with, above all an unpleasant document attacking Charter 77 that was being circulated by the Party, and he would not tell lies. It was, though, only after the November Revolution that he summoned the nerve to tell his father-in-law what he had done. In the long run such unwilling members did the Party more harm than good: always passive in its defence, they eventually exploded in anger against the organisation that was the cause of their humiliation.

Of all the Parties the greatest sham was undoubtedly Romania's, the most serious (though still with plenty of sham about it) East Germany's. 'What does the slogan "Death to Communism" mean to the four million Romanian Party members?' a Bucharest journalist and ex-Party member asked rhetorically after Ceausescu's death. 'The Party card was simply an ID card. You couldn't do anything without it.' 'To be a Party member in Romania was purely a bureaucratic matter,' agreed Andrei Plesu, the highly regarded literary critic who became the first non-Communist Minister of Culture. The Romanian Party approached recruiting in a straight-forward way. Under pressure from Ceausescu to have as many members as possible – only the East German Party was as large in proportion to the population – it bribed and bullied people into joining. All good students in higher education were enticed into membership by the promise that they would get extra marks for 'Communist activities' and improve their general academic rating and therefore chances of a good job on graduation. Getting out was another matter. 'It was easy to join the Party,' a well-known Bucharest professor of literature explained with winning frankness but 'almost impossible to leave it because that meant abandoning both social life and one's profession. An intellectual who left the Party had two choices, to emigrate, or to become marginalised.'

The East German approach was almost the exact opposite to the Romanian. At universities education was meant to be matched to political reliability. The Technical University in Dresden grouped its brightest students in 'master classes' with the aim of producing a 'socialist performance elite'. No question here of simply picking the cleverest young people. Selection was handled by the Rector and the head of the University's FDJ, the Communist youth organisation. It was not enough to be, for example, a good engineer. A student had to be involved in 'the social strategy of his country', a muffled way of saying politically reliable. Asked what he thought about Deng Xiaoping's aphorism about a cat's colour not mattering as long as it caught mice, the Rector looked surprised. The idea was new to him but he quickly found an appropriate rejoinder. Not so, he said, in the German Democratic Republic not all the mice were, so to speak, neutral and only a cat of the right colour would know the ones to pursue.

Although the East German Communists ended up with more reliable students – as a group they were of little importance in the turbulence leading to the overthrow of the Honecker regime, and quite a few became grateful followers of Gregor Gysi – there was the same cynicism in society at large. If in Romania you joined the Party because it meant so little, in East Germany the independent-minded young stayed away from university and anywhere else where Party membership and political reliability were demanded. A university degree became a positive disadvantage when travel to the West became easier, for the regime was fearful of losing expensively educated specialists by defection, hence the Dresden Rector's earnest search for cats of the correct colour. In Poland, as one might expect, the system broke down more extensively than elsewhere. A sociology professor at Warsaw University, where Marxism-Leninism had not been seriously taught since the mid-1970s, found himself having to explain such basic Marxist concepts as the 'superstructure' to students who had never heard the term before. In Hungary, in spite of the more relaxed ways introduced by Kadar, the old system of formal indoctrination of the young remained in force until the very end. Children were pulled into it at the age of six by an organisation with the cute name of the Little Drummers, the Pioneers followed at fourteen, the Communist youth organisation, Kisz, at sixteen, and some would even have joined the Party before entering university two years later. Small wonder that when the system collapsed students in particular felt an extraordinary liberation. 'They don't want to be the disciplined members of any organisation,' the rector of a provincial university said. 'They are scared of being in a herd again, scared of any group that has a boss who gives orders.'

A young Pole passing the Central Committee building in Warsaw in early 1989 gestured at the policemen standing guard. 'Why do they bother? Don't they know they're defending a lost cause?' By then the Party fortresses no longer awed the people who lived outside their walls. Deprived of the best counsel that the national intelligentsia was capable of, the Communist regimes were sure of survival only as long as they were ready to use force to put down any uprisings. Small wonder, when the fortress walls collapsed, that the once mighty commanders inside were revealed to be as harmless, though by no means as appealing, as the Wizard of Oz when Dorothy and her friends at last tracked him down. They were men unable to make sense of the world from which they had for so many years been hiding. They no longer even possessed a language that could describe what they saw happening. What did 'socialism' mean? 'A political ideal has become a magic formula, and the magic formula has become a synonym for all that is bad.' That was Havel's view. Others pointed out that 'socialism's' artificial language had created an illusory world on which whole nations had become grammatically dependent. No one should have been surprised that they stumbled so often in the real world for they had no words to describe it. It was typical that Milos Jakes, interviewed by Western journalists just before the free elections in the summer of 1990, insisted that the Czech opposition had come to power 'by the same methods as the Communists in 1948. The only difference is that we won the election and then took power whereas they took power and are now holding elections.' It was a travesty of what had happened, but his mind was unable to perceive things in other than the old artificial patterns.

Honecker had from the beginning of his time as Party leader chosen the media and state security as his prerogative area and yet his loss of contact with reality was almost total. He had used the press only to reflect his own opinions, intervening in the smallest details of the Party paper *Neues Deutschland*, the proofs of whose first two pages he checked daily even when on vacation. After the weekly Politburo meeting Honecker went off alone to another room with the security chief Erich Mielke where, a Politburo colleague said, they 'gossiped over the intimate security details of socialism with the same lip-smacking that other men talk about women's underwear'. The image was apt. How else was Honecker to approach his people except by this act of voyeurism? – but like the voyeur he saw only what was already in his own mind, never the thoughts of the nation he spied on. He outraged even colleagues hardened to his ways when, in conversations with Gorbachev during the celebrations of East Germany's fortieth anniversary in October 1989, with crisis fast approaching, he continued to boast of East Germany's superior achievements in microelectronics and added his favourite barb about East German labour productivity being so much higher than the Soviet. And yet it was moving rather than ridiculous to see Honecker at the anniversary parade standing ruler-straight to sing all three verses of the *Internationale*, apparently as happy as when he and his sister had led the May Day parade of the Red Front Fighters' Union through Wiebelskirchen fifty-nine years before. For a moment one could almost understand the young East German woman who had confided to a friend that she found the seventy-year-old Honecker attractive – '*Das ist ein Mann für mich!*'

None of the other Communist leaders at the time of the crack-up had the smallest bit of pathos. Jakes was an uncomprehending, unpleasant dumpling; Jaruzelski too opaque (or was it shifty?); Zhivkov merely a traditional Balkan manipulator. Honecker was of course corrupted like all the others by Stalin's bargain. He too fell victim to that most efficient but banal corrupter, power (Western consumer goods in the supermarket at the Wandlitz compound, the huge hunting estates where he was known to go shooting from his car at night). But one could still see in him traces of the wreck of an idealism and a great social movement betrayed.

The greatest betrayal was that in the end Honecker's survival depended on him using the machinery of force that had kept East Germany stable for so long. In the late summer of 1989 Erich Mielke held a meeting with the State Security's regional heads to discuss the growing discontent in the country. Leipzig was already an obvious trouble spot and Mielke asked the commanding general there to report. 'The atmosphere is wretched,' came the reply but 'so far as the question of power is concerned, Comrade Minister, we have things firmly in hand.' After the regime's collapse one of the State Security Ministry's deputy chiefs remarked that the Stasis were sufficiently well armed, organised and prepared to have cleared the East German demonstrators from the streets and re-establish order. But in spite of the immense power of the secret police throughout East Europe 'the question of power' was at last irrelevant. For force to be effective there had to be the will to use it, and by 1989 that had vanished in all East Europe except Romania. Not all of Honecker's colleagues were as isolated from reality as he, nor did they all fail to understand that Gorbachev had broken the Soviet end of Stalin's bargain. Moscow would neither use its own force to help them, nor encourage them to use force to help themselves. By the autumn of 1989 the process of change in East Europe had become like a fire driven by the wind from building to building. That fire's first small flames had appeared in Budapest, in the spring of 1988.

5

God Bless the Hungarian

JANUS
The notice on the door of the house in the East Hungarian town of Debrecen gave news of a death with a difference.

With joyful heart we announce that Communism passed away on 25 March 1990 in its forty-second year. Our hated deceased has been put to eternal rest this same day at midnight.
The happy family: the Magyar people.
Address: Hungary,
Europe, 1990.

The slow death of Magyar Communism, finally registered in March 1990 when the Communists, by then split into two parties, won only twelve per cent of the vote between them, surprised no one more than the Hungarians by the smoothness of its course. Indeed the last two years of the old Hungarian Party were much concerned with peaceful, though significant, funerals. The first was a political one: the removal of Janos Kadar, Hungary's ruler for thirty-two years, from the leadership of the then still united Communists in May 1988 – the moment that the fire already smouldering throughout East Europe broke into flame. To appreciate the irony of that occasion, and the miscalculations behind the manoeuvres that brought it about, it is best to begin with another, though later, funeral, that of Janos Kadar himself.

Kadar's death in July 1989 provoked a spasm of public sympathy for the old man, a most disagreeable surprise for the new Communist leadership under Karoly Grosz which had calculated it would win popularity by removing the old man from power. It also came at an inconvenient moment, for a visit by President Bush, on whom great attention had to be lavished, ended the very day that Kadar's lying-in-state began. There was never any doubt about where to lay the old leader to rest. *'Temetni tudunk'*, we know how to bury people, is a popular Hungarian saying and the Communists had early decided that their heroes deserved no less than the capital's Kerepesi Cemetery, the Hungarian pantheon where Kossuth lay and also Batthyany, the aristocratic Prime Minister shot by the Austrians after the failure of the 1848 uprising, and Deak, 'wise man' of Hungary and father of the Compromise of 1867 that brought the country unheard of prosperity as co-ruler of the Habsburg Empire. Deak's tomb, a great classical cube topped by a dome and a verdigris-tinted angel clutching a laurel wreath, was calmness compared to the passion of Kossuth's memorial. The supreme Magyar and father of the 1848 Revolution lay in a vast barrel-lidded coffin beneath a classical stone canopy that rested on what might have been the base of an Aztec temple. On its very top stood a gigantic male angel, wings apart and pinions spread, a flaming torch in one hand and in the other a chain attached to a roaring, larger-than-life lion. The Communists, no less ambitious as mausoleum builders, completed their Pantheon of the Working-Class Movement two years after the Soviet troops had shot down the Hungarian workers of Pest in 1956. Six flanking white-stone walls led the way to a low stone building in front of which the bronze figure of a man led a hesitant woman by his left hand while his right arm supported the slumped figure of a man. 'They lived for Communism and the people,' read the inscription behind the statues, whose poses suggesting life had almost got the better of them would never have done for Kossuth. Star-marked graves of dead Communists lay in rows in front and to both sides but the true ambition of the site was only revealed to those who entered the low building and descended to its underground halls. Here was space for the ashes of generations of Party heroes yet to come. At weekends respectably dressed elderly ladies could be seen looking at the urns that were already in place, murmuring the first names of the people whose ashes they contained as though it were a family tomb.

Kadar's funeral left the new Hungarian leadership no choice but to be present themselves in this place so blatantly dedicated to a cause and a class that some were already trying to distance themselves from. Grief, however, they left to the widow, a small, lost-looking figure in a black Germanic pork-pie hat, and to parts of the public, in particular a group of sturdy middle-aged women in summer frocks who at the end when the military band began to play the *Internationale* joined in, hesitantly at first, and then with confidence. These eyes, at least, were damp. No handkerchiefs were needed on the other side of the grave where the new men of power stood.

Uncomfortable moments were unavoidable at the funeral of a man whom, ever since his retreat from power, they had tried to make the scapegoat for almost everything that had gone wrong in the country. A quite unnecessary vexation, though, were the unforeseen crowds who turned up to pay their last respect to Kadar while his body lay in the great hall of the Central Committee building. On the first day people queued for three and a half hours in order to file past the corpse to the sound of Mahler, only stopping to make a little bow or more rarely a sign of the cross, or to place a flower at the foot of the coffin. Some villages hired buses to take them to the capital and the hall had to be kept open till one in the morning. At midnight, Budapest radio reported in some awe, a young man of twenty wearing jeans asked to touch the coffin and was allowed to. At first the young man seemed to come in handy to the new leadership, as did the other young people there, among them even children in sandals and clean ankle socks. 'Have you noticed the young?' asked an excited secretary of the Central Committee when he came across a foreign acquaintance watching the mourners file by. 'People say only the old and the middle-aged liked him, but do you see the young?'

He interpreted the presence of the young as a sign of hope for the Party, but everything the mourners said on leaving the hall suggested that was nonsense. 'He led the country for over thirty years. He did good things and things people didn't like, but in the end everyone said, as long as Kadar is here nothing bad can happen.' This remark of an elderly educated woman, never a Party member, set the tone. A couple of young women, also not Party members, thought he had given the country 'security and peace and love. We looked up to him.' An athletic-looking young man explained that he and his friends had come 'because of Kadar's human side. Now they're trying to put the blame on him and of course it's true he stayed too long in power. But he will be remembered as a great leader of Hungary.' Ordinary people mourned Kadar's going as one mourns the passing of youth or one's working life. They sensed that things would never be the same again. All Hungarians born before 1950 had memories of horror: the Bela Kun revolution and the white terror that followed; the loss of Transylvania and other parts of the old Kingdom; the economic hardships of the 1930s; war and again a Communist revolution; Stalinism; 1956 and its aftermath. Kadar had brought peace and a certain stability. Whatever his crimes he had in the end allowed the country almost to forget the terrible Stalin years when tyranny (the name of a poem written at the time by Gyula Illyes) penetrated everywhere.

There is tyranny in the cradle,
In the father's advice
The smile of the mother
The answers a child gives to a stranger . . .

In the farewell kiss
In the way a wife says:
When will you be back, dear?

Understanding neither the political manoeuvering at the top nor the depth of the crisis facing the country Hungarians knew that with his death an era was over, an era that for people living on an exposed plain in a perilous region of Europe had not been bad as history had accustomed them to expect.

Some very clever Hungarians shared that opinion too. Istvan Bibo was one of the most gifted Hungarian political thinkers but scarcely ever allowed by the Communists to publish: he told friends that when the time came to put up his tombstone they should write on it, 'He lived between 1945 and 1948', the only years in which he could work freely. Yet Bibo compared Kadar to Admiral Horthy and the last great Habsburg Emperor, Franz Josef. All three had begun with bloody suppression (Franz Josef of Hungary's 1848 Revolution, Horthy of Bela Kun's short-lived Bolshevik regime of 1919), yet all had gone on to win popular recognition. Bibo allowed that intellectuals may have accepted Kadar 'with a good dollop of resignation, scepticism or even cynicism' but he achieved perhaps the best compromise possible. A leadership which after the 'great trauma of 1956' had become 'disillusioned, resigned, no longer wanting everything at any cost', did a deal with a country that had become 'disillusioned, cynical, and striving for direct tangible advantage'. The result, Bibo concluded, was the 'most cleverly governed dictatorship of the proletariat in history'.

Kadar had two faces. He was the old Communist, the battler of and for the working class who in his later years reached the limits of his comprehension and could only be wheedled into anything new by copious use of the epithet 'socialist'. No one had ever mistaken him for a democrat. He hated the rigged assembly that in his day passed for Parliament and very seldom spoke there. While his policy of 'he who is not against us is with us' allowed most Hungarians to make an accommodation with the regime, his secret police pursued and persecuted without mercy the few men and women who openly continued to resist the regime or submit it to testing criticism. These rare, tough characters considered the deal described by Bibo to be humiliating. 'Kadarism,' according to one of them, 'was not just accepting the lesser evil: it meant having to love it too.' It certainly meant accepting that share of guilt implied by silence over the fate of Imre Nagy and the others executed with him. That Kadar felt guilty about Nagy was beyond dispute. It was not only the eventual execution of Nagy and four of his associates in Budapest in 1958 that left a foul taste in the public mouth but also the shamefaced silence that covered everything to do with the matter until 1989. Nagy and the others, manacled hand and foot, were hanged in the transit jail on Kozma Street the morning after they had been sentenced to death. Their bodies were hidden in the jail until 1961 when they were tipped face down into new coffins and secretly reburied in unmarked graves in the plot for murderers and unknown suicides in the public cemetery of Rakoskeresztur next to the prison. Some three hundred insurgents were also buried in plot 301, some of them workers too young to be executed at their time of capture but whom Kadar nevertheless sent to the hangman as soon as they reached their eighteenth birthday, a memory that would always darken the Pest working class's feelings about the old leader. These men lay together for twenty-eight years, their bodies at best marked by two pieces of metal piping lashed together to make a cross, in the most distant part of the huge necropolis where grass and shrubs grew wild and tall, and pheasants and even the occasional deer were more frequent visitors than human beings. Three months before he died Kadar surprised the Central Committee by turning up at a meeting to make an incoherent hour-long speech that returned again and again to the matter of what he called his 'responsibility', above all for the death of the man whom he could not bring himself to name and referred to only as 'the person who has since deceased'. Small wonder the city gossips told stories about the old man getting up in the night to wander about the rooms of his villa on Rose Hill looking for the seal he attached to the document condemning Nagy to death.

In the end most Hungarians chose to see the other face of Kadar, the face that peasants saw when they made naive sculptures of him delivering a speech, or going hunting in a carriage drawn by five grey horses. The latter was a fantasy for he was no Honecker when it came to hunting, but the imagined coach was appropriate for a man whose length and peacefulness of reign were only matched by kings of Hungary who had been dead five hundred years. It seemed natural when a rock musical was put on in 1983 that, though ostensibly about Istvan, Stephen, Hungary's first king, it was a clear allegory of Kadar's coming to power. *Istvan the King* used history to conjure up an emotional justification of the tragic ruler of today. It was easy for audiences to see not only Kadar-Stephen on the stage but Nagy too, and all the blood-soaked choices of 1956. The chorus representing the Hungarian people had the last word:

Our day has come, Istvan our Lord's
Merciful light grows upon us.
Our heart sleeps, we are happy to sing
Beautiful Hungary, our dear home.

This genuine popular benevolence extended only to the person of Kadar, never to his supporting colleagues and certainly not to socialism. A survey carried out in 1982 showed that only one in ten people could identify more than three members of the Politburo, although their names were every day in the papers and their faces almost as regularly shown on television. Surveys suggested people were not even sure what the Politburo was supposed to do, and although they knew they could not get rid of the Party élite they resented it as unnecessary. Although Hungarians would express affection for Kadar, and even believe he had a decently human attitude towards them, they had no such feelings about the system he had done so much to keep in place. Perhaps a character in a film made in 1978 summed up the popular attitude: 'Socialism is like a voyage on the ocean; one can throw up, but it is impossible to get off the ship.' 'Even if [the Hungarians] know and understand that this is the best they can have,' wrote a sociologist in the mid-1980s, 'emotionally they largely reject the system.'

The limited economic reforms that had been pushed through in the teeth of Soviet disapproval were beginning to create a new rich class resented by ordinary people, not least the traditional working class the Party was supposed to favour. There was also a worsening mood among the intellectuals and artists who had been seduced by Kadar's cunning but cultured old Politburo friend Gyorgy Aczel, a literary collector who liked to be given manuscripts even by those whom he censored. Issues had come up that disturbed people who till then had made do with a little more freedom, including freedom of travel, and a few more comforts, or who had come to terms with the regime on a far more elevated plane like the Marxist philosopher Gyorgy Lukacs. The eminent thinker had joined the Nagy Government as Minister of Popular Culture but later recanted and sought intellectual security by reconciliation with Kadarism (and for his pains was condemned by the émigré Polish philosopher Leszek Kolakowski, once a 'revisionist' Communist himself, as 'the most striking example in the twentieth century of what may be called the betrayal of reason by those whose profession is to use and defend it'). One of the new and troubling issues was the proposed dam at Nagymaros which more and more people considered a dangerous anachronism that no truly Hungarian Government should have allowed. Even more feeling was provoked by the regime's silence over the Hungarian minority in Transylvania whose situation deteriorated sharply throughout the 1980s. Kadar never allowed his Government to address this problem openly, partly because as an old Communist he disliked nationalism (particularly the pre-war revanchist Hungarian kind) and accepted the Soviet-bloc rule that no member should publicly criticise another, and partly because he feared the Russians would exploit a Hungarian–Romanian squabble.

The subterranean pressure exerted by these and other issues affecting the fate of the Magyar nation was one underlying cause of the successful coup against Kadar at the Party conference in May 1988. Kadar had been accepted as a genuine Hungarian leader, a man who had done as much for the nation as difficult circumstances had allowed. But if respect for him as a man remained, the feeling was growing that new times presented the country with both new chances and dangers. The popular joke about the old man wanting to pass the country on to his successors in the state that he had found it caught this feeling that Kadar was out of touch and had better depart quickly. None of the men who now came into prominence had a fraction of Kadar's status. The new Party General Secretary Karoly Grosz was a sharp, cold-eyed apparatchik led by ambition to exaggerate his chances of success (a failing revealed again and again by all East Europe's Communist leaders in this twilight period of the system). The economist Rezso Nyers, who had fought for reform for over twenty years, was a decent man but not a natural leader. Imre Pozsgay, the politician Kadar had always refused to let into the Politburo, saw furthest into the future and for that reason was the most enthusiastic reformer. But all three understood what Kadar no longer could. It was simply not enough to 'preserve' Hungary by keeping loosely in step with the Soviet Union and maintaining the system more or less as it was. That had saved the country after 1956. In 1988 it was killing it.

PATRIOTIC ALARM

By the end of the 1980s all the regimes of East Europe knew they were approaching economic and social crisis. Even in Romania and East Germany, where Ceausescu and Honecker refused to allow such things to be discussed, there were nevertheless some members of the Party élite who understood how bad matters were. It was typical of the underlying unease that in Prague, where the leaders' speeches were of an untroubled tedium almost till the end, a research institute headed by Valtr Komarek was allowed to produce increasingly dire forecasts of what would happen if economic policies were not changed. As for Hungary, after Kadar's removal from the Party leadership the Communists almost completely lost control over the press by the end of 1988, and by the following year people were finding it hard to distinguish between the programmes of Budapest's Radio Kossuth and the Voice of America. The new Party leaders themselves plunged into the business of explaining how desperate the situation was, expressing it as an international economic challenge that could no longer be ignored. A leading Party intellectual and member of the Academy of Sciences remarked during the 1988 Party conference that the Party would have to follow the example of earlier Hungarian élites and make sacrifices for the good of the nation. 'When the challenge is dramatic – adapt or collapse – you find a readiness for change.' The Hungarian nobility had been willing to give up some of its privileges for the national cause in 1848. Now it was the Party's turn.

Even the conservative Politburo member Janos Berecz, responsible for ideological matters, was convinced by theoretical studies carried out under his direction in the early 1980s that while capitalism was capable of almost endless renewal 'socialism' had come to a dead-end. Communists had for years regarded state ownership as the most 'advanced' form of property. The truth was that cooperative and private ownership were in every respect more useful and productive. The still limited private sector (to be found in farming, services and construction, the state having almost abandoned building houses) was creating a third of the country's wealth while most of the majority of the subsidised state industries found it difficult to sell their products anywhere but the Soviet bloc. It was also becoming obvious that a declining economy was having a disastrous effect on every aspect of national well-being. Half the population had two or more jobs. This opportunity to increase earnings was offered by the growing private economy, but it meant that every other Hungarian spent an average of sixty hours a week at work and a sizeable number as many as eighty or even a hundred hours. But although people were obviously working themselves into chronic ill-health, the Hungarian state spent less on medical services than any other country in East Europe except Romania. The two most frequent causes of death were alcohol and respiratory troubles, the latter usually caused or aggravated by heavy smoking. Hungarian men had a lower life expectancy than anywhere else in East Europe, and only in Romania were prospects worse for women. As a result the Hungarian population was no longer growing. Between 1983 and 1985 the number of Hungarians living in Hungary had decreased by 150,000.

The statistics were bad for all East Europe. Even the supposedly successful East Germany looked good only compared to the rest of the Soviet bloc; compared to the industrial West its economic and social achievements were, with some striking exceptions, shabby. Decaying factories; outrageous levels of pollution; inadequate housing; demoralised and underfunded schools; a neglected industrial and social infrastructure; an unhealthy diet and massive addiction to alcohol and tobacco – this was the common legacy East European Communism left to the governments that took over in 1989 and

1990. All the Communist regimes had reasons as strong as Hungary's to take alarm at the situation and move towards a reform of the entire system. Why was it that Hungary's Communist leaders moved quicker than anyone else?

One reason was the Hungarian Communist Party itself. When the Party got on its feet again after 1956 it became possible, under Kadar's relatively benign leadership, to argue the reformist case in the Party once more. By 1968 the reformers, led by Rezso Nyers, were able to introduce considerably revised economic policies. But even when the tide turned against the reformers, and Nyers lost his seat on the Politburo, they were not driven from the leadership circles, still less out of the Party itself. Nyers remained a member of the Central Committee, a position he used to good effect as Kadar's forced retirement drew near. Together with Pozsgay, also a Central Committee member in spite of views that Kadar disliked, Nyers supported a group of young Party academics who in 1987 wrote a study on the economy called *Turn and Reform*. This put the blame for the country's difficulties on the leadership's economic policies and argued that the only solution was social and economic reform based on an honest dialogue, lacking thus far, between Government and people. These ideas did not appeal to the Party apparatchiks, but because the Party had not undergone the drastic loss of talent experienced by the Polish and Czechoslovak Parties there were people both within its bureaucracy as well as influential Party members in industry and Government who were capable of appreciating them. Although they remained a minority in the Party up till the very end these 'Reform Communists', as they later called themselves, were eventually able to seize the initiative within the Party and help set the agenda for Hungary's revolution. By the spring of 1989 it was no longer a surprise to hear from men like Pal Vastagh, newly elected Party leader in the southern county of Csongrad, dire predictions to the effect that without 'quick and radical change in all aspects' of the nation's life, Hungary would be no more than 'a little island with an exotic language'.

Vastagh and others like him were not just speaking as worried Communists. Theirs was the tone and language above all of worried Hungarians. And important though the Hungarian Party's comparative tolerance was in making smooth change possible, its members' rediscovery of Hungarian feelings and instincts counted for more. Four decades of talking about an entity called East Europe had accustomed many West Europeans to supposing there was something naturally coherent about the other half of the Continent. Few if any Hungarians had ever believed that. They knew they had been, and always would be, odd men out. The Slavs belonged to a large family. They might feel trapped among disagreeable relations, but not isolated. Romanians believed they had cousins in Italy, Spain and France, and that they were, as President Iliescu said at his inauguration in 1990, 'a European country of Latin expression'. The only kinsmen Hungarians had in Europe were the extremely distant Finns and Estonians. The latter's tribes had set off to the West from the same area of the Urals as the Magyars but the similarities of the languages they spoke were recognisable only to linguistic archeologists; and it cannot be said that Hungarians were greatly interested in their supposed Scandinavian cousins. That certainly was the experience of a Finn who visited Budapest towards the end of the 1980s. 'The Hungarians,' he decided 'are a small people with a big power mentality. They said goodbye to us [the Finns] somewhere in the Urals and have not really wanted to know us since. We are not worthy of them.' The observation hinted at the unstable balance between vulnerability and ambition that marked the Hungarians and their history, for their small size and linguistic isolation were compounded by the land-locked plain that Arpad, leader of the seven migrating tribes, chose to settle on at the end of the ninth century. Even Admiral Horthy had been known to criticise the venerated national ancestors for not having picked 'the right place for a kingdom'.

Although Hungarians often talked as though their history of the last two hundred years had been one of unbroken tragedy, the briefest acquaintance with Budapest or some of the main towns in the provinces suggested that this was not quite the whole truth. Between the Compromise of 1867 and the beginning of the First World War, Budapest was the fastest growing city in Europe. In 1815 Metternich had pointed at the road leading east from Vienna and declared that that was where Europe ended, but by the turn of the century Budapest was unquestionably a European city, partly thanks to its rich and talented German and Jewish communities that were rapidly becoming Magyarised. Budapest liked to build big. The Stock Exchange was the biggest in Europe though it did considerably less trade than even Vienna's. The almost Gothic Parliament was the biggest in the world although it served more as a temple to Hungarian self-esteem than as a house of representative democracy. The Opera, although seating almost 1,300 people, was regrettably not quite as large as that of the imperial capital, Vienna, on which it was partly modelled. Even the gentry of a provincial town like Kecskemet commissioned the famous Budapest architect Odon Lechner to build them a town hall in the Magyarised Art Nouveau manner that included a council chamber where they could sit in Gothic pews surrounded by portraits and statues of earlier Hungarian heroes. The architecture of the provinces, like the creations of country pastry cooks, may not have matched the capital in size, subtlety of colour or proportion, but it was only the money and skill that fell behind Budapest's, not the pretensions. It was a Hungarian connoisseur of Budapest who put this astonishing burst of building down to a combination of untypical, (for Hungarians), optimism and a much more typical 'myopic feeling of Hungarian omnipotence'.

The Dual Monarchy of Austria and Hungary that was created by the Compromise allowed Hungarians to press for ever more power within the Habsburg Empire and eventually to behave, some historians have thought, as though they owned it. Towards the end the Hungarians were almost demanding a separate army, while refusing any rights to the numerous national minorities in their kingdom. The Austrian Archduke Franz Ferdinand, whom the Magyars found humourless, was driven wild by them ('the so-called "decent Hungarian" *simply does not exist'*) and they even managed posthumously to get under the skin of such a humane writer as Edward Crankshaw:

> [The Hungarians] ruled over half the Empire, in which they occupied a position of extraordinary and indeed disastrous privilege, under a King to whom they professed romantic loyalty while doing their best to stab him in the back. They paid less than their share of everything; they had enjoyed more than their share of influence when it came to policy-making . . . They contributed nothing but some dashing regiments of cavalry, a large number of surpassingly beautiful women, and an infinity of woe.

And then came the shock of the Trianon Treaty of 1920, and the loss of Transylvania, of what had just become Slovakia, and a good deal more besides. All Hungarian history has since that day swung between the two impossible poles of reversing or accepting Trianon, and the result was to increase the danger of the country isolating itself even more from the concerns of the rest of Europe. Trianon strengthened what one Hungarian historian called 'the fatal Hungarian tendency to self-centredness'. The Hungarian-born Arthur Koestler, writing in 1939 about the suicide of the poet Attila Jozsef, evoked the feverishness of being Hungarian after the surgery of Trianon. 'The hopeless isolation of this nation breeds its talents, its will to assert itself, and its hysteria; to be Hungarian is a collective neurosis.'

Not that the ruling classes of pre-war Hungary accepted that recovering the lost territories was impossible. France was held primarily responsible for Trianon and to this day Hungarians can be found who explain everything by the fact that Prime Minister Clemenceau had a Hungarian daughter-in-law whom he hated. Destabilising the French Republic therefore seemed desirable; a semi-official scheme for flooding France with forged francs ended farcically when two Hungarian army officers in civilian clothes were caught trying to exchange packets of the false banknotes in a Brussels bank. Hitler seemed a more serious bet. Well to the right itself, though distancing itself from Hungary's own full-blooded Fascists, the Horthy regime became Nazi Germany's ally in exchange for getting back the better part of the lost territories. The result was that Hungary's position in 1945 was as bad as at the end of the First World War. Unlike Romania, which joined the Allies at the last moment, Hungary fought on the German side till its own collapse. The lands it had recovered and ruled for at most six years were taken away again. Communism came to Hungary to punish a nation as much as a class.

The country thus began its life under Communism with a profound sense of national grievance, feeling utterly alone and at others' mercy in a way that no other country in Europe did. 'The slandered of history', 'constantly disparaged', 'inculcated with a sense of defeatism and an inferiority complex', are phrases Hungarians still use to describe how the country felt at that time. Having failed before the war to develop a proper community among social classes, and lacking a national church such as Poland's to bind them together, the granulating effect of Communism was all the greater. It was Kadar's skill to tempt the demoralised and gloomy Hungarians with a more relaxed and comfortable life. Magyars are not Slavs who sometimes care more for what they see in their minds than in the world around them. A Hungarian intellectual who had built up a profitable if ironical relationship with the regime liked to recall that his Polish translator once said to him, 'We Poles may not know how to live, but we die magnificently.' His answer had been, 'Well, we Hungarians prefer to live.' He might have said 'prefer to live well', for Magyar self-esteem came into play here. There is a story by the nineteenth-century novelist Kalman Mikszath about a wedding among the provincial gentry, a celebration that at first seems worthy of the greatest aristocrats. There is a plethora of servants. Guests arrive in splendid four-in-hands, and some give the bride and bridegroom cheques worth tens of thousands of florins. The ladies wear dresses from Paris, the bride an emerald necklace. By the time the party ends all this evidence of luxury is proven to be false. False beards, moustaches and a variety of uniforms turn a handful of servants into an imposing retinue. The coaches have been hired, the horses have come from the cavalry stables, and the only thing Parisian about the dresses were the boxes they were packed in. The grand gentlemen worked as clerks in the local bureaucracy; the cheques are worthless; and the bride's necklace is borrowed from the bank. The wedding has been pretence from start to finish. All know it, but all feel better for the hours of borrowed grandeur they believe was their real due.

Kadarism at first succeeded in gratifying Hungarian self-esteem by raising living standards. Many middle-aged Hungarian men may have worked themselves into ill health or an early grave but in return there was a visible increase in prosperity. In 1960 there were 18,000 private cars in the country. By 1970 this had grown to over 200,000; by 1985 to one and a half million. There was a similar explosion in the ownership of other household consumer goods. Sociologists who studied the more fevered aspects of this accumulation marvelled that while conspicious consumption usually came at a late stage of capitalism it had already arrived in Hungary. Taboos against wealth were weakening; showing it off both gratified the Hungarian taste for grandeur and made up for the decades in which such instincts had to be stifled. The Government took pains to smarten up the famous parts of Budapest on either side of the Danube which not only attracted foreign tourists but also pleased Hungarians. There was, though, an echo of Kalman Mikszath's story about this, for a minute's stroll behind the celebrated Opera brought one to streets of real poverty, and by the beginning of the 1980s a good deal of Mikszath-like sham was being revealed in the whole Kadar boom.

Hungarians were realising that the improvements in their lives for which they worked so hard were modest compared with the changes taking place in West Europe. Kadar had given increased freedom to travel and by 1988 passports were issued virtually on demand. Hungarians poured into Austria to go shopping: eight hundred thousand made the trip in just one week in April 1989 to beat higher customs duties about to come into force on the Hungarian side. Instead of being grateful for the chance to buy abroad what could not be got at home Hungarians asked why Austrians, of all people, should live so much better.

The mood of self-questioning pessimism was caught in a column published in a Budapest newspaper in the summer of 1989 under the title 'What kind of country?'

> We are a country of extremes and would like to be one of sobriety. We are exaggerated in every exaggeration, and impatient in demanding patience . . . We really love only our dead and especially if they are victims. We are splendid at burying, but poor at rebirth . . . We stutter in our sorrow: why is misfortune alone faithful to us? . . . Why are our numbers steadily decreasing? And why does only our consumption of *palinka* [brandy] increase? Why do we eternally meditate on our excesses, our tragedies and our impotence? Why does the outside world see our talent, our smartness, our proficiency and yet we hardly see it at all?

This self-pitying querulousness of the second half of the 1980s was not new. Had not the national anthem long invoked God's blessing on the Hungarian because a nation that had 'already done penitence for both past and future' deserved to be spared from any more suffering? But this querulousness was also turning into something more positive, into a patriotic alarm that for some at least was a call to action. The highly regarded poet Sandor Csoori, who liked to talk about the Hungarian nation as though it were long-uncultivated soil, declared the modern Hungarian to be 'someone who is a genius or would like to be one'. Admitting this might sound a 'shocking desire', he suggested it was nevertheless necessary because only great aims 'can get us to take off'. A small and diminishing nation like Hungary could only, Csoori thought, be kept alive by its 'consciousness'. Each night Hungarians experienced a shock when they saw their country's map on the TV news. Hungary had been 'trimmed right round'; now was the time to recognise that their future conquests had to be internal: 'We can still conquer ourselves.'

If there was one Communist politician who could turn such thoughts into political language and a political programme it was Imre Pozsgay, the man Kadar considered 'impertinent' precisely because he was the most intellectually daring among the Party leadership. Pozsgay alone among the Communist leaders had the talents needed to become a public moralist, and fitted into the Hungarian populist tradition of a leader who defined the needs of the nation. Within a few months of his election to the Politburo Pozsgay would be speaking of the need for an 'anti-catastrophe policy' and a little later calling for a million new Petoefis, Deaks and Kossuths to make a reform that would at last clean the 'mud-spattered Hungarian flag'. Pozsgay and Csoori were in fact old friends and bound by something else almost as strong. Both had been favourites of the great Gyula Illyes. The poet who as a young man had wanted flood waters to carry off the rotten pre-war society later reached an accommodation with Kadar, but he had come to stand for the best in old Hungarian life and culture. On his death bed Illyes told his wife to take care of two people – the poet Csoori and Pozsgay the politician. In no other country in East Europe was there a similar apostolic succession running from a grand old man of national letters to a Communist leader who pledged himself to undo the damage wrought by Marxism-Leninism on national values and the national spirit.

THE SLIPPERY SLOPE

The clear-out of the old guard at the May 1988 Party conference went beyond the most optimistic calculations of the Party reformers. Eight old men, including Kadar, were removed from the Politburo and five of them also failed to win a place even in the new Central Committee. The latter body lost about a third of its previous members including one, Antal Apro, who had joined the Politburo under Hungary's own little Stalin, Matyas Rakosi, and stayed there undisturbed like the Dormouse at the Mad Hatter's Tea Party for over thirty years. Kadar himself seemed scarcely able to understand what had happened, the melancholy of his last meandering speech emphasised by the plaintive rhythms of the Hungarian language in which words tumble like tennis balls bouncing out of their container.

For all the drama of this changeover, the conference still appeared to remain within the bounds of Communist decency. Nyers, re-elected after an absence of fourteen years to the supreme leadership, told journalists that while a multi-party system was in theory possible, and that the Party would probably one day concede to it as it already had to the idea of the market economy, it was still hard to imagine the steps by which it might be reached. Nyers said he did not expect to see this transformation in his lifetime. Pozsgay was more forceful. He could think of 'no arguments in favour of a one-party system except practical and historical ones'. The Party had shown at the conference that it was ready for 'pluralism' and as for democracy, he could not 'imagine a society based on human values that is without it'. Nevertheless Pozsgay still said he believed Hungarians wanted socialism, although admitting he was a little less sure about the younger generation.

The man who emerged on top, though, was the fifty-eight-year-old Karoly Grosz who kept the premiership while becoming General Secretary of the Party. Grosz, a worker's son from North Hungary, seemed a familiar East European figure. Short and energetic, his eyes had the hardness that sometimes came to an apparatchik after years of proximity to raw power. It was Grosz, not Pozsgay or Nyers, who represented the Party establishment. Nevertheless on appointment as Prime Minister he had shown untypical skill at public relations, talking at length to newspapers and television about how the old leadership had made the mistake of appearing 'colourless' (although this was scarcely true of Kadar), and making unusual confidences about such matters as the sleeping pills he took each night. Most people supposed that Hungary was set for a new stage in a not unfamiliar battle to reform the socialist economic and political system, and that moving Hungary back towards the company of modern nations depended on whether Grosz and the radicals like Pozsgay and Nyers could work together to this end. Few imagined that the virtual disappearance of the Communist Party was on the agenda. Pozsgay himself spoke of the need to bring a pluralism of ideas and organisations into Hungarian life while in private he suggested that the Party might one day become a purely inspirational force 'like the Roman Catholic Church' (the idea sounded bold at first, but on examination suggested – if genuinely meant – a remarkable over-estimation of the potential authority of an organisation kept in place by a foreign power). But both Pozsgay and close advisers such as the sociologist Mihaly Bihari talked as though the old 'socialist dictatorship', which they openly recognised as a 'historical cul-de-sac', could be done away with by allowing pluralism within a much more relaxed Communist Party. Pozsgay certainly believed that a multi-party system would come eventually but he seemed to imagine that when it did a new-look Communist Party would remain as the dominant force within it. Meanwhile what counted was to create a system in which debate and conflict of ideas could prevent the Party from the trap of taking wrong decisions in enforced unanimity which, he would say later, was 'the basic cause of our troubles and our problems'.

It was true that much more radical forces were at work outside the Communist ranks but there can have been scarcely anyone then who foresaw that within a couple of years they would be the two biggest parties in a democratically elected Parliament. The group that attracted most attention abroad was gathered round the handful of experienced dissident intellectuals of Budapest like Janos Kis and Miklos Haraszti, who had begun their *Samizdat* journal *Beszelo* only in 1981. The late start was a consequence of the relative success of Kadarism which, as Kis said, allowed Hungarians to think 'they were better because they had butter', and to suppose that the path to change lay through gradual socio-economic advance and not political confrontation as in Poland. By the end of the decade the position of Kis and his colleagues had been greatly strengthened by the realisation that Kadarism, far from being a solution, was in fact only 'a postponement of a crisis that affected the entire Soviet bloc'; and that the postponement had actually made the crisis worse. These early dissidents were now joined by environmentalists fighting against the Nagymaros dam, and students and young academics who had created Fidesz, the ambitiously named Federation of Democratic Youth. There was also the new independent trade union, actually an interest group of scientific workers, that reflected the disadvantageous position of the intelligentsia in Hungary as throughout East Europe. It was from these people that a new party, the Association of Free Democrats, would be formed before the year was out. The future Free Democrats and Fidesz (which became a party in its own right) were classic parliamentary democrats and their Hungary belonged fair and square in modern Europe. They were as firmly committed to non-violence as their dissident friends in Prague and Warsaw, although somewhat more right wing in their unqualified enthusiasm for the market. Their leaders were men of talent and principle, and the study they gave to the machinery of a future Hungarian democracy ensured that when the unexpectedly speedy transformation did happen the country was not entirely unprepared for it. Their power of political analysis allowed them to spot quicker than others the regime's weakness, and when talks between the Communists and the new political groups began in the mid-summer of 1989 it was they who forced the pace. Confident by then that time and the internal processes of Hungarian society were working against the Communists they were able to prevent the opposition from making unnecessary compromises.

Some of the future Free Democrat leaders were Jewish; others had once been Communists and even Marxist philosophers. This, together with their openness to Western thinking and aversion to nationalism, marked them off from the Hungarian Democratic Forum, another radical group that had taken shape at a meeting the previous September in the village of Lakitelek outside Budapest. Like the soon-to-be formed Free Democrats the Democratic Forum was a result of the realisation that Kadarism was part of Hungary's problem, not its solution. The Democratic Forum was also committed to non-violence: Sandor Csoori, one of the Lakitelek meeting's inspirers, insisted on the need to break away from the pattern of violent, tragic revolution set by 1848 and 1956. But there the likeness between the two groups ended. The choice of a village for this gathering of intellectuals signalled that the pre-war gap had opened up again between the intellectuals of the capital and those who either lived in the provinces or, like Gyula Illyes, were as so-called Populists concerned with the plight of the provinces and country-side. Some Forum members saw the nation divided into 'deep' and 'shallow' Hungarians, a distinction elaborated by one of the pre-war Populist thinkers, and which most obviously meant that anyone without pure Magyar blood, like Jews and gypsies, belonged in the second category. Almost all Forum members believed in the restoration of the Hungarian nation, religion and 'Hungarian values', the latter no less precious for being difficult to define. When in 1990 the Forum came to pick candidates for the elections they often chose doctors, lawyers and teachers – the same provincial intelligentsia who had supported pre-war Populism. It was never a surprise to learn that these men (women candidates in this tradition-conscious party were rare) often had more children than average, for were not they the Hungarians most concerned about the future of a threatened nation? It was quite appropriate, too, that some turned up to the first day of the new democratic Parliament dressed in the white and black costume made fashionable by Kossuth.

The Democratic Forum seemed a phenomenon unique to Hungary. The Forum's guiding lights, let alone its ordinary members, were not dissidents in the sense of people who, having taken a stand on principle against the Communist regime, paid a price for it, and then devoted the rest of their lives to changing the system. Jozsef Antall, the leader who took the Forum into the elections of March 1990 and then became Prime Minister, came from a pre-war political family. He took part in the 1956 uprising at the age of twenty-six, was arrested and lost his job as a high-school history teacher. But Kadarism eventually allowed him to become a respected member of society as head of the Semmelweiss Museum and library, a distinguished medical collection well-known abroad. Antall would not have described himself as a dissident, nor had he moved in the same circles as the leaders of the Free Democrats. Did the Forum fit into the theories of those opposition thinkers in Prague and Warsaw who had hoped for the creation of an alternative society, which through a myriad independent structure would live its own life, almost as though the Communist regimes did not exist? Only partly. What might be called the classical thinkers of dissent were above all interested in democracy; and until the Party could be removed from power they were interested in democracy's practice at the micro-level, in such things as local union activities, unofficial education or the not-so-underground press. The Forum stood for something different. It wanted democracy, but that desire was absorbed within the much more powerful and emotional impulse for Hungary to be Hungary again. Democracy was attractive because it was seen to be prestigious, modern and the opposite of anti-Hungarian Communism. It also offered a chance to the most active spirits in the Forum, including the provincial intelligentsia, to break into the positions of power and influence that had for decades been monopolised by local Communist oligarchies. The success of Kadarism had been never to push such men and women so hard that they were radicalised and took up dissident activities. Instead of becoming members of an alternative society, as some of their Polish counterparts had done, they waited in the wings, potential leaders of what they believed was the still suppressed real nation.

When the Forum met in March 1989 for its first congress (representing a national membership of some 13,000) speeches in the glass-roofed aula of Budapest's Karl Marx University returned again and again to themes of national spirit and identity. Quoting an Endre Ady poem Zoltan Biro, one of the Forum's founders, declared that Hungarians had been scattered not just physically across the world by frontiers and emigration but spiritually too. Ady said this scattering had taken place before the Hungarian 'temple' could be built. This was what they needed now – a temple, not a party headquarters which, if it came later, must stand in the temple's shadow. With Karl Marx's statue hidden behind a vast Forum banner the university itself almost seemed a temple. A mixture of neo-Renaissance and cast-iron, it was an epitome of late nineteenth-century Hungarian confidence. As for the audience, their intensity and their sobre dress – no dissident jeans and T-shirts for the Democratic Forum – suggested servants of a cult as much as ordinary politicians. 'Self-centred and backward-looking,' remarked a disenchanted foreign observer at the end of the proceedings, but he was not Hungarian.

As for the Communists, their new leading ensemble not only soon ran into trouble; it almost equally quickly began to lose the attention of the nation. Although it sat at what was supposed to be the centre of the national stage the music it played was for the most part boringly familiar and little by little would be swamped by the exciting sound of patriotic airs coming from the radical bands in the wings. The important Central Committee meeting in February 1989 was an example. For the first time in the history of Communism a ruling Party decided to surrender its 'leading role', up till then considered the essential foundation of its power, and to introduce instead the multi-party system that Rezso Nyers nine months earlier had said would not come in his lifetime. This step had been discussed late the previous year, when even the conservative Berecz had been in favour of the revolutionary change. Grosz, however, was at that time against it and if he switched in February he certainly still believed that, with a little deviousness here and there, the Communists would come out on top in competition against other parties. A Party official who watched the steady Communist decline from the heart of the Central Committee summed Grosz up as a man who 'understood the rules of the liberalisation of the Kadar system, but never the rules of the quite different system when the Party had no leading role. He lacked the imagination to understand this – and anyhow he didn't want to.' That might have served as an epitaph for the bulk of the Party membership which was unnerved by such changes but was also scared of what the nation might do if there was no change at all. And if Grosz still believed the Party would emerge victorious from real elections so, too, did many even of the reforming minority among Party members. Indeed lack of imagination – about what the country really felt about the Party, and about the chances of Communists, after forty years running a dictatorship, ever again being accepted as ordinary politicians – was as striking in Hungary as elsewhere in East Europe. The truth was that the old hardliners like Prague's Vasil Bilak, who repeatedly told his colleagues, 'If we start liberalising they'll string us up', were right. The system could not survive liberalisation. Once you took away the Party's leading role, and the instruments of power that went with it, there was a risk of losing the whole game, and quickly. Even a man like Pozsgay, who was undoubtedly sensitive to the national mood, could one day reveal 'infamous data' about how 600,000 Hungarian peasants had passed through prison or internment camps between 1950 and 1953, and the next talk as though the countryside had forgiven the Party and would vote for it in a free election. A little more imagination and Hungary's Communists might not have gone so quietly.

The politically awakening part of the nation, however, pocketed the Communists' offer of a multi-party system as something inevitable while becoming excited about another Central Committee decision to the effect that 1956, far from being a counter-revolution as the Party had always said, was in fact a 'popular uprising' and therefore to be honoured by the people. It was Pozsgay who pushed the Central Committee into this shocking break with orthodoxy. He had supervised the group of Party historians charged with re-evaluating the past four decades that reached this conclusion, and made it plain in private that he meant to use it to identify and isolate those he called the Party's 'Stalinists'. It was an immensely popular coup, and one that seemed to fit the man who made it. Pozsgay was the only national leader with a foot in both the Party and the radical camp outside. Invited as honoured guest to Lakitelek in 1987 he had delivered a speech calling for constitutionally guaranteed freedom of expression that was bound to infuriate Kadar. By keeping links with the Democratic Forum – through leaders like

Csoori and Zoltan Biro, once his close associate – he seemed on the brink of developing a national constituency. His country origins certainly did him no harm. Born in 1933 into the family of a village tailor, he had been brought up among smallholders whom it was once again permissible to regard as the salt of the Hungarian earth. The Pozsgay family had preserved relics of 1848: 'Kossuth banknotes', printed by the brief revolutionary Government and a fine chest of drawers that his ancestors buried to save from the avenging imperial army. Having joined the Party at sixteen he quarrelled with his family about collectivisation although in his own village even the lofts had been swept clean to ensure compulsory delivery of entire crops. Later he admitted he had 'shut his eyes' to what Communists had done to the countryside. He was highly intelligent, knew how to win over people and, unlike some colleagues grown too used to the Party cloisters, seemed to enjoy publicity. A big man with a round, flat face, he would turn towards photographers with the sensuous pleasure of a large cat stretching itself in the sun.

Pozsgay's coup over 1956 made him the most popular politician in the country. If the political system was to be modified there would be new elections and Pozsgay was the Communists' obvious candidate for President. In fact friends were already advising him in February to leave the Party and run for the country's leadership as a genuinely national figure. That Pozsgay always rejected the advice tells a good deal about the difficulty not only Communists had in anticipating the future in 1989. When the Free Democrats met to draw up a programme in March they decided that, 'given the total unpredictability of the next elections', there should be arrangements to prevent either Communists or opposition being shut out of political decision-making. Pozsgay's special skill was to see ahead more clearly than anyone else in the Party but though the Communists' prospects steadily weakened, he still would not jump ship. He remained after all a man of the Left and the new Social Democrats, comically divided among themselves, did not offer a serious alternative home. Nor was he, or anyone else, under the pressure of popular demonstrations. Certainly there was dread of violence on the streets – 'Hungary is a nation born for self-immolation' was a typical remark of the time, this from a well-known Budapest journalist – but there was no violence. The elections of March 1990 passed off amid a good deal of indifference and public puzzlement (there were over fifty parties, most of them meaning-less). If almost two-thirds of the electorate turned out for the first round, less than half bothered to vote in the decisive second one. Political activity was mostly confined to the small number of people, perhaps 100,000 throughout most of 1989 according to some esti-mates, who had joined the various new parties. Pozsgay seemed to believe that a real political party could be made out of the more than 800,000 Communists. But at an important meeting of Party reformers in Szeged in the springtime not even an open-air rally at which the Molnar Dixieland Band played Pozsgay and Nyers onto the stage with 'Tiger Rag' produced the artificial excitement that is expected on such occasions in the West. Members were already leaving the Party. The country at large was unlikely to be seduced by the reformers' idea of adopting a winsome red rose as the Party's new emblem, let alone the Szeged reformers' overdue discovery that a 'type of Asiatic despotism' had been established in Hungary in 1948. Perhaps Pozsgay was misled by the easy way reformers set the agenda for the Party's internal debates, for the conservatives were mostly elderly and not very bright and the majority of Party members in the middle, few of them ever convinced Communists, were apprehensive but passive. It was one thing to belong to a Party whose meetings were held in the office during work hours, quite another to be faced with trailing after work to some remote district office and being told to distribute leaflets. They had not joined the Party for that, and the truth was Communists had few if any of the skills needed in a proper political party that survives by winning elections.

There was a very different atmosphere in Budapest and other cities on 15 March when, for the first time in forty years, the country was permitted full-blooded celebrations of the anniversary of 1848. Eighty thousand people gathered in a capital city that might have been designed for a patriotic pilgrimage, so full was it of stirring monuments and memories. The crowd, largely middle-class and with plenty of children and dogs, flowed from monument to monu-ment partly re-enacting what Petoefi and the original revolutionaries had done. Like them they had a list of twelve demands. Read out from the steps of Hungarian Television, whose building was declared symbolically occupied, they included a multiparty system, democratic liberties, independence and neutrality, a national holiday on 23 October to mark the 1956 uprising, and rehabilitation of

1956's leaders. Another halt was made outside the Parliament where from the base of Kossuth's statue Janos Kis declared that 'History has pronounced its sentence on the system called socialism.' Kis, who looked like the austere philosopher he was, had returned for the occasion from a teaching fellowship in America, a sign the opposition was also having difficulty keeping up with the pace of change. On the previous 15 March police had beaten up demonstrators. That Kis could now say such things publicly without fear of the police, without even a uniformed policeman in sight, was evidence of the regime's loss of control over the public debate. In the evening young people led by Fidesz marched over the Chain Bridge from Buda to Pest and climbed up the hill to the Castle holding candles and singing Kossuth songs:

> Lajos Kossuth has sent a message:
> His regiment is no more.
> If again he sends a message
> We'll join him in the war.

They made a charming sight, and tourists watching from the Danube embankment may have thought it was a carnival or some quaint folk custom. It certainly did not look like a revolution.

It was said of Imre Nagy that he had always been a step behind the people, and the same was true of the Grosz regime. Having lost a chance to win popularity by at once abandoning the Nagymaros project it changed its mind and ditched the scheme in May. While delaying the legal and political rehabilitation of Imre Nagy it made a half-hearted attempt to regain credit by having Pozsgay and the new Prime Minister Miklos Nemeth attend the June ceremony on Heroes' Square where Nagy's coffin lay before reburial. After an internal tussle the regime had allowed flags reminiscent of those carried by the 1956 Freedom Fighters, with the Communist emblem cut out of the centre, to be hung from the semi-circular colonnade at the end of the square. Laszlo Rajk, son of Rakosi's most famous victim, had draped in black the classical façade of the Art Exhibition Hall in front of which lay the coffins of Nagy, his defence Minister Pal Maleter and four others, one of them symbolically empty for the unknown Freedom Fighter. Rajk had also constructed a dart-shaped white cloth, a singed black hole at its centre, that jutted out into the square. This represented that old Hungarian friend, a ray of hope soon proved forlorn. It was on this day, when Hungary's 'good Communist' was finally honoured by the people, that the Party's chance of winning back national respect seemed to vanish for good. That the mood was melancholy was to be expected. Many older people brought memories of the uprising that were still painful after thirty years, and some were angry that anyone from the Government should be present. The most applauded speaker was a young Fidesz leader who ridiculed Communist politicians for thinking that 'touching the coffins' of the dead men would bring them good luck. When the ceremony moved for the re-interment to Rakoskeresztur Cemetery, where the Government had with guilty speed and generosity relandscaped the once desolate plot 301, speakers called Nagy 'Uncle Imre', and remembered the endearing way he twiddled his moustaches and addressed the people as 'my little Hungarians'. But as the day went on the last doubt about who and what was being commemorated faded. One of the graveside orators quoted Nagy's supposed last words: 'If my life is necessary to prove that not all Communists are enemies of the people, then I willingly give it up.' Hungarians did not want to hear that. Judit Ember, a film-maker who had just produced a documentary about 1956, was among those who watched Nagy being returned to his grave. 'The miracle,' she thought, 'was that this real Party man imagined Communism could be combined with humanity, democracy and the Hungarian spirit. It can't and it's a pity. Mankind has lost another dream.' The funeral served to bury the dream, not revive or mourn it, and the nation's grief concentrated on the symbolic empty coffin, covered with a flag from 1956, that was buried close to Nagy, and on the others who already lay in plot 301. Their names and professions were read out that chilly afternoon – toolmaker, driver, soldier, miner, peasant, and electrician, 'formerly an officer in the Hussars'. These were the real Hungarians, went the message of that day, and they were Communism's victims, not its well-meaning but misguided supporters or reformers.

GOING QUIETLY

These public rituals, unthinkable a year earlier, did not take place free of fear. Several speakers at the Democratic Forum's congress had spoken of peasants still cowed by 'the puffy-faced Party secretary who smells of brandy'. One delegate had confessed to

being frightened himself but added that 'after forty years of oppression' no one should be amazed by that. A speaker told the calm
crowds on 15 March that 'being a democrat means not being afraid',
but nervousness that hardliners in the regime might use violence still
stopped some people going to Heroes' Square for the Nagy funeral.
Even some who did could not help wondering if police might open
fire from the rooftops, as they had in 1956, or even whether there
could be a Hungarian version of the massacre of Tiananmen Square
that had just taken place in Pekin. Some fears were less specific, but
no less revealing of the anxiety that penetrated the texture of daily life
even under Kadar's brand of Communism. A student on the square
that day had learned only the night before that both his mother and
grandmother took part in the fighting of 1956: their years of silence
were meant to protect him from possible retaliation.

Why was there no violence? The changes in Hungary were by
mid-summer far in advance of the rest of the Soviet bloc except
Poland. There, the week before Nagy's reburial, Solidarity had
crushed the Communists in elections. Nevertheless a pre-arranged
allotment of seats assured the Polish Party and its allies a majority
in the key lower house, evidence of Solidarity's belief that it was far
too early to dream of ousting the Communists from power. There
was scarcely a breath of perestroika anywhere else in the bloc.
Hungary's only advantage was that, without a common border with
any NATO country, it was not of major strategic importance to the
Soviet Union. Nevertheless Hungarian like other East European
dissidents had never underestimated the regime's capacity for force:
Adam Michnik's warning about the Polish regime having feet of
clay, but hands of steel, applied throughout East Europe. Something
new had happened in Hungary. The decision to move to a multiparty
system undermined the Party far faster and far more thoroughly
than anyone anticipated. It quickly made the Party look almost
illegitimate and superfluous, while Parliament became the most
important forum because its predominantly Communist MPs,
though originally Kadar's placemen, were stimulated by thoughts
of a real election ahead. When the opposition began to pick away at
the regime's network of power – above all the Party cells and
commissars in the army, police and factories – the hardliners found
it hard to resist because Pozsgay and the reformers refused to back
them, because such privileges made nonsense if there was to be a
multi-party system, and because it was plain they could expect no

support from Gorbachev's Moscow. The negotiations between the regime and opposition on the mechanics of transition to parliamentary democracy were complicated and not finally decided until a referendum in the winter. Forced through by the Free Democrats this produced an overwhelming majority in favour of taking the Party out of the workplace, redistributing the Party's considerable property and abolishing the Workers' Militia, a red guard created to support the regime after 1956. (The referendum also decided, though in this case by a whisker, that the new President would be elected by Parliament, not directly, much to the delight of the Free Democrats who partly feared the emergence of a new Horthy but also wanted to scupper the waning presidential hopes of Imre Pozsgay, whom in spite of his liberal views they abominated as a discreditable turncoat.) Hungary's fate, however, had been decided before that. Already in September a leading Free Democrat felt confident that the battle was over. The Party had 'imploded' and the opposition found it 'hard any more to meet a point of resistance'. We shan't hate the Communists, a Budapest newspaper commented jovially the next month, 'because if there ever were any they certainly haven't existed for a long time'.

As an old dissident the Free Democrat in question felt a certain distaste when, for example, the Interior Minister stood up to tell Parliament that freedom to travel was a human right although this contradicted everything the man had said in the past. The Communists, he said almost with regret, 'simply don't believe anything any more'. But this collapse of belief was a blessing to Hungary, for the instruments of force that the Party still possessed were only harmless as long as there was no will to use them. The army, not surprisingly, was particularly open to patriotic alarm about the country's decline, had no reason to love Russians, and was also aware of the traditional corruption (nothing original – chiefly luxury villas and drunken parties in hunting lodges) of some of its generals. At least one conscript who attacked the officer corps as Stalinist was told he was knocking on an open door. The opposition had plenty of experience of the Ministry of Interior and its subordinate State Security Service, especially the III/3 department for internal security whose members were recruited whenever possible from the families of industrial workers and old revolutionaries. But Party control of the Ministry was abolished as early as May 1989 in the wake of the decision to move towards a multiparty system. It seems to have been inertia, rather than a serious attempt to halt change, that led III/3 to tap opposition telephones during the negotiations with the Government for, as a security operative confessed to a Budapest journalist, 'it's hard to stop the work you're used to'.

There were rumours of coups and much suspicion of the 60,000-strong Workers' Militia, but none of the rumours stood up to investigation; as for the Militia, when their time came they folded up with no more resistance than a tent at the end of a summer holiday. The Militia had last been out in force on Budapest's streets during Kadar's funeral. Middle-aged and often overweight, they might have been bus drivers had it not been for their red ties and the red star on their soft-topped caps. Charged with defending the Revolution the Militia declined into a benevolent association for workers who had not done very well out of the Revolution – two-thirds of its members were fathers of large families on the edge of the officially-defined minimum wage. They were a typical organisation of the decaying Communist state, over-funded with public money and occupying real estate, including a new head-quarters on a fine site in the Buda Hills and a holiday centre on Lake Balaton, out of all proportion to their usefulness. Their weapons, which ranged from 60,000 machine pistols to machine guns and grenade launchers, together with the 20,000 handguns issued to senior state and Party officials, turned out to be no more dangerous than the teeth of an elderly lion too confused even to open its mouth to yawn. In late October the army removed this arsenal to their own depots and the paper proletariat was unarmed.

If the atmosphere in 1989 was not conducive to hardline resistance, it was Hungary's good fortune that social developments actually favoured the taking-over of power by one group from another. From the moment the Party's loss of power looked likely the danger was not from ardent Communists determined at whatever cost to defend the Revolution. It came, as a Party reformer put it, 'from those people who have power and equate socialism with their holding on to it'. There were fears that if people lost their jobs they would be driven to desperation. Troubling incidents did occur when officials who had been turfed out of good jobs in the diminishing apparat were turned down for work elsewhere, but senior state and Party bureaucrats were more nimble. Power in the old days had come from controlling state property, but the growth of private and cooperative ventures and the transformation of state enterprises into joint-stock companies in preparation for a market economy offered new opportunities. Thanks to the opportunities given by the earlier Kadar reforms, by the end of the 1980s ten per cent of the population was getting more than twenty per cent of overall income. Chances were that if an ageing Party leader could not make the jump into this world himself, his children could and perhaps already had. Elemer Hankiss, one of Hungary's best-known sociologists, concluded from a study of the profitable private boutiques in the centre of Budapest that two-thirds of them were linked in some way to senior officials. He summed up his conclusions by imagining the family reunion of a Party bigshot. There would be the daughter, owner of the Budapest boutique, and a son who managed a joint venture with a Western firm. Brother-in-law was director of a new joint-stock company while mother-in-law had for years been coining money with her private boarding house on Lake Balaton. There was, the sociologist noted, nothing unusual about this. Ruling classes had always made way for others as long as they also found room for themselves under the new sun. It was only shocking to people who had thought that the laws of social development had come to a stop with the creation of People's Hungary.

Because of the greater progress that Hungary under Kadar had made in reforming the socialist economy, its old élite were less scared than their counterparts elsewhere in East Europe by the profound changes brought by abandoning socialism. Money, its value, and the making of it had proved a stumbling block to Communists everywhere. The Hungarians, with characteristic ingenuity, were the first East Europeans to accept that to be an entrepreneur and to become rich was the way of the modern patriot.

6

Money Matters

AN ALTERNATIVE ECONOMY

The Polonia Express, due to leave Budapest's Keleti Station at five-past six in the morning, to no one's surprise was late. As the name suggested it was a Polish train that began in Warsaw and a Hungarian railwayman, interrogated as to the likely time of its arrival in the Hungarian capital, shrugged at the foolish question. 'These Poles! Everything's kaput with them.' Things might have been worse, for even at this hour on a freezing morning in November 1988 the station was stirring into promising life. Raw-faced men unpacked bundles for a large news stand, and there were decently wrapped sandwiches and pastries to be bought at the booth next door. A hole-in-the-wall buffet offered espresso coffee, though most of its customers bought shots of brandy which they downed in a gulp. The place had a rough liveliness that suggested people determined to provide themselves with the small but intricate conveniences of city life in spite of a system that scarcely bothered about such things. When two Soviet soldiers in long-skirted greatcoats and high boots stalked through the busy Hungarian crowd they looked as out of place as a cassocked priest among Puritans.

The same air of unofficial diligence hung over three clean blue Hungarian carriages that were waiting to be coupled to the Polish train. The middle carriage was a second-class sleeper whose attendant's cabin had been turned into a makeshift buffet. A blue-uniformed attendant, suave and moustached, supervised the loading of supplies. There were crates of soft drinks; plastic bags of salad and other greenery; and cylinders of gas for a small stove. This was Hungary on wheels, and foreigners were not invited aboard. When the Polonia Express did arrive, vaguely green beneath its antique grime, eventually to pull out of Budapest a mere two hours late, bursts of laughter and smells of Magyar cooking would tantalise the corridors of the comfortless Polish carriages. Private enterprise, though, could not be lacking from any East European train crossing international borders at the end of the 1980s. As the express was about to move off, a door on the opposite side to the platform burst open and a couple of young men scrambled up dragging behind them heavy-looking bags and two large objects wrapped in brown paper. The couple were Albanians from Yugoslavia, the mysterious wrapped objects the bumpers and wings for a Polish baby Fiat. They had been on an ordinary East European shopping trip. First they had gone to Warsaw to acquire parts for their damaged car at home in Pristina. On their way back they had stopped in Budapest to buy men's boots to fill their bags. Sold on returning home the boots would cover the cost of the trip.

The weak spot in their plan were the Yugoslav customs and as the train approached the border the Albanians went into the corridor to spy out assistance. They found it in three Libyans, a friendly insurance agent who was accompanying his sister and nephew on a hypochondriacs' tour of East European doctors. Introducing themselves in broken English as fellow Moslems the Albanians explained that since they had a large part of a car in their carriage it would be a good idea to leave their bags of boots with the Libyans. Having checked to examine their contents the polite Libyan agreed. Yugoslav customs had long been trained to detect the duty-avoiding tricks of their citizens but the Libyan's sister was pale and very beautiful. The top of a fine white blouse showed above the neck of her long black dress and on her feet, kept warm by grey wool tights and thick ankle socks, she wore delicate black patent-leather shoes. The young customs officers' eyes never reached the luggage rack on which the bags of boots were stowed.

The Albanians, though ingenious, were mere amateurs of private commerce. Poles were the acknowledged experts. A hundred years earlier it used to be said in Hungary that 'every respectable castle must have its refugee Pole'. Now that Poles had their own country again they were still becoming temporary and not so temporary refugees in ever greater numbers. Allowed more freedom to travel earlier than other East Europeans they soon discovered the advantages of the international division of labour. Between 1981 and 1988 a quarter-million Poles had gone abroad never to return; another quarter-million each year prolonged temporary foreign visits in order to earn more money at some job. Surveys carried out in 1989 suggested that half of all young Poles were ready to work abroad for a long spell, and that a further eight per cent wanted to leave permanently. By the end of the 1980s as many as half a million Poles visited West Germany each year where most of them worked as illegal labourers for a while. The growing gap between the official and black-market exchange rate of the Polish zloty meant that a few weeks spent on a building site for what West Germans thought unacceptably low wages could set a Pole up nicely for a winter in Krakow or Lodz. Many others worked 'black' (no taxes paid) in the sugar-beet and soft fruit fields of Sweden, only a short ride away on the Baltic ferry. Even professional couples would pack their children into unreliable cars and brave the sneers of the West Germans on their autobahns to spend a working holiday picking grapes in a French vineyard. What they earned could make the difference between scraping by and a decent Warsaw life with such comforts as a car, a video and a home computer.

It was, however, as traders that Poles were most visible in the other countries of the East. Some of those who got off the Polonia Express in Belgrade took their bags up the hill to a market where they soon made a little corner of Polish stalls. A young lathe operator from Zyrardow was in Yugoslavia for the sixth time. His trips began by stocking up with whatever marketable goods he could find in Poland. Textiles were promising, and so were ski-boot fasteners and instruments like spanners and screwdrivers. Soviet watches, which he might cross the border to acquire, were always popular. Yugoslavs bought such things because his prices, like those of the other Polish traders, were low. With the proceeds he acquired Yugoslav brandy (everything else was too expensive) which he would sell in Hungary. From Budapest he took back clothes, especially good knitted sweaters, to Poland or sometimes to the Soviet Union for if he bought enough watches there he was ready to start on another trip. The lathe operator's was a modest business. Poles who had cars and could lay their hands on vodka, cheese and butter loaded up and made their way to West Berlin where they needed no visas. They sold their wares cheaply to Turkish emigrants and other less well-off people but a couple of days' profit of 200 Deutschmarks converted to black-market zloties was the equivalent of three months' Polish wages. Many Poles flew about their business, for the already low East European air fares became exceedingly cheap if bought with zloties acquired on the black market. These flying traders were easily recognised at airports. Usually women in early middle age, they took as many heavy bags onto the aircraft as they could and smoked their cigarettes until the last moment before boarding.

Naturally there were no Government figures for the value of this private commerce but in Istanbul, a favourite destination, officials calculated that Poles bought goods worth $300 million a year, three times more than official Turkish exports to Poland. Since there were so-called Polish markets not only in the East European capitals but in provincial towns too, it was not surprising that here too private trade in some consumer goods exceeded the amount that went through official commercial channels. As for Poland itself, a visit to the Sunday market in Warsaw's SKRA stadium at first suggested that the regime had found a way without cost to itself to remedy the shortcomings of socialist commerce. The Warsaw shops did not have much to offer in the spring of 1989 yet Poles, by their own enterprise, managed each week to turn the sports stadium into a respectable department store full of goods that were seldom seen in state shops. There were bananas, grapefruit and pineapples; good German coffee and coffee-grinders; Russian caviar in jars of every size up to a one-kilo tin. You could buy Lacoste shirts, hair-dryers, shoes, watches, Pampers, video tapes, spray deodorants, throwaway razors, bathroom scales, car stereos, condoms, French pendulum clocks, maps, cameras, leather rocking-chairs, Russian 'Malysh' accordions and on one spring Sunday even a white plaster reproduction of a Roman portrait bust. On consideration this unexpected cornucopia made the visitor ill at ease. An elderly lady who stood a little to one side held a bar of Russian chocolate in one hand and a chocolate *galette* from Nedel in the other. Nedel was a rare Warsaw establishment that still made good confectionery and the woman would have had to queue since before dawn to obtain one of their much sought-after specialities. Some of the traders had only a little pile of goods at their feet, usually articles that could have been crammed into a suitcase at the end of a holiday abroad. Although those traders at the stadium who were professionals may have made good money, many people went there to make a hard life just a bit easier.

Poverty and border-line legality were even more obvious at other markets in the city. At Zabkowska Street across the river in the working-class district of Praga official notices warned it was illegal to sell video cassettes and books or to trade standing up and without a proper stall. No one paid any attention. Three rascally-faced young women in straw hats and oddly demure frocks leant against the wall of a shed on which they had hung a selection of Western clothes. People squatted round sweaters and brassières piled on the ground under the eye of a blonde girl in pink, eating seeds from a great sunflower head that rested in her lap. It was a scene familiar from Asian markets, yet the Chinese and Indian traders in the provincial towns of pre-Communist Laos or Cambodia had put on displays a hundred times better. Poles knew this perfectly well. 'That's just what we say,' an acquaintance agreed with gloomy satisfaction. 'We belong to the fourth world now.'

The growing freedom to travel and visits by more Western tourists meant that two things the Communists had always hoped to do without – money (real money, that is) and the market – were re-introduced from abroad with a vengeance. They had never been entirely done away with. From early on the East European Governments had allowed a number of shops to sell Western goods for hard currency. These were originally meant for Western tourists and the small number of their own citizens who brought back hard-currency savings after working officially in the West. Later the shops were expanded so that local citizens with relatives in the West, of whom there were naturally many in East Germany, but also in Poland, Hungary and Czechoslovakia, could spend hard currency sent them from abroad. This system expanded with great speed in Poland where the home market was chronically ill-provided and the Pewex shops eventually sold a wide range of foreign goods. When the narrator of Tadeusz Konwicki's *A Minor Apocalypse* prepares to set himself alight on the steps of Stalin's Palace of Culture as an opposition protest it is in a hard-currency store that he proposes to find the matches. It was not long before wits were suggesting that the quickest way to reach the West was to jump over a Pewex counter and claim asylum. Foreign currency also allowed people to move to the front of the queue to buy domestic cars and even apartments. The result was to create a new class division, never imagined by Marx, between those East Europeans with some access to hard currency and those with none.

The regimes were not altogether happy about this development and in East Germany Communists, normally required to wear their Party badges at all times, were supposed to remove them before going into one of the hard-currency Intershops. Western money had become to the Soviet bloc what sex was to some Victorians – a source of profoundly guilty pleasure. In spite of evidence that hard currency was driving their own money into a corner, the Communist regimes continued to act as though dollars and Deutschmarks were temporary visitors. An elderly Hungarian who had survived very comfortably under Kadar's socialism once remarked of Communists that they considered money and everything to do with it, such as profits and prices, to be 'like masturbation: something you give up when you get to the real thing'. The real thing, in its original form at least, included an element of austerity that had always attracted true believers. More important, though, was sheer political will-power. It was a characteristic of many of the great schemes of socialism, like collectivisation and the great construction projects in both the Soviet Union and East Europe, that while they often did not make conventional economic sense they did make sense as demonstrations of political will. Intended or not, the decision of East German Communists to set up their Party headquarters in the immense building previously occupied by the German Reichsbank symbolised this financial revolution. Under socialism words would replace money and the job of ministries of finance was to express political decisions in accounting terms. 'The party-state,' admitted Hungary's last Communist Prime Minister somewhat late in the day, 'wanted to exert an influence in almost every sphere of social and economic life, and for this it needed budgetary sources that could be distributed or taken away.' As for prices, even the Czecho-slovak Communist Prime Minister, Ladislav Adamec, confessed that no one had cared much about how they were formed. Money became the commands of the leadership expressed in a different language: it was certainly never meant to talk for itself.

So satisfactory was this system to the men in power – for it was the very basis of their power – that certain inconveniences such as frequent shortages or persistent cases of corruption were ignored as phenomena that would vanish with time, like the private plots that were regarded as unfortunate necessities until collectivised farming reached its full potential. The explosion of private trade in the 1980s was the extension abroad of venerable domestic black markets that themselves had been made necessary when planners first set prices and began to rob money of real value. Anything that was not in abundant supply eventually acquired a second, hidden price. In

Warsaw canny people had their 'little men' who came in from the countryside selling – at a real price – farm sausages of rough-chopped pork or sharp-nosed eels from the Mazurian Lakes. Well-organised inhabitants of Bucharest would make summer rounds of peasants they knew to buy meat that they stored for winter in their deep-freezes. Services beyond the most routine were unobtainable at the official price. 'If you want your car repaired,' the East German writer Stefan Heym liked to say, 'you have to pay an entrance fee – a smoked eel, for example, or a West German edition of a novel by Stefan Heym.' Hungarian sociologists made studies of this sort of corruption. People might pay, or give presents, to get a bed in a hospital, a place at university, and licences of any kind. It was usual to give certain sorts of officials, like the customs, a present merely for carrying out their ordinary job, because one never knew when a little extra might not be needed from them. Economists calculated that by the mid-1980s Hungarians spent each year on bribes and corruption as much as the entire national budget for social insurance. Bribery, cynical East Europeans said, not only saved the socialist system but humanised it too. In Czechoslovakia, where there were very few legal opportunities for private business, the grey economy in which moonlighters, skilled craftsmen and a good number of criminals operated was estimated by Marian Calfa, President Havel's appointee as Prime Minister, at 'tens of billions of crowns' (Czechoslovakia was spending fifty billion crowns a year on defence and security).

By the end of the decade hard currency had broken the leash the Communist regimes had hoped to keep it on. Local currency, even in sizeable amounts, was often not good enough for bribes and more and more private trade was conducted in Western money. In Romania, where isolation and surveillance limited the supply of foreign notes and coins, a substitute had long existed in Kent cigarettes. Kent became an early favourite of the Romanian élite. At Ceausescu-era Party Congresses it seemed the only cigarette judged suitable to smoke. But a packet of Kent was as good as cash. It could pass from hand to hand for months even though the original American cigarettes might have been removed by gypsies who had discovered a way to re-seal packets to look as good as new. In other countries increased travel abroad and a growing number of Western visitors created plentiful supplies of currency and speeded the collapse of local money. In turn the growing gap between the latter's official and real worth encouraged ever more people to deal on the black market. Even in Hungary, which had the strongest national currency in the bloc, only half of the money spent by Western tourists in 1988 was exchanged officially. As for Poland, hard-currency savings in official bank accounts amounted by then to four billion dollars. Estimates of how much more was hoarded at home ranged from another five to fifteen billion dollars (the Polish foreign debt that was cause for so much lamentation amounted to forty billion dollars). The advantages of hard currency began to show itself in ever more alarming ways. Hungarian police complained that they in their little Soviet-made Zhiguli cars could not be expected to catch criminals driving BMWs. Equally striking as a symptom of decline was the way in which the privileges of the ruling élite, originally defensible as necessary to free overworked men and women from daily worries, became increasingly a matter of access to foreign goods and money. Alexander Schalck-Golodkowski was irreplaceable in the life of Erich Honecker and his colleagues thanks to his skill at providing the sweet things in life. Trained, appropriately, as a pastry-cook and never losing his own passion for sticky cakes Schalck, state secretary at the Foreign Trade Ministry, made available eight million Deutschmarks a year for running of the Politburo compound at Wandlitz and keeping its supermarket stocked with imported goods. Some of the Communist privilegentsia regardless of dignity pursued dollars to the end. Poland's first non-Communist Foreign Minister Krzysztof Skubiszewski found, on visits to his embassies abroad, he was meeting middle-ranking diplomats who had once been ministers and deputy ministers in the Government in Warsaw. They considered it normal for an ex-minister to accept a humbler job if it gave access to hard currency. Skubiszewski declared it demeaning, and something that 'did not happen anywhere else'.

In the end the placid pattern of official East European trade was upset. In November 1988 travellers arriving at Prague airport were greeted by a notice from the Czechoslovak customs listing forty-five items whose export had been newly banned. At first glance it did not seem so out of the ordinary. Personal computers, video recorders, even cars and motorbikes were known to be in short supply and might tempt visitors from the Soviet bloc. But toothbrushes and toothpaste? Canned fish 'from non-socialist countries'? Windows and doors? Sewage pipes? The explanation was that while markets throughout East Europe suffered from more and more shortages the growth in foreign-currency holdings and the difference in national price-levels encouraged cross-border shopping raids on a hitherto unknown scale. The East European brothers had begun to beggar each other and the governments responded in the spirit of the Balkan saw, 'Brotherhood is brotherhood but for cheese you must pay.' But these tough Czech customs regulations proved inadequate and one of the last acts of the old Communist Government in 1989 was to halt all weekend group excursions to Czechoslovakia from the Soviet Union, Poland, Hungary and Yugoslavia.

'It is not money but the lack of it that is the root of all evil in socialism,' a Hungarian economist remarked as the socialist experiment in his country was coming to an end. It was a painful lesson for Communists who had once thought that man would be better off without it. In fact money's absence had created yet another alternative society – not the high-minded one of would-be citizens proposed by the dissidents, or the one only slowly starting to be expressed of nations long neglected, but a human, selfish, struggling society that looked after itself as best it could because Government had failed to do so. It was an anti-society, without human cohesion, that only the thickest skinned could live in without a sense of bruising and of being almost daily dirtied by the need to bribe or exploit connections or, simplest of all, steal. Its finest possible achievement was private comfort achieved at the expense of socially useful labour, as typified by the effort put by two million Czechoslovak families into their summer cottages. 'That's where they work, that's where our famous "golden hands" have gone,' Czechs would say ruefully. 'On Mondays people are so tired from their weekend labours they can hardly work, and on Thursday they are already looking for the things they will need to take to the cottage on Friday.' Many East Europeans would have understood the Romanian intellectual who believed that the greatest damage Ceausescu had done his country was to attack its innermost 'moral cell', just as they would have nodded in agreement at the remark of Gorbachev's close adviser, Aleksandr Yakovlev, that it was 'not only the emptying shelves, but also emptying souls' that made change imperative.

DEAD END

The subject of the Polish Economic Society's calendar for 1981 was a bald man wearing a suit of camouflage green and a red tie.

Blindfold, he stood at the beginning of a maze in whose very centre was a tempting picture of a handsome tree beneath blue sky. Even had the man been able to find his way through the maze he would never have reached it, for closer examination revealed there was no entrance to the space enclosing the picture. And that was really all that needed to be said about the chances of rescuing the economies of East Europe, as long as the Communist Parties remained in power. Attempts at reform had always run into trouble. In Hungary the Russians had objected though so, too, had the powerful lobby of Hungarian trade unions and managers of heavy industry. Economic reform had been given a bad name forever among Communists in Czechoslovakia because of its associations with 1968. Successive Polish Governments talked of reforms but they could never keep a steady course. It was typical that although from the mid-1970s Warsaw encouraged the thirteen million Poles who lived abroad to invest their money in private companies in Poland, taxes were raised whenever these undertakings showed signs of success. In the end it was considered best not to mention the word reform at all. The changes that were attempted were given unalarming names like a 'new economic mechanism' or a 'set of measures'.

There was no doubt what the problems were, though it was not clear how well they were understood at the top of the political leadership: certainly Erich Honecker and Nicolae Ceausescu were not always given true figures by subordinates. The condition of the East European economies was suggested by the pictures on the diminutive banknotes of the German Democratic Republic. The fifty-Mark note showed a venerable chemical plant with pretty clouds streaming from its chimneys; the twenty-Mark had a girl intently watching an antiquated control panel; the five a squad of combine harvesters at work, quite modern apparently, but part of a food chain that was shown to be entirely uncompetitive when the time came for unity with the West. There had been progress in the Communist economies until the 1970s and it was particularly plain in countries like Poland, Hungary and Bulgaria where a large peasantry had been drawn into new industries. 1970 was the first year in Poland's history when townspeople outnumbered those living in the country. In Hungary in 1949 workers and white-collar professionals made up only forty-seven per cent of the population. Twenty years later they accounted for four out of five Hungarians.

Such changes improved the lives of many, for people preferred to work for steady wages in a factory in a town than to exist as a poor peasant in some run-down hamlet. These were genuine social revolutions but having achieved them the Communist regimes became lost. Mieczyslaw Rakowski, Poland's last Communist Prime Minister, once explained the outdated structure of Polish industry by saying that the first industrial generation everywhere in the world had been 'fascinated by heavy industry'. Communism's problem was that it never got over that fascination. It was difficult for a Honecker, Jakes or Ceausescu to understand that the steel mills and coal mines that they as young men had admired as evidence of strength could become economic burdens, but the trouble went deeper than old men's minds. However hard the Party's experts tried they could not think up a safe way to move into the new economic structures pioneered in the West after the oil shock and the subsequent technological revolution. Almost every change that encouraged economic and technological initiative threatened the Communist political system which depended on protecting the industrial working class while reserving all significant power to the upper echelons of the Party. Awareness of this trap eventually produced the radical idea, embraced only by the most daring Communist leaders like the Hungarian Imre Pozsgay, that economic and political reform were inseparable, and that if the market was the only effective medicine for the economic disorders, political sclerosis had to be cured by democracy. Recognition that one unpleasant pill could not be taken without the other meant that the regimes were even more scared to move, while those who understood the extraordinary pressing need for change became ever more dejected. In the summer of 1989 one came across Prague intellectuals who felt as desperate as men watching an avalanche gathering above an unsuspecting village without being able to do anything about it. They foresaw an economic catastrophe of such proportions that only the devastation Czechs had known at the end of the Thirty Years War could be compared to it.

At first sight the Czechs' alarm seemed exaggerated, for their living standard was good by comparison even with Hungary, and incomparably better than Poland's, let alone Romania's. But the alarm was justified, and had much to do with a feeling of lost dignity and worth that would play a powerful subterranean role in the November revolution. Czechoslovakia, a federal state of two different Slav peoples, the Czechs and the Slovaks, was not able to produce the unalloyed national flamboyance of the Poles and Hungarians, still less the patriotic passion of Romanians in which paranoia was never far away. What the Czechs, inhabitants of the advanced regions of Bohemia and Moravia, did have were national memories against which the present day looked more and more shabby. Bohemia and Moravia had been the industrial heart of the Austro-Hungarian Empire. In 1938, twenty years after the Empire's collapse, the Czech lands enjoyed a higher standard of living than Austria. By 1968 the Austrians had reached Czech levels, and twenty years after that Czech standards were the lower by a third. Some members of the Prague Government understood the meaning of this gloomy tale and it was in the wake of Gorbachev's announcement of *perestroika* in the Soviet Union that Prime Minister Strougal, though himself lacking the power or nerve to try to push through reforms, arranged for Valtr Komarek to set up his Forecasting Institute. Komarek was an unmistakably Central European figure, a cross between Trotsky and Freud to look at, and a determined, skilful political manoeuvrer. He soon began to spread a message of measured doom through the Institute's publications as well as in conversations with anyone who cared to knock on his door. Born in 1930, like many economists of his generation Komarek had burned his fingers in 1968, and he now gathered round him younger men who were much more radical supporters of the free market than he and who would later occupy key Government jobs after the November revolution.

It was, he admitted, theoretically possible to maintain the living standard for another decade without substantial reform because some improvement could be made merely by raising quality of production a little and cutting back the large amount of waste. Bringing in younger managers might help, as would some application of foreign technology. The problem was that unless far more substantial changes were made Czechoslovakia would lose contact with global developments. It was, he liked to argue, 'not so much a question of preserving living standards as a choice between progress and backwardness. It is not reform or death, but reform or stagnation, and we know from history that whole nations have fallen into stagnant periods that lasted for centuries.' Such a prospect, unappealing for any nation, was unbearable to Czechs who had known such a brief national revival. The twenty years of independence between 1918 and 1938, the culmination of so much hope and effort, now seemed to have been fool's gold. Even the achievements made while under Vienna's rule were being wasted. Such feelings of opportunity lost were common throughout East Europe, for the twentieth century had at first brought high expectations to almost all the countries only to destroy them later. Poles and Hungarians knew how to wrap themselves with memories of tragic but glorious defeat. That was not the Czech way, and it was in Prague of all the capitals of East Europe that the visitor most felt the bitterness of a small, talented nation that feared it was condemned to slow decay.

At that time Komarek prudently talked of a market system that preserved 'socialist traits', and of private firms with a maximum of thirty employees. But by stressing that Czechoslovakia 'should behave like a developed, not a developing, country' he was saying no less than far more radical economists like Poland's Jan Winiecki. One of the first East Europeans to understand that the socialist economies had entered a period of terminal decline, Winiecki pointed out that while other countries had decreased the share of heavy industry in the national product as the living standard rose, this had not happened in East Europe. Instead the region was trapped in a wasteful but self-supporting cycle of investment in classical industries which in turn called for ever more raw materials to be used by ever bigger engineering and construction industries. Czechoslovakia was making almost a tonne of steel for each of its fifteen million inhabitants. Romania was putting up its fourth steel mill. It was only after the November revolution that the Czechoslovaks learned the consequences of this short-sightedness both for society as well as the economy. Several of the new leaders, but particularly the Federal Prime Minister, Marian Calfa, and the former Chartist, Petr Pithart, as Premier of the Czech lands, spoke with moving indignation about the state of the country they had inherited.

What did it mean to be, in Calfa's words, a 'second-class country'? Pithart, typically, stressed the social and human degradation. Forty-five per cent of women in Bohemia and Moravia were working, an example, Pithart suggested, of 'equal rights granted without mercy' because men's wages alone were insufficient to feed families. Only five and a half per cent of the national income was spent on education, and the proportion of students over fifteen remaining in education was half that of Japan. Students had been obliged to spend one in every ten periods studying Marxism-Leninism and the quality of teachers, often chosen for political reliability, had declined. After forty years under Communist rule people were eating several times more meat and eggs, and also drinking more alcohol, but they ate scarcely any more fruit and, hard though it was to believe, less vegetables. At the end of the 1960s Czechoslovak working hours were among the lowest in the world. By 1989 Czechs' annual holidays were ten days shorter than in Austria, and at the end of their vacations they returned to apartments that were on average a third smaller, to say nothing of often being in ugly and run-down estates, where repairs were carried out with delays of ten or even twenty years (there was also a good chance they would be coming back to homes without telephones, for which there was a waiting list of 400,000). Although there were proportionately more doctors than in parts of West Europe, the rate of illness was growing and the average age had dropped. Pollution was a major cause of health problems. New residential areas were built without sewage plants, soil erosion affected over half the cultivable land in Bohemia and Moravia, and acidity was even more widespread. Rivers and underground water were polluted by an ever-growing amount of industrial and agricultural waste and as a result genetic changes had already appeared both among farm animals and country people. A third of the country's forests were threatened, scarcely surprising since sulphur emissions were the second highest in the world, a consequence of using brown coal to produce energy that was consumed at a far higher rate than in West Europe. 'The whole country,' Pithart was to exclaim not long after taking office, 'has changed into a chaotic, disorganised and dirty workshop', in which ever higher production was pursued, 'regardless of quality and even without fear of the possible consequences'. Specialists believed that living under these conditions was gradually robbing the population of its general immunity to disease. Pithart, not a man inclined to melodramatic statements, called this a risk even greater than AIDS: it was 'the most dangerous time-bomb facing the population'.

The combination of political and economic pressures turned the family into the last hideout for many East Europeans. Family cohesion, Pithart remarked, was 'a form of defiance, an attempt to create a defensible intimate space'. The family house or summer cottage and garden also encouraged working together, arguably a strong need for the majority of East Europeans who retained the instincts of people who had only recently left the land and whose family farms had been destroyed by collectivisation. But the family fortress bred selfishness as often as solidarity, and concentration on physical survival and material gain meant, in Pithart's judgement, that children did not always find 'moral support within it against the disintegrative pressures of a totalitarian regime'. What Czechs liked to think of their 'traditional good family' was weakened in another way too. While the divorce rate was rising throughout East Europe, in the Czech lands by 1987 there was one divorce for every 2.7 marriages.

The industrial structure that was at the root of these problems had become a sorcerer's apprentice. In advanced countries over half the workforce was employed in small- and medium-size companies, but these scarcely existed in Czechoslovakia where the average enterprise had 3,500 employees, approaching a world record. In the forty years since the Communists came to power the share of heavy industry in Bohemia and Moravia's economy had grown from forty-five to fifty-three per cent, while food processing and consumer goods, once Czech specialities, had fallen from fifty to twenty-five per cent. The structure of exports resembled that of a developing country, for over half were made up of raw and production materials. Engineering, another old Czech pride, had lagged so far behind that the products that were still exportable sold in the West at only a quarter the price of similar Austrian goods. Membership of Comecon, the Soviet bloc's pale equivalent of the Common Market, reinforced this decline because the Soviet market was happy to take out-of-date engineering products they had become used to, and in some instances objected when the Czechs tried to improve them. The large defence and security establishment (there were country-wide 62,000 security personnel, and a prison population proportionately almost three times that of Britain or France) together with the state administration, and political organisations like the Communist-directed National Front consumed nearly a third of the national income, twice as much as government had cost on the eve of the Communist takeover in 1948. It was only to be expected that in the 1980s there ceased to be any more real growth in the national income. By 1989 a Czech had to work four times as long as a West German or Austrian to buy a suit or a pair of shoes, and five times as long for a refrigerator or television set.

Czechoslovakia's decline from its previous place among the more developed nations of Europe was a poignant example of the way Communist economies got out of control and began to destroy the well-being of their supposed masters. East Germany had the same experience of relative decline as Czechoslovakia, and its economy's failure to keep up with world developments became unmistakable from the end of the 1970s. By 1987 the share of state-of-the-art machine tools and electrotechnical products in East German exports to the Federal Republic had sunk to ten per cent, a damning comment on a regime that once boasted of overtaking the West. But there was a similar feeling of being prisoners of their own industrial machines even in those countries where the simple fact of industrial-isation had profoundly altered national life, and at first for the better. This growing alarm had one consequence that almost no one foresaw. The moment the Communist bluff was called a new squad of economists at once presented themselves, trained and self-confident, for national duty with ideas that stood the previous economic wisdom on its head. Unknown to most people the mini-stries and institutes of Communist East Europe had been nurturing a school of passionate free marketeers and monetarists. In Poland the Catholic University of Lublin, the only university in East Europe to be almost outside Government control, had protected Jan Wieniecki and like-minded colleagues, but Leszek Balcerowicz, Poland's first non-Communist Finance Minister and mastermind of the escape from the Communist dead end, had been conducting seminars at the old Institute of Planning and Statistics which Wieniecki and other economists of similar opinions were able to attend. These Poles knew the men at Prague's Forecasting Institute like Vaclav Klaus, Vladimir Dlouhy and Karel Dyba who would all move into senior Government positions. Even in Romania there was a small group of talented specialists like Eugen Dijmarescu who had been protected by Bucharest's Institute of World Economy. Together with similarly minded Soviet colleagues these East Euro-peans had formed an almost secret society, keeping up-to-date with Western thinking and acquiring new specialist literature on trips abroad and exchanging ideas among themselves. When Ceausescu made foreign travel almost impossible younger Romanian econom-ists had managed to keep abreast of ideas by listening to foreign broadcasts. The phenomenon suggested the completeness with which Communism had lost its intellectual hegemony, a loss that contributed greatly to the speed of its final collapse, for apart from the self-interest of the rulers there were no more arguments to be mustered in its favour.

The new men were no longer bothered with finding a way through the socialist maze: they simply proposed cutting it down, and the sooner the better. A Western journalist came away from a discussion in post-Revolutionary Prague reflecting that these economists were like the pilots of B-52 bombers, decent men who would never have to see close up the result of their work. For the result was bound to be bloody, which was why Communist leaderships had always refused to undertake it themselves, not so much out of tender-heartedness as concern for their own survival. Only five months before the Communist downfall in Prague a senior Party ideologist privately conceded that to re-restructure and modernise the Czechoslovak economy some two million workers, chiefly in the metallurgical branches, would have to lose their jobs. The only trouble was that 'we lack the men of courage to say what must be done about it'. What else did he expect? Two million workers represented a quarter of the employed population. To bring about the loss of even half that number of jobs would have been to destroy the social contract which guaranteed Communist power quite as much as the Party's control over a politically indoctrinated army and police.

UNBREAKABLE CONTRACTS

Whatever happened in East Europe in 1989 it was not a workers' revolution. Although workers eventually participated in the great demonstrations in East Germany and Czechoslovakia they neither originated nor led them. In Hungary apart from the celebration of patriotic anniversaries, mainly a student and middle-class affair, there was scarcely a hint of political battle on the streets. The young workers of Bucharest did play an important part in the fighting before and after Ceausescu's overthrow but it was not exclusively their victory: almost everyone in Romania had a score to settle with the *Conducator*. Only in Poland did an opposition develop out of working-class protest and that was because the Polish Government had failed to carry out its part of a social contract that was no less binding for never having been written down. The Gdansk strikers in August 1980 presented Warsaw with a list of twenty-one demands whose most eye-catching points were political – independent trade unions; the right to strike; a free press; the release of political prisoners. The eighth demand switched attention to the falling living standard. The strikers wanted more money and wage indexation; better food supplies and, as a temporary measure, meat rationing; paid free Saturdays; and reduced waiting time for new apartments. When the Polish strikes had begun the previous month in protest against higher meat prices their motive had been almost entirely economic. It was the Polish opposition's unique link to the working class that led the movement in a more general political direction. The Government's original mistake had been to mismanage the economy so badly that it could no longer give the workers what they had come to expect as their right, above all sufficient cheap food and housing. Another right, seldom spoken about at that time because it was so entirely taken for granted, was permanent employment. If the Polish Government's special failing was its inability to provide the worker with cheap pork, socialism's reward for a peasantry that had accepted to be industrialised, its second was to believe it could solve the problem by raising prices. This ruse had brought trouble upon previous Polish Governments and was known to be deadly dangerous ever since the massacre of striking workers in Novocherkassk in 1962, the result of Nikita Khrushshev's attempt to increase the price of Soviet meat.

The socialist social contract did not mean that the working class of East Europe enjoyed fine conditions. It had been the introduction of higher norms that touched off the East German workers' revolt of 1953, and what really went on in factories remained a sensitive matter for all the regimes. When Miklos Haraszti wrote in 1972 an account of conditions at the Red Star tractor factory in Budapest a furious Hungarian Government brought him to trial on the charge of provoking hatred against the state. Haraszti had shown that the socialist employer practised the same manipulation of norms and piece rates to extract more work but without paying the higher wages that Hungarian capitalists had. Deprived of real trade unions and under the permanent eye of Party cadres and if need be security police, workers had no way to defend themselves apart from idling, petty theft and the occasional unofficial strike which at best won temporary concessions from the Government. But as the failure of East Europe's economies to keep pace with the West became more obvious the working class acquired immense passive power as an obstacle in the way of change.

Solidarity showed Communists what happened once they lost control of the workers. The Polish Government's life was further complicated when the official unions grouped in the OPZZ, and supposedly loyal to the Communist Party, realised that demagogic defence of working-class living standards (such as they were) was the best way to compete against Solidarity. By 1989 the OPZZ leader Alfred Miodowicz, whose sharp wits matched a taste for sharp clothes, had become adept at populist argument and was attacking both the Communist and opposition leaderships as 'élites'. Miodowicz would complain that the new Polish Parliament elected in June 1989 was only a 'quarter democratic' because it had fewer workers and peasants, 'the salt of the earth', than the pre-war Sejm. 'Democracy,' Miodowicz liked to warn, 'should not be instead of, but together with, the welfare of the working people.' Similar arguments could be heard from his Hungarian opposite number Sandor Nagy whose university degree in economics allowed him to put them with greater sophistication. By the autumn of 1989, after the Hungarian Communists had renamed themselves Socialists at their Party congress, Nagy talked scathingly of politicians who had 'lost touch with everyday problems'. Trade unions could not afford such an 'aristocratic approach' and were less concerned with the following year's elections than with how a worker was 'to make ends meet on a salary of three thousand forints [about $50] a month'. When the rest of East Europe went to the polls in 1990 the discredited Communist Parties often tried to save themselves by appearing as defender of sacred working-class rights which, in their last months in power, they gave sign of wanting to salvage. It was made easier for them by the appearance during election campaigns of radical ideas that were deeply shocking to many East European ears. A candidate of the Hungarian Free Democrats, old-fashioned liberals in economic matters, confided with the frankness of a man fighting his first election that his programme was for 'the rich to get richer and the poor poorer for at least six to eight years'. The upshot was that the Communists lost less badly than some expected: the East German Communists got fifteen per cent of the March 1990 poll; Hungary's reformed and unreformed Communists, split into two parties, between them took only a little less; even the particularly despised Czechoslovak Communists picked up almost fourteen per cent of the votes; while in Bulgaria the Communists in the renamed Bulgarian Socialist Party won a majority of seats in the new Grand National Assembly.

The Communist tactic was dishonest for their leaders understood by then that their old policies were leading to disaster. They knew there had been efforts in the past to dismantle the interlocking structure of artificially low prices and high subsidies which brought social and political calm but ever poorer economic performance. They knew that none of them had pulled it off. Each of the three Polish attempts to raise prices between 1970 and 1980 ended in trouble. The Hungarian reforms of 1968 started a political battle that lasted ten years between far-sighted economists led by Rezso Nyers on one side and Party and trade-union apparatchiks loyal to what they called a 'workers' policy' on the other. It was at the end of this tussle that one of Kadar's advisers reflected on the irreconcilability of efficiency with equality that in the end would fatally weaken the Communist system. He admitted that Communists had promised too much in the 1950s, for they had supposed then that 'a new man' who worked to benefit others and not just himself would prove as productive as capitalism's self-interested Adam. The Party had since learned that this sort of 'new man' would always be a minority, and the problem now was to give incentives to the most skilful without damaging the less talented. But how did you achieve that when people said 'we're living in socialism and that means everyone should have things'? The Hungarian Party never found the answer, and nor did anyone else. As late as October 1989, when Honecker had already fallen, one came across East German academics still sweating over the same conundrum. Yes, socialism most regrettably had not solved the problem of efficiency but the market economy that some said was the answer 'cannot be the way because it sacrifices social aims to purely economic ones'. It was no surprise to find members of the Czech opposition worrying gloomily over the working class and its place in a society that had degenerated, in the words of the philosopher Ladislav Hejdanek, into a 'conspiracy of the untalented'. Like many Chartists a natural and mild-mannered democrat, Hejdanek looked pained as he pronounced his judgement: 'I'm afraid only the intellectuals are interested in changes – the working class is no help at all.' But by then even some members of the Czechoslovak Government were ready to talk about the need to take 'painful measures', not least because lack of pay differentials and the old bias in favour of workers and against white-collar workers were at last being recognised as damaging. A worker in a steel mill in Ostrava was paid five to six thousand Crowns a month; a miner twice that. A teacher with a university degree earned only three thousand Crowns at the age of thirty, precisely a hundred crowns more than a factory electrician in his early twenties. Not only was there no encouragement to talent and qualifications in the wages structure but the subsidy system itself represented a massive redistribution of the national wealth regardless of effort and achievement. In East Germany price and housing subsidies in 1988 worked out at a monthly 945 Marks for every employee, almost as much as the average wage. No one was surprised when sociologists discovered that nine out of ten East German industrial workers had little or no interest in performance and productivity.

Not much changed because the Party leadership did not want it to. In East Germany old men's arrogance and self-delusion had a good deal to do with it, but in Prague it was a considered calculation. In October 1989, the month before his world collapsed, the Czechoslovak Party leader Milos Jakes told his Polish counterpart Mieczyslaw Rakowski that Czechoslovakia would avoid the troubles affecting other parts of East Europe. He allowed there been some difficulty with 'small groups of intellectuals' influenced by the West but 'as long as we are in control of prices and wages, as long as there is food on the shelves, then there is nothing to worry about'. Had the public learned of this cynical and short-sighted remark there might have been a revolution on the spot, for it entirely ignored the economic problems that Jakes's own Government had itself begun belatedly to struggle with. It was true that there was food and beer in the shops, though the supply of some other goods, as the new Czech customs regulations mentioned earlier made plain, was much less satisfactory. Even Jakes should by then have understood the price the country was paying for its relative well-being. Czechoslovakia was living on tick. Its foreign debt was approaching eight billion dollars, small compared to Hungary or Poland's, but large for a leadership that had always tried to avoid borrowing abroad. The country's engineering and machine-tool industry had been kept going by Government credits worth several billion dollars – of which only a fraction was recoverable – to politically favoured countries like Iraq, Syria, Nicaragua and Cuba. Though attempts were made to keep money supply under control there was no way to discipline an enterprise that went into debt to pay workers' wages. 'It was typical of the socialist economy,' remarked one of the experts called in to clear up the mess, 'that neither the debtor nor the creditor was really worried.' Worst of all, the country was living on the credit represented by the achievements and efforts of past generations. Little was done to maintain let alone add to the patrimony that the Communists had inherited in 1948. Money that should have been invested for the benefit of future generations was simply consumed. It was not even a matter of eating the seed corn, Petr Pithart liked to say, but of devouring tomorrow's breakfast.

The leaders of other countries saw the problem more clearly but as long as they hoped to maintain the Communist system they could do little about it. This explained the comments alternating between waspishness and despair about their countrymen's ignorance of economic reality. In Hungary the reform Communists moaned about the difficulty of persuading the working class of the need for change, while their inspirer Imre Pozsgay was ready to declare that the myth of the working class had 'imprisoned politics and did not work. We should ask instead who is for progress.' In Romania it was largely Ceausescu's insistence on paying off his foreign debt by forcing austerity on his workers that left him friendless in his final crisis. His successor Ion Iliescu won the May 1990 election largely by restoring the old Communist concessions to the working class, but it was a sign of the times that the Prime Minister Petre Roman felt obliged to sound a warning immediately after the victory. You can't eat what you don't produce was his message, though in the obligatorily rotund language of Romanian politics what he actually said was 'the fact that products exist only if they are created does not always seem to be clearly present in the thought processes of all members of society'. It certainly had not been present for decades in Polish 'thought processes'. As early as the 1970s one came across Warsaw Poonah-Commissars who complained about the fecklessness of the Polish worker without stopping to wonder if this might not be a deformation of the system. At the end of forty years vainly trying to master the Polish worker the Party's bitterness knew no limits. Here is an outburst, passionate by any standards, from the early autumn of 1989:

Socialism's achievement was that at first it gave everyone an equal chance so the peasant kids went to school, benefited from a free health service and so on. But since the 1960s the system became increasingly inefficient. Equality for all meant giving everyone a little, but in reality this little turned out to be nothing. The tragedy of socialism in the last twenty years was that it became a system of the lumpenproletariat. Our professional classes got far less than in the West. Only the lumpenproletariat gets more, for they're guaranteed work, health care and education. The Party's great mistake was that in times of crisis it always flirted with these people, and this gave them a feeling of power. Economic reform means that the main price must be paid by the lumpenproletariat. Unfortunately there are millions of them, and they are very noisy.

The speaker, the thirty-five-year-old Aleksander Kwasniewski, had just won more votes in the elections to the new Senate than any other Communist candidate, though still not enough to gain a seat. Solidarity intellectuals like Adam Michnik respected him, and in early 1990 he became chairman of the new-style Communists under the appropriately classless name of Social Democrats. But the damage was done and Kwasniewski, as member of the last Communist Government under Rakowski, had to bear some of the responsibility, so perhaps there was guilt hidden in the virulence of his words. Much of the foreign debt Poland acquired in the 1970s had been spent on maintaining living standards. When the West would lend no more the regime tried to repeat the same trick by printing zloties. Wages soared, control was lost over the money supply, and goods disappeared from the shops. Faced with an election in 1989 the Rakowski Government allowed wages to rise by over two hundred per cent in the first seven months of the year, more than twice the rate of inflation. While Rakowski made speeches deploring the budget deficit and insisting the time for deceiving society was over the Ministry of Finance simply omitted to collect taxes from factories so that the new inflated wages could be paid. The result was a massive deficit in the budget, a third of which went on subsidies. In July prices began to increase at the rate of forty per cent a month, the pace being quickened by the Government's decision, once it had lost the election, to let subsidised food prices go up six-fold. By the end of the year the cost of living had grown by two hundred and fifty per cent.

Other Communist Governments behaved little better. The Hungarians had also gone heavily into debt, though the real amount was never revealed even to the Politburo while Kadar was in power.

Hungary's borrowed dollars, like Poland's, served to keep the workers happy; by Imre Pozsgay's estimate only a tenth went on investment, while 'the rest was spent on the maintenance of social peace which hid the need for reconstruction'. One time-honoured way of keeping the social peace was to subsidise loss-making heavy industries. The 1968 reforms had avoided tackling this problem and even the last Communist Government led by Miklos Nemeth dared only to talk about it. East Germany, so self-satisfied in the face it presented to the world, was no less surely than Czechoslovakia devouring its own riches without thought for the future. Honecker was proud of his slogan about the 'unity of economic and social policy' which he believed other Communist regimes, above all Moscow's, had ignored. But the share of subsidies and services provided from the East German budget grew throughout the 1980s at a rate far beyond the country's means. Again it was a case of social peace bought at the cost of future economic growth, something only fully understood when, poised for reunification with the West, East German managers had to face up to the uncompetitiveness of their out-of-date factories. Calculations by West German experts suggested the impossibility of long continuing in this way. In spite of the artificially cheap prices, rents and other services, by 1985 four out of ten East Germans were living a rather uncomfortable life in households whose income was under the already low national average. Elsewhere there was real poverty. By 1989 a million people – one in ten Hungarians – lived on or below what was defined as the minimum subsistence level which assumed enough money for staying alive and a change of clothes but nothing else. The luxuries affordable by another two million did not stretch beyond an occasional newspaper, cup of coffee or packet of cigarettes. In 1990 the Family Aid Centre in a working-class Budapest suburb called Ujpest constructed for the Museum of the Labour Movement in Buda Castle a model of a poor family's two-room tenement. Living conditions in Ujpest were almost twice as bad as in the capital: two people to a room; half the homes without a bathroom, and scarcely a single telephone. Yet there were parts of Buda where people could afford in 1989 to pay the equivalent of almost half a million dollars (the average monthly wage was $175) for a three-storey house equipped with gymnasium, sauna, and a kitchen for the guard dogs, and if there was no swimming pool it was probably only out of fear of provoking the taxman.

The poor of Hungary, like those of other East European countries, were not usually very visible. They were the old on small pensions or no pensions at all; the unemployed; the gypsies; the single-parent families. It was typical that as long as Kadar was in power these problems could not be publicly discussed. When in 1979 a group of Budapest intellectuals set up a private organisation called SZETA to help the poor many of them were hounded out of their jobs and some forced into poverty themselves. They nevertheless discovered that some of the modern poor were descendants of the pre-war landless peasants who had simply moved into the cities bringing their poverty with them. Yet it was 1985 before the Government allowed the first Family Aid Centre to be established in the capital. The sort of people who might be its clients could be seen at the cheaper markets waiting to buy fruit and vegetables that had been spoiled, or chicken heads and feet to make a stew. The elderly among them had worked all their lives performing the classic duties of the industrial working class, and a woman who complained to anyone who would listen that she could only afford some half-rotten *kohlrabi* might have been speaking for all of them. She had worked for thirty-five years in a textile factory; it was people like her who had built up the country after the war and put meat on the tables of the Government ministers; and yet now they were being treated as though *they* were lumpenproletariat. That was the word she used. Between the anger of the young Kwasniewski at being held to ransom by his lumpenproletariat and the bitterness of an old woman who could not understand why, after a lifetime's work, she felt like one of that despised group herself, lay the measure of the damage done by the social contract to which the Communists had bound themselves.

Believing that power allowed them to treat money as they wished, the Communists were in the end brought to their knees by their disregard for it. Political systems are often called bankrupt, but rarely is this both metaphorically and literally the case. Re-establishing money therefore became the priority of those who took over from the Communists. Speaking to the Sejm in January 1990 the new Polish Prime Minister Tadeusz Mazowiecki said:

> We must rebuild the categories and institutions of money. This is to be money in the fullest sense, with which everything may be bought; with which we can measure the value of human labour and goods; in which

savings may be invested . . . money which is the universal equivalent of commodities and which transforms everything which is produced into a commodity.

It was fitting that these words in praise of money should come not from an economist, let alone a businessman, but from a Catholic intellectual whose attitude to wealth was as sceptical as that of his friend Karol Wojtyla. Mazowiecki was reminding the Polish people that honest money was necessary to the moral order of state and society, and his dry words were as much a death sentence for the old system as any declaration of democratic intent. When in the summer of 1990 East Germans gathered up the last of Honecker's diminutive Mark notes for replacement by the Deutschmark they were being every bit as revolutionary as the men and women who had begun to knock down the Berlin Wall down eight months earlier.

7

Letting Poland Be Poland

SOCIALIST SURREALISM

What was there to be said about Poland in the summer of 1988 that had not already been said ten thousand times? Why not repeat what Poles were saying eight years before, when Solidarity had been born? In August an official at the Wujek mine near Katowice insisted that a visitor look at the shrine of St Barbara, patron saint of miners. 'We are a Catholic country with Communist characteristics,' he explained in the tone of a man who only states the obvious. After the declaration of martial law the following year seven Wujek miners were killed in fighting with the police but that did not diminish the accuracy of the remark. Poland remained what Stalin, using other words, had always said it would be: a Catholic beauty dressed up in unsuitable Communist clothes. Adam Michnik described the situation in Poland at the end of 1980 as 'a compromise between a non-sovereign government and a sovereign society'. It was the same idea differently expressed. Poland was one thing, her masters another. Not many people were deceived by the fact that the non-sovereign Government had all the attributes of power. Visit an official of the Government trade unions that were then fighting for their life against the newly born Solidarity and one would be shown into a comfortable office with Russian dictionary and Polish translations of Lenin on the bookshelves, and presents brought back from numerous trips abroad boastfully displayed. A secretary would bring excellent coffee unobtainable in ordinary shops; the host might offer his guest a packet of Marlboro cigarettes brought out from a locked cupboard. In such ways did a man display his modest share of power. In a suburb at the other end of Warsaw an activist from KOR who was organising peasants for Solidarity was working one evening in the sitting room of his little semi-detached house, the floor covered with piles of paper, a primitive rural woodcarving of Christ surveying the disorder from an over-burdened side-table. 'It's always like that with these people,' said a Polish acquaintance when the activist, as untidy as his room, disappeared to lead two straw-haired children up the stairs to bed. And because so much in the country, not only the life of the opposition, was still 'always like that', with no apparent hope of change, by 1988 even the Poles had begun to get tired.

The previous year the Pope had made his third visit home. 'Time for a miracle,' said a friend, but without much hope. Karol Wojtyla did work his usual personal miracles of making each Pole who saw him feel it was Easter. He moved around the country as though it were a neglected but beloved old house, picking up forgotten objects or blowing the dust off pictures to show his countrymen how beautiful they were. He recalled old kings and heroes. He honoured Poland's newest martyr Jerzy Popieluszko, murdered three years earlier. He praised the Polish peasant, whose land and work he called 'an image of God'. He also praised the Polish worker, seeming to find in the parable of the farmer hiring labourers for his vineyard a divine precedent for the Gdansk agreement of 1980. He tried to comfort the women textile workers of Lodz, ugliest and least Catholic of Polish cities. People travelled miles to see him, or waited hours to be one of a million for whom he would celebrate an open-air mass, and then went home happy.

He did what he could, which was reassure the opposition that he would not let himself be used by the Communist regime. Old fears had returned about the Church's readiness to cooperate more closely with the Government, and rumours were spread that the bishops had agreed to prevent Solidarity banners being unfurled at any of the papal masses. The Church's timescale was, after all, eternal, and man could attain salvation under any regime. Even when Cardinal Wyzsynski was alive there had been similar moments of nervousness when loyal Catholic laymen like Mazowiecki had felt it necessary to repeat that there could be no dialogue between Church and state if there was none between state and people. The Primate, the little jug-eared Cardinal Glemp, was particularly suspect in opposition circles. 'Glemp is tempted to work with the Government,' people told each other, 'because he thinks they would be quite decent chaps if they weren't Communists.' But the Pope, particularly when he spoke in Gdansk, made it plain that Solidarity belonged in his Polish pantheon, and that he would always speak out for those unable to speak for themselves. And as if to make plain how he ranked Primates, the first stop he made on entering Warsaw was at the newly unveiled statue of the invincible Wyszynski, whom he called 'the Primate of the Millennium'. But even this Pope could not break the Polish impasse. One might say that he even blessed it, for he was after all a pope and not a politician, and he urged the young in particular to develop 'the power of the spirit so as not to yield to resignation, indifference, or hopelessness'. Then he left and what else, apart from another papal visit in four or five years' time, did the Poles have to look forward to? Would that be enough to stop more and more young Poles pinning their hope on emigration to the West?

November 1987 had seen a disastrous attempt by the Government to win support for a programme of economic reform that even the opposition allowed had some merit. In return for introducing some reality into the economy the Poles were to be asked by a referendum to accept an overall price rise of about forty per cent. Carried away by its unusual flirtation with democracy the Government decided to show it was man enough to jump the biggest hurdles and ruled that more than half of all the registered voters must approve the new programme. In the event two-thirds of the electorate turned out on voting day of whom two-thirds voted yes to the economic proposals. It was a respectable result by the more modest standards of Western democracies but not enough to win the day for the Government for it amounted to only forty-four per cent of the electorate. The incident was yet another example of the regime's loss of political touch. General Jaruzelski had thought he could use the Pope's visit to bolster his regime and was made to look foolish. Thinking it could win people over by offering them a moment of democratic choice the Government had destroyed the slight chance of its survival that lay in bringing back order to the economy. This lack of any feeling for reality – the political equivalent, it seemed, of the unreality that permeated the economy and so much of Polish life besides – was to play a large part in determining Poland's fate in the two years ahead. Bronislaw Geremek, the historian who had advised Walesa from Solidarity's earliest days in the Gdansk shipyards, remarked after the Pope returned to Rome that 'the Government has physical power but no moral influence over society, while society has moral strength but no physical power'. That went far to explaining the regime's chronic loss of touch. It knew how to deploy its policemen, but it could not marshal words in any manner that might convince the Poles it so badly needed to talk to.

July 1988 brought reinforcements for General Jaruzelski in the shape of Mikhail Gorbachev, the first Russian leader Poles had not hated. Because of Gorbachev Poles were studying the once despised Soviet press and some even admitted remembering the Russian language they had learned with gritted teeth at school. But the Soviet leader could not both support the General and please the Poles. The country watched with disinterest as Gorbachev visited the only Lenin museum in the country and the wooden house in the Tatra foothills where Lenin and Krupskaya had spent summers before the First World War. Poles sniggered when he urged young people at a gathering in Krakow, Poland's most Catholic and conservative city, to find an example 'in Lenin's life and struggle'. People were so disappointed at Gorbachev's avoidance of the matters that interested Poles, above all the Soviet NKVD's massacre of the Polish officer corps at Katyn, that few bothered to consider the new logic of Soviet policy and what the Russian might have said in his private talks with the General. It was Gorbachev's custom to show irreproachable restraint while travelling in East Europe – he had managed it even during the disagreeable days he spent with the Ceausescus in Bucharest the previous year – but the Soviet Union's relationship with its Communist allies was already a matter of open debate in Moscow. Soviet authorities on East Europe like Academician Oleg Bogomolov had rejected the Brezhnev doctrine that allowed Moscow to restore Communist order in the bloc on the pretext of 'proletarian internationalism'. 'We gave too much advice to our partners,' Bogomolov confessed, 'and it was actually very damaging to them. It's time to keep our advice to ourselves.' If the Soviets kept their advice to themselves it meant they would keep their tanks too. And without the threat of tanks or even of the sort of Soviet advice disguised as brow-beating that the Polish regime had been submitted to in 1981, what was left of the famous Polish *raison d'état*? This was what had kept the Polish Communists going, the belief – shared by most Poles – that only if Poland was socialist could it survive even as a partly independent country. In the summer of 1990, after the old East European regimes had been swept away, the Soviet Foreign Minister Eduard Shevardnadze wrote somewhat self-defensively in *Pravda* that 'neither socialism,

nor friendship, nor good-neighbourliness nor respect can be produced by bayonets, tanks or blood'. We do not know how fully
Jaruzelski appreciated, in the summer of 1988, the revolutionary
ideas at the heart of the new strategy of Gorbachev and his like-
minded colleagues. One may guess that at that time neither Gorbachev nor Jaruzelski saw how far and how quickly Moscow's logic
would carry them all. It is certainly true that the Polish opposition,
at each stage in their unplanned advance to power, would remain
wary and prudent, and at no time behave as though Soviet reactions
could be discounted. But it is hard to believe that after Gorbachev
had gone home and Poland entered a period of new turbulence that
Jaruzelski, a man sensitive to changes in political atmosphere, did
not understand that he was on his own in a way that no previous
Polish Communist leader had been before. If that is true, it was a
powerful contribution to the peaceful resolution of the long struggle
between Communist and non-Communist Pole.

At the time few in Warsaw caught this glimmer of hope. The
atmosphere in the city had long been quite different from that in
any other capital of East Europe. The opposition in Prague, let
alone East Berlin or Bucharest, remained under constant pressure.
In Budapest the dissidents were isolated as much by the determination of many educated Hungarians to lead the best life that
circumstances allowed as by police surveillance. In Warsaw it was
the regime's officials who seemed isolated from the normal life of
the city. The writer Konwicki liked to tell the story of how in 1979
he received a mysterious summons from an admirer who wanted to
give him a reward for his novel A *Minor Apocalypse* that had
just appeared in *Samizdat*. He was taken to a large house in the
countryside where admiring guests, caviar, champagne and a gold
medal awaited him. The admirer turned out to be one of Poland's few
successful private businessmen. After the reception the businessman
showed the novelist round his estate, pointing out everything from
the swimming-pool to his stable of horses. 'Do you know why I do
it?' he asked Konwicki. 'Because it is my way of getting back at the
Communists.' The businessman was at that time a member of
the Party. Later he would become a minister in Poland's last
Communist-led Government. Little more need be said about Polish
socialist surrealism.

Poles were frustrated because they felt in so many respects free
yet were not able to be free. They spoke their mind even on the

telephone, which only the most committed of regime opponents in Hungary did. Warsaw University continued to pay salaries to Solidarity leaders who had long been barred from teaching under Party pressure. The authorities had little choice but to tolerate *Samizdat* because it was so widespread and was by now even publishing magazines for children, one of which ran a comic strip called 'Rambo and Julia' about a little girl whose mother went to work in the West to earn hard currency while her father was busy in underground publishing. In 1980 and 1981 the country had sung a song written by Jan Pietrzak, Warsaw's best known cabarettist, called *'Zeby Polska byta Polska'*, 'So that Poland may be Poland'. Jaruzelski had tried to kidnap the idea in his speech at the 1981 Party congress, saying that 'for Poland to be Poland it must be a socialist Poland'. It was because people knew beyond doubt that the real Poland was not socialist that putting up with the Communists had become so enervating.

How do Poles feel? I asked a friend. 'Cheated,' he replied without having to think about the answer. 'The old feel cheated of what their past might have been. The young feel cheated of their future.' The most random consideration of the facts of Polish life was likely to induce depression. Poland's hard-currency exports per capita for 1987 had amounted to $324. The figure for Singapore was $1,500. Poland had almost five million cars and 125 miles of motorway. A junior scientific worker earned half as much as a teenage policeman in his first year of service. The increasing dilapidation of public life could sometimes be amusing. Cockroaches were familiar inhabitants of Warsaw's public buildings but when a young Polish woman spotted a monster insect in the office of a senior official of the Party Central Committee she had a tale to dine out on for weeks. Watching a film made by British television about Ryszard Kapuscinski in which the Polish writer demonstrated how on his travels in the Third World he made a sustaining nest in his hotel room before setting out into the confusion of the streets, something seemed familiar. It was the hotel. For the film Kapuscinski was using Warsaw's Hotel Europejski, and he was right. It had acquired the same atmosphere of decay and approaching disaster that permeated hotels I had known in some of the unhappiest countries of Asia. My old acquaintance G. would sometimes sink into black moods in which the apparent hopelessness of the situation darkened even his view of his fellow countrymen. 'Poles are dirty, lazy and don't know how to work. They say it is only the circumstances, and that if things had been different they would be different. But it's not true. They are dirty, lazy and don't know how to work.' Everyone knew the extenuating arguments by heart. The Germans could make any system work but Poles had to have a system that suited them, otherwise they would never be efficient and hard-working. History had taught the Poles to thrive on crises and resistance. A crisis was almost as good as a papal visit for lighting up their eyes, for they were at their best when they were not bored. Resistance was a good in itself. 'Here it's always good to be against the state,' said a resigned Party leader, hoping perhaps to draw some sympathy from a foreigner. 'Here it's always good to go on strike.' But in 1988 even the organised resistance represented by Solidarity was tiring. People were weary. Activists who had been fighting since the 1970s admitted to being weary. How many members were there in the union that on the eve of martial law had numbered ten million members, the majority of working Poles? Perhaps two million were left in a Solidarity hanging on, in spite of being officially still illegal. Even in Gdansk the union's membership was less than half what it had been in 1981, and figures for other regions were considerably worse. And membership was often passive: factory committees were thought to be doing well if five per cent of their pre-martial law members paid the union dues. Nor was the union attracting the social mix that earlier had given it a national character. Professionals no longer joined which meant there were fewer people qualified to run the union's affairs. And there was growing apprehension about the rising generation, too young to have known the excitement of 1980–1 and now growing up in the hopelessness of the end of the decade.

Older Poles were discovering that the educated young, while interested in learning from them about the past, thought that the previous generations had got just about everything wrong. A fifteen-year-old-boy, bright, from the intelligentsia, told a family friend that his class at school were into anarchism and pacifism. They combined forces to oppose members of other classes who called themselves Fascists, dressed in black and preached Aryan superiority. Nothing surprising about that, for such phenomena had been observed in Soviet-bloc schools for some time. But what did the boy think about Solidarity? He groaned. 'It's Dad's Army.' If Solidarity was worried about the young so were the brightest

Party officials like Alexander Kwasniewski, who drew a picture of aggressive sixteen- to twenty-year-olds with precious little respect for Walesa or Cardinal Glemp, let alone General Jaruzelski. What had they to lose? Nothing. Solidarity agreed. A May editorial in the union's main (illegal) newspaper *Tygodnik Mazowsze* spoke of a 'generation with absolutely no prospects'. Young men had taken to wearing masks in clashes with the police, something unthinkable in the old days and which made people who watched pictures of these battles on television most uncomfortable. In the spring the well-known Solidarity leader Henryk Wujec had warned of the appearance of increasingly radical groups among young workers. 'I think the situation will continue to evolve,' Wujec wrote in a *Samizdat* journal, 'with a strong tendency to become more radical . . . What is bad is that these young people have learnt that the authorities only yield to force.' Some of the better educated young expressed the same dead-end feelings in nonsense street happenings. The Orange Alternative theatrical company in Wroclaw, following the slogan 'socialist surrealism is the reality in which we live', mounted demonstrations that sent up the regime by seeming to support it. Sometimes they dressed as policemen and caused chaos by helping direct traffic. On other days they appeared as gnomes or Father Christmases, demonstrating for worthy causes like an eight-hour day for members of the security service and mocking martial law with slogans like 'support the ideals of December 1981'.

Fear that a new young generation might forget the opposition rules of self-restraint and non-violence became particularly oppressive in August when strikes which had hit various industries throughout the year took hold in the mines of Silesia. Many if not all of the striking miners were young, and very often neither they nor their leaders were Solidarity members. The Government and miners began a battle of nerves in Silesia in which Jan Litynski, who had spent much time there in the first Solidarity years, was one of several activists who also took part. What he saw explained a good deal about the strikes' unexpected outcome. When Litynski got to Silesia he bluffed his way through the police lines surrounding the July Manifesto mine at Jastrzebie and offered his services as an adviser. He soon discovered that the immediate cause of the strike was the immensely complicated pay system, understood by few miners, which had just caused wages to be reduced. Conditions in this mine as in others had reverted to what they were before 1980, and

Litynski's account of the miners' complaints was familiar to anyone who had visited the Silesian coalfields in the year of Solidarity's birth. Huge bonuses for working on Saturdays and Sundays, always detested by the miners as 'bribery' and abolished under Solidarity pressure, had been reintroduced. Most of the other changes affecting work practices won by Solidarity in 1980 and 1981 were no longer observed. The official trade unions were passive and the mine management had won back all the power that had been prised from it. The old 'Prussian discipline' the Polish Communists had inherited when they took over Silesia from Germany in 1945 had returned with a vengeance. Nevertheless the Solidarity committee in the July Manifesto mine had not been influential before the strike – it was shunned for being too 'political' – and it was some days before the miners decided to include the re-legalisation of Solidarity in their demands. What followed was a tussle between strikers and the authorities that revealed the weaknesses of both. It was difficult to keep an occupation strike going. At the peak of the action only half the workforce of five thousand stayed at the pit day and night, and eventually the occupiers dwindled to a mere few hundred. Conditions were bad, people were nervous, and some of the strikers' families were urging them to give up. Security forces flooded into the neighbouring town of Jastrzebie and one night searchlights were turned on the mine, giving rise to fears of an attack by the ZOMO riot police, whose tactic on such occasions was to send in non-striking workers first and, after scuffles broke out, charge in themselves to 'restore order'. Litynski and two other experienced Solidarity activists advised the strikers to organise self-defence squads armed with pick handles, and to create an impression of further strength they dreamed up a 'Service-S' which appeared to give orders to the strikers over the mine loudspeakers but in fact did not exist.

Litynski, however, soon became convinced that the other side was bluffing too and that General Kiszczak never intended to use force to break up the strike, a hunch proven correct when on 25 August a Catholic intermediary arrived in Gdansk with an overture to Lech Walesa from none other than the Interior Minister. Out of these contacts developed the proposal that the Government and what Kiszczak called 'representatives of various social and workers' groups' should gather at a Round Table. Although the regime was at first vague about whether Walesa himself would be allowed to sit at this table, no one doubted he would if the Government was serious about talking. And the Government had every reason to be serious. The summer strikes, though only a limited threat in themselves, promised a far bigger and more radical strike wave in the future. The true nature of the economic crisis could not be indefinitely disguised by printing increasingly worthless zloties, and no financial help would come from the West until the regime talked to Walesa and Solidarity. If Solidarity was weak so was the Party: only seven per cent of its members were now under thirty. And nothing was to be expected from Moscow, unless it was the revolutionary advice to look for a political settlement. If there was optimism about the success of any future talks it was because, as Litynski put it, 'both sides are weak and both are sober'. Litynski himself was the same slight, tense figure he had been ten years before, but the hair in which he had a habit of twisting his finger was getting grey and his teeth were stained by countless cheap Polish cigarettes, some of which were notorious for their toxicity because the tobacco came from fields drenched by fall-out from the Huta Lenina steelworks outside Krakow. This looked like being his generation's last chance to achieve change without violence. The Communists, too, thought they had a chance, still believing they could survive as a power in the country. They were wrong, but the illusion was useful to Poland, lessening the temptation of a desperate regime to resort once more to force.

A GAME OF HIGH NOON

When the Round Table was over a member of the Communist Party Central Committee called it 'the first post-war Polish Parliament that worked'. There were moments, though, when it seemed it would never get started, and it was not till 6 February that fifty-seven people sat down at the vast doughnut-shaped table in the offices of the Council of Ministers. Both Government and opposition had to fight to rally their forces behind the talks, though Jaruzelski's battle proved much the harder. Walesa had only to persuade the strikers to go back to work and entrust their future to him, and in December 128 well-known intellectuals and Solidarity leaders formed a Citizens' Committee to act as his support staff. A little greyer and stouter than when martial law had swept him off the national stage, he nevertheless soon showed he had not lost his incomparable political instinct, and for many Poles a glimpse of his

Pilsudski moustaches and beady eyes was enough to make them feel they were in safe hands. The team he prepared for the talks was well known: Mazowiecki and Geremek, Michnik, Kuron and Bujak were there, as were new Solidarity stars like a young miner from the July Manifesto pit called Alojzy Pietrzyk. But the longer the negotiations' start was delayed the more people wondered why Jaruzelski had made the unexpected decision to talk. Had he really meant it? Mazowiecki, charged with organising the Solidarity team, never dreamed there might be talks until the summer strikes began. In August Kiszczak had convinced him that he understood a compromise was necessary to 'save the country'. But in the autumn there were daily attacks in the Communist press against Solidarity leaders – Michnik was called a 'historian-pyromaniac' – and Mazowiecki, who would be smoking three packs of cigarettes a day when the talks did start and whose El Greco face seemed most at home when worried, began to fear traps. Would the regime torpedo the talks and try to put the blame on Solidarity? Or was its aim to manoeuvre Solidarity into a position of co-responsibility without power, for he was sure the Party was not ready to give up power?

Jaruzelski's problems were of a different kind. The ambitious and combative Prime Minister Rakowski, keen that his new plan for economic salvation should occupy centre stage, liked to give the impression that the Round Table was only a sideshow, an argument also offered with aggressive self-assurance by senior official trade unions and the middle-ranking Party apparat, both of whom feared the re-legalisation of Solidarity. After much discussion opposition leaders decided that Jaruzelski and the Party were talking because, as one of them put it, 'they have seen the abyss. They know they face economic disaster without more Western money' (the availability of Western money obsessed both sides, and Solidarity was wondering whether its re-legalization might make it easier to attract Western assistance). The Solidarity leadership also believed that the Gorbachev visit had been crucial, for the Soviet leader could only have told Jaruzelski to expect no economic help from Moscow. The Central Committee meeting in January produced cries of alarm at the prospect of Solidarity's re-emergence. There were rumours of a split within the ranks, and a fifth of its members voted against the leadership's proposals for a 'socialist parliamentary democracy' even though the weasel word 'socialist' signalled the Party's intention to remain the ultimate boss. Some speakers tried to reassure Committee members that the country was not entirely on Solidarity's side (which Solidarity leaders readily admitted) but it helped little. Rakowski urged the Party to retain its power by becoming 'a strike force' for reform but many speakers were possessed by the fear, although seldom clearly articulated, that the Communist power machine could only survive under the familiar old conditions. The Central Committee's nervous mood had not been helped when a few days earlier a gathering of young people chaired by a Central Committee secretary was taken over by members of the still banned pro-Solidarity Independent Students' Association and turned into an all-out attack on Communist rule. A week before the Round Table was finally due to assemble General Kiszczak warned Walesa there was a chance that everything would collapse and the talks not be held. All he could promise in that event was to give him two days' notice. Was Kiszczak unsure of Jaruzelski's commitment to the talks? Did he fear there could be some destructive provocation from the Party or security services, even though the latter were supposed to be under his control? Or was it a last piece of psychological warfare to put the opposition into a more grateful frame of mind when the Round Table did begin?

It was appropriate that the talks were led on the regime's side by an Interior Minister who had spent his life as a professional intelligence officer. Kiszczak's subordinates in the security services were suspected of many more murders than the proven one of Father Popieluszko; yet this handsome, smooth-mannered man claimed to consider the infamous anti-Semitic campaign contrived by Party conservatives in 1968 a 'disgusting event covering [Poland] with disgrace'. Like most intelligence officers at the summit of their profession he was essentially a mechanic of power, and as such a more reliable tool for Jaruzelski than the abrasive Rakowski or a senior Party apparatchik unable to forget his ideology. And no one else knew the opposition leaders better than Kiszczak who for years had been both their gaoler and close student. The question was, what use did Jaruzelski mean to put him to? Bronislaw Geremek had commented a couple of years earlier that Jaruzelski, unlike previous Communist leaders, 'knows the true state of the country; he knows the mood of society'. Realism had always served Jaruzelski well. As a schoolboy in pre-war Warsaw he had urged his classmates in the spirit of the times to take up 'the heroic heritage of the scouts who died in 1920, fighting the Red [i.e. Russian] invader'. Four years later, after deportation to the Soviet Union, he became an officer in the newly formed pro-Soviet Polish army. Remaining in the army to destroy what was left of the anti-Communist resistance he made a brilliant and rapid career, nicknamed by contemporaries Little Jesus for his assiduousness on the courses essential to an officer's promotion. The events of 1968 that disgusted Kiszczak carried off among others the Defence Minister of the day, Marian Spychalski, and allowed Jaruzelski, aged only forty-five, to step uncomplaining into his shoes. Later he would talk of martial law as 'a thorn' he would always carry within him, but almost the first thing he did on appointment as Prime Minister in February 1981 was to begin planning for it. Yet Walesa would speak of a 'current of understanding' when he first met the General that same year, something that had never existed in his contacts with the then Party leader, Stanislaw Kania.

Was it not possible that Jaruzelski – his aides' rather ridiculous whisperings about his impeccable Polish credentials apart – was, by his own lights, a patriotic Pole, and even just perhaps a tragic patriot, forced to wound what he loved in order to save it from a far worse fate? The very idea enraged many Poles, even though the collaborator who believed he was doing the best for the nation was a character well known from nineteenth-century Polish history. It certainly seemed unlikely that in 1989 Jaruzelski would prefer Marxism-Leninism to realism which was perhaps why he appeared at Party gatherings to be as solitary and stiff a figure (a bad back requiring him to wear a surgical corset) as he did on most public occasions. His attempts to unbend – when together with Gorbachev, for example, working the crowds and stooping to kiss the hands of women – could be winning because they so clearly cost him effort. Some women said they found him attractive because he looked vulnerable but he was far from handsome, with bad skin, a shifty-seeming way of speaking from the side of his mouth and the wings of hair on each side of his bald head suggesting a clown's make-up. The dark glasses, whether worn to protect eyes weakened by the dazzle of Siberia snows or not, added to the air of shiftiness. It was apt of history to cast this equivocal figure to lead Poland's Communists to the electoral slaughter, and yet survive himself as first President of the revived Polish Republic – the only Communist leader of East Europe still to hold a leading position in the new post-Communist order.

That both sides emerged reasonably content with the results of the two month-long negotiations suggests how hard it was for either to see the future clearly. The regime went into the negotiations with one chief purpose: to persuade the opposition to join the system as an authorised but minor player who would be permitted to take part in controlled, 'non-confrontational' elections. This, it was supposed, would give the Communists a better chance to bridge the gap that had for so long separated them from most Poles and allow them at last to carry out a programme of reforms. Solidarity's first goal was its own re-legalisation as a trade union, but it had important subsidiary demands including local self-government, media access, and court and legal reform. All these points aimed in the time-honoured manner to enlarge the civic freedoms in what everyone assumed would still be a Communist state, for Solidarity's guiding principle from the very first session was that there could only be a transition to democracy by the gradual construction of self-governing bodies. The summit of the deal concerned a new Presidency and a two-chamber Parliament. The Communists and their satellite parties would have sixty-five per cent of the seats in the Sejm, the key lower house, while the remaining thirty-five per cent of the seats could be freely fought for by the opposition but also by Communists and anyone else. This idea of a role, albeit as a minority, in the Sejm had intrigued Mazowiecki and other opposition negotiators from the start. They were less interested in the second house or Senate which was to be freely elected, while they positively disliked the strong Presidency which would be in Communist hands. It was typical of the myopia of the moment that one of the most contentious issues was whether to override the Senate the Sejm would have to muster a three-fifths majority, easily achievable by the Communists and their allies, or a harder to achieve one of two-thirds. The regime's agreement to the latter was seen as an important concession. Events were soon to make it quite irrelevant.

The Party leadership appeared satisfied with the agreement although it had not achieved its original aim of Government and opposition going into the election campaign on a joint programme. A Politburo member told a Soviet journalist that it nevertheless provided the Polish Party with impregnable 'lines of defence'. The bloc of Communist and satellite deputies in the Sejm prevented any change in what was still a socialist constitution; and the President, with the army under his command, was the final guarantee of socialist control. The regime thought it had been clever to force a quick election which would pose problems for Solidarity as it emerged from illegality but not for the Party with its unmatched organisation and resources. As for Solidarity, much depended on how the agreements on such matters as media access or the independence of the courts were applied; certainly no one supposed the regime would yield more ground anywhere than it was obliged to. The opposition took some comfort from the understanding that the next elections would be completely free, though few were making serious calculations that far ahead, and the opinion polls were encouraging too. According to the liberal-leaning but official newspaper *Polityka* the publicity gained by the opposition during the Round Table had done wonders for its popularity by the end of March. Walesa's rating had risen to seventy-nine from twenty-four per cent the previous spring, and he was now second only to Cardinal Glemp, the obligatory first choice for most Catholic Poles. Approval of Solidarity had jumped by an almost identical amount over the same period, and it too trailed only behind the Church in institutional popularity. Yet it certainly did not seem ridiculous for a Politburo member to declare Poland was on the brink not of a change of system but 'a change towards democracy while keeping the basic values of socialism to which Polish society has become accustomed'. Although the Hungarian Party had just voted in favour of a multiparty system few people in Budapest yet understood that this meant a speedy end to Communist rule. In these circumstances the agreements reached by the Poles at their Round Table seemed remarkable enough, not least to an opposition no longer sure that its powers of resistance were inexhaustible, and which only the previous summer would have dismissed the very idea of a Round Table as fantasy.

It soon became clear that the regime's first mistake was to suppose it could benefit from Solidarity's unpreparedness. The Citizens' Committee that was technically running the election (rather than Solidarity the trade union) acquired a national headquarters on Fredry Street. A dilapidated, leprous building whose pediments had rotted away above the windows, it nevertheless occupied a commanding position next to Victory Square, and the red and white Solidarity banners on the roof might have been royal standards proclaiming the return of a king from exile. Inside was the urgency, confusion and excitement of life as Poles preferred to lead it. Desk tops were littered with plates of unappetising food, wolfed down as though it was caviar and then as quickly abandoned. Desk drawers soon acquired the obligatory untidiness of a schoolboy's pocket. Old women sat in corners clipping newspapers to no apparent purpose; young people smoked and struck poses of importance. A hundred volunteers, including many of the 'devoted ladies' who had typed manuscripts for *Samizdat*, had got the first edition of Solidarity's newspaper *Gazeta Wyborcza* ('Election Gazette') onto the streets on 8 May as planned. The motto beneath the title was the old one of 'There is no freedom without Solidarity' and the front page carried a photo of a genial, round-cheeked Walesa saying with no great originality 'for things to be different and better we must win these elections'. A tabloid, *Gazeta Wyborcza*'s short news stories and comments revolutionised the language of the Polish press by being clearly, and above all freely, written. Reading it made people realise how much censorship and self-censorship there still was in the official Polish papers; to be able to buy such a newspaper from a kiosk (admittedly at first very difficult even in Warsaw) was in itself a liberation from the double world of private and public truth that Poles had for so long lived in. The next evening brought Solidarity's first election programme on television. A clever evocation of old Solidarity images and emotions, its undoubted star was Walesa, as compellingly watchable speaking as when kneeling in prayer, his eyes for once at rest, during a spectacular mass in Father Jankowski's church. The ginger-bearded Professor Geremek emerged as another TV star, sounding and looking as reassuring as a Conradian sea-captain in an address to the Parliamentary candidates in the hall at the Lenin Shipyard where Solidarity was born.

The Communists' election tactics were a mixture of caution and confusion. Believing they could count on the support of at most thirty per cent of the voters (all those people, including bureaucrats and soldiers, whose way of life depended on the old regime), they hoped to increase their vote by having among their candidates people who would not be immediately thought of as Communists but were local or national personalities in their own right: the director of Wroclaw Zoo who had a popular wildlife programme on television was considered a successful choice of this kind. At the Central Committee in Warsaw the tranquil corridors remained undisturbed by signs of election bustle, partly because here as in every other Party office throughout the country no one had much idea of how to fight a real election, partly because the leadership believed they were going to do well enough. Zygmunt Czarzasty, the Party secretary running the campaign, forecast that the Communists would get fifty-five per cent of the seats in the Senate, and that over half of the limited number of openly contested Sejm seats would be won by independent candidates unconnected with Solidarity. At the time no one thought this a ridiculous forecast. The Solidarity leadership felt sure of the support of only a quarter of the electorate, and supposed it might win half of the Senate places and the same proportion of those seats it was able to contest in the Sejm. But it was telling that in spite of his reputation for realism even Czarzasty was confused about the future of the Communist Party. At one moment he admitted liking what he called the 'moral principles' taken up by Solidarity in 1980, and to admiring both Adam Smith and Father Tischner, the Krakow theologian close to the Pope. At another he insisted that the Communists had to become the 'intellectual élite of the nation'. He was proud of having lectured Party conservatives on the need to accept Solidarity unionists back into the factories, but himself argued that the Party had to keep its political monopoly in the army and police. And he found nothing contradictory in asserting that two out of three Poles still wanted socialism as long as it could be made both 'productive and ethical'.

So much for the view from Warsaw. Out in the provinces it was soon clear that the Party was in trouble. In mid-May, with the first round of the election little more than two weeks away, the Government coalition's campaign in the West Polish city of Poznan was almost invisible. Jan Kolodziejczak, a well-known industrial manager and reformist member of the Central Committee running for the Senate, knew the game was up the moment he understood that people were going to vote for sides, and not for individuals as the Party had hoped. And while Walesa and his close colleagues had picked all the Solidarity candidates, the Communist Party, in its attempt to cover its tracks, had allowed any Party member able to collect sufficient qualifying signatures to stand as a candidate. They were then left to run their own campaigns as they wished, which produced some quite contradictory propaganda. While Kolodziejczak's ideas were not very different from those of left-leaning Solidarity economists, a young Party journalist called Marek Krol who was running for the Sejm expressed as much admiration for a clever but eccentric far-rightist called Korwin-Mikke ('Our Reagan is younger,' was his supporters' slogan) as for a famous liberal publicist who had advised Walesa to 'get into power on the backs of the workers and then declare capitalism'. Krol's motto matched his elegant military appearance. It was blood, sweat and tears, and if he had talked to Aleksander Kwasniewski he would probably have added 'and to hell with the lumpenproletariat'. Irritated at being asked why he had ever become a Communist he answered with a dashing lack of logic that he favoured social democracy, that the old Communist policy of equality and planned affluence did not work, and that what he would like to see was capitalist production matched to socialist distribution (he did not repeat the Party sneer that Solidarity wanted the opposite: capitalism in the shops, socialism in the factories). The nub of his cloudy but increasingly Fascist-sounding argument was that while Solidarity was handicapped by having a working-class constituency the Party, if it had had the guts to impose martial law, should not be frightened now of imposing a free market.

The Communists' passivity and lack of coherence made Poznan's Solidarity team look invincible. They held well-attended meetings, had plenty of posters and enjoyed the discreet support of the Church, and it was after Sunday mass that the campaign to collect signatures in support of candidacies had produced the most spec- tacular results. Both Solidarity candidates for the Senate were celebrated local academics and both had been interned during martial law. What Pole, asked the Communist Kolodziejcazk in a humorous monologue of woes, could resist that? 'We are a nation which should never be told no, a nation that is sensitive to any form of oppression. Those two professors can dress up as sufferers, almost as saints. They can play on all the elements of the Polish psyche that a rational man like me can't.' True, but not really fair to Janusz Ziolkowski, an eminently rational man and distinguished sociologist who until his internment under martial law had been rector of Poznan University and was now one of Poznan's Solidarity candi- dates for the Senate. To watch Ziolkowski speak in a secondary school on the outskirts of the city was to see Solidarity, and what perhaps was going to be a new Poland, at their most magical. Seventy people, an ordinary crowd, sat listening to this courteous white-haired gentleman dressed in a tweed suit complete with waistcoat. A mother had brought a picture book and crayons to keep her small daughter quiet. Some children from the school were not quite sure whether they were bored or not, and the old women who had come in from nearby housing estates seemed puzzled. But just as the evening sun made the bare schoolroom glow so Ziolkowski's quiet words for a few moments conferred purpose and dignity on these ordinary people and their far from satisfactory lives. He said that Poland wanted no more than to be a 'normal country'; that they had slipped far behind Europe and that now even Asians like the Japanese were better educated – the audience rustled into life at that. He recited the well-known dates of protest and defeat: 1970, 1976, 1980 and 1981. Everyone knew them by heart as though they were part of a prayer. And at the end he said, very simply, that everyone should remember that 'the state is us'.

Was it really possible that forty years of history made by armies, and secret policemen, and revolutionaries turned autocrats could be brought to an end by tweed-suited professors addressing gatherings of people who had never had power and who certainly would not be convinced by one election campaign that they were indeed the state? Where, asked Poles who had attended similar meetings and also been moved by them, where were the hard men of the regime, the so-called 'concrete' which never showed its face or talked in public but everyone knew was always there? Would they allow Ziolkowski and his little meetings to walk away with their power? Ziolkowski was worried too. He had expected the regime to protect itself with much greater skill and determination. He was amazed at the risk the Communists were taking with their sloppy campaign, for he already had a fair idea of how disastrous the results would be for them. The explanation was that the Party believed the agreement reached at the Round Table meant it could not lose in any way that mattered. Had not Politburo members repeatedly said that the elections, far from changing the system, would bring cooperation between Government and opposition, and 'a political order that should guarantee economic calm'? Jerzy Urban, the bizarre but nimble-minded Government spokesman who delighted in making waspish, unpopular remarks, was telling visitors that the new Parliament, whatever its composition, was unlikely to be the centre of the country's political life. His argument was that over the last three hundred years Poland had had just eight years of proper Parliamentary rule and they were a failure. Why trust one's fate to it now? On the eve of the election Solidarity would put up its wittiest poster – a black and white still of Gary Cooper wearing both sheriff's star and red Solidarity badge above the words 'W *samo południe*', 'High Noon'. But when designing the poster Solidarity knew as well as the Party that it couldn't really be high noon for the point of the Round Table had been to make sure that the election was a duel with a pre-arranged result, and that neither side's gun was loaded with real bullets.

On Saturday 3 June, the day before the elections, England played Poland at football. Not even the late substitution of a young Solidarity supporter, who had just written an article for *Gazeta Wyborcza* and crossed himself before running onto the field, could save Poland from a three-nil defeat. 'We were humiliated,' said G., watching the game on television with friends whose interest in politics was almost matched by their passion for football. They took more comfort from the election prospects. Jan Litynski, who was managing the Solidarity campaign in the capital as well as running for the Sejm from a Silesian mining constituency, had private poll figures suggesting easy victories for all the opposition's Warsaw candidates, and Solidarity's estimates were being revised upwards throughout the country. In G.'s sitting room the consensus was that Solidarity could win eighty per cent of the Senate seats, six out of seven of all the seats available to it in the Sejm, and that a good many names on the Government's so-called national list, although all running unopposed, would fail to win the votes of the necessary fifty per cent plus one of the registered electors. Curiosity was aroused by a news report broadcast during half-time that Cardinal Glemp had received two candidates from a tiny new Christian Democrat group who happened to be running in the same constituencies as Kuron and Michnik, but an appearance on the evening TV news by Walesa (who as union leader was himself not standing for Parliament) seemed much more significant. Walesa's remark that he intended to vote for those candidates on the national list whom he knew to be supporters of reform was the clearest sign so far that Solidarity, in spite of all the precautions of the Round Table agreements, was worried about the possible extent of the regime's defeat. The news also showed pictures of Jaruzelski and Rakowski with world leaders and subtitled 'no one relies on the weak'. Since Urban had taken over direction of television such blatant insertion of election propaganda into news programmes had been common, but this was interesting as the last attempt to scare people with the old Communist argument of Polish *raison d'état*. Rakowski had fallen back on it in his campaign speeches, on one occasion even claiming that Cardinal Wyszysnki before his death had compared Poland to a man living between a Slav and German wall, and that he preferred to rest against the Slav one. The same theme was sounded by Jaruzelski in his final TV address, though it was chiefly remarkable for his failure to use the words 'Communist', 'socialist' or 'Polish United Workers' Party'. As the Party's moment of truth approached the provident General gave every sign of distancing himself from it. Solidarity's last word that night came in its final election programme and ended with an image recalling the atmosphere that had blessed Professor Ziolkowski's meeting in the dreary schoolroom in Poznan. It showed an old man walking slowly into a church and kneeling down to pray. 'Solidarity,' said the words that flashed onto the screen, 'the hope of all.'

GENTLEMEN IN VICTORY

On a fine Sunday morning General Jaruzelski and his wife vote in the polling station closest to their home. Set up in a neo-classical mansion that once belonged to a famous sculptor it lies in a small park well out of sight of any Gary Cooper posters. Since the weather is so good they walk home, to the excitement of the television crews who stretch their long microphones towards Jaruzelski like bees desperate to extract pollen from a rare flower. But the General is the last man in the world to reveal his hopes or fears on this or any other day, and long before the couple have reached their plain little villa on Ikara Street they are almost alone except for the General's empty black Peugeot that follows dog-like behind. People in the village of Debnowola south of Warsaw are scarcely more forthcoming, not least because there is a plague of hangovers after three large weddings the day before. The village priest supports Solidarity but he has not fired his congregation with his enthusiasm. 'Can you change anything in Poland?' a young farmer asks, not bothering to answer his own question. Other peasants say they don't care who is in power as long as prices don't go up for the goods they have to buy, though naturally they wanted more money for the food they produce. As is to be expected the capital is more lively. A friend's wife, watching a special TV news bulletin from Peking about the massacre in Tiananmen Square, puts her hand to her head and groans, 'My God! These Communists.' The family's young son comes in with a friend from delivering Solidarity flyers. On the way they have picked up some Communist leaflets and want to know what to do with them. 'Shall we burn them, Dad?' the boy asks hopefully. There is something of the same combative spirit at a polling station near the Ursus tractor factory, where Zbigniew Bujak made his name as a working-class leader. People take particular pleasure in telling how many names they have crossed off the national list, which already looks like being yet another embarrassing Communist mistake. A young woman says she put a line through them all. Her mother grins and pointing a finger at her says, 'She's a real Turk, that one,' but she has done exactly the same. At the nearby Church of the Holy Mother of Fatima, a temporary breeze-block hangar beside a huge brick church that has yet to be completed, a young priest bearded like Geremek and wearing a pink shirt with his black clerical trousers explains that when speaking from the pulpit he tells his parishioners only that they should 'be in the truth of Jesus Christ'. It is hard, though, holding back like this and if they ask him privately he tells them to vote Solidarity. He says there is a minority in this industrial suburb who believe in the election and will vote for Solidarity; and another Communist minority who also take the polls seriously. But most people are indifferent and (like the farmers of Debnowola) do not believe their vote can change anything. 'The system has left its mark here, particularly the fear caused by the years of martial law.'

Outside a polling station in the Kuron constituency of Zoliborz two teenagers in Solidarity T-shirts hand out cribs showing which names should be left on the ballot papers and which crossed off. A girl in a Kuron T-shirt worn with an ankle-length skirt and bobbed hair is showing an old woman how to vote under the disapproving stare of a sallow young woman wearing the badge of Sila-Nowicki, the Christian Democrat who received the Primate's unexpected blessing on election eve. It's no good asking young people here who they have voted for – they are solid for the opposition – but an elderly lady in a flowered dress looks as though she might have voted for Cardinal Glemp's favourite Sila-Nowicki. The suggestion shocks her. 'Goodness no! I voted for Kuron. He's a Polish hero.' And the national list? She blinks and purses her lips together at the pleasure of the memory before taking a pencil from her handbag and holding it up for inspection. 'All out. I crossed them all out. I took this pencil with me to use as a ruler and I crossed them all out.

After all these years it was such a relief.' Later I learn that even the sagacious G. could not entirely resist this temptation. While leaving most of the not-so-bad guys on the national list Polish conscience compelled him to score through the name of Czeslaw Kiszczak, pivotal figure in the Round Table perhaps, but also never to be forgotten as the smooth technician of martial law.

When the polling results became known it was hard to tell who was more alarmed, the Party or Solidarity. Ninety-two of Solidarity's candidates for the hundred-seat Senate had won outright, and all but one of the rest would get in after the second round two weeks later. Solidarity failed to win first-round victories in only one of the 161 Sejm seats open to free competition. Most humiliating of all for the Party were the results for the uncontested national list, where all but two of their thirty-five most senior candidates failed to win sufficient votes, among them eight Politburo members (including Kiszczak, Rakowski and the Defence Minister General Siwicki) and the leaders of the satellite United Peasant and Democratic parties. One of the two who did get through, a high legal official, may have owed his luck to being the last name on the list and therefore missed by all but the most careful voters like the lady from Zoliborz who had the foresight to equip herself with a ruler. During the confused days that followed the Party's stubborn disregard of Solidarity's warning about the perils of sticking to the national list provoked an uncharacteristic outburst from the usually impeccably gentleman-like Geremek. It was, he said, 'a monstrous political and technical mistake', the consequence not only of lack of imagination, but also of 'the sin of pride'. The other disconcerting result was the high abstention rate: four out of every ten Poles had not bothered to go to the polling station at all, a proportion that neatly matched the Warsaw priest's estimate of the indifferent ones in his parish who did not believe their vote would change anything. Mazowiecki, who had declined to be a Parliamentary candidate, found this particularly disappointing. The 'psychological breakthrough' among ordinary people that he had hoped for had not taken place.

The Party's first reaction was a measure of its shock. Like a man climbing from his car after a smash it tried to pretend it had not happened. One of the Politburo's more reasonable members explained that emotions had got the better of people. 'Is the sum of individual decisions an expression of collective will? I think not.'

But even the Polish Party, never famous for its sense of shame, lacked the heart for a new magical-dialectical justification of their minority rule, and the old argument of Polish *raison d'état* was adapted to make a more sensible line of defence. As phrased by Jerzy Urban, it was that although the Party could in theory tell Solidarity to form a government this would damage the cause of reform in East Europe by signalling to the rest of the Soviet bloc that democracy was dangerous to Party rule.

Yes indeed; and what else, one was tempted to ask, should one expect? But in June 1989 Urban still seemed to have a point. The Round Table agreement was constructed on the acceptance, at least until the next elections, of continuing Communist rule albeit over a society with greater rights of self-organisation. Communist Party rule was still the unbroken norm throughout the Soviet bloc except for Hungary, and even there it was not plain that the multiparty system approved by the Party in principle would mean Communist loss of power in practice. G. was speaking for many Poles when he said that 'the Communists got what they deserved and asked for. One should not feel sorry for them.' But at the same time there was apprehension about these emotionally so pleasing results. In the almost bare office where he was preparing to edit Solidarity's new weekly paper (a fruit of the Round Table) Mazowiecki, grey-faced with fatigue, worried that the victory might be too big. He could not forget a remark by the earlier Communist leader Wladyslaw Gomulka that once the Party had power it would never give it up. Had their mentality really changed? Mazowiecki doubted it. 'We must hope the worst won't happen.' Some feared it already had, and that Poland was back on the old switchback ride in which a new Solidarity revolution was bound to end in another bout of martial law, this time all the harder to bear for being repeated. Others could not forget the recent bloody events in Peking.

None of these fears were ridiculous. One of the results of having such a strong opposition was that the Polish Party and security apparatus were more easily scared and enraged than in other countries in the bloc. Conversations with Party apparatchiks often revealed a streak of guilty malice towards their incorrigible fellow countrymen, above all in the never-ending dispute as to who were the true Polish patriots. Even Mazowiecki and the other best minds in the opposition still did not see clearly the way to a peaceful exit from Communist rule. Adam Michnik thought there were two relevant patterns. There was the Spanish, in which members of Franco's old regime were offered the chance of a decent place in the new society; and there was the way of post-Second World War de-Nazification, meaning punishment and revenge and which in Polish conditions threatened either a new dictatorship or violent resistance from those who were purged. In fact something like the Spanish way was already being repeated in Hungary, driven not so much by conscious planning as by the Magyars' urge for survival and talent for accommodation. There were far fewer signs of this in Poland, although some enterprise managers were beginning to exploit the Rakowski reforms to take over ownership of factories by a process of speedy privatisation that was extremely advantageous to them and their partners.

The existence of a large army and large security machine under Communist control, combined with prudent respect for Soviet interests as they were then understood, seemed to leave Solidarity no choice but to ignore the election results and observe everything that had been agreed at the Round Table. Solidarity would meanwhile put its hope in what Geremek called 'the gradual construction of democratic bodies'. In fact within days of the second round of voting in mid-June Solidarity was called to act as a mattress to break what had become the Party's helpless tumble from power. The new MPs from the satellite Democratic and United Peasant parties very soon understood the disadvantage for them in being tied to the dying Communist duck, and as a result the old regime coalition upon which all Round Table calculations had been built started to break up. The first moment of danger came on 19 July when the abstentions and in a few cases even hostile votes of some Democratic and United Peasant deputies almost prevented the election of Jaruzelski to the new post of President, even though it was generally agreed that Polish stability and Soviet tolerance depended on the General getting the job. In the end Jaruzelski won the absolute minimum of necessary votes thanks only to absenteeism and counter-abstentions stage-managed by the Solidarity leadership in the Sejm and Senate. The next question was whether the Communists could form a government. Even before Jaruzelski scraped into the Presidential apartments in the Belvedere, Michnik had shocked his Solidarity colleagues with an article in his newspaper headlined 'Their President, our Prime Minister'. It was shocking because it seemed to disregard the Round Table, but Michnik's purpose was the opposite of provocative. A rapid, stuttering talker, still as untidy as a student in spite of his election to the Sejm, Michnik remarked just after the election that he had felt safer when he was in prison, and the nub of his argument was that under the new circumstances only a Solidarity-led coalition government that included the reform wing of the Party could manage a non-violent transition to a new system.

Jaruzelski himself precipitated the next crisis by a final and fatal demonstration of Communist pride and lack of imagination when he proposed General Kiszczak as the new Prime Minister. How, after such elections, could Poles have been expected to accept as the first President and Prime Minister of the new Poland the two men most responsible for martial law? This time it was Walesa who cushioned the Communist fall with a surprise mattress of his own making: he proposed that Solidarity form a government with the Democrats and Peasants whose Parliamentary rank-and-file were by now in almost in full revolt. Again there was shock at first: what about the Round Table, for Walesa seemed to be leaving out the Communists altogether? This little shock served Walesa well for it was essentially his formula, significantly adjusted to appease Jaruzelski, the Communists and (it was widely supposed) Moscow by the appointment of Generals Kiszczak and Siwicki respectively as Ministers of the Interior and Defence, that led at the end of August to the election as Prime Minister of Tadeusz Mazowiecki, friend of the Pope, adviser to Walesa, and quintessential Polish Catholic intellectual.

On 12 September, the day Mazowiecki introduced his Government to the Sejm, it took me forty-five minutes of queuing to buy the morning newspapers, bread and milk. It was a good thing that only milk was needed that day for the self-service grocery had nothing else to offer apart from questionable fruit juice, vinegar, soup powder in drab brown packets and bags of crisps and neon-coloured sweets. The memory of the wretched shops and the punishing daily life of which they were a part returned when, three-quarters of an hour after Mazowiecki had begun his speech, he faltered, seemed to gasp for air and was led out by the Speaker under the expressionless gaze of Jaruzelski seated in appropriate solitude in the new Presidential box above the chamber floor. It was almost an hour before Mazowiecki came back to resume his speech by joking that 'a few weeks' intensive work have reduced me to the same state as the Polish economy'. The mood relaxed when he read out the names of his chosen ministers; Jacek Kuron, expelled from the Communist Party twenty-four years earlier for being impossibly critical but now on the way to becoming a national mascot, receiving the greatest applause as the new Minister of Labour. But the apprehension caused by the Prime Minister's attack lingered on, and there was much worried talk when the deputies adjourned to the Sejm dining room for lunch. It was only to be expected, said a woman who turned out to be a Communist deputy, given the way the new Premier had been living, with cigarettes by the packet, too much stress and too little sleep. But something else troubled her more, even though she was a Party member. As Mazowiecki was helped from the chamber she could not help thinking that some ill fate hung over Poland, and wasn't it because other deputies had felt something similar that they, too, had shuddered and for a moment been scared? For some Communists the sight of the frail sixty-two-year-old Prime Minister gasping for breath was the moment they understood that they had surrendered Poland into other hands, and that those hands had to be given a chance.

Almost from the moment of General Kiszcak's failure to construct a Communist-led government grunts of disapproval were to be heard from Czechoslovakia and East Germany. In Romania the reaction was old-fashioned Communist melodrama. Immediately after Mazowiecki's nomination as Premier the Polish ambassador was summoned to the Romanian Central Committee where he was told that 'socialist Romania' could not consider the developments in Warsaw to be a 'purely internal affair', and that the time had come for all Communist Parties to cooperate to prevent 'worker-peasant power' being handed over to Polish 'reactionary circles'. Behind these ugly old words lay a perfectly correct assessment by the Romanian dictator of the meaning of the Polish Party's defeat for Communism in the rest of East Europe, and Ceausescu dispatched his thoughts to all the brother Parties in the apparent hope of reviving the old Brezhnev doctrine. But much as the East German and Czechoslovak Parties disliked what was going on in Poland they understood there was no chance of a Warsaw Pact intervention unless the Soviet Union wanted it, which even they by then understood it did not. If Jaruzelski's staff were to be believed the East German leaders did not even think it worth conveying privately to the Polish Party their dislike of the changes in Poland.

Nevertheless some of the Solidarity leaders, among them Geremek, now leader of the Solidarity deputies in the Sejm, still believed that a sort of Brezhnev doctrine remained in place. The Polish Central Committee had tried to make much out of a telephone conversation just before Mazowiecki's Sejm confirmation in which Gorbachev and Rakowski (fresh from election as Party First Secretary) were said to have agreed that Polish problems could not be solved without the participation of Poland's Communists. What did that mean? Geremek believed there was still a 'red line' that Poland could not cross with impunity, and he described his role as that of a sapper who tested by trial and error where the line now lay. In September 1989 Moscow no longer drew this line at exclusive Communist Party rule – as the East Germans, Czechs and Romanians would still have dearly liked – even though the Round Table had not agreed on a multiparty system. What concerned Moscow, Geremek supposed, were the vital Soviet interests protected by Poland's membership of the Warsaw Pact and its other security and economic obligations. Mazowiecki had acknowledged these interests by the appointment of Kiszczak and Siwicki, and even his appointment of the law professor Krzysztof Skubiszewski, a so-called independent, as Foreign Minister was meant to be reassuring, for the Foreign Ministry would at first largely remain in the hands of its old Communist officials. Would Moscow have been more agitated by the Polish election results and the emergence of the Mazowiecki Government if it had foreseen the speed of coming events in East Europe? There is no doubt it was this speed that disarmed those Soviet generals and Communist Party conservatives most likely to object to what happened, and it took them till the Soviet Party Congress in July 1990 to express their disapproval in a forceful public manner. By then it was too late. They could grouse and propose hunting for scapegoats, but scarcely suggest the reconquest of an empire they had lost almost without noticing. Whether Gorbachev would have behaved differently had he possessed second sight is doubtful. Like all Soviet leaders before him, in matters of foreign strategy he relied heavily on bluff. The slower East Europe changed the better for him, and he accordingly avoided doing anything to speed it up unnecessarily. That the Poles were still so cautious in September 1989 was a measure of his success. But he never had the intention of intervening himself to save Communist Parties he judged to have failed, and once his bluff was called he gave in with grace.

There was certainly no sign of resistance among the new leadership of the Polish Party chosen shortly after the Parliamentary elections. As was to be expected Rakowski fired off some bitter words in the first moments of defeat but by the time the Mazowiecki Government had taken office the inevitable was coming to be recognized for what it was. Marek Krol, now one of Poznan's deputies in the Sejm but also newly elected to the once powerful post of Central Committee secretary, claimed that all the leaders – in the Politburo, the army and the security services – understood that the time for solutions imposed by force was gone for good: one more go at martial law and the Party would be finished for ever. Rakowski and his men were put out by their failure to get Communists appointed to head the Foreign Ministry and state television, but little by little their attention was demanded by more pressing if more humble concerns. For instance, how much longer could the Party afford to occupy the huge Central Committee building and its other well-appointed offices throughout the country? They had called in the businessman who fêted Konwicki for *A Minor Apocalypse*, and his advice was 'no more Party temples'; sell them off. Krol was delighted. He found the atmosphere in the huge Central Committee unbearably gloomy, particularly towards evening when it was almost deserted and the only company left for the statues of Marx and Engels in the marble entrance hall were a bronze trio of workers in combative poses that must have made Aleksander Kwasniewski think of the lumpenproletariat each time he passed them. But what was to be done with such a place? Turn it into a hotel, another Central Committee secretary suggested. They could call it the Hotel Bolshevik, and charge guests double for staying in rooms once occupied by members of the Politburo. But wasn't that a last flash of the old Communist pride, for who, in years to come, would want to pay extra for a room once occupied by people of that kind?

8
Saints and Scoundrels

FORGOTTEN BEAUTIES

One summer day towards the end of the 1970s a dapper little Yugoslav was talking to a Western visitor in the lobby of a Belgrade hotel. He was in fine mood, for all seemed to be right in his world. Marshal Tito, with whom he had worked closely for many years and gave every sign of being immortal, would soon be appearing to universal applause in customary white suit and diamond rings to preside over yet another congress of the League of Yugoslav Communists. But the immediate reason for the little man's pleasure was Kosovo, the autonomous province in the south of Yugoslavia inhabited mainly by Albanians. He had just come back from Pristina, the provincial capital, delighted by what he had seen. Federal aid was helping change the face of this most backward part of the country but even more dramatic was the transformation of the young people. Albanian teenagers were now no different from their Serbian contemporaries. They wore the same blue jeans, and danced to the same pop music. Watching the evening promenade up and down Pristina's main street he could scarcely tell the two nationalities apart. Tito and socialism (in that order, he let it be understood) were at last smoothing out the national differences that had for so long brought conflict and bloodshed to this part of the Balkans.

Ten years later the Serbian politician Slobodan Milosevic became the first Communist leader in Europe to show that a Communist Party could survive by turning itself into a national crusade. The trick was not unknown in other parts of the world. If Vietnamese Communists seemed invincible it was because they had early on hijacked the passions of Vietnamese as they fought to free themselves from French colonialism. Arguably one European, Albania's Enver Hoxha, had done something similar by breaking relations with all powers, Communist and non-Communist alike, whom he suspected of wanting to dominate his tiny country. But Milosevic was a different animal: he was a Communist who specifically disavowed the international spirit of the original Communist movement in general and as it had been practised by Tito in Yugoslavia in particular. His target was not just insubordinate Albanians but Slovenes, Croats and any one else in Yugoslavia whom he thought slighted Serbian dignity. Milosevic called Serbs 'the only people who lost their nation in time of peace', and even Serbian intellectuals disenchanted with Communists were likely to agree with him. Like Milosevic, they believed that Serbia, the dominant nation in pre-war Yugoslavia, had been dealt an unfair hand in the post-war Communist state by the half-Croat, half-Slovene Tito, and was further discriminated against when Voivodina (with a Hungarian minority) and Kosovo (with its overwhelming Albanian majority and small Serb minority) were later partly detached from Serbia to become autonomous provinces within the Serb Republic. They traced this Communist distrust of Serbs back to the pre-war Cominform which, against all Marxist logic, had treated the entire Serb nation as a class enemy; and they saw the same distrust in the way Tito treated Serbia even during the war against Germany, for the Yugoslav leader, they said, 'never lost his Bolshevik reflexes'. Were they being nationalistic? Certainly not, retorted a Belgrade journalist who later became Milosevic's Foreign Minister, 'these are the facts'.

In a poem about the period of the Turkish invasions the contemporary Serb poet Miodrag Pavlovic imagines soldiers of the last Serb garrison saying,

Let us sing and remember ourselves,
Others have forgotten us.

Let the law of the constant heart reign
Beside the ruined town.

Under Milosevic's impulse Serbian singing and displays of constancy once more took on dramatic forms, and soon it was as though Tito had never existed. Milosevic seldom mentioned the dead Marshal's name, and eventually his photograph replaced – in Serbia, but not in the rest of Yugoslavia – the once ubiquitous pictures of the Marshal in his Ruritanian uniforms. Belgrade resumed building the vast shrine to Saint Sava, Serbia's patron saint, that was begun before the war but whose completion Tito had forbidden. The remains of the martyr King Lazar, killed fighting the Turks on Kosovo's Field of Blackbirds, remembered as the blackest day in Serbian history, were removed from the Orthodox cathedral in Belgrade and processed from monastery to monastery in preparation for the battle's six hundredth anniversary in 1989. A pre-war scholar had remarked that the God to whom Serbs prayed was apparently so concerned with their fate that he might have been made to serve them alone, and in spite of forty-five years of Communism this seemed still to be true. Nowhere was Serbian feeling more self-righteously passionate, or more directly pitched at a Serbian God, than in matters concerning Kosovo, once the heart of medieval Serbia and still the centre of Serbian Orthodoxy for all that its ravishing little churches were surrounded by Moslem Albanians. Serbs insisted that Kosovo was and always would be an integral part of Serbia – and indeed in 1990 was re-established as such by Milosevic – in spite of its dwindling Serb population and though even at the beginning of the century some of its most famous towns were, as an English traveller noting the Albanian predominance put it, as lost to Serbia 'as is Calais to England'.

At meetings and demonstrations people sang songs in praise of Milosevic. 'Loved by big and small,' the words of one went – as long as Milosevic was alive Serbs would never be slaves again. 'People are asking who will replace Tito. Everyone knows the answer – Slobodan is his proud name!' At first sight he was an unlikely politician to lead a nationalist revival that apparently contradicted the main line of European development at the end of the twentieth century. Westerners found him charming, partly because his English was excellent, partly because he had the knack of appearing easy and unassuming in private. He had travelled a good deal while working as a banker (in Yugoslavia at that time a political appointment) and had well-placed friends in Washington. His wife's family came from the inner circle of Tito's partisans and was herself an avowed Communist who supervised ideological matters at Belgrade University. It was much harder to say what he was. Certainly a skilful and if need be unscrupulous politician who knew how to wrap nationalist policies in Communist jargon. He was not a remarkable speaker and in public actually tried to avoid smiling, apparently because he thought it made his babyish face insufficiently mature.

Nevertheless even sophisticated Serbs sometimes found tears coming to their eyes at his meetings. He gave the impression of an ambitious man who had filled a personal emptiness with Serbian passions powerfully concentrated by long years of suppression under Tito.

Those East Europeans who knew of Milosevic found him a troubling portent. They saw a man riding to power on the problems of multinational Yugoslavia which in many respects were also those of the Soviet bloc. Different nations, languages, religions and histories had been crammed together in forced brotherhood and the consequent problems ignored or suppressed in Soviet East Europe just as in Tito's Yugoslavia. If Serbia had suffered 'historical injustice', as Milosevic said, could not Hungary or Poland claim the same? 'Martyr' was a word that came every bit as easily to the lips in many parts of East Europe as it did in Serbia. What would happen if East Europe were to produce its own versions of Milosevic, politicians more skilful at exploiting the narcissism of small and oppressed nations than interested in constructing modern democratic societies? It was partly to allay these fears that so much fuss was made about the East's 'return to Europe'. Westerners might find the East and the Balkans colourful. Intrepid Victorians had revelled in it, and even sung a song about it.

> We're back to the Balkans again.
> Back, where tomorrow the quick may be dead,
> With a hole in his heart or a ball in his head –
> Back, where the passions are rapid and red –
> Oh, we're back to the Balkans again!

It was another matter to be living there at the end of the twentieth century. 'I'm afraid for my country,' a young Slovene said during a difficult moment in the late 1980s. 'It's the Balkans here.' For a Slovene or Catholic Croat daily life demonstrated in so many ways the lack of common bonds with Serbs to the East. Slovenia's Central European culture was charmingly demonstrated by the city museum in its capital, Ljubljana, which recorded the German-style shooting clubs whose painted wooden targets went back two hundred years. 'Good God, Seppi! That's not a buck!' said the German-language caption under a picture of one man shooting another in the bottom while a deer scampers off untouched. Would they have thought that funny in Belgrade where Vuk Karadzic, the nineteenth-century creator of the modern Serbian language, was at about the same time having his portrait painted wearing a Turkish fez? It was quite natural for a couple of elderly women in a picture gallery in Zagreb, capital of Catholic Croatia, to cry, 'Look! There's Sisi!' when they spotted a portrait of the Empress Elizabeth, Franz Josef's difficult wife. Patriotic Croatian intellectuals had by 1989 concluded that after forty years of Communism the most important characteristic of Yugoslavia remained the old divide between Rome and Byzantium, between Habsburg and Turkish empires. Serb roots remained in the East (or so these Croats argued), while Slovene and Croatian faces naturally turned to Rome and Vienna. Croat nationalists brought to power the following year by free elections believed that politicians who ignored or tried to overcome the Croat-Serb divide were condemned to be tragic figures rejected by both nations. Was their Croatia part of Europe? Certainly. Was it still part of Yugoslavia? Perhaps.

If Croats and Slovenes saw Europe, by which like most other East Europeans they meant the community growing up around West Europe, as their escape from an unwelcome past, so did most of the Soviet-bloc nations who also had a great many undesirable things to flee from. Most immediately it was Communism which they now saw as Soviet semi-Asiatic rule incompatible with their Christian, European natures. But beyond that were the pre-war decades of faltering democracy, uneven economic development and unre-formed feudal societies, and further back still centuries of domi-nation by Turks, Russians and Germans. East Germany, the odd man out in so many things, was nevertheless a would-be escaper too, in its case from the Nazi and Prussian inheritance. But escaping promised to be a difficult and competitive business. Prime Minister Mazowiecki liked to say that by choosing democracy and a market economy Poland was returning to 'the mainstream of history – to its own history'. But a Polish diplomat, weary from trying to persuade West European Governments to grant visas more readily to the citizens of this new and fully European Poland, complained that 'we may want to fill our lungs with European air – but Europe doesn't want it'. The 'return to Europe' was one of the first themes in Romanian newspapers after Ceausescu's overthrow. 'Romania has moved with the times, has rejoined Europe with its head up', was a typical sentiment, but doubts about how much Europe wanted

Romania, and even Romanians' confidence in their own Europeanness, were not far below the surface. It only took West Europe to
hesitate over aid to Romania for a leading Bucharest journalist to
explode in self-pitying indignation:

> A new martyrdom begins for Romania. No sooner has the
> burden [of Ceausescu] been lifted, albeit incompletely,
> than another heavier cross is put upon its shoulders.

Was Romania, he asked, the country that had 'uprooted totalitarianism . . . in just one wink of history', now to become 'a victim on
the altar of its own victory'? Romania had a 'new Cross to carry on
its shoulders, the Cross of humiliation'. But Romanians were not
beggars, and would certainly not go seeking alms at the 'high
imperial courts' of the West.

Hungarians seemed more adept and self-assured in dealings with
the West than Romanians, and in the course of rediscovering their
patriotic feelings Hungarian Communists naturally made much
of their intention to bring the country back into the European
mainstream. One of the last acts of the Communist Government
was to move Hungary's celebration of the end of the Second World
War from April (when the Germans were driven out by the Red
Army) to May, the anniversary commemorated in the West. When
in March 1989 Prime Minister Miklos Nemeth introduced in Parliament the new constitution establishing Hungary as a multiparty
state he recommended it as 'an undertaking which can propel us,
again, into the vanguard of European development', while for his
Justice Minister 'Europeanness' meant no less than the 'pillars of
civilisation'. Europe was an old Magyar preoccupation. The literary
journals of the 1920s and 1930s were full of essays on Hungary's
rightful place as a European power. It was partly because of the
wish to exorcise centuries of Turkish rule. But it was also partly
self-reassurance for people who knew their roots went back to Asia,
and that much of their folk culture and pentatonic music remained
of the East. 'But our heads are Western,' added K., a Budapest
friend. The question was, would the West understand that? Some
thought not. A Hungarian sociologist writing after the defeat of the
Communists in the March 1990 elections sounded almost as bitter
about the West as the Romanian journalist, even if his language was
less melodramatic.

Most people think that returning to Europe means living standards similar to West Europe's but it is not true. Hungary will belong to the place where it is geographically, that is Central Europe. It is a better place than it used to be but not as good as people expect it to be . . . Compared to West Europe, East Europe will always be considered the world of dirt and dust, just as it was in the past.

Czechoslovakia was more self-confident – remember Valtr Komarek's boast to Soviet friends that his was an 'educated European nation' – but it was also divided by Europe, though less tragically than Yugoslavia. 'Slovakia ties us Bohemians and Moravians to the East, and keeps us apart from the West where we belong.' That was the opinion of a member of Charter 77 several years before there was any sign of the collapse of Czechoslovak Communism. The long-industrialised Czechs were used to thinking that Slovaks were economically and politically more backward. Slovakia's intense Roman Catholicism had not saved it from becoming during the war what R. W. Seton-Watson called a 'backwater of ignominy and subservience' in which the Presidency of Father Jozef Tiso 'brought dishonour upon the priestly cloth by his connivance with Nazi blood-lust' (fifty thousand Jews were deported from Slovakia under the Tiso Government). Slovakia was given a better deal by the Communists than the rest of the country after 1968, and there were mutterings in Prague that as a result Slovaks had not pulled their weight in the opposition movement. When a Slovak bishop unveiled a plaque to Tiso in the summer of 1990 Czech doubts about the suitability of Slovakia as partner in the return to Europe could only increase.

The idea of Europe, and being recognised as European, was pleasing to the pride of nations, most of them small and all of whom were inclined to see their history as a repetition of failures and defeats. Their self-esteem would be increased by 'joining Europe', just as a self-made businessman is gratified on gaining entry to a grandees' club. Although there were Poles and Hungarians who saw the new institutions of West Europe as a welcome window through which they could escape from stuffy rooms grossly over-furnished with national myths and prejudices, it is doubtful that most East Europeans felt that way once the Communists were out of power. Claudio Magris, writing about the countries along the banks of the Danube, remarks that while small nations have to shake off the indifference of those that are (for the moment) great they must also try to get rid of their own complex about being small.

> Those who have long been forced to put all their efforts into the determination and defence of their own identity tend to prolong this attitude even when it is no longer necessary. Turned inward on themselves, absorbed in the assertion of their own identity and intent on making sure that others give it due recognition, they run the risk of devoting all their energies to this defence, thereby shrinking the horizons of their experience, of lacking magnanimity in their dealings with the world.

Communism, the creed that was supposed to overcome national barriers through class solidarity, strongly reinforced the tendency of East Europe's nations to look inward. A Hungarian writer argued that for Hungary and its neighbours the nation had always been the 'basic value in life' because it had been under more or less permanent threat from greater powers. Four decades of Communism had strengthened this tendency to see the nation as 'a special value'. The Communists destroyed even that amount of social space, sometimes considerable, allowed by earlier rulers like Turks, Habsburgs and Russian tsars. Under these circumstances it was scarcely remarkable that the most striking quality of the Polish Church was not its social conscience, valuable as that would have been in an increasingly impoverished country, but its identification with the national cause. Only the nation was left, but most often as a sort of secret society which could never be properly acknowledged yet all knew to be there. The nation lived its life in language and memory, in pride and grief, but also at its most shadowy depths – because nothing could be brought for proper examination into decent light – in suspicion, hatred and prejudice. If the forty years since the end of the Second World War had been for West Europe a process of overcoming old antipathies by cooperating in a common beneficial cause, the opposite was the case in the East. The institutions of the Communist East, from the Warsaw Pact to Comecon, came increasingly to be seen by all except Communists, and eventually by a good many of them too, as forced participation in endeavours that damaged the national interest. If some prescient East Europeans waited for the collapse of Communism with trepidation it was because they feared that pent-up nationalism might be the only force capable of occupying the empty seats of power.

The question was why, if Milosevic had prolonged the life of
Serbian Communism by turning it into a national crusade, the
communist leaders of East Europe could not have done the same.
Of course they flirted with national sentiment. Soon after 1956
Janos Kadar brought back the pre-war Hungarian military cap as
Jaruzelski was to do later in Poland. Later Kadar won popularity
by negotiating the return of St Stephen's crown from the United
States. In the last year of their power the Hungarian Communists
tried to make amends for insufficient patriotism in the past by
allowing the old Hungarian coat of arms to replace the star-topped
version brought in by Kadar in 1957, though even that was meant
to be slightly more Hungarian than the original Soviet-style arms
of 1949. People took pleasure debating whether the new coat of
arms should be the simple version of the so-called Kossuth arms
displayed by the Magyar revolutionaries in 1848 or a more elaborate
one topped by the crown of St Stephen. Budapest pastrycooks
decorated their shops with huge marzipan crowns and coats of arms
while postcard sellers did a good trade with reproductions of old
prints showing the crowned Kossuth arms being carried to heaven
by angels. But none of this would persuade Hungarians of the
Communists' national credentials, for there were two important
differences between them (and the other Soviet-bloc Parties) and
the Serbian leader. Milosevic belonged to a Communist Party that
had come to power by its own efforts in a war of liberation (that it
was also a savage civil war was another matter). And when Milosevic
allowed Tito's reputation to be destroyed in Serbia he did not
damage his own claim to power but strengthened it, for he was
proving himself to be the 'good Serb' that Tito neither was nor
could have been. The opposite was true for the Communists of the
Soviet bloc. In their case it was Moscow that had put them in
power; to challenge Moscow's authority was to destroy their own
justification for staying there. The Bulgarian leader Todor Zhivkov
once remarked on a visit to the Soviet Union that it was 'always
a good thing to check one's watch with Moscow time'. East Europeans might have thought of a different metaphor: the best that
could be said for their Communist Parties was that they were
umbrellas, necessary to protect them from Soviet storms. But if
Soviet storms were no longer so terrible, or had been dispelled
completely by the Gorbachev sun, the Party-umbrella could
be thrown away. Even Ceausescu, although in his early years

playing a cryptic version of the Milosevic game, understood this. He never quite gave up the fiction of bloc solidarity based on proletarian internationalism and, as we have seen, even resorted to it in a quixotic attempt to keep Communism in power in Poland.

Who was to inherit these long-scorned nations, to care for them and tell them they were still beautiful? The recognised anti-Communist oppositions led by intellectuals whose names were known to the world were not in the business of playing up to national neuroses. On the contrary by their efforts to establish contacts among themselves, and which eventually linked East Berlin, Warsaw, Prague and Budapest, they were at last establishing common goals for nations that had never had much in common. They might not have completely agreed with Dr Johnson that patriotism was the last resort of scoundrels but they would have sympathised with his drift. Could such people really inherit nations that were bruised, uncertain, and eager for flattery after years of neglect? The answer was in some cases probably no, and there were even signs of this in the victory of the apparently saintly Solidarity in Poland's summer election.

BLAMING OTHERS

One morning shortly before the Polish elections three old Polish farmers were sitting in silent bad temper in a room off a muddy courtyard in Radom. It was a warm day but the most imposing of them, a rather frail figure in spite of fine Pilsudski moustaches, wore a dark brown suit, terracotta cardigan and tie. Jan Pajak, seventy-two years old, a Catholic father of five and grandfather of nineteen, owner of thirty acres and chairman of Rural Solidarity in Radom county, veteran of the Polish army's hopeless attempt to stop Hitler's invasion and then of the guerrilla Home Army under the codename 'Robak' ('Worm'), had unexpectedly found himself a rebel Solidarity candidate for the Senate. The story of how this personification of the Polish countryside Solidarity claimed as theirs found himself fighting against the man chosen to run for the Senate by Lech Walesa attracted little attention at the time. At elections, and at this election above all, one closed ranks, and Solidarity sent many of its stars to persuade the electors of Radom not to be deflected by the Pajak campaign. In truth the old man was something of a puppet. It was the forces and emotions behind him that deserved to be watched.

The immediate cause of the trouble in Radom was the literary critic Jan Jozef Lipski, a well known member of the opposition and co-founder of the Workers Defence Committee (KOR) that was set up to help workers and their families after the strikes of 1976. The food price rises of that year provoked protests throughout the country and some of the most violent were in Radom, where factory workers were joined by crowds in the street when they broke into the Party headquarters and raided its well-supplied restaurant before setting it alight. Four people died in the fighting that followed. Police beat up the strikers, some of whom were jailed while others lost their jobs. Radom had certainly not forgotten this in 1989. In 1981 the city had laid the cornerstone of a memorial to those who, in the inscription's words, had been 'crucified' after the workers' protest. Since then nothing had changed in the city according to the young man who was running Pajak's campaign and also doing most of the talking for him. The Communist Party headquarters remained the best painted building in the town 'and the best supplied with ham and cheese'. Why then did Solidarity in Radom not welcome Lipski as an old friend and supporter? The most obvious reason was that he called himself a socialist, albeit in the West European sense, and had helped revive the old Polish Socialist Party. This was difficult to stomach even for the people running Radom's official Solidarity campaign. Why, wondered its hard-pressed manager, had the leadership forgotten when picking Lipski that 'Polish society cannot distinguish between good and bad socialism; that it only knows one socialism, the bad sort it's had for the last forty years'? How, he asked, was he to run a campaign in which the four-man Solidarity ticket (two for the Sejm, two for the Senate) was split between 'three Christian candidates and one socialist'?

That a socialist of any kind could not be Christian was self-evident to the three farmers gathered in the little room whose only decorations were blurred pictures of the Saviour and the Virgin Mary. The other two sat immobile as Indian chiefs as Pajak explained that Walesa had too many advisers of 'socialist and atheist orientation' and so could not know what was going on outside Warsaw and Gdansk. He produced a well-fingered cutting from *Polityka*, and the old men nodded with approval as Pajak's manager read out some paragraphs that had been carefully edged in ink. Their gist was that the well-known Solidarity intellectuals Michnik, Geremek and Kuron had as boys been members of the Communist-sponsored Red Scouts, and at their meetings joined in singing Polish and Russian socialist songs. Later Michnik had contacts with Lipski, whom he called his spiritual father. Of course none of this was a secret in Warsaw where many intellectuals had been Party members in their youth, but it seemed damning evidence to these old farmers. Even if they had understood that Lipski himself was never a Communist Party member it would not have changed their opinion of him: it was enough that he called himself a socialist. It was not surprising that *Gazeta Radomska*, the local Catholic paper, had printed a photograph of the Bishop of Sandomierz and Radom with Pajak and the three official Solidarity candidates who were Catholics, while the Bishop had only agreed to receive Lipski, with no photographer present, because the latter had asked him to. Radom had for some years been home to a working men's ministry whose aim was to help Solidarity mothers during martial law but also to counter what one of the mission's young workers called 'the socialist stream in Solidarity that wants to institutionalise atheism'. Small wonder Pajak's manager seemed to think Lipski's worst crime was to present himself as a candidate on the eve of the arrival in Radom of a relic of St Kazimierz of Wilno, the city's patron saint. What business had a socialist in a town that was about to play host to a saint?

Pajak won enough support to force a second round of voting but Lipski got through on the second, which was not surprising, for whatever Catholic Radom's dislike of the so-called Solidarity socialists they had not turned away from Walesa. A schoolmistress working in the official Solidarity headquarters said the affair was all the more 'painful because we are united with Lech, he's our symbol, he is within us'. Even Pajak's angry young manager said he still felt the same about Walesa and did not regret having christened his son after him.

This feeling that Walesa and some of his most important advisers stood for different things did not break sufficiently into the open to unsettle the opposition's national campaign, and Solidarity's victory left unanswered the question of who and what had actually won. Radom was not the only place where questions were asked about who represented Solidarity and what it really stood for. The editors of *Gazeta Wyborcza* were relieved to have obtained for their first issue a statement by Cardinal Glemp saying that abortion should not be made a political issue, but there had been election meetings at which Solidarity candidates were asked their opinion on the matter, and also whether they and their children had been baptised. Solidarity's newspaper was not only independent of the Communist Party; it was that equally rare thing for Poland, a legal publication in no way sponsored by the Church, and there was some doubt whether either the bishops or the Polish public were ready for it. It was a disagreeable shock when Cardinal Glemp received on election eve the avowedly Catholic candidates who were competing against Kuron and Michnik, but it was not entirely unexpected either.

The truth was that Solidarity had never been a united movement with a common ideology. Its unity lay in opposition to the Communist regime; and to the world outside it had always seemed more liberal (in the political sense) than it really was. The fusion between intellectuals and workers that led to its creation was largely the work of men and women of leftish inclination who were keen to teach trade unionism to Polish workers. Some like Kuron and Geremek had once been Communist Party members; others like Michnik and Litynski came from families with strong left-wing traditions. But although Walesa took these men as advisers no one had ever doubted that his own politics, and probably those of most Polish working men, were a mixture of Polish and Catholic conservative instincts. The relationship between these advisers and Walesa had seldom been easy and even before martial law sighs were to be heard about the difficulty of working with him. 'Of course we need him as a symbol,' people said privately even then, 'but if only he would be just that. He has such an odd idea of democracy.' Later the criticism became sharper and more public. Walesa was as 'capricious as a beautiful woman', contemptuous of knowledge, convinced that he always knew best. Martial law and the years of Solidarity's illegality that followed served to press the disparate strains in the opposition together again. Those years also disguised the fact that much of Solidarity moved to the right in the 1980s, when Friedman, Hayek and other conservative authors became fashionable among intellectuals, and the tough attitude to Communism of President Reagan was valued as a contribution to the system's weakening. At the Round Table the union had still been represented by left-leaning economists who favoured wage indexation and workers' self-management, but they were growing out of touch with times that produced wall graffiti like 'Proletarians of the world, enrich your-selves!', and it was economic liberals who took all the key ministries in the Mazowiecki Government. Mazowiecki himself was and always had been a man of the centre right, which his supporters defined as a synthesis of national and Christian values combined with the conservative and liberal thought of the West. But there was another right wing, quickly visible in some speeches in the new Sejm, that was more traditionally Catholic and conservative, inclined to populist rhetoric and much more guarded in its attitude to the liberal societies of the West. None of this was very clear while the election was going on, for the key figure in Solidarity's campaign after Walesa himself was the social democrat-inclined Geremek. Once the polls were over Walesa's inclination for more conservative advisers became obvious and it was one of them who questioned whether Solidarity's left wing had any real Polish roots at all. Was it not just a reaction to the aberration of Polish Communism itself, an attempt to repair the irreparable? And once the Communist Party had lost power would not these opposition leftists lose their reason for existing?

Like the other nations of East Europe Poland emerged from its Communist experience facing growing impoverishment, with its national dignity and self-confidence impaired, and uncertain what its real capabilities were. That similar doubts and uncertainties had haunted East Europe before the war could only further darken the tones of this introspective mood. Writing after the June election Adam Michnik argued that the greatest threat to democracy in East Europe was no longer Communism but 'a combination of chauvinism, xenophobia, populism, and authoritarianism, all of them typical of great social upheavals'. If Solidarity and the Polish Church held firm, Poland should avoid the danger seen by Michnik, but what if one or the other wavered? These fears lay behind the open split in the summer of 1990 between Walesa and some of his best-known advisers and colleagues. After Michnik had accused the Solidarity leader of wanting to become 'monarch of a post-Communist empire', Walesa attacked Solidarity Parliamentarians, all of whom had been picked as candidates under his supervision, for trying to be 'guides set above us, above society'. They should watch out, he warned in an unnervingly demagogic turn of phrase, because just 'one blast from the miners or the farmers will blow all your regulations and documents into the dustbin'.

Doubts about the Church had surfaced even earlier. The election of Karol Wojtyla as Pope had been particularly welcome to those Polish intellectuals who saw it as a guarantee that the Church would not lapse into self-admiring Catholic nationalism but remain open to the rest of Europe. They wanted to believe that when Cardinal Wyszynski died Karol Wojtyla would be seen as the real new Primate of Poland. It did not work out like that; Cardinal Glemp, installed as Primate in his palace on Miodowa Street, almost turned the problem of a tiny Carmelite convent in the old Nazi extermination camp of Oswiecim-Auschwitz into an international controversy about the character of the new Poland. No one paid much attention when the nuns first acquired an old warehouse adjoining the camp wall in the mid-1980s. This was Poland, vocations for the contemplative orders were growing, and it was natural for existing convents to send off groups to found new ones. Nevertheless protests soon came from Jews abroad who said it was wrong for any faith to set up a house of prayer in a place where God had been shown to be silent, and particularly wrong for Catholics, a minority among the dead of Auschwitz and its twin camp Birkenau. That the nuns had also chosen a building where the Germans stored the poison gas that killed the camp inmates was seen as a further unpardonable error. Polish Catholics could not understand the Jewish theological objection about the muteness or absence of God, but in the end the hierarchy, respectful of the unique Jewish experience, agreed it would be better for the nuns to move to a 'centre of education, meeting, information and prayer' that would be built a few hundred yards away from the camp. The storm broke in July 1989 when American Jews tried to break into the Carmelite convent that by then had acquired a pretty garden of dahlias and roses, a neat white statue of the Virgin Mary, and a well-stocked vegetable patch. The Jews wanted to publicise the fact that no progress had been made in moving the nuns, which was true. They also brought out a side of the Polish Primate that had occasionally been glimpsed before. In a sermon preached on the eve of the fiftieth anniversary of the outbreak of the Second World War at the Jasna Gora monastery in Czestochowa, Glemp rebuked Jews for talking 'as a superior nation' to the Poles. Their protests about the convent were an infringement of Poland's 'hard-won sovereignty'; they should not use their 'power' over the foreign mass media to turn it into 'seedbeds of anti-Polonism'; and anyhow it was in Birkenau, not Auschwitz, that most Jews had died. The uproar that followed only made the Primate dig in his heels. He could not understand why the nuns should be moved, he told an Italian newspaper, for it was like going into another person's house and telling them to move a wardrobe. As for the Archbishop of Krakow, Cardinal Macharski, who had negotiated the agreement to move the nuns, he had acted 'a little too hastily' and the whole matter needed re-examination.

Anyone who cared to visit the offices of the Polish Episcopate in Warsaw discovered that Glemp was saying what many senior churchmen thought. A bishop, so upright and soldierly in bearing one expected to see campaign medals on his cassock, explained that moving the convent was a 'touchy business' because Poles remembered the days when 'Bolsheviks' and before them Nazis had driven nuns out of their convents. If the sisters were to move the planned few hundred yards what would the Jews demand next, for certainly they would not be satisfied. The world outside ought to understand the Polish emotions that had been aroused. 'We are a people who have long been humiliated. In our living memory there have been the Germans, then the Communists, and now when Poles are becoming aware they have their freedom again the Jews start with their requests – you may pray anywhere in your country except there, in Auschwitz.'

While waiting for the bishop his secretary, a curly-haired young priest with a face like unbaked bread, had wanted to debate the question of the best language in the world. He suggested Chinese – best by strength of numbers – but eventually settled for 'the language of the heart that needs no words'. Whether his bishop was or wanted to be fluent in that language seemed open to doubt. He had more pressing matters on his mind, above all Poland's dignity for which he, as one of the Church's generals, had campaigned so long. To ask for meekness from Poland's bishops now was perhaps as foolish as to expect it from Soviet marshals in the moment of their victory over Hitler.

The affair of the Carmelite convent worried reflective Poles. It was no secret that old Catholic prejudices lingered in some corners of the Polish Church, that there were parishes where one could buy anti-Semitic literature and sometimes that hoary fake, the Protocols of Zion. Polish Jews had tales to tell of anti-Semitism, and even of their children being attacked at school, 'because you Jews killed Jesus Christ'. Ten per cent of the pre-war population, and as much as forty per cent in Warsaw, there were now only a few thousand Jews in all post-Holocaust Poland. Until early 1989 there had not been a Chief Rabbi for over twenty years and the new incumbent, a survivor of wartime ghettos and extermination camps who found refuge in Israel, was only a temporary visitor. Yet during the election campaign anonymous leaflets had circulated attacking Solidarity candidates as Jews; many of Kuron's posters in Zoliborz had been defaced with the word 'Jew' or with Stars of David even though he wasn't Jewish. Here was a clue to both the logic and the emotions at work. Suspicion of the Jews was a symptom of much less well-targeted fears: of outside forces that threatened the nation's independence but were beyond its control; of internal forces that seemed always to rob true patriots, long-disfavoured, of the wealth and power that seemed at last within reach; of everything unusual and different that might threaten established ways of thinking, feeling and behaving; and, for those who were believers, of everything blasphemous that threatened the final security of faith. Such fears exist, more or less well-controlled, in all societies but in the peculiar historical and geographic soil of East Europe they had put down particularly strong roots. Whenever Poland was in crisis someone suggested that Jews were to blame. Communist hardliners had used this tactic in 1968, even daring to include the Minister of Defence on their list of crypto-Jews. Years later they still believed they had been justified, and in self-defence would ask rhetorical questions like, 'Can you imagine a Great Britain in which as many as eighty per cent of the most senior authorities were Irish?' The Polish security service regularly tried to pin Jewish origins on people they disliked. When the strikes began in the summer of 1980 the secret police spread rumours that the workers leading them had Jewish wives. No one doubted that they, too, were behind the whispering campaign directed against Kuron and other Solidarity candidates in 1989. In this they were remaining true to their unscrupulous selves, but they were also demonstrating a widespread belief that Poles were receptive to such whispers.

Old East European prejudices against Jews had been powerfully reinforced by a peculiarity of the Communist takeover in East Europe. The liberal economist Jan Winiecki remembers spending a holiday with his family in the Tatra Mountains soon after the Communists had come to power. The peasant who picked them up at the station in his cart pointed to a large well-lit house. 'It must be the Government,' he said, 'because they're Jews and they've been singing Russian songs.' The association of Jews with Communism began – in East European minds – at the Russian Revolution. In the short-lived Hungarian Council Republic of 1919 thirty-two of Bela Kun's forty-five Commissars had been Jewish. In a tiny pre-war Communist Party like the Romanian most of the leading members were Jewish or from Romania's German, Hungarian and Ukrainian minorities, and perhaps the oddest thing about the young Nicolae Ceausescu when he joined the Party in the 1930s was that he was a full-blooded Romanian. Discrimination against Jews and members of national minorities was common throughout East Europe so it was natural for some of them to be drawn into a political movement in which class, not race, became the test of salvation. The Jews of the newly independent Poland were pleased to have escaped from Tsarist rule, but they were still banned from the Polish army and civil service, and their numbers were also restricted in most professions (Poland's Ukrainian and Byelorussian minorities were arguably even worse off). It has been said that Hungary's Jews, well under ten per cent of the population at the beginning of the century, were 'hounded into success' as businessmen because it was one of few occupations open to them. One of the most astute, Manfred Weiss, magnate of the Budapest industrial suburb of Csepel, even became a baron and joined an archduke, a prince and a count as member of the quartet of Hungary's richest men. In the late 1930s, when Hungary moved closer to Nazi Germany, anti-Jewish laws were introduced that drove many Hungarian Jews out of their jobs, not only from the professions accessible to them but also from the businesses they had created.

It was not surprising that at the end of the war the Russians, needing reliable local Communists to execute their policies in East Europe, often picked members of the minorities or Jews (the situation was different in East Germany and Czechoslovakia, where the pre-war Parties were stronger and with more genuine national roots). In *The Seizure of Power*, his 1953 novel about the Communist takeover in Poland, Czeslaw Milosz imagines one Jew warning another against joining up with the Communists.

> If there's ever a change, the Poles will get their knives out and there won't be any Jews left. And why do you think they need people like

you? Because they haven't any others, any Poles? When they've trained enough new Communists they'll promote anti-Semitism on the quiet.

The Polish Communists who exploited anti-Semitism naturally preferred an argument more flattering to themselves; and it bore some resemblance to the one Milosevic would later use in Serbia although his enemy was Tito. It was, they said, the Jews and not Communism itself that had done so much damage to the Polish nation, while they as truly Polish Communists had always wanted to link themselves with national traditions.

East European reluctance to re-examine these fears in 1989 was compounded by guilt, often suppressed to the point of denial, about treatment of Jews during the war. Jews were not normally accepted into Poland's guerrilla Home Army, and even risked being hunted down by ultra-nationalist resistance groups. The misery of Jews at German hands in Nazi-occupied Poland has been well documented but a recent book (*I Remember Nothing More* by Adina Blady Szwajger, London 1990), describing the life in the Jewish resistance of a young woman who was able to operate outside the Warsaw ghetto only because she looked Aryan, is a particularly chilling reminder of how some Poles could not be counted on not to betray Jews. After a short while as a courier in Warsaw for ZOB, the Jewish Fighting Organisation, she wrote

> That is what everyday life was like: people, problems, forever running round – and fear. Already then there was fear. Every familiar face was hostile. The whole town, my town, my own town, that I had grown up in, was strange, hostile, and every corner I turned might be my last.

Yet forty-five years after the end of the war Poles could still be tempted to look for Jews as cause of their problems. The logic was simple: because there were problems there had to be Jews, even though in reality almost none existed any more. Two old men were overheard swapping complaints in Powazki Cemetery at the 1989 unveiling of the monument to the leaders of the Warsaw Uprising. They agreed that life was terrible and getting worse: 'but what else can you expect,' one asked the other, 'with all these Russian Jews running the country; these Jaruzelskis, Rakowskis, Kurons and Michniks?' It was a classic example of Communist being taken as a synonym for Jew because Michnik, the only one of Jewish parentage among the four, was also the only one never to have joined the

Party. No one should have been surprised that after the new Government's first painful measures people began asking whether Prime Minister Mazowiecki might not also be a Jew. One man in the street was convinced of it. It had its advantages, he thought, because Jews were clever; on the other hand the country deserved to have a truly Polish leader.

Nations that feel hard done by and that have survived against the odds are not inclined to have much pity for others. As G. liked to say, Communism had allowed Poles to indulge their old habit, acquired during years of foreign occupation, of blaming others while feeling free of sin themselves. Solidarity, as an opposition movement, had in some ways been a celebration of that sinlessness, a skilful composite of Christian faith and Polish patriotism that masked or ignored the more self-critical tendencies that the union also contained and that to a considerable extent were its brains. Once in power the opposition could not remain blameless. Its maturity depended on the readiness of its leaders to explain to Poles that freedom meant a chance to rejoin the company of ordinary human sinners.

COMPETITIVE SUFFERING

When the Hungarian Democratic Forum emerged as a political party in 1989 there was speculation, angrily denied by the Forum, that some of its members were anti-Semitic. 'What the hell,' was the comment of a worldly-wise Hungarian journalist. 'In this part of the world everyone is a bit anti-Semitic, including the Jews themselves.' Hungarian Jewry had learnt that a feeling for irony was a useful companion in life. Having done much to give the country a modern bourgeoisie and the economic skills associated with it, they were rewarded between the wars with the anti-Jewish laws that eventually banned not just marriage but even sexual intercourse between Jew and non-Jew. It was the Hungarian Jew's misfortune that, unable to be accepted as a *mely Magyar*, a 'deep Hungarian', in spite of cultural assimilation greater than in the rest of East Europe, he inevitably suffered as a result of the Hungarian misery and rage caused by the award of Transylvania to Romania under the 1920 treaty of Trianon. Hungarians blamed the loss of Transylvania on France in particular and the Western allies in general, and Jews were associated with both the Western ideas of parliamentary democracy and economic liberalism that much of the Hungarian élite had never cared for. Nevertheless, it was largely thanks to Admiral Horthy, no monster in spite of not being very bright, that while most of the Jews from the Hungarian provinces eventually died at German hands, a good many of those who had made up twenty per cent of pre-war Budapest's population were saved.

Horthy's decency counted for little in the first years after the war. Hungarians, who unlike the Romanians remained Germany's allies until the end, felt they had not only been defeated but also lost their independence. Jews returning to Hungary could suppose there had been a victory, but what did they find? In 1944, when Horthy had been forced to accept a fully Fascist Government, the houses and other property of all Jews were confiscated or plundered in what the Hungarian historian Victor Karady has called 'a sort of institutionalised looting'. The scene was set for further sadistic twists of fate in the story of the two peoples. According to Karady,

> Home-coming Jews were received in Hungary by silence, and not simply by silence, but by some sort of reproachful silence. Institutions, churches and various public bodies did not join them in their immeasurable mourning, on the contrary Jozsef Darvas for instance argued . . . that the sufferings of Jews were nothing special because the entire Hungarian nation had suffered under the old regime.

Darvas was a Communist writer and a post-war Minister of Culture, and if he was unapologetic towards the Jews it is not hard to imagine how non-Communist Hungarians felt: often dispossessed themselves; forbidden by the new Communist regime to mourn for the Hungarian dead lost fighting against Germany; belonging to classes and indeed a whole nation that Stalinism treated as Fascist, what pity did they have to spare for Jews? And what did the Jews who returned home do? The Communist Party needed their skills, for most of them were professionals or white-collar workers, while they themselves were naturally drawn towards any left-wing movement that was anti-Fascist. It is possible that these highly qualified Jews whom, unlike the old Hungarian professional classes, the new regime could trust, saved Hungary from some of the usual consequences of revolution, like the disruption of government services, but it earned them no thanks from ordinary Hungarians. They simply saw Jews occupying many high places, not least in the security service, under a hated 'foreign' regime. It counted for nothing that the Jewish Communists tried to destroy their own Jewishness. Silence at home – children were often not told they were Jews – was matched by silence in public, where for twenty years the Jewish question was very rarely discussed.

As the Communist regime grew weaker and weaker in the course of 1989 the Jewish issue took on a new but not unexpected form. Although Matyas Rakosi was the last Jew to head the Communist Party Jews remained an important element within it, not least in its cultural establishment. Gyorgy Aczel, the writers' Svengali and confidant of Kadar, was Jewish, as was Gyorgy Lukacs, the most celebrated of the world's Communist philosophers that still kept the faith. When Karoly Grosz rose to power the story went round that he began a talk to a group of Party officials with the words, 'My name is Karoly Grosz and I am not a Jew' (his father's family was in fact German). This would have appealed to those Party apparatchiks who felt they had to contend with a Jewish lobby within the Central Committee. It would also have appealed to a young Hungarian in his thirties who like so many others had joined the Party to further his career. Intelligent and well-travelled though he was, he saw Jews as a freemasonry within and without the Party. He believed Kadar had only been 'an expression of their interests', and that Jews were by definition unpatriotic and also out to frustrate the ambitions of all good Hungarian lads. Yet someone like himself had little chance outside the Party, even though the Jews were powerful within it.

This sense that the Jews, although numbering no more than 80,000, less than one per cent of the population, were an obstacle to the self-advancement of true Hungarians became one of the partly hidden issues of the March 1990 elections. The original Hungarian opposition, the intellectual dissidents who were in contact with the Solidarity thinkers and the Chartists of Czechoslovakia, included several extremely talented Jews, often the children of Jewish Communists. Miklos Haraszti's working-class Communist parents were among those Jews who, having fled Hungary to escape the Nazis, returned when the war was over. This opposition, apart from containing Jews, was also liberal (in the economic and political sense) and open to the West, the same qualities that pre-war Jews had been associated with, and disliked for, by those who saw themselves as upholders of Hungarian values. If in Poland the two chief tendencies within the opposition to Communism – Western democratic and Polish Catholic – could at first be contained within Solidarity, the two comparable Hungarian trends never had the same chance to come together. The Hungarian Democratic Forum became the obvious political home for anyone who believed that Hungarian independence would bring careers for every *mely Magyar* who had been discriminated against during the Communist years. It was inevitable that the Forum would be suspected of tacit anti-Semitism, and just as inevitable that the Forum would deny it. Nevertheless before the vital second round of the Hungarian elections – the Democratic Forum and Free Democrats were almost evenly placed after the first – Zoltan Biro, a Forum leader who had once been a Communist and remained close to Imre Pozsgay, wrote (in the Free Democrats' own newspaper) that the predominance of Jews in the Free Democrat leadership had a 'special significance' because the chief men of Bela Kun's Council Republic and of Rakosi's post-war regime had also been Jews. It was only to be expected, Biro wrote, that the presence of Jews at the top of the Free Democrats would awaken bad memories in people, 'memories of two national catastrophes'.

There was no doubt that Biro expressed the fears of the provincial intelligentsia of doctors, teachers and technicians who had either never been Communist or only for form's sake, and who saw the Democratic Forum as the entrance to public responsibility and power denied them by the Party apparat. The Forum's provincial candidates in the elections displayed a telling mixture of self-confidence and uncertainty. Delighted to have escaped the Communist world in which they felt, as one of them put it, that they were always 'running into a stone wall and life was a constant defeat', and proud of being able to speak up at last for their idea of Hungary, they were far from confident they would be able to cope with the modern world outside, from which Communism had so long shielded them. They were shy of rapid economic change that opened Hungary to the West because they feared this would benefit only the best educated and those with knowledge of foreign languages (which few of these younger Forum candidates possessed, for the Communist regime in the 1950s and 1960s had for political reasons discouraged the study of Western languages in spite of the suicidal implication this had for a nation trapped in what my friend K., who loved his native tongue dearly, called 'this prison of a language').

They used the word 'cosmopolitan' and when asked what it meant said 'those who are a minority, who are alien to the nation', people who were Hungarian but had given up their national character, 'neither Hungarians nor Jews' but a 'layer' different from the majority. By this of course they meant the Free Democrats, or at least their leaders. In Debrecen in eastern Hungary, a centre of both Hungarian tradition and Hungarian Calvinism, a doctor who was a Forum candidate explained that while Free Democrats 'say the homeland is where life is good, we say that life must be good where the homeland is'. The Jews – the doctor used the word for the first time – had as many homelands as there were countries in the world but Hungarians had only one (the latter sentiment was developed by the nineteenth-century romantic poet Mihaly Vorosmarty into a celebration of Hungary as unique cradle and if need be tragic grave, a poem that became a second anthem and was once more frequently sung at public meetings). The danger, the doctor said, could not be greater: the Free Democrats had to be stopped in these elections because this, after 1919 and 1945, was the third attempt by the Jews to seize power in Hungary.

There were one thousand Jews in Debrecen. Before the war there had been twenty times as many, and they had twenty synagogues to pray at. In 1990 there were just two synagogues left, and the biggest, a late nineteenth-century building lugubriously painted in beige, brown and orange, was only used on holidays when seldom more than half its four hundred seats were filled. It was an ageing Orthodox community, looked after by a solid young rabbi from Israel who had been an army chaplain, with a kosher butcher and baker, and a centre next to the big synagogue where people could have lunch at tables laid with handsome white cloths. The last thing to be expected from the old men talking with the rabbi there was surprise at anti-Semitism. Orthodox Jews, one of them said, had never been assimilated in Hungary whereas reformed Jews had 'and thought they would be safe'. He shrugged, though whether at the sadness or stupidity of the idea was difficult to tell. As long as there were Jews there would be anti-Semitism: that was the rabbi's opinion and the others nodded. None of them were the least surprised that a local newspaper had printed articles blaming Jews for all the problems and mistakes in Hungary over the past forty years, from the excessive weight of school satchels to each lost football match.

How was one to link these wry ghosts left behind by one of the most productive Jewish communities in Europe with the fears of the doctor and his friends who saw power once more about to be snatched from the hands of good Hungarians by brilliant multilingual Jews? It was not, perhaps, so difficult. Jews were not the problem. It was the uncertainty of a new generation of would-be Hungarian leaders who had not yet had a chance to test themselves in power, and who realised they were provincials in the increasingly international world of the other Europe to the West. The uncertainty was all the stronger because it repeated the guarded attitudes of a more traditional world towards the powerful and potentially subversive cultures of West and Central Europe that had been common in the politics of pre-war Hungary and other East European countries. When crowds gathered in front of Parliament in Budapest on 23 October 1989, the day the new non-Communist Hungarian Republic was declared, they heard speeches full of self-congratulatory patriotic phrases expected on such occasions but at the end they sang the national anthem as mournfully as ever, without any sense of elation or, it seemed, of hope. The twentieth century had taught Hungarians the frailty of hope, and they did not approach the March elections with the *élan* that might have been expected from a nation at last given the chance to vote freely. But there was no doubt that the Forum was the party with the best claim to represent the nation, for its support was well-balanced between town and country, age groups and occupations. That it also did better in the tradition-minded counties of the east than in western ones more exposed to Europe came as no surprise.

A country that for many years had little control over its destiny and is unsure of its ability to flourish under new conditions of freedom holds on to old heroes and idols as though they are mantras whose potency depends on their form never changing. Traditions from the Church-controlled education of the nationalist pre-war decades had survived and it was considered inappropriate to recall such matters as the syphilis that contributed to the death of poets like Vorosmarty and Endre Ady. It was only to be expected that a veil was drawn over a brilliant but eccentric poet called Janos Vajda who, ignored in his lifetime, made a bequest on his death to the Hungarian Academy of Sciences of the collection of glass bottles in which over many years he had each day sealed his faeces. The summer of 1989 saw a classic reaction to an attempt to re-adjust the myths surrounding the greatest hero of all, Sandor Petoefi, poet of uncontested genius and revolutionary of irresistible charm. Having touched off the Revolution of 1848 Petoefi was to die on the battlefield at the age of only twenty-six, his body then thrown into a common grave from where it was never recovered. Petoefi's invocatory poem to the National Assembly summoned after the Revolution was read at the opening of the new democratic Parliament of 1990 and with its image of a homeland that had ceased to exist but 'whose name wanders among us like a ghost' was a perfect evocation of a country on the brink of recuperation from the Communist experiment. It was thanks to Petoefi, noted Paul Ignotus, that 'Hungarians thereafter could hardly conceive of a social reform movement, let alone a war of independence, not inspired by a poet'. That Petoefi had died at the hands of the Tsarist Russian troops added to the poet's allure for a nation under Soviet domination.

But what if Petoefi had not died a soldier's death; if he had been taken as a prisoner to Russia, later to be exiled to a distant settlement in Siberia where he married the postmaster's daughter, fathered a son, and even wrote poems in Russian? The man bold enough to advance this subversive theory was a self-made manufacturer of boilers called Ferenc Morvai, a type only possible in the semi-reformed Hungary of the late Kadar period. Morvai's suggestion scandalised the well-developed Petoefi industry in Budapest, partly because it was a boiler-maker who had dared disturb the perfect hero's memory, partly because Morvai had the gall to pay for an expedition to Siberia that turned up a grave with a skeleton whose measurements seemed to match what was known of the living Petoefi. To judge by letters in the Budapest press ordinary Hungarians were no less enraged. Petoefi was such a perfect patriot, wrote one, that if he had been taken to Russia alive he would if necessary have crawled home on his knees. How could he have given up the fight against the Russians? How could the sublime Petoefi have lived in a wretched Russian village 'looking after post horses and repairing leaky gutters'? How could he have remarried after warning his wife that his ghost would grieve if she married again after his death (which in fact she did, and was fiercely criticised for it)? If the boiler-maker carried out his plan to bring this skeleton back to Hungary, another reader warned, there could only be 'a funeral in the souls of all Hungarians'.

Morvai's theory was not original, for the Horthy regime had

rejected a previous version of the poet's Russian exile, and in the end it seemed probable that the body in the Siberian grave was a woman's, as the critics had maintained from the start. But the uproar showed that Hungary was in no state to have its legends tampered with, as some Hungarian commentators well understood. The nation's heroes had been kept alive in legends that were stronger than facts, a journalist wrote, and 'if it were not so we would long ago have lost the ground from under our feet, because our history would have had no chief players who would not have turned out to be different'. Perhaps the poet had died in Siberia, but it was unimportant because people wanted him to die on the battlefield. 'These are beautiful fairy tales which cannot be denied . . . and facts have nothing much to do with them.' Morvai stood as an independent candidate in the March elections from Petoefi's birthplace of Kiskoros. During the course of the campaign he was ambushed and beaten up. He did not win.

Apprehensive of the future, Hungary was in danger of falling back into the patterns of a past furnished with legends. There was one particular temptation that was as dangerous as it was powerful. Just as most Hungarians wished to keep their shining image of Petoefi so they clung to the belief that the loss of Transylvania in 1920 represented an unparalleled wrong. 'Hungary protected the West from the Turks for a thousand years, yet was raped at Trianon. It was the greatest injustice of the twentieth century, as bad as giving Paris to Germany.' Many, perhaps most Hungarians would have agreed with the conservative politician who said that in 1990, but where did the injustice lie? Pre-Trianon Hungary was co-ruler of one of the European land empires that finally collapsed at the end of the First World War. As part of the Habsburg dual monarchy Hungary had ruled over a population of almost twenty million people, of whom only half were Hungarian. The remainder included almost three million Romanians in Transylvania, two and a half million Serbs and Croats and nearly two million Slovaks. Hungarian policy towards its subject peoples had grown increasingly repressive at the end of the nineteenth century. Most Romanian Transylvanians were peasants and as such barred from voting. Romanian-language education was restricted and advanced education could only be had in Hungarian. Yet the Romanians had been a majority in Transylvania at least since the eighteenth century, and when in the chaos at the end of the war they took matters into their own hands they were joined by the important German minority in voting for an autonomous Transylvania within a Greater Romania. Nevertheless if the collapse of the Austro-Hungarian empire was inevitable and Romania's claim to Transylvania from the demographic point of view strong, Hungary did have reason to feel hard done by. Trianon left it with a population of seven and a half million, almost all full-blooded Hungarians, while nearly half as many Hungarians were left behind in Transylvania and what became the new states of Czechoslovakia and Yugoslavia. Many of the Hungarian settlements in Slovakia were divided from the motherland only by the Danube. In Transylvania, though, the areas of most concentrated Hungarian population lay 170 miles east of the new border and neither then nor now was there any practicable way to include them in Hungary.

Transylvania is one of those parts of the world destined by its history, culture and beauty to be the cause of conflict. Hungarians rightly argued that it had played a vital part in their civilisation, but Romanians could also claim it as the cradle of their national revival in the eighteenth century. Up till that time national distinctions counted little. It was a Romanian Vlach from Transylvania, known in Romania as Iancu of Hunedoara, but called Janos Hunyadi by Hungarians, who became Hungary's regent and father of Hungary's great Renaissance king Matthias Corvinus. Istvan Szechenyi, one of the nineteenth-century creators of modern Hungary, wrote that there was scarcely a Magyar

> who is not transformed into a madman and even more or less deaf to the laws of fairness and justice, whenever the question of our language and nationality is raised.

Nevertheless Latin, the language of the court of Corvinus, remained the language of administration within the Hungarian kingdom till the early nineteenth century, when Budapest's attempts to substitute Hungarian provoked opposition from non-Hungarians. When the Soviet secret police chief Ivan Serov told Sandor Kopacsi, head of the Budapest police during the 1956 uprising, that he was going to have him hanged, the Hungarian cried out 'Vae victis', 'Woe to the defeated', to show the Russian he was dealing with an educated man (the point was lost on Serov who did not understand). Today educated Hungarians still use Latin tags more often than their counterparts in Germany or Britain. Nevertheless people have a selective devotion to their history, and in this century Hungarians have thought less about their multinational, though feudal, past but obsessively about the more recent times of avowedly Magyar empire. Hungary's ruling class failed to reflect on the social, political and economic changes that made the loss of their land empire inevitable, and spent the 1920s and '30s manoeuvring to recover it. Travelling through Hungary in the early 1930s Patrick Leigh Fermor found that the very mention of Romania made his well-bred Magyar hosts 'boil over'. They warned him not to go to a country full of crooks and robbers where 'whole valleys are riddled with VD' (anyone planning to visit Romania before and after Ceausescu's death were likely to hear equally lurid warnings in Budapest). As for the noble Hungarian families of post-Trianon Transylvania, Leigh Fermor found them living in a 'backward-looking, a genealogical, almost Confucian dream and many sentences ended with a sigh'. Should one wonder, then, at the Hungarians' extraordinary romance with the British press baron, Lord Rothermere, who in 1927 wrote an article in the *Daily Mail* headlined 'Hungary's Place in the Sun' to support Hungarian claims to Transylvania and the other lost lands. Hungary, Rothermere wrote, was a country of ancient traditions and 'not to be treated like a newly formed Balkan state of upstart institutions and inexperienced politicians' – an obvious dig at Transylvania's new ruler, Romania. Budapest named a street after the British peer; a Hungarian composer wrote a Rothermere march; and numerous organisations, among them the Industrial Society of Coffee House Keepers, dispatched finely illuminated addresses of thanks to the *Daily Mail*. A movement began to give Rothermere the Hungarian crown but with the emergence of Hitler a more promising partner seemed at hand. Like Hungary a 'victim of Versailles', Germany's revanchist aims were a perfect match for Hungary's and in the two Vienna Awards of 1938 and 1939 Hitler allowed Budapest to recover part of southern Slovakia with a Magyar majority, northern Transylvania with a Romanian majority, and a piece of the Carpatho-Ukraine with scarcely any Hungarian population at all. Seldom has there been a more disastrous triumph, and by 1945 only ghosts remained of what was once the Admiral's Kingdom.

Hungarian Communists believed that silence was as correct a cure for Magyar territorial nostalgia as for Hungarian anti-Semitism.

Kadar also feared Moscow might exploit the Transylvanian question in its subterranean feud with the independent-minded Ceausescu, and he did not wish either himself or Hungarian emotions to be exploited for this purpose. Transylvania thus remained the most heavily censored of all sensitive issues, and nothing could be published about it in Hungary without the permission of the Central Committee. The Party realised too late the damage this was doing to their claim to be a legitimate national leader and last-minute attempts to repair it – even to the extent of fuelling rumours in 1989 that Ceausescu was acquiring nuclear missiles for use against Hungary – achieved nothing. The failure of the Communist attempt to destroy old national emotions became plain during Hungary's March elections when some conservative candidates were happy to admit they considered the Vienna Awards to have been just, and that they could not imagine Transylvania except as part of Hungary.

Hungarians interpreted Ceausescu's plan to 'systematise' the villages of Romania (in fact only a few villages were touched before he died) as the last, mortal attack on the Hungarians of Transylvania whose minority rights had been whittled away by the Government in Bucharest over a period of thirty years. Many of the Hungarian communities were in hilly country untouched by large-scale collectivisation and the villages with their handsome old churches and peasants who still observed old customs made the region all the more precious to Magyars because such things scarcely survived in the plains of Hungary after forty years of socialist modernisation. After Ceausescu died Hungarians were impatient to believe that the condition of their Transylvanian brothers and sisters would inevitably improve, only to plunge into despair at the first sign that national tensions had survived the dictator's fall.

When the March elections formally swept the Hungarian Communists from power no responsible political leader, regardless of how strongly he felt about Transylvania, admitted to revanchist aims. 'The question,' said a Free Democrat in a typical formulation of the problem, 'is not where the borders are but what they look like.' If Romania became a proper democracy, giving Transylvanian Hungarians free access to the motherland and assured minority rights the problem would fade away, or so optimists hoped. But there were other voices to be heard. On the eve of the Hungarian elections the distinguished Budapest journalist Pal Bodor, born in Transylvania and a rare impartial expert on Romanian affairs, could imagine a more gloomy future. The next century, he speculated, might be the 'century of fundamentalists – fundamentalists of language, religion and race. If there is another world war it could well be something as irrational as one between blue-eyed and brown-eyed people.' Hungarians and Romanians were trapped in each others' insecurity, in the bitterness of their past defeats, and in the conviction that their greater suffering gave them the strongest claim to have ancient wrongs corrected in their favour. Hungarian unhappiness about Transylvania was bound to contribute to the weakening of a Communist regime that could not admit such passions were legitimate. The ordinary Hungarian believed that Hungary's survival depended on the well-being of the more than three million Hungarians outside the national borders as well as of those within. It was to be expected that others would forget this; but all the more reason why the Hungarians should, as the Serb poet said, 'sing and remember' themselves. But the Communists had neither sung nor remembered and for that reason opposition in Hungary was not so much a matter of an alternative *polis*, of alternative structures as imagined by dissident philosophers, for such things scarcely existed in a country where outright dissent had been rare. In Hungary opposition was lodged in an alternative nation, the real (though invisible, because it lacked means of self-expression) nation as opposed to the mock one of international proletarian solidarity that Communists celebrated in slogans that Vaclav Havel mocked as 'friendship for fences'. It was this alternative, or real, nation that also held the key to the revolutions soon to come in the rest of East Europe, not least in East Germany where many people only came to understand this slowly, and with considerable pain.

9

Deutschland, Einig Vaterland

ESCAPE

On 3 September 1989 Christoph Demke, Evangelical Bishop of Magdeburg, just back from family holidays in Bulgaria, sent a letter to the clergy of his diocese that only a few weeks earlier he would not have dreamed of writing. Many of them, he wrote, would have returned home to find friends and colleagues missing. Like him they would have heard reports of the growing number of East Germans leaving for the West. Yet when they picked up East German newspapers, or watched the TV news on *Aktuelle Kamera* what did they find? 'A few bad-tempered reactions' and an attitude of

> 'Everything is in order here; it is others who are at fault.' Not a word of what is to be heard in conversations even between strangers in the trams and shops, namely the worried question, 'Where are we drifting to?'

Some six thousand East Germans had illegally crossed the frontier between Hungary and Austria when Bishop Demke sat down to write his pastoral letter. Another fifty thousand had emigrated legally to the West in the first six months of the year. Tens of thousands more were still on summer holiday somewhere in East Europe and it seemed probable that many of them too would eventually head for the border to the West. Three thousand had already made their way to Hungary where, having applied for the West German passports to which the law of the Federal Republic entitled them, they were waiting in refugee camps organised by

Bonn's embassy in Budapest. Many of them were young couples; some were even on their honeymoon. For the most part skilled workers, they were the sort of people who saw they had a chance to make a decent life in the West, and nothing more to hope for in the East. Their attitude was that their parents had wasted their lives believing there would one day be a change for the better, but they were not going to be caught in the same trap.

All the Communist regimes of East Europe as they approached their end survived on inertia. They were like ocean liners whose captain and senior officers refuse to notice that the engines have almost stopped and fires broken out below decks, while the crew is scared or passive and the passengers helpless. The difference in East Germany was that the more agile passengers now had a chance to escape. West Germany was standing by as always: the novelty was that Hungary had provided rafts and lifebelts with which to reach it safely. It was typical of East Berlin's loss of contact with reality that it failed to foresee the consequences of Hungary's announcement in May 1989 that it was going to dismantle the defences along its frontier with Austria. The East German regime assumed this only meant pulling down some barbed wire, and that Hungary would continue to patrol the border and observe its 1969 agreement not to allow East German citizens to leave Hungary without valid visas for a third country – in other words go on helping prevent East Germans escaping to the West. Goodness knows what reports the East German embassy in Budapest was sending back to Berlin, for by midsummer the Hungarian Government was plainly pursuing newly re-discovered national interests and actually relishing each occasion when these clashed with the interests of the hardline members of the Soviet bloc. The summer had seen several quarrels between Prague and Budapest. Hungary's belated decision to suspend work on the Nagymaros dam brought reproaches and counter-claims from the Czechoslovaks. Hungarian TV broke the old Soviet-bloc rule of silence about each other's internal problems by broadcasting interviews with Vaclav Havel and Alexander Dubcek. And when two Hungarians were arrested in August for taking part in the Prague demonstration on the anniversary of the 1968 Soviet invasion of Czechoslovakia, the Budapest media turned them into heroes and a protest sit-in was begun to general applause outside the Czechoslovak embassy in Budapest.

'Prague,' a Budapest newspaper wrote, 'fears the democratic

changes in Hungary as a devil fears incense.' The tone of delight was unmistakable, and not only in the comments of journalists. True, there was some concern that Hungary was in danger of provoking an anti-Budapest alliance similar to the pre-war Little Entente of Czechoslovakia, Romania and Yugoslavia (all countries that then feared Hungarian revanchism), though now the Yugoslavs had been replaced by the East Germans. But even that prospect was not entirely undesirable. It was proof that Hungary was running its own affairs again, and in fact not much danger was involved. Each East German or Czechoslovak attack made the West more favourably disposed to Hungary and the West was Hungary's main interest now, a point Budapest made with its enthusiastic welcome for President Bush in July. As for Moscow, the Hungarian Government knew that their conservative critics would get no sympathy from Gorbachev. Asked at the end of August if he was worried that Hungary might become isolated, Foreign Minister Gyula Horn admitted the possibility existed but went on to say that it 'should not divert us from our selected political course, as it would infringe on our freedom of action'. This was no surprise coming from Horn, an ingenious diplomat and outspoken Pozsgay-style reformer who had come to accept that Hungary could only be saved by scrapping the old socialist system and replacing it with Western-style democracy.

By August the flight of the young East Germans had become a major preoccupation of the regime in East Berlin. It was obvious that the Hungarian patrols were not trying very energetically to stop East Germans getting into Austria. The Hungarian public, which saw East Berlin as an enemy of change, entirely approved, and was much enjoying stories like the one about a border guard who took an East German mother and her baby home so his wife could change the child and help with the breast-feeding. The East German Politburo knew that another 120,000 of its citizens had applied to leave the country for the West. Secret tests of public opinion suggested growing disillusion among the young, and among citizens in general a declining sense of common interest with the East German state. Most of this information came from Egon Krenz, the Politburo member responsible for internal security and who at fifty-two was both the youngest member of the leadership and Honecker's most likely successor. Krenz did not dare show Honecker all the raw material on popular discontent but there is no reason to suppose anything would have changed if he had. The old man dominated the Politburo and, as the next few months were to show, was already past the stage where he could alter ideas or policies to meet new circumstances. In the middle of August Honecker was unexpectedly forced to go into hospital for a gall-bladder operation and he appointed Günter Mittag, the Central Committee secretary responsible for the economy, to chair the Politburo in his absence. In spite of having lost a leg as a result of diabetes Mittag was an energetic dictator of the economy, notorious for his rages against subordinates unwise enough to suggest his policies might be mistaken, and himself careful never to let any but prettified statistics reach Honecker's desk. It was hard to imagine a man less well-equipped – unless it was Honecker himself – to cope with the bomb that Hungary was about to explode.

Negotiations between Hungary and East Germany over the fugitives in Budapest reached their climax on 31 August when Horn flew to East Berlin for talks with his opposite number Oskar Fischer. A more ill-matched couple was hard to imagine. Fischer had for many years served a state whose identity was supposed to derive from class rather than nationality. The Hungarian had become spokesman of a classic nation and thus a dangerous spoiler of the laboriously preserved decencies of the Soviet bloc. Did Fischer anticipate the likely consequence of his refusal to guarantee that, if Hungary sent the escapees back to East Germany, they would eventually be given permission to leave legally? It seems not. Having heard the German out, Horn said that in Hungary's view the United Nations convention requiring free passage for refugees accepted by a third country overrode the 1969 agreement to turn East Germans back from the Austrian border. Hungary therefore had no choice but to open the border and let the East Germans pass into Austria and West Germany beyond. At this point, according to Hungarian accounts, Fischer turned white as chalk and clutched the arms of his chair, but all he could offer as an objection was 'that wouldn't be very nice of you'. Since neither Mittag in a meeting with Horn the same day nor Honecker in a telegram sent later from hospital to the Hungarian leadership would give the necessary guarantee on the fugitives' right to leave East Germany, Hungary opened the border on 11 September. Within hours 20,000 East Germans had crossed to the West. Honecker would later call it a betrayal. 'We trusted [the Hungarians] but they betrayed us and did not inform anyone, not even the Soviet Union.'

This simple act had immediate and dramatic results. At one stroke it destroyed the ecology of the Soviet bloc which depended on each member being prepared to do the other's police work for it when necessary. The consequences were particularly dire for East Germany because it was a different sort of country, indeed scarcely a country at all but an idea maintained by determination, the readiness to use force in its defence, and ever-increasing amounts of self-deception. The border dividing Europe was originally supposed to be like the one between Poland and the Soviet Union that so impressed the young Erich Honecker when he crossed it on his first visit to Moscow in 1930. The moment when Red Army soldiers replaced the Polish border guards on the train had for him, he would say later, 'immense symbolic force'. He understood that this was no ordinary border but a 'state frontier of a quite special kind' separating capitalism from the new socialist world. By 1989 it was obvious that East Germany's border with the West was of a particularly 'special kind'. Hungary and Czechoslovakia would remain on the map if their frontiers ceased to be socialist, but what would happen to East Germany? Could East Germany survive as other than a socialist state? Otto Reinhold, East Berlin's leading theoretician, had asked and answered that question in August, 'What right to exist would a capitalist German Democratic Republic have alongside a capitalist Federal Republic? None, of course.' East Germany's existence depended on it remaining socialist and that meant preserving, in Reinhold's words,

The political power of the working class . . . the leading role of the Marxist-Leninist Party, social ownership of key means of production, social direction and planning, and the dominance of socialist ideology.

Communism was East Germany's nationalism, its reason for existing. East German dissidents and churchmen would not have accepted all Reinhold's formulation, but even most of them agreed that East Germany had to be different, preserving a modified form of socialism with a German face. It was only to be expected that the frontier between East and West Germany should be designed to instil in people the same awe that Honecker felt crossing into the infant Soviet Union. The elaborate system of watchtowers, fences, and open strips served as a decompression chamber to accustom travellers to the different air on the other side. Naturally the

Communist Government would control closely all who came and went across this frontier, although under pressure from West Germany on whose economic assistance East Germany had come increasingly to depend, and also in an attempt to calm growing discontent at home, the regime had begun to ease its travel controls. In 1988 a record 1.2 million East Germans under retirement age (pensioners could travel freely) visited West Germany. The same year the Government took the daring step of publishing the secret regulations that laid down who was and who was not allowed to visit relatives in the West. Letting more people go to West Germany on temporary visits was supposed to diminish people's wish to leave the German Democratic Republic altogether, but it did not work out that way.

The number of those getting out for good had begun to increase in the mid-1980s and in 1988 reached almost 40,000. Three-quarters of these went through the intentionally laborious business of applying for official permission, while most of the rest escaped through third countries. Only 589 managed to escape across the East German border itself. A further 1,094 were political prisoners bought out by West Germany, a practice that had gone on for years, though the prices had risen, an East German scientist or doctor costing over $50,000 by 1989. (One of the accusations later made against Honecker was that the money from these sales was kept in a West Berlin bank account over which he had sole control.) In September, when Hungary opened its border with Austria, it seemed likely that 1989 would see as many as 100,000 East Germans leaving with or without permission, a number approaching the intolerable annual exodus before the Berlin Wall had gone up under Honecker's supervision in 1961. The quality of those who were leaving hurt as much as their number, for most were skilled workers or professionals whose departure had already begun to affect the work of factories, hospitals and schools.

The East German Politburo learned of Hungary's intention to open the border at its meeting on 5 September. Perhaps because Honecker was not present the ghastly news stirred its members into what one member later confessed was their first discussion in which unfavourable developments were not just blamed on the incompetence of an industrial manager or the 'laziness of a minister' but laid at the door of the system itself. The unusual debate continued until its sacrilegious nature proved too much for the regime's overseer of ideology, Kurt Hager, and he brought it to an end it with the remark that it was unseemly to discuss such matters in the absence of the General Secretary. The leadership's agony was increased by the approach of 7 October, the fortieth anniversary of the founding of the German Democratic Republic. Honecker's pride demanded that this celebration to which he attached so much importance go smoothly, and he was understandably furious at the foolish and ungrateful citizens who threatened to spoil the occasion by their flight. It was to remove another scandal that might disturb the coming celebrations that Honecker agreed at the end of September that 2,500 East Germans who had taken refuge in the West German embassy in Prague should be allowed free passage to the West. In fact East Europe had reached that dangerous stage when developments in one country were threatening to affect events in the others and the Czech regime, worried about the mood of its own people, was itself keen to get rid of the troublesome young East Germans before their bad example became contagious.

At this moment Honecker's arrogance led him into two mistakes. He could not let the escapees go without letting the world know what he thought of them and he had the official East German news agency publish a commentary reviling them for having 'trampled moral values with their feet' and adding – in words chosen by Honecker – that no tears deserved to be shed over their going. These remarks offended not only those East Germans like Bishop Demke who were anxious about where the country was heading but also rank-and-file Party members who knew how sour the national mood had become. The second error was Honecker's belief that the evacuation from Prague could be handled in a way that preserved East German dignity. Instead of letting them go straight to West Germany Honecker, against the advice of Politburo colleagues, insisted that the three trains be routed conspicuously via Dresden so that the escapees could be duly stripped of their citizenship during the passage through East Germany. It was to be Honecker kicking them out, not their leaving of their own accord. When Hans Modrow, the Dresden Party leader, learnt of this plan he at once saw its 'madness' and rang the Minister of Transport to ask him to stop it, but a mere Minister counted for nothing in such matters. Modrow's worst fears were realised when the three trains passed through the main Dresden railway station on the night of 4 October. Thousands of people tried to board them but were driven away with considerable brutality by riot police. The fighting continued on and off for the next two days in the worst violence of the East German revolution. Over 1,300 arrests were made.

The battle of Dresden was an important lesson for Modrow, the man already spoken of as a possible East German Gorbachev. By Modrow's own admission he was still in the grip of old *Feindbilder*, preconceptions about the 'enemy', when the Dresden riots began, and did not at first realise how badly the police had over-reacted. But within a very few days the experience led him to establish a working relation with Church and opposition leaders in Dresden. From that moment the city saw no more violence and it was only a matter of days before Modrow and other local Party and Government leaders were walking at the head of one of the huge demonstrations that had become a weekly event in Dresden and many other East German cities. Without yet knowing it, East Germany had found the man who would keep the country calm while Communism, and Modrow's own last remaining illusions and *Feindbilder*, collapsed. The other lesson of the Dresden riots was that Hungary's decision to open its border had altered the balance of power within East Germany. By persisting in their determination to get out of the country the East Germans had at last acquired the whip hand over their Communist masters. East Germany's crisis would be driven to its resolution by the proven readiness of its citizens to desert if the pace of change failed to live up to their expectations.

A GERMAN DREAM

In the months that have passed since the collapse of East German Communism, much has been spoken and written about its iniquities and incompetence. Extraordinary levels of pollution, which before were virtually a state secret, are now measured and published daily in local newspapers. The viciousness and all-pervasiveness of the Ministry for State Security has been documented, and the frightening length of its reach demonstrated by stories like that of Wolfgang Schnur, the civil rights lawyer who became leader of Democratic Awakening, one of the new East German political parties allied to Chancellor Kohl's Christian Democrats, before it was learnt that he was an old Stasi informer. Günter Mittag is said to have told Honecker, 'Erich, I'm going to make this country into a second Japan' – and the old man believed him. Yet Honecker's boasts about East German labour productivity and other economic achievements were shown to be nonsense when East German industry and farming almost collapsed upon union with the West. Why was it, then, that many intelligent and concerned non-Communist East Germans at first believed their country could still become the fulfilment of a dream, and what they usually called a socialist dream at that?

The explanation lay in the nature of the dream. At its heart was the desire for a German state free of German guilt. East Germany, with all its faults, was supposed to be that state, hence the growing apprehension when it seemed to be losing the battle to survive. An old Party member was not just speaking for Communists when in December 1989, alarmed like so many others by the speed of change, he broke into a lecture on German recidivism, on the ineradicably dangerous nature of the German people. He feared that Germans were once again showing they were incapable of learning from the past; that they were heading for another Weimar Republic and goodness knows what worse disasters beyond. It was an awful thing to say, he concluded, but perhaps Winston Churchill was right and Germans only knew how to creep or to dominate. The middle ground of responsible nationhood could never be theirs.

The East German regime successfully transferred a good deal of the fear of what it meant to be German onto West Germany. Its anti-Western propaganda was not very different from that used by other East European Communists but its audience, because it was German, was more receptive. As a result many East Germans who were neither Communists nor even thought of themselves as anti-Communist displayed what might be called classic leftist instincts and reactions. The Evangelical Church (which included both Lutherans and Calvinists) was particularly prone to this, and even the cleverest of its clergy sometimes found themselves drawn into ludicrous positions as a result. The young Wittenberg pastor Friedrich Schorlemmer was a courageous critic of the regime whose twenty theses, delivered to a regional synod in 1988, represented one of the most daring programmes for change that ever came from Church circles. But Schorlemmer had no fondness for West Germany. When he looked at the Federal Republic he did not see a normal democracy that was imperfect, of course, but arguably the most successful German political creation of the century. He saw what he liked to call a gross Titanic of a society, greedily consuming more than its share of world resources. The West German Titanic, he argued, was heading for ecological disaster and no sensible East German should want to board it. Yet East German industry was by any measurement a far more prodigal consumer of the world's resources than the West. It mined more highly polluting brown coal than any other country even in East Europe, and the energy this coal produced was used with a wastefulness that would have been intolerable to any West German business. East German cars were the dirtiest in Europe; its rivers among the most poisoned. The production of uranium near the Czechoslovak border by the Soviet-German company called Wismut had for years taken place with only minor safety precautions.

The Schorlemmers of East Germany knew, or suspected, all this – the struggling dissident groups had had some success in publicising environmental problems – and yet found it impossible not to believe that the West was irreparably flawed, and that their duty therefore was to make a different, better Germany. This combination of moral disapproval of the West with indulgence to the imperfect East German state because it still embodied a dream showed up in discussions about the Third World. It was understandable that an elderly Communist journalist, as the storm gathered strength in the autumn of 1989, should comfort himself with thoughts of the West's 'immoral exploitation' of developing countries. Even Sweden – admired by Russians and Poles, he added in a typical East German aside, only because they did not know the facts – exploited the Third World by putting its dirtiest industries there. But what about the eminent Protestant theologian who, speaking in a little church in the southern town of Erfurt just after the Berlin Wall had been opened, called Third World exploitation the 'grim back yard' of Western capitalism? Perhaps he did not know about the contribution of East German security advisers to keeping some of the most repressive Third World regimes in power, but one wonders what difference it would have made if he had. The point the theologian wanted to make was that although 'the meaning of socialism must be kept open' there had to be an alternative to the capitalism whose 'glitter' so many East Germans had had a chance to see for themselves since the border had been open. Capitalism, however many agree-able things it offered, was not a dream, and the East German regime and most of the East German opposition were united in their insistence on having one. If there was no dream then Germany was beyond redemption.

East Germany's first non-Communist Prime Minister, the Christian Democrat Lothar de Maizière, addressing the problem of the state that imposes too much on its citizens, quoted Hölderlin's *Hyperion*:

> You grant the state too much power. It must not demand what it cannot enforce. And what love and the intellect give cannot be enforced. It should leave this alone, or people will take its law and pillory it. By Heaven, he who wants to make the state a school of morals knows not how he sins. After all, what has turned the state into Hell is that man wanted to make it his Heaven.

The reproach was of course aimed at the Communist Party which, like all the regimes of East Europe until they degenerated into systems for the maintenance of power, had seriously tried to inculcate a collectivist morality. De Maizière's words should also have flicked the conscience of dissidents and churchmen. Believing that West Germany had failed, indeed never tried, to become a decent 'school of morals' and for that reason still harboured the old German ills, they too were convinced of the need for a purer state in the East. This explained the guarded attitude of both dissidents and the East German Churches to those who wanted to leave the country. The remark of a Roman Catholic bishop in September 1989 that emigrants were 'choosing the easier way' expressed an opinion long held by churchmen. The Churches felt it their duty to help those who fell foul of the state because of their desire to leave, but they took care never to be seen themselves as advocates of emigration. The motto of the Evangelical Church was, after all, 'not to be a Church near or against socialism but a Church *in* socialism'. And when in September the Roman Catholic and Evangelical Churches made their first joint demand for political reform they did not say the growing exodus was justified but only that it was 'the visible evidence of a much more deeply felt demand for change'. Many local churches launched campaigns in September to urge young people not to leave, one youth mission in Thüringen putting out flyers that read

STAY IN THE COUNTRY!
Develop yourself with honesty

Offer resistance each day
But do not become violent

and ended with the encouraging thought that 'Even the GDR is not a godless land.'

As for the tiny dissident groups, the greatest disaster that could befall any of them was to be forcibly expelled to the West. At the beginning of 1988 the regime arrested on charges of treason a young songwriter called Stephen Krawczyk and his wife, the theatre director Freya Klier, only to release them within days to the West. The announcement that the couple had chosen to emigrate caused dismay among the small dissident community for whom Krawzcyk was a hero. In fact the couple had been threatened with jail sentences of up to twelve years if they did not leave, but it suited all the other parties – the East German regime, the West German Government and the churchmen who acted as mediators – not to spell this out. (There was always a danger in these affairs, a leading East German churchman admitted, of the Church being trapped 'between truth and politeness', not a problem that bothered the Communist regime.) As long as it was so easy for the East to get rid of troublemakers there was no chance for dissident leaders to develop. Indeed the West was seen by some dissenters as the cause of many of the East's problems. If it were not possible to receive West German radio and TV throughout almost the entire country then perhaps East Germany's own media would have to give a more realistic account of affairs. If it weren't for the West German books that were smuggled without much difficulty across the border East Germans would have had to develop their own *Samizdat*, which would inevitably have drawn some of the literary establishment into complicity as well as promoting a culture of conspiracy. If West Germany was not always there to help solve in a hundred discreet ways East Germany's problems – there was a suspicion that West German industry preferred to make profits out of East Germany as it was – then the East German regime would be under more pressure to carry out reforms itself.

The two young men who in the summer of 1988 outlined such wild hopes were members of a group called the Peace and Human Rights Initiative that had members throughout the country, but was puny even by comparison with the limited world of Hungarian dissent. They were typical inhabitants of Prenzlauer Berg, a district of East Berlin where after misty evening rain the cobble streets glistened like wet sand beneath the cliffs of crumbling soot-black terraces. Neither repairs nor decorations had been carried out in this part of the city since the end of the war, and the houses, with faded signs of pre-war shops like forgotten messages still visible on the walls, could have attracted no one except those young West German squatters whose delight was to take possession of ruined buildings. The two men were talking in an austere but not unfriendly pub where a waitress, who had not very long ago been pretty, smiled each time she brought more beer. There was little choice, only beer, potato salad and sausages resting on a cushion of pale mustard. What was it an East German teenager had said? 'You have to remember that here one gets always only what one needs and seldom what one wants.' This pair, though, might have approved of that as a recipe for a good life. The younger had a duckling's hair and grey eyes, the elder was sallow and bearded. Both smoked without cease as they talked with admirably dignified pessimism about how little support they had among the ordinary public. They did not complain, as a leading Lutheran layman had done, that 'civic courage is not a traditional virtue in Germany', but they knew they could not count on the sympathy of the large-stomached men around them who emptied their litre mugs like long-suffering animals after a day's work. What else could one expect in a country that raised its citizens to be docile as children? Their group tried to operate independently of the Church which they regarded as too cautious and conservative, and out of touch even with the growing number of its own young members. But their isolation did not end there. Unlike the other dissidents of East Europe they got no encouragement from anyone within the country's cultural establishment. The novelist Stefan Heym had unrivalled freedom to travel to the West. He was even a regular performer on West German television talk shows where he made what appeared to be daring criticisms of East German policies. But after one short look at the tiny dissident world in the capital Heym had nothing more to do with it, retiring to his house on the agreeably wooded Rabindranath-Tagore-Strasse on the far outskirts of the city. Disorder and unrest in East Germany, Heym was arguing in 1988, were the last thing the Soviet bloc needed at the moment when Gorbachev was trying to reform the socialist system. 'Of course the young people don't take that into consideration, but mature writers know that things must be done carefully.'

There spoke a man who had lived a long life against the odds by *Fingerspitzengefühl*, instinct and sureness of touch in situations where the less wary had perished. Heym's heavy face did not lie when it suggested someone who had seen close up many of the alarms and horrors of the twentieth century. Both Jewish and left-wing, he escaped from Hitler's Germany to become an officer in the American army and then, after a series of political somersaults that could have broken a less agile man, found himself back in East Berlin in the early 1950s. Heym knew by heart how to manoeuvre in a world where Communism was accepted as something permanent although hopefully open to modification. It was only to be expected that he and other 'mature' East German writers and intellectuals should be at a loss when the system, against their expectations, was seen to be on the edge of collapse. But in one matter he did see eye to eye with the two young men from Prenzlauer Berg. The latter's isolation extended to the opposition groups in the rest of the Soviet bloc. Though they did manage to send representatives to some of the East European dissident gatherings that were occasionally arranged with considerable difficulty, they had never met with real understanding there. They felt they were treated with condescension because they had, by the standards of the others, so few followers and such minor successes. The reason was obvious. Poles, Czechs and Hungarians had national feeling to fall back on, and a self-consciously national constituency to cultivate. Many of East Europe's leading opposition intellectuals found much to criticise in their own national traditions, but if there was bad Polish or Hungarian nationalism there was also laudable patriotism, a distinction that both the two young East German dissidents and Heym the elderly novelist were unwilling to make about the German Democratic Republic. The last thing they intended was to appeal to German national sentiment of any kind.

It was fitting that this tiny East German opposition with its peculiarly German inhibitions should have first come together as one group with the purpose of checking the escape of their fellow citizens to the West. When New Forum was set up after Hungary's opening of the border to Austria, one of its founders explained that because 'a majority of the refugees had given up every hope of an improvement of the situation in the GDR', New Forum wanted 'to help prevent this fire from growing'. The painter Bärbel Bohley, another of the founders, described the Forum and its supporters among the demonstrators in the street demonstrations of October as

> a rebellion against the principle that anyone who thinks differently can do nothing but leave the country. 'We want to stay' [a slogan still heard from some of the demonstrators at that time] means: we want to take on responsibility for our own lives here. For me, it also means we have found our identity, whereas until now everyone kept looking at the West, trying to imitate the life-style of the consumer society.

New Forum's general aims might almost have been drafted by West Germany's Greens. East Germany should neither be debtor to the West nor 'plunderer' of the developing world. Unlimited economic growth should be abandoned in favour of greater frugality and friendliness towards the natural environment. People should be expected to work conscientiously but not at the cost of the socially weak. Although it spoke of democracy and justice the first statement did not attack the socialist system and failed even to mention the Communist Party. One phrase seemed particularly characteristic of East German dissent: 'We want opportunity for economic initiative but not degeneration into an elbow society.' This dismissive phrase, the 'elbow society', was to repeat like a rondo's theme throughout the opposition's discussions and declarations. Elbows, uncomfortable and ugly things, were not the stuff of which East German dreams were made.

Another of New Forum's founders was a lawyer called Rolf Henrich who had been a Communist for twenty-five years before quarrelling with the Party and publishing in West Germany a critique of the GDR called *The Paternalistic State*. The striking thing about men and women like Henrich was that they were social moralists, not politicians. The fervent Henrich, with hair cropped close on his large head, could have passed as a Reformation cleric. New Forum made it plain from the start that it was not and would not be a political party (Henrich said parties were out of date) but would remain a 'Citizens' Initiative' performing the function of a forum or meeting place where Communist Party members and others could discuss public problems. After the Forum's founding Henrich retired to a canal lock-keeper's house in the countryside where he planned to grow cereals so he could make his own muesli. His departure from the Communist Party had been part of a revolution against what he believed to be the phoniness and contradictions of his former way of living. A remade life based on eating healthily and giving up smoking seemed to him a necessary step towards a new way of thinking. Considering East Germany's problems Henrich came to the conclusion that there were advantages in backwardness. For example it should be easier to convince the East German in his Trabant of the advantages of speed limits than a West German in a Mercedes Benz. The meagreness of East German shops was better preparation for a frugal, environment-friendly economic policy than the cornucopia supermarkets of the West.

Such ideas and attitudes had little in common with the drift of dissenting thought in the rest of East Europe. Solidarity in Poland was a civic crusade but with the Polish Church at hand it never pretended to be a spiritual one too. The politics of Michnik, Havel or Hungary's Janos Kis certainly had a strong moral content. Havel in particular had tried to show how a man or woman could lead a decent life under a profoundly indecent system. But their chief purpose was to create a civilised democratic order in which citizens would be free to wrestle with their own souls as they wished. One could not see many of these East Europeans retiring to a cottage to make their own muesli, let alone giving up tobacco and alcohol. Compared with other East European dissenters there was, to adapt Adam Michnik's expression, something too 'angelic' in the approach of Germans like Henrich; and too little awareness that politics was practised by sinful men with unavoidably sharp elbows for whom the imperfect vehicle of the ordinary political party was in fact well suited. It was typical that other New Forum supporters imagined the Citizens' Initiatives becoming a watchdog over Government, almost its super-ego, but not actually dirtying their own hands with practical politics.

On the other hand Henrich's idea of socialism was not enirely incompatible, as far as it went, with that of the East German official ideologist, Otto Reinhold. Henrich himself defined socialism as having 'its basis in the common ownership of the decisive means of production'. Was there not the making here of an understanding between dissenters and the Evangelical Church on the one hand and the Communist Party on the other? Both sides wanted East Germany to remain a separate state with its own identity. No one had more credibility than the Church and New Forum when it came to urging East Germans not to flee to the West. Yet even after Honecker's resignation in October his successor Egon Krenz would tell a meeting of the Party's regional first secretaries that there was no question of recognising New Forum, that in no case was it to be treated as a partner for negotiations at any level, and that its 'demagogic and anti-socialist demands' had to be demolished. As for the Protestant clergy, agonising between the demands of truth and politeness, the State Security chief Erich Mielke reported to the Politburo that the Church was a threat because it continued to be 'the most important point of departure' for attempts to unite the opposition movements.

From its point of view the Party was right and even Bärbel Bohley, whose greatest desire was for the German Democratic Republic to continue its existence, wanted what the regime could not give. Typically reluctant to have New Forum tagged as a conventional political opposition, Bohley did allow that it was an 'opposition to this dreadful sclerosis, this apparent irreversibility of the status quo, this perennial shelving of the problems of society . . . [with] not a trace of self-criticism'. How could the Party concede she was right? The system was of a piece. No one part could be altered without threatening all the rest. Until the mid-1970s the Party Central Committee had a Public Opinion Institute, some of whose work was used by the newspapers. It was closed down, a Party member recalled, 'because it got too interesting'. Yet there was logic in this apparently suicidal decision, for it was the business of Communists to create new reality, not to bow before the existing one. Control of information was just one part of a tightly interrelated system. This conundrum of how to change the inherently unchangeable had stumped all would-be reformers of the Communist economies, and in the end made the very word 'reform' taboo in decent Party circles. It was what had broken the East European revisionists who hoped to democratise the system, and in this sense New Forum, which had a number of Party members among its leaders, can be seen as East Europe's last and shortest-lived revisionist flower.

These dissidents loyal to East Germany supposed it would be possible to keep what they liked in the system while changing everything else. What they liked most was the opposite of what they believed they saw in West Germany. This was a long list of old and new German devils, starting with militarism and a potential for renewed Fascism, and continuing with commercialism, consumerism, dominance of have-nots by haves, and the absence of disinterested community feeling. A provincial member of New Forum, a music teacher who greatly disapproved of the West's lack of state-funded music schools, had been astonished during a visit to West Germany by how little neighbours knew about each other. 'They knew what cars the couple next door had, and how much they earned, but not what their problems were.' In the East, she said, they helped share the burden of each other's troubles, and this fostered a sense of community which they were frightened of losing if East Germany disappeared. A warmer, more intense life among family, friends and neighbours – other East Europeans, and some visitors from the West too, sometimes saw this as an advantage of socialist societies. But they and the nice music teacher, whose plump cheeks and fair hair drawn back in a bun suggested she was indeed an admirable neighbour, failed to see that this was a by-product of a dictatorial and economically inefficient state. Neighbourly self-help was necessary to both physical and spiritual well-being. The little communities of decent people, long a feature of life in the semi-Asiatic world of the Soviet Union, were a faint modern echo of those villages that kept certain freedoms even under ancient Oriental despotisms.

And even these apparently precious parts of life could so easily be contaminated by the system. What of the Ministry for State Security's 109,000 'unofficial collaborators', in other words informers, the number officially admitted to when the Ministry's organisation was revealed, though the true figure was generally supposed to be higher? Wolfgang Schnur, the short-lived leader of Democratic Awakening, lived a double life as a respected defence lawyer of dissidents and a Stasi informer. He was a typical creature of the East German state, not an exception. It was thanks to people like Schnur that the Ministry was able to keep files on five million people, the great majority of East Germany's active population. Those parts of East German life that New Forum's supporters appreciated were like the creepers and flowers that seed themselves and manage to survive on the walls of a great fortress. Some of the blooms were pretty but their roots grew in the system of Party dictatorship. And it was the fortress walls, not the charming flowers, that were the reality of this German dream.

COLLAPSE

From the moment of the opening of the Hungarian border events in East Germany were determined by a contest between two uneven forces. On one side was a population that, whether it realised it or not, had the regime in a half-nelson, for by continuing to leave, or even just threatening to leave, it was able to apply irresistible pressure for change. On the other was a regime whose resolve to resist was being eroded both by panic in the Party and the unaccustomed challenge of a newly emerged opposition movement, above all New Forum to which thousands rallied within days of its appearance. By 7 October, the day of the fortieth anniversary celebrations, the regime had reached a point at which all choices looked dangerous. To prevent its citizens escaping it could make travel more difficult to other countries of the Soviet bloc, while using whatever force was needed to suppress protests as it had in the recent battles in Dresden; or it could try to pacify its citizens by tolerating the exodus while making popular reforms to reduce the number of those wanting to leave to an acceptable minimum.

Discontent within the Party, above all in the Berlin organisation, had been growing for some time. In 1988 the capital's First Secretary, Günter Schabowski, had tried to start a discussion in the press on the problem of poor quality in industry but was at once squashed by Mittag, who also sabotaged any attempt by industrial managers to convey their worries about the deteriorating economic situation to Honecker. Although East German Communists feared Gorbachev might lose control of events in the Soviet Union, many were shocked by Honecker's unprecedented order to ban the Soviet German-language press digest *Sputnik* on the grounds that it no longer made 'a contribution to German-Soviet friendship'. But what really opened Party members' eyes were the May local elections in 1989 which produced both an unbelievably massive turn-out and a ninety-eight per cent vote for the Party's candidates. Such foolish trickery made Party members uncomfortable, not least for the doubts it raised about the leadership's good sense. The elaborate celebrations of the fortieth anniversary with yet another march past of young people as well as an old-fashioned military parade would on their own, given the Party's troubled mood, have stirred further doubts. Coming after the shocking exodus of the summer they seemed almost intolerable. The two men in the Politburo most responsive to such feelings were Schabowski and Egon Krenz, and it was their manoeuvres from the end of September up till Honecker's resignation in mid-October that unknowingly set the Party off on the road to self-extinction. Gorbachev's meeting with the East German leadership during the celebrations gave the nervous conspirators the final encouragement they needed. The Soviet leader reacted blankly – disbelievingly, some accounts said – to an arrogant lecture from Honecker on East German successes, but he later let it be known that he had warned the East Germans that 'life punishes those who arrive too late'. A clearer sign of Moscow's disapproval of Honecker's stubbornness could not have been wished for.

It is scarcely to be wondered that Krenz and Schabowski failed to understand the forces they were about to let loose. Krenz was a man of limited ability and imagination. At fifty-two the Politburo baby, his only strength lay in being sidekick to an old autocrat. There was little sign of either wisdom or sincerity in his long face and uneasy wolf's grin, and though a passable performer in the cardboard events that served as public life in East Germany he had no idea what to say when faced with crowds of real angry people. Schabowski was a clever bruiser but crippled by too many years within the Party machine. Notorious when editor of the Party newspaper *Neues Deutschland* for printing a record number of pictures of Honecker, he lacked the nerve to act against the old man when something might still have been saved. Later Schabowski was to admit his errors: the Party, he confessed, had been like a monastic order whose members had too often 'believed' and not 'thought'. He was one of very few East European Communist leaders who acknowledged both guilt and the need for repentance.

But what, realistically, should Schabowski and Krenz have foreseen? The Polish Communists' defeat at the June elections seemed to have been contained by the appointment of Jaruzelski as President and the preservation of Communist control of key ministries (though the presence at the fortieth anniversary celebrations of Skubiszewski, the gentlemanly professor of law who was the new non-Communist Polish Foreign Minister, should have seemed a disturbing omen). It was true the future of the Hungarian Party did not look good, but since when did an East German Communist think he had anything to learn from Poland or Hungary? Moscow, informed by the conspirators of the final moves against Honecker, saw no more clearly into the future. When Hans Modrow, by then Prime Minister, talked privately with Gorbachev during a Warsaw Pact meeting in early December, the two men agreed that the 'democratisation' of East Germany would strengthen socialism. (In fact Modrow was already nagged by the fear that it might also work the other way, but he did not admit this to the Russian.)

Having resolved to get rid of Honecker it made no sense for the new leaders to adopt his policy of driving the demonstrators off the streets. Someone thought it worthwhile to spread the story that Krenz had countermanded an order from Honecker for the security forces to fire on the Monday demonstration in Leipzig two days after police and Stasi plainclothes men had attacked demonstrators in East Berlin on the evening of the fortieth anniversary celebrations. (There is no evidence Honecker gave such an order, and Krenz himself later denied that live ammunition had been handed out to the security forces.) Krenz and Schabowski knew that the Party was in self-questioning mood. In Dresden after the train riots and in Leipzig since the 9 October demonstration, local Party officials had been talking with Church and opposition leaders in an effort to avoid violence. The cultural establishment, docile for years because of their commitment to the existence of the new German state in the East, was at last daring to demand reform. And the Party leadership had no doubt that using force would earn them Soviet disapproval. It may be the case that the officer commanding Soviet forces in the Leipzig area informed the East German authorities during the crucial October days that his troops would be confined to barracks, meaning there would be no Soviet support for the 'Chinese solution' that so many East Germans at the time still feared. True or not, it fitted the logic of Gorbachev's policy, and no East German leader in his right mind could have expected anything else. There was also the question whether the security forces, in particular the ordinary police and the army, could themselves be relied on indefinitely, even if the Stasis remained firm. Towards the end of the fighting in Dresden some police units had refused orders to use their truncheons. It is also possible that the army general staff refused an order from the Minister of Defence to deploy a motorised rifle division to help close the Berlin Wall again two days after its opening – the order would have had to originate from Krenz, who might indeed have panicked after so many East Germans rushed into the West, even though most returned. The speed with which the demonstrations grew in October was another argument against using force. Erich Mielke reported to the Politburo that between 16 and 22 October there were twenty-four 'unauthorised demonstrations' country-wide in which 140,000 people had taken part. Two weeks later this had grown to more than two hundred demonstrations – they were being held regularly on different days in different places, like markets in country towns – with over one million three hundred thousand participants. To arrive in a town on the evening of a demonstration – they were always held after work – was like going back to the turbulent Germany of the 1930s, except there was no violence and, after a while, not even the apprehension of violence. Many of the streets had changed little since those days, and the rare lights illuminated the crowds that moved quickly towards whatever square the meeting was to be held with the dramatic emphasis of an Expressionist painting. These were extraordinary displays of anger built up over years and now expressed with masterful restraint, thanks in large measure to the churches and the soon-to-be deceived idealism of the opposition groups. It was as though a light that had long burned red in East German heads had suddenly turned green, making it harder to stay away from the crowds than to join in. As the numbers increased, people's fear vanished entirely, and without fear the system could not be effective.

Even the 85,000 strong Ministry for State Security was not designed to cope with protest on this scale, and it seems possible that its centre was overwhelmed by the variety and number of reports coming in from all over a once passive country. Honecker had brought Erich Mielke into his Politburo in 1971 since when his greatest achievement may have been industrial espionage. If Honecker's fantasy about becoming a power in microelectronics was not already dead it was partly thanks to Stasi ingenuity in obtaining prohibited Western technology, including in 1988 a glamorous four-megabit chip East Germany was finding it difficult to make for itself. Mielke had once been an able secret policeman in the classic Communist mould. There is a chilling account of his interrogation in 1950 of a leading East German Communist who had to be sacrificed in the Stalinist purges. The victim survived to recall that after Mielke had persuaded him to confess,

I suddenly felt a hand stroking my hair almost as tenderly as if it had been a woman's. It was the same hand that just before had beaten me worse than a dog. [Mielke] gave me a long, kindly look with his fine eyes from which all the harshness, all the meanness, had suddenly disappeared.

In 1989 Mielke was eighty-one. He was accustomed to playing a game for which he devised the rules, and with the support of a secret bureaucracy that seemed all-powerful. Party members of an earlier generation had always recognised the danger of security work for Communists, for those entrusted with it enjoyed to the full the frightening gift of the Party's absolute power. Such a 'licence and freedom to act practically without any kind of control,' one of Poland's first post-war leaders remarked, 'spoils and rots'. How it had coarsened Mielke may be guessed from the disagreeable detail that he called his private dining room at his Ministry's Normannenstrasse headquarters the Villa Hügel, the name of the palace in Essen belonging to the Krupp family, greatest of the German arms-makers and industrialists. Within weeks of Honecker's resignation Mielke would be revealed as a garrulous, almost senile, old man lost in a world he no longer understood.

Honecker agreed to resign at a Politburo meeting on 17 October. Krenz, Schabowski and their allies had primed its members and they all spoke against him, even Mielke, who accused his friend for not paying attention to his warning signals. The deposed leader apparently offered little resistance, though both then and later he refused to admit wrong-doing, and warned his successors they had led the Party onto the road to disaster. Honecker's departure seemed to lift a spell from the country. It revealed how strong the forces for change already were, and allowed them to develop with such speed that the opening of the border with the West became the only way to prevent an explosion. These passions so suddenly laid bare surprised those travellers who had become used to Honecker's East Germany. It had long been a place where people grumbled, the young more than the old, about lack of freedom to travel, about the many inconveniences of life like having to wait two years to buy a colour television that even then could not be used with a video recorder. But East Germans were, by comparison with the Germans in the West, so quiet, so pale – their little children even wore old-fashioned sun-bonnets – and apparently so resigned that it was easy to understand the gloom of dissidents like the two young men in Prenzlauer Berg. And there seemed to be a peacefulness and security about the country's life that spoke to anyone who remembered the West Europe of the 1950s and 60s. Neglect and lack of money had blessed towns and villages with changelessness. Those lucky enough to escape damage in the war had become Sleeping Beauties, darkened by the dust of coal smoke, untouched by new paint, but as magical as any treasure that is unaffected by time. The pleasures such places offered were as dated as they were modest – in this sense the frugality urged by the puritans of New Forum seemed already to have arrived. People still went riding on tandem bicycles. You could buy an old-fashioned Bee's Sting cake in a tiny private bakery or, with some luck, find a small café for a cup of Romanian coffee (a questionable mixture of coffee, cocoa and alcohol) or even a glass of East German gin and tonic, but not much more. A journey through this country where there was no escape from the melancholy smell of coal smoke suggested that the imagined security of childhood might not, after all, be lost.

To live there was another matter. Few East German cities were more ravishing than Erfurt in the south-west yet here, as in Leipzig, Dresden and many other places less well known, an unstoppable process had begun at the end of the summer. The story of how these many small streams of protest began, how they were at first channelled and guided by the churches and the new opposition groups but later overflowed to become a spontaneous movement is the story of the collapse of East Germany. On 20 September, a little more than a week after the opening of the Hungarian-Austrian border, a message almost revolutionary in its content was pinned on the notice board outside Erfurt's Gothic cathedral that stands on a small hill overlooking a glorious spread of ancient houses below. An open letter from Johannes Braun, Roman Catholic Bishop of Magdeburg (in whose diocese, for obscure reasons of German history, Erfurt lay), it was far more outspoken than the earlier letter of his Evangelical colleague, Bishop Demke. Braun summed up the complaints and questions that were being put throughout the country. Everyone had been shattered by the westward flight of fellow citizens, the bishop wrote, but the press was not reporting it properly. The Government would still not explain why people could not travel when they wanted. Many other questions remained unanswered. Why were people not rewarded properly for good work? Why did there have to be just one political party? The Government said it provided social security and freedom from the fear of unemployment, but life was made wretched by the daily hunt for necessities, and also by the fear people felt in their dealings with the authorities.

Erfurt was unusual in that about a third of its active Christians were Roman Catholics, and it was in the Catholic Lorenzkirche that the city's public revolt began. For eleven years an ill-attended Thursday 'prayers for peace' had been held there. When after many years of silence the Catholic hierarchy spoke out on political matters the service attracted more people, the most militant being students from the Catholic theological college, the only one in East Germany. Sensing that emotions were rising and to stop people taking to the streets, another Catholic and two Lutheran churches also began Thursday peace prayers. At the end of September the Evangelical Church for the first time allowed the local branches of New Forum and Democratic Awakening to hold meetings in church buildings – there were quite simply no other places for them to gather. The atmosphere was tense. The local Party boss, Gerhard Müller, was a hardliner long suspicious even of the local churches. The mayor, 'Red Rosi' Seibert, was equally unpopular, even a gentle Lutheran clergyman allowing himself to call her a 'terrible woman'. New Forum and Democratic Awakening were as worried as the Church leaders by the prospect of street demonstrations and it was the theological students who at the end of the Lorenzkirche service on 19 October, ten days after the nerve-wracking demonstration in Leipzig, seized the initiative and led part of the congregation in a march to the Stasi prison. In the same week the actors of Erfurt's theatre took what was then still the brave step of passing a strongly-worded political resolution that resonated through the city's intellectual community.

The following Thursday, 26 October, the congregations from all four churches walked through the narrow streets towards the vast square at the foot of the hill on which the cathedral stood, and Erfurt's Thursday demo had become an institution. Although travel freedom and the regime's silence about the escape of so many of its citizens abroad dominated the first meetings, hatred of the local leadership soon made itself felt. 'Red Rosi' was booed down when she tried to speak. The city's Christian Democrats, for decades obsequious allies of the Communists, declared their independence and demanded the mayor's resignation. 'After years of silence,' remarked one of the clergymen most closely involved, 'it was as though people could be silent no more.' Nothing was taboo, from the special shop stocked with Western goods on the Eislebenerstrasse for which a written entry permit from Müller was needed to the First Secretary's own hunting lodge at Kammerbach. It was the Party's local paper that published the first pictures of this furtively enjoyed privilege, for the critical mood had also swept through an alarmed Communist rank-and-file. When Müller resigned shortly after the opening of the Berlin Wall thousands of Party members gathered outside the Erfurt Central Committee building to shout 'no resignation without accountability'. People even began to ask questions about Mikroelektronik, the state conglomerate Honecker hoped would put the country at the front of world technology and whose headquarters were in Erfurt. Until now as untouchable as the local offices of the Ministry for State Security, Mikroelektronik employed 8,500 people in Erfurt and was rumoured to have paid immense bonuses to its senior staff. Yet the management refused to answer enquiries from Erfurt inhabitants and no one really knew what was going on there (the firm's secrecy was understandable, for its products depended on many Western components, some acquired illegally at great expense, and were quite uncompetitive on the world market). Children were drawn into the excitement of the moment and compiled their own programmes for school reform. Openness, truthfulness and a more relaxed atmosphere featured high on their list of demands. As for the old city, a conservationist lobby soon appeared to publicise the state of near collapse of many of its buildings: the limits of the unconscious Communist policy of preservation through neglect had been reached.

Erfurt's mood had the unmistakable purity that usually marks the first stages of a revolution. It was, a young Protestant pastor thought, like living through 'one long wedding'. Yet in Erfurt as everywhere else it was still a revolution without real leaders. The Churches and the opposition groups provided some organisation – apart from the Communists only the pastors and the priests had much organisational experience – and they were a reliable brake against violence, but they were not leading opinion. The young pastor understood this. He had seen how easy it would have been for him to take power into his own hands and it worried him. New Forum's distaste for conventional politics diminished its capacity to exercise clear leadership, but there was the even greater problem of its message. What did anyone who listened to its representatives hear? That East

Germany was about to embark on something the world had never known before, the combination of democracy with the social ownership of the means of production; that what only a short while ago had been a boring country was about to become one of the most interesting in the world. Was it what the people of Erfurt and East Germany wanted to hear? A young Catholic monk, a behind-the-scenes force in Erfurt's Democratic Awakening, had been analysing the speeches and slogans at the demonstrations on the Cathedral square. They called for the abolition of the one-party state; a democratic society with competing political parties; an economy revived by the introduction at least of 'market elements' and by links to West Europe; the legalisation of private and various cooperative forms of property. But if all this was achieved, what would distinguish the German Democratic Republic from West Germany? And these were only the demands of what could be called the city's middle classes, for neither the Churches nor the opposition movement had reached out far beyond them. What did the working class want? The monk shrugged. All he was sure of was that 'we have reached a traumatic moment'.

THE GERMAN REALITY

A revolution will always in the end find its leader, but who was to be leader of East Germany's? Certainly not the Party. There is no reason to suppose the cleverest Communist could have regained control, but Krenz was dim enough to believe he would be applauded simply for not being Honecker. Once it was plain that he had no ideas of his own – and that was very soon – he was forced into the trudge of retreat that was becoming familiar for all East European Communists. Nothing he did was enough. When at the end of the first week in November the old Politburo resigned, its replacement contained names of such unpopularity, among them local Party leaders already being openly reviled during demonstrations, that four of them had to resign within forty-eight hours. New travel regulations for which much had been promised turned out to include some concessions, but the document was phrased in the old tortuous style that suggested trickery was intended. There was applause for Modrow's appointment as Prime Minister, but it did not diminish the flow of young East Germans to the West, many of them now crossing the Czechoslovak border into Austria. Fifty thousand had reached West Germany through Hungary, Poland and Czechoslovakia by the time East Germany's own border to the West was opened on 9 November.

Krenz was trapped between pressures that were impossible to reconcile. The demonstrators were already shouting *Egon raus* and 'Communist Party bye-bye' had become a popular slogan everywhere. The more intellectual and anguished Party members, many of them young, had also started to demonstrate outside the Central Committee in Berlin. They were fired by the not unfamiliar dream of a democratised Party, free of bureaucrats and purged of the 'guilty', a word increasingly to be heard. They demanded a purifying Party Congress – the last thing Krenz wanted – and after that, as one of their slogans innocently put it, 'We want to win free elections.' More cautious Communist theoreticians, while admitting that the Party was discredited, feared that if blame spread from the old leadership to the system itself everything would fall apart. Artists and writers organised a big demonstration in Berlin on 4 November in support of a reformed but still socialist East Germany which was addressed by New Forum members, well-known intellectuals, including Stefan Heym, and Party stars like Schabowski and Markus Wolf, the ex-head of foreign intelligence in the Ministry for State Security who had revealed himself as a Party reformer. Schabowski was booed and so was Wolf, an experience that clearly both surprised and displeased the smooth spymaster. The decision to open the border on 9 November was taken in considerable confusion. A major purpose was to stop the embarrassing exodus across the territory of other members of the Soviet bloc. The leadership apparently did not foresee that the border posts, particularly in Berlin, would be rushed by huge crowds who did not have even the passport or visa the new regulations demanded, and that once that happened the guards, confused by imprecise orders, would have no choice but to let everybody through. Perhaps as many as five million East Germans went to the West in the week after the opening and almost all came back, their shopping bags stuffed with the irrational yet satisfying purchases of people who for years had been forcibly protected from the evils of consumerism.

As was to be expected the *Volkskammer*, the East German Parliament, erupted into self-protective activity, with the old satellite parties fooling no one by their claim to be long-frustrated democrats. What was genuine, however, was their keenness to forget the humiliation of their past subordination to the Communists, a humiliation all the more sharply felt now that it was spiced with danger for them. It was this Parliament, till now assembling only for rare formal sessions, that at the beginning of December voted to remove the Communist Party's constitutional right to a leading role. The press, not least Communist journalists anxious to find the guilty men, did not have to dig very deep for stories of scandalous behaviour, and the regime's reputation suffered further from the confessions of members of the old Government. At the beginning of December, Krenz and his Politburo resigned and the Party's affairs were entrusted to a working commission led by Gregor Gysi, who had remained a Party member in good standing in spite of acting as defence lawyer for dissidents, until an extraordinary Party congress met later than month. The congress showed a Party almost paralysed by panic (there had been many threats against Communists, and even some physical attacks) and more determined than ever to find someone to put the blame on. Delegates gave the impression they would have jumped into a bath of anyone's blood if they thought it would wash them white in their fellow-countrymen's eyes. This disagreeable mood was caught in a remarkable letter published in *Neues Deutschland*. Its author was an eleven-year-old girl called Anne Zimmermann whose mother and grandmother were both Communists while her father was a member of the satellite Liberal Democrats.

> Mummy and Daddy have told [me and my brother] that to lie and to steal are the worst things possible; and that we must always be industrious and do our work honourably so that peace may be more secure in the world . . .

The Zimmermann family's happiness was shattered the day Anne's father came home from work and, warning the children not to disturb him, turned on the television to watch the *Volkskammer* hearing explanations from Honecker's old ministers.

> I noticed that my Daddy had tears in his eyes and was very depressed, something I'd never seen before. I have recently heard that Erich Honecker and our old Government were not honest, and that they told lies to the people of the GDR. That's why I am writing this letter. I would like Erich Honecker, Günter Mittag, Erich Mielke . . . and all the old men of the old Government to be punished so my parents can

be happy again. All of us must work more diligently, more honestly and conscientiously and do their duty so that our GDR stays a socialist country and we children can have a secure future.

It is difficult to imagine such a letter appearing in the newspaper of any other East European Communist Party, but then East Germany's Communists were displaying all the treacherous symptoms of love betrayed. There were of course many opportunists among the more than two million Party members but there was also a greater proportion of true believers than in the other Parties, above all because to be Communist was to prove oneself free of the old German sins. The congress delegates listened unwillingly to the few speakers who tried to suggest that Party members themselves bore some of the guilt for what had happened. Delegates' attempts to have the disgraced leaders appear before them had to be deflected by the congress chairman Wolfgang Berghofer, mayor of Dresden and one of the city's peacemakers who was soon to resign from the Party. Berghofer appeared to understand that the Party could not survive the spectacle of the Communist rank-and-file tearing to pieces the old masters whom they had for so long obeyed. And Berghofer had to lecture petulant delegates before they agreed to listen to a ghost from the past they wanted to forget – Rudolf Bahro, imprisoned and then dumped in the West after saying in 1977 that the Party was no better than an almighty bureaucracy. The congress did, however, extract some blood by expelling from the Party Honecker, Mielke, the ingenious manipulator of Western money and goods Schalck-Golodkowski and several others, among them Erfurt's hated Gerhard Müller. Later the Party managed to take further revenge on Honecker, now a sick man though in control of his wits, by refusing to provide him with a new home when he and his wife had to leave the Wandlitz compound. It was said that Gysi, the new Party chairman, tried and failed to find accommodation for them but the Evangelical Church which took the couple in when no one else would was not impressed by his efforts and publicly rebuked the Communists.

It is a poor token of the former ruling Party . . . that those who only a few months earlier praised him to the skies should today deny him a place to live . . .

If the Party leadership had been guilty of injustice and violation of human rights, this had only been possible because

many others, both Christians and non-Christians, were silent when they should not have put up with injustice. In the present situation of this country guilt belongs to all.

If the Party had demonstrated its unsuitability to lead the new East Germany, the opening of the border knocked the confidence out of New Forum and the other left-wing opposition groups. It was difficult to feel pity for the Communists: however badly informed by their leaders they should have understood some of the realities on which the Party's power rested. The opposition could claim with more justification that it was like the lover of *foie gras* who has little idea of what a goose must suffer to produce it. They thought they could produce their socialist *foie gras* – subsidies, controlled prices, full employment, free social services – without having to oppress geese, without needing the Party-dictator and the substitution of commands for economic common sense. The open border was a threat to everything these men and women hoped for, hence the bitterness of Bärbel Bohley when she accused many of those planning to go to the West of wanting nothing more than a nice little house and a life of unlimited consumption. The growth of public protest had seemed miraculous to opposition activists who for so long had been fighting on their own. 'We saw in a few weeks,' one of them said, 'how a prudent sense of national identity began to take shape' – he meant, of course, an East German identity. After the border was opened people had deserted East German streets for West German shops but he knew that was not the only explanation of the change of mood. This man, as gifted as he was serious, had also crossed into West Berlin where he felt for himself the 'overpowering emotions' of experiencing the coming together of a divided country. Modrow as Prime Minister would soon set up a Round Table in which both the old political parties and the new groups took part, and which was supposed to reach consensus on the country's future. The Government put at the latter's disposal a large building on the Friedrichstrasse, next door to the offensively luxurious Grand Hotel that Schalck-Golodkowski had designed to seduce Western businessmen. Christened the House of Democracy the building never lost the smell of student protest and the newly revived Social Democrats, proud of their old political traditions, quartered themselves elsewhere. An East German writer commented that the opposition's 'dilettantism' was 'sometimes touching, more often embarrassing' and he accused it of conducting itself with almost as much arrogance as the Communists because it, too, had been 'legitimised by no one but itself'. It was an unfair crack – who legitimises whom in a revolution? – but these were the weeks of dying illusions. 'It is impossible now to conjure up a future for ourselves,' an East Berlin intellectual who supported New Forum confessed in the New Year. 'All our values, all our ideals, have collapsed. There is nothing more to imagine a future with.'

The bitterest blow came from Leipzig, the 'hero city' that had blazed the path of peaceful mass demonstration and was supposed to stand for all that would be best in the new East Germany. But there had always been ambiguity about the Leipzig movement. For several years East Germans who wanted to leave the country but were refused exit visas by the regime had gathered regularly at the Nikolaikirche in the centre of the city. Leipzig's magic, for those who thought like New Forum, was that when people took to its streets in October it was because they wanted to stay in the East in order to change it for the better. But the early demonstrations also attracted people who were happy to stay where they were on one rather different condition: that the two Germanies unite. *Deutschland, einig Vaterland* (a line from the East German national anthem whose words were no longer sung after the Berlin Wall made nonsense of them) made its appearance as a slogan very early on, as did others like 'Rather a market economy than a black market and shortages', even though most still concentrated on the iniquities of the Communists and the Stasis. Opinion surveys conducted in the late 1980s by West Germans suggested that almost three-quarters of the people in the East wanted unification, which was only slightly less than in the West. It was difficult to say what such figures meant, for at that time no one supposed a coming together of the two Germanies was more than the remotest possibility. But the strength of support for a better though still socialist East Germany was also deceptive. Because of the regime's expulsion of troublemakers to the West and the possibility for some emigration a process of natural selection had taken place. The members of the East German intelligentsia who might have favoured unification were for the most part already in the West. Even so it was not rare to come across educated East Germans for whom unification was an obvious good. They pointed out that the East German regime, after boasting for years about overtaking the West – the unity promised in the East German anthem was to be on Communist terms – had only itself to blame if its citizens now made unfavourable comparisons between the two. A prescient psychiatrist commented that East Germans who knew how many problems they would bring into a united country probably had more reason to want unification than Germans in the West.

Anxiety about unification at first affected all the opposition, including men like the Berlin pastor Rainer Eppelmann, a leader of Democratic Awakening that was to become an electoral ally of the Christian Democrats. Eppelmann's chief worry was that the rest of Europe was not ready for a united Germany, and that 'it would be terrible if for the third time in this century the Germans put a bomb in the basement of the European house'. The Left-inclined opposition and the East German intellectual establishment was against unification under any conditions, and it was not surprising that by the end of November a group of East German celebrities, including Stefan Heym and the writer Christa Wolf, felt the need to draft a petition called *For our Country* in support of an independent German Democratic Republic. The West German Chancellor Helmut Kohl had just published a ten-point plan for gradual unification but more worrying for the East German intelligentsia was what they saw as the dangerous change in the mood of the demonstrations, especially in Leipzig. Heym, who had originally marvelled at the aptness of the demonstrators' cry '*Wir sind das Volk*', now feared it would soon become '*Ein Volk, ein Reich, ein Führer*'. He publicly reflected on the 'savageries' in the German people and imagined the brief East German dream turning into a nightmare. In a conversation with Hans Modrow in December he asked the Prime Minister if he thought it conceivable that the pair of them might one day find themselves hanging from neighbouring trees. In Heym's opinion it was only too probable.

Knowing what the old novelist had seen during his lifetime one could only sympathise with him, but his gloom was no less misplaced for that. It was true that by the end of November the Monday demonstrations in Leipzig, and those in some other big cities too, had escaped from the control of their original organisers among the clergy and the new opposition groups. In Dresden the demonstrations had originally begun with a service at the Catholic cathedral that stood like a Baroque Noah's Ark on the banks of the Elbe, but the prayers of comfort, the songs of quiet resistance, the bells that filled the tall nave to warn the powers-that-be and encourage the oppressed had served their purpose and were no longer needed. Before long the demonstrators were gathering outside the walls, confident they could look after themselves. The crowds in Leipzig's Karl-Marx-Platz reacted with increasing impatience to the speeches made from the Opera House and it was not just because of the presence of a noisy group of young men with close-cropped hair and German tricolour flags, some of them certainly members of the right-wing Republican party from West Germany, or because of the football match atmosphere, with chants of 'Reds out of the demo' and a triple clap routine after the cry of *Deutschland*. Although there were occasional scuffles with students who passed out hysterical leaflets warning against the coming wave of Fascism the crowds gave the impression of people who knew that violence was not necessary. Important ground rules had been set in Leipzig and elsewhere by local Citizens' Committees that ensured, among other things, that the local Stasi headquarters were not ransacked, but what set the tone was that the borders were open and all who wanted to had seen the West. How were people supposed to go on believing that there was something so special in the East that needed protecting from the West? A fashionable East German playwright could still argue in December that West German democracy was directed by the Deutsche Bank but that kind of argument was unlikely to impress people who had experienced the convenience, civility and cleanliness of West German life. Wasn't it obvious now, if it hadn't been before, that Germany was one country? Even Hans Modrow was to admit that his knowledge of German history and culture had made it impossible for him to accept the Communist theory of two German nations, one socialist and the other capitalist. And what were the supporters of a separate East Germany offering? Friedrich Magirius, vicar of the Nikolaikirche, was saddened by the thought that East Germany might not be given the chance to 'try out something on its own'. But one thing the ordinary men and women in the Leipzig demo and elsewhere did know was that they had had enough of experiments. 'Why this arrogance?' asked the mild-mannered man interviewed on East German television. 'Why this insistence we should go our own special way, and not the normal way?'

The Modrow Government slogged down the familiar road of retreat. Elections set by the Round Table for May 1990 had to be brought forward to March for fear that order could not be maintained any longer than that. As the Government failed to produce plans to dismantle the socialist economy the outflow of East Germans to the West continued, reaching 60,000 in the first month of the new year. In February Modrow himself pronounced the words *Deutschland, einig Vaterland*, even though Gysi's Communists, renamed the Party of Democratic Socialism, continued to preach a 'third way'. It was understandable that some young people, out of a mixture of idealism, German guilt and infection by the old propaganda should see Fascism in every cry for a united Germany. But it was a sign either of the barrenness of Communist thinking or of plain unscrupulousness that an intelligent man like Gysi should have tried to start a scare about the new Fascist danger in East Germany. That some East Germans were gripped by a disagreeable nationalism was beyond doubt. Part of them joined the conservative German Social Union (DSU), a new party that won twenty-five seats in the new *Volkskammer* (twice as many as the alliance that included New Forum) and whose founder, a Leipzig pastor, later resigned in protest against its growing raucousness. But there had long been a core of right-wing extremism in East Germany, though the media were never allowed to mention it.

The outsider watched with mixed feelings this uneven battle between the remnants, mostly corrupted but a few still not, of an old German idealism and the new German reality. Whatever the politicians and the demonstrators said there was a feeling of a country finding itself again, not least in the way the regions were rediscovering their old identity as *Länder*, the historical regions abolished by the Communists. At first it was a shock to see the green and white flag of Saxony hoisted over the walls of Königstein fortress where King Augustus the Strong imprisoned Johann Böttger while he worked to discover the formula of a porcelain to rival China's and whose profits would help make Saxony a cultural centre of Europe. It was not long before the fresco on the walls of Dresden's royal palace depicting all the Saxon princes ceased to be a curiosity and revealed itself as a link with a past that people were grateful to rediscover. Even the words of the inscription seemed apt. 'You ancient house,' it ran, 'as in all times your people vow to you the old German loyalty' – not to be taken literally, perhaps, even though the *Sächsische Zeitung*, formerly the Party paper but by 1990 promising to be 'independent and open to dialogue on all questions', had taken to quoting the former kings with approval. What counted was that Augustus the Strong and his successors had made Saxony European, and that was something Dresden and Saxons had not felt for years.

If the six *Länder* were to revive, their natural home was in a federal Germany. If the old satellite parties like the Christian and Liberal Democrats were to come to life again, their natural home was in union with their old sister parties in the West, as was also true of the recreated Social Democrats. But the past collaboration of the former ('I always have to prove I'm not a thief', an old Christian Democrat worthy complained to a visitor in 1988) and the obscurity of the latter made it unlikely they would produce a leading figure to take control of the revolution and guide East Germany towards the unification that was its obvious fate. The leader, by default, was Helmut Kohl, and he was recognised as such by many East Germans after his first visit across the border to meet Prime Minister Modrow in Dresden in December 1989. Kohl's largest meeting of the March election campaign was held on the same square in front of the Leipzig Opera from where the demonstrations that shook the Honecker regime began. The West German politician who best knew how to speak to the average German was revealed as the natural leader of those East Germans for whom being average and German was happiness enough. Kohl, introduced as 'our Chancellor', told them what they wanted to hear: that it was natural for Germans to come together; natural to want to live decently; and stupid to talk of a Fourth Reich because Germans had learned their lesson from history. Throughout the speech a group of about forty young men and women at the back of the square blew whistles and kept up a constant barracking but the Chancellor's words were carried over what was now called the Augustus-Platz by such a mighty pair of loudspeakers that the noise bothered no one.

The East German Christian Democrats and their allies won forty-eight per cent of the votes in the elections, Gysi's Communists sixteen per cent. New Forum and two allies, one of them the Peace and Human Rights Initiative to which the young men in Prenzlauer

Berg belonged, obtained just twelve seats in the new Parliament. A German dream was dead. Reality, not as terrifying as the dreamers feared, had returned to Germany.

10

Perfect Prague

VILLAINS

It is tempting to see the dramatic events of November 1989 that so quickly swept away the unloved Czechoslovak Communist regime as a flawless uprising by a nation frustrated for decades in its desire for democracy. And so, to some extent, it was. Unlike East Germany's revolution, Prague's was not haunted by the *angst* inevitably present whenever the future of the German people hung in the balance. It was entirely free of the violence compounded of fear and desire for revenge that would poison the overthrow of Nicolae Ceausescu the following month. The millions of Czechoslovaks who took to the streets of their cities showed themselves to be disciplined, witty and determined. They knew whom they opposed and whom they supported, and once they made that plain the Communists had no choice but to go. 'Here we are! Here we are!' the Prague crowds shouted in answer to the church bells and factory sirens signalling the start of the general strike on 3 December that gave the final push to a tumbling regime. Indeed they were, but was it out of order to ask where they had been for the previous twenty years? The Communists were scared of the people but almost till the end remained confident they could bully and bribe them. The opposition acted in the people's name but was not sure of their support until the very last minute. The Czechoslovaks' genius was to emerge at the right moment, but that moment came at the end of a long drama in which the Communists gradually lost ground both to reality and to an intelligent, stubborn opposition. The people's part was to appear on cue to boo the villains off the stage and cheer the heroes. It was not itself a heroic part, though it was an essential one, and excellently played. The story of the Czechoslovak revolution rightly begins with the decline in the fortunes of the villains, and the consequent divisions among them. Without this the final act might not have passed off so peacefully.

By the early summer of 1989 even the most cautious of those Czechoslovaks who had long been hoping for change were sure it could not be far away. 'All we need,' said a typically cautious member of Charter 77, 'is a catalysing event. After that everything could move very fast.' His confidence was based on a shift in the balance of forces, no less real for being barely visible in everyday life. The Party was weakening, the opposition growing stronger, and it seemed that neither trend could be reversed. The year before a new journal called *Kmen* had published a most unusual article about Moscow by Eva Fojtikova, wife of Jan Fojtik, ideological expert in the Party Presidium. A teacher of Russian who travelled regularly to the Soviet Union, Mrs Fojtikova had been horrified by what she saw on a recent visit to the Soviet capital. Moscow, she wrote, had collapsed into 'an unmanageable eruption of emotions'. Old gods were being pulled down and a 'childish desire' for business enterprise had brought all sorts of shoddy traders onto the streets. She herself had paid for her picture to be taken outside the Bolshoi by a photographer who, she noted, did not have worker's hands, and she was surprised (and perhaps disappointed) when the prints were sent to her as promised in Prague. She understood what she had seen: it was the beginning of counter-revolution. But did the Russians understand, for they had not had the priceless educative experience of the Hungarian Communists in 1956 or the Czechoslovaks in 1968? Mrs Fojtikova obviously thought not.

This was an astonishing piece of impertinence coming from a Czechoslovak Communist. Since the crushing of the Prague Spring by Soviet tanks the Czechoslovak Party had been more dependent on Moscow's support and goodwill than any other Party in the bloc. The most it could hope for where its own people were concerned was not to annoy them by asking for harder work or by lowering the standard of living. It was typical that when Milos Jakes became the Party's General Secretary in December 1987 he should have spoken ardently of the need to learn from Soviet experience, not something most other East Europeans cared to stress any more. Some people in Prague found Fojtikova's article sinister. A well-known writer declared it was always dangerous when a woman 'without an atom of sex appeal' turned to politics. Others enjoyed it as evidence of the growing strain in the regime's relationship with its Soviet patron. That strain became very much worse the following spring when Jakes went to Moscow to be told by Gorbachev that Moscow's re-appraisal of its past foreign policy had to include the 1968 invasion of Czechoslovakia. Jakes, horrified, said this might tip Czechoslovakia into civil war and he pleaded with the Soviet leader not to raise the matter in public. In one of his essays for the *Samizdat* press the writer Ludvik Vaculik, commenting that the Government always seemed to be frightened, had innocently asked, 'Why does it not conduct itself so that it does not have to be afraid?' The answer was 1968. To make Czechs happy by questioning the rightness of the Soviet invasion was to question the regime's own right to exist. When the dangerous date of the invasion's anniversary came round in August 1989 Soviet press comment, while containing interesting new details of the Soviet operation, was with one intriguing exception discreet.

Izvestia interviewed one Valeri Nefedov who had taken part in the Soviet invasion as a teenage conscript of the Seventh Guards Airborne Division. Nefedov recalled how after talking with ordinary Czech people he had felt 'ashamed' of what he had done, and added 'Forgive us, Prague'. A month later *Izvestia* published a letter from Jiri Hajek, Dubcek's Foreign Minister and now a pillar of Charter 77, thanking the ex-paratrooper for 'having the courage to tell the truth about the tragic event which caused the most profound alienation between the peoples of our countries in all the centuries of their friendly relations'. Hajek ended his letter with breezy good wishes 'for the complete success of your restructuring'. This was a revolutionary use of a newspaper's letters column, and warning of worse to come. The following month the same paper published a scathing analysis of the Brezhnev doctrine that ended with the, for Prague Communists, chilling judgement that 'the Molotov-Ribbentrop pact, the invasion of Czechoslovakia and the "international assistance" to Afghanistan are links in one the same chain which cannot be separated'. The Soviet Union's 'moral health', the author concluded, depended on overcoming the 'imperial syndrome'. Within days the Soviet Foreign Minister Eduard Shevardnadze was telling Adam Michnik in an interview for *Gazeta Wyborcza* that it was not Moscow's business to tell Prague to re-assess 1968. It was the least he could say – and consistent with the 'hands-off principle' of Gorbachev's 'new political thinking' in diplomacy – but Moscow's real feelings about its intervention against Dubcek and the Prague Spring were plain enough.

It was usually said that there was no Party in the Soviet bloc less likely to change than Czechoslovakia's. Most of its leaders had taken part in the suppression of the Prague Spring. Jakes himself was a classic apparatchik, an accomplished fighter of bureaucratic battles in the dark Party jungles, but clumsy and comic once he stepped into the sunlight of public appearances. With a face that might have been carved from a potato and a tendency to ungrammatical nonsense whenever obliged to speak impromptu he was not the person to lead the Party into a more open relationship with a cynical Czechoslovak public. The Party's middle-aged members were scarcely more promising for many of them had begun their careers as hardline youth leaders in the years after 1968: small wonder some Czechs wrote the Party off as a 'conspiracy of the unqualified'. It seemed typical of this Party that when its members met they still used the Stalin-era salute *'Čest práci'*, 'Honour to labour', whereas common sense had long ago led the Hungarians to drop their *'Szabadsag, elvtars'*, 'Freedom, comrade' (by the 1960s polite Hungarian Communists were greeting women with a mongrel 'Kiss the hand, Comrade'). This was a Party that carried obedience to the Soviet line to ridiculous extremes, as when at the height of Moscow's quarrel with Peking it banned publication even of the Chinese classics and ordered a freshly printed edition of Chinese cookery recipes to be scrapped. But nothing is constant in politics, and there was always life even beneath the seemingly frozen political wastes of East Europe. How else to explain that the first elected Prime Minister of the new non-Communist Czechoslovakia would be Marian Calfa, deputy Prime Minister in the last Government of the old Communist regime, yet a man with whom Vaclav Havel found it a delight to work? In fact by 1988 there were unmistakable signs that some people within the Party understood that changes had to be made even though they were still at a loss how to bring them about without endangering the system. In the autumn of that year a senior apparatchik called Rudolf Hegenbart published a most unusual article criticising the Party leadership, albeit in general terms, and senior Party academics began to suggest even to foreigners that Gorbachev's reforms had their admirers in Prague. One of the directors of the Central Committee's Institute of Marxism-Leninism was ready to admit there was no future for a

king-like Party and an all-pervasive, all-powerful bureaucracy. He
even expressed admiration for Czechoslovakia's long-ignored pre-
war democratic experience. But he warned against expecting anything to happen quickly because at the top of the Party there was
still an 'exaggerated cautiousness, a desire to avoid mistakes that
would be difficult to correct'.

By the following year Czechoslovak Communists were being
pulled ever more strongly in different directions. The old mulish
instinct not to budge was reinforced by events in Hungary and
Poland. Jan Fojtik called the June funeral of Imre Nagy an attempt
to 'bury socialism'. The appointment of Tadeusz Mazowiecki as
Polish Prime Minister two months later provoked him into still
gloomier reflections on the condition of both Hungary and Poland,
and he warned that anyone who advised Czechoslovakia to follow
their example was proposing the same 'counter-revolution' that his
wife had spotted traces of in Moscow. Jakes himself gave notice that
no one should try to use slogans about *perestroika* to weaken
socialism and the Czechoslovak Party's leading role. The same
thought was put more crudely by the old hardliner Vasil Bilak who
was said to be telling any colleague who would listen that 'if we
liberalise they'll string us up'. The forces tugging an unimaginitive
and nervous Party in the opposite direction took much of their
strength from the increasingly obvious need for economic reform. In
the course of 1989 Prime Minister Ladislav Adamec's speech-writers
came increasingly under the influence of the dire prognoses of Valtr
Komarek's Institute of Forecasting, and a Presidium that could
never forget that economic reforms had triggered the crisis of 1968
found it more and more difficult to agree on the drafts of Adamec's
Prime Ministerial statements. There was also a flow of reports in
the Party press suggesting that many lower-level Party organisations
were passive and that the number of those giving up their Party
cards was increasing. It was getting harder to attract both young
workers and young intellectuals.

None of this was a surprise to those few Czechoslovaks who were
interested enough to keep the Party under observation but it was
unusual for such matters to be brought out into the open. It
suggested that at least some people at the top of the Party understood
that life could not go on as before. Another straw in the wind was
the increasing readiness of artists and intellectuals with official
positions to contribute to a cultural column in *Lidove Noviny*, the

main opposition *Samizdat* paper, to the great satisfaction of those Chartists like Petr Pithart who had always believed it vital to bridge the gap between the official and unofficial worlds. Representatives of the official world had also begun to accept invitations to speak to students' groups at the same time as members of Charter 77, something unthinkable a couple of years earlier. By the middle of 1989 the Institute for Marxism-Leninism was distinctly edgy about the possibly paralysing effect on reforms in Prague of developments in Poland, Hungary and above all the Soviet Union where Czechoslovak Communists, like the East Germans, feared a collapse into chaos. Nevertheless, senior members at the Institute for Marxism-Leninism were ready to say in private that the time for political change had come. The ghost of 1968 had now to be laid by the Czechs themselves, because everyone knew the Soviet Government was preparing its own re-assessment of the invasion. The Party had to face up to the fact that the old leadership was associated to greater or lesser extent with 1968 and was therefore a 'handicap'; most of its members should go. The country's situation was about to become 'very dramatic' and it would be necessary to have 'an enlightened, wise leadership' that was not 'isolated from the people', and had enough courage to explain the painful measures needed to rescue the economy from decline. The Institute saw a battle already shaping up between reformers and the Party's strong conservative wing that made up perhaps a quarter of the 1.7 million members, a formidable proportion given that most Party members were passive. The Presidium itself was split between those who wanted reform and those who feared it, and it was the conservatives who had managed to prevail and prevent the recognition of *Obroda*, a group of Communists expelled from the Party after 1968, who nevertheless kept some Marxist-Leninist sympathies. *Obroda*'s founding meeting in a Prague restaurant in June 1989 was frustrated by the usual secret-police tricks. Yet at the Institute for Marxism-Leninism this group's programme was described as something any Party member could attach his name to.

By mid-November Honecker's fall and the collapse of the Berlin Wall increased the pressure on those among the leadership who accepted the need for reform. Adamec was one, for as Prime Minister he could not ignore the unpleasant economic statistics as easily as other members of the Presidium. The Prime Minister, though, was a late convert to daring ideas, for he had resisted the Prague Spring reforms when he was head of the Central Committee's Economics Department and as a result was moved out of the job by Dubcek. Vasil Mohorita, head of the Socialist Youth Union and a member of the Central Committee secretariat, was another likely supporter of change, though his Youth Union was a typical Communist mass organisation, designed chiefly as a tool of control and in the judgement of the daring men at the Marxism-Leninism Institute 'corrupt and purely formal'. Miroslav Stepan, the Party leader of Prague, would have liked to be a reformer too, but there was something Walter Mitty-like in the belief of this thick-necked, instinctively authoritarian man that he could become the Czechoslovak Gorbachev. The brutality with which police had put down recent demonstrations in the capital had won Stepan no popularity and he made matters worse by boasting at Party meetings that he had taught a lesson to demonstrators whom he called 'young thugs'. (It was Stepan's illegal orders to security forces during demonstrations in October 1988 and the following January that earned him a four-year jail sentence after the collapse of the Communist regime.) Stepan himself was to claim later that the Presidium was divided into three groups, with hardliners led by Jakes and Fojtik; 'respectful' reformers like himself and Mohorita; and the 'impatient' ones like Adamec. Stepan did not mention Rudolf Hegenbart, head of the Central Committee department that supervised the army and security services, but his unusually critical press debut the previous year made him a likely candidate for a place among the reformers.

The forces for change in the leadership were scarcely impressive but they were sufficient to perform the useful function of dividing the Presidium once the final crisis began. This reduced even further the chance that an already demoralised leadership, isolated in the Soviet bloc – apart from the unacceptable Ceausescu – would use force to keep control. But did the reformers try, at the last possible moment, to do more, in the style of Krenz and Schabowski conspiring against Honecker or of the Hungarians Grosz, Nyers and Pozsgay (with far better timing and foresight, but in the end no better luck for themselves) against Janos Kadar? And if they did, what part did Moscow play? The new Soviet policy towards its East European allies was in principle one of strict non-intervention. Worried delegates to the Twenty-Eighth Soviet Party Congress in July 1990 asked Shevardnadze whether the collapse of socialism in East Europe was not a 'severe defeat for Soviet diplomacy'. Quite the reverse, he answered. It was not the Soviet aim to oppose 'the elimination in other countries of administrative-command systems and totalitarian regimes imposed upon them and alien to them'. The remark won him applause, and he went on to explain that even if the changes in East Europe had been counter to Soviet interests – which he did not think they were – there could have been no Soviet intervention because Moscow's policy was to recognise 'not in words but in deeds' the sovereignty and equality of all nations. Did the Soviet leadership know what was likely to happen in East Europe?

> Yes, we had in principle predicted all this. We sensed all this. The time will come when it will be possible to pick up the recordings of conversations of [Gorbachev], when it will be possible to . . . look at . . . the telegrams which passed from the various capitals of these countries. We felt that if serious changes did not take place then tragic events would be the result. In principle we sensed this, we knew this.

The only way Moscow could not have been well-informed about the drift of East European events was if the Soviet leadership itself had not understood, or not wanted to understand, the information at its disposal. This might have happened in the Brezhnev days, but not under Gorbachev. There was a huge Soviet presence in all these countries, not least inside their security services, where there were official KGB liaison officers and without doubt also unofficial KGB agents. Western allied intelligence services liaise with each other too, but this is usually done through embassies. In the KGB's case their men sat inside the Hungarian, Czech and Polish headquarters; and it was the Hungarians who were the first to ease them out, achieving this in the summer of 1989 when Budapest still had a nominally Communist Government. The East European services were also obliged to maintain their own liaison teams at KGB headquarters in Moscow, and many of the bloc's security personnel were trained in the Soviet Union. But until November 1989 in Prague there was no hint of the KGB trying to shape events in East Europe, or of Soviet leadership going beyond warning of the danger of resisting change, advice that in the case of Honecker and Jakes was ignored.

In this light, it was curious that Viktor Grushko, one of the deputy chairmen of the KGB, was having dinner with Lieutenant-General Alojz Lorenc, the Czechoslovak first deputy Minister of Internal

Affairs and head of the StB, the State Security Service, on 17 November 1989, the evening that violent police attacks against a peaceful student demonstration touched off the revolution. The two men met in a Prague safe house belonging to the StB, and Grushko made almost two dozen telephone calls to Moscow in the course of the evening as reports of the police operation against the students came in. Lorenc himself had been to Moscow in August and September where he had met the KGB Chairman Vladimir Kryuchkov. This might mean that Czech and Soviet spooks actually planned the unusually brutal suppression of a peaceful student march as a classic 'provocation' that was supposed to act like dynamite under the Jakes regime; or that there was a Soviet plot to get rid of Jakes and install a new Communist leadership that would carry out speedy reforms in the hope of keeping Czechoslovakia safe for socialism, even if the rest of the bloc was crumbling. If the latter, then Moscow must be working together with the chosen alternative team, perhaps using Hegenbart as the go-between, for his work as the Party's man overseeing security matters gave him perfect cover. (The Soviet leadership would not have bypassed the Czechoslovak Party to work directly with Prague's security service.) It was possible, therefore, that Gorbachev and his colleagues were sufficiently worried about the collapse of their East European alliance to forget the principles of the 'new political thinking' that Shevardnadze expounded so sympathetically and to revert to old-fashioned covert interference in an ally's affairs.

Until further facts emerge, only incorrigible addicts of conspiracy theories will believe that these things were happening, for it goes against the grain of Soviet behaviour in general during the prolonged East European crisis. Equally there may have been a conspiracy between the Party reformers and Lorenc to oust Jakes, with the conspirators merely keeping Moscow informed as the East Germans had done over Honecker. This is something to remember when the November events are recounted, though a warning is in order. Like so many other conspiracy theories, it exaggerates the power of politicians, spies and secret policemen to manipulate events at those moments of crisis when it is easy to launch a 'provocation' but far harder to control all its consequences. What was beyond doubt was the weakness of the Communists as the November drama approached. The leaders were divided, and a crisis could only divide them further. Having reached the top by proving their unoriginality they were even less likely than other Communists in the bloc to produce a credible plan of salvation; indeed we know that, metaphorically speaking, Vasil Bilak was right. There was no safe half-way stage between keeping the system unchanged and scrapping it altogether. Lieutenant-General Lorenc was later asked about the plot he was supposed to have played such an important part in. He denied its existence, which was not surprising, but went on to say that though the State Security could have stopped a coup it was quite another matter to check a fast-moving revolution. That had the ring of truth. The revolution's speed was assured by the presence of two new forces; an opposition that after years of isolation realised that its strength was growing fast; and the readiness of a nation to return to public affairs after a twenty years' absence on private business.

HEROES

The fair-haired young woman in the café on Malostranske Square had become boring with her endless talk about the difficulties of learning Swedish in Prague, but the ability to bore was perhaps useful to someone who was likely to be called in for interrogation by the police. Certainly interrogations didn't scare her; anyone with strong nerves could survive them, she thought, though she allowed it could be tougher in the provinces. A librarian by training, she earned her keep working night shifts in the Post Office but she was often able to finish by midnight which left plenty of time for her 'other activities'. In September 1988 these chiefly involved working for Democratic Initiative, a group that was a year old and in spite of having only a dozen proper members was already being mentioned as a subversive organisation in confidential instructions to local Party committees. Her 'other activities' had begun as a teenager when she became involved with the Jazz Section, a young people's cultural group that had some 5,000 members by the late 1980s and claimed to influence a great many more. Its original interest in jazz had broadened into the wilder areas of pop music and all kinds of experimental art. It had a *Samizdat* publishing house that among others things brought out works by Bohumil Hrabal, considered by most Czechs their greatest living writer; the authorities thought them unsuitable for printing. A small monument that the Jazz Section put up in Prague in 1985 to commemorate the fortieth anniversary of the end of the Second World War and the founding of the United Nations touched off a farcical battle with the city authorities who in the end removed it. The Jazz Section had no political aims except to be left alone and pursue its own interests but in Communist Czechoslovakia that was in itself an unacceptable political claim, and in 1987 the regime sent some of its leaders to prison on contrived charges.

The fair-haired girl now acted as Democratic Initiative's link with the Jazz Section but she also had contacts with the Independent Peace Association, one of whose leaders, Tomas Dvorak, had just been arrested for his part in the demonstration on the August anniversary of the Soviet invasion. Dvorak was a twenty-three-year-old who had first set up a pacifist organisation named after John Lennon, around whom there was a Czech cult of some years' standing. Every December young people gathered to remember his death in the Kampa, a charming island of gardens and old houses below Prague Castle by the edge of the Vltava. The authorities eventually gave up trying to erase the slogans they wrote on an ancient wall there, and 'Hey Jude', 'Give Peace a Chance' and the friendly Czech greeting *'Ahoj Johnny!'*, 'Hello Johnny!', remained all the year round like faint cries to the forbidden but increasingly familiar world beyond socialism's borders. Dvorak had called on the veteran opposition activist Petr Uhl for advice, but Uhl, though ready to help with the publicity a new independent group needed as protection against police action, refused to give him any. True to his belief in liberation through self-organisation Uhl told Dvorak to do what he thought best, and the result was the creation of the Peace Association in early 1988. All its members were in their twenties and they soon made contact with a more established Polish group called Freedom and Peace that was fighting for the legal right to conscientious objection. Freedom and Peace's members were also young and occasionally a cause of heartburn to the middle-aged leaders of Solidarity.

The young woman in the café eventually finished the story of her search for Swedish grammars and went off for a karate lesson, disappearing behind the vast St Nicholas Church that Kilian Ignaz Dientzenhofer's father Christoph had built for the Jesuits who were bent on returning the Protestant Czechs into the hands of Rome. For someone accustomed to meeting members of the small band of Chartists it was a surprising encounter. Perhaps the girl seemed so self-confident just because she was young. There was not a word of complaint from her about feeling isolated in an indifferent society. And because she was young and had no career that could be damaged by her independent opinions there was none of the melancholy one sensed in men and women who for years had not been able to practise a loved profession. This girl did not seem to distinguish much between working not very hard in the Post Office, learning Swedish and karate, and her 'other activities': all seemed equally normal to her. And she proved to be a portent of the future. By the spring of the following year there were at least thirty independent groups in Czechoslovakia. Several were connected with Charter 77 or had Chartists among their members, and the membership of many of the groups overlapped, but they were evidence of a growing appetite for independent activity. Their names suggested the variety of their interests: the Association of Friends of the USA; the Children of Bohemia (at first thought to be Dadaists, they eventually revealed themselves as supporters of a revived Central European monarchy); the Christian Union for Human Rights; the Committee to Protect the Rights of the Hungarian Minority; the Group for Labour Union Solidarity; the Independent Ecological Group; the John Lennon Peace Club; the Masaryk Society (another group formed to promote the officially suppressed legacy of Czechoslovakia's pre-war President included Havel among its members); the Society for Happier Present Times ('happenings' arranged by young people); the Society for the Study of Democratic Socialism.

What was going on? Not so very long before one heard experienced members of the opposition complaining that young people no longer even knew who Masaryk was. After the demonstration in August 1988 they were more likely to exclaim that the appearance of someone like Tomas Dvorak was a miracle. Havel's friend, Zdenek Urbanek, had been amazed during the crisis of 1968 to find that young people whom he supposed had forgotten the 'Czech tradition' could speak more eloquently than he. He felt the same surprise now, because after the Soviet invasion he had seen so many of the clever young return to the cynical pursuit of careers. Thank God for good Czech genes, he said. By the following summer the older generation had a clearer picture of the younger one: they were unafraid, very idealistic though in a vague way, and highly moral. They appeared to be reacting against their parents who had either sold out to, or compromised with, the regime after 1968. The

Chartists and their sympathisers who sometimes unofficially taught these young found it a time-consuming business. To an older person who retained some traditional learning their minds were *tabula rasa*, but that still did not make their appearance any the less miraculous.

Some of the young had been encouraged by the Roman Catholic Church which had slowly increased its following over the previous fifteen years. In spite of Catholicism's ancient role as destroyer of the Czech spirit, the Church had made amends by its conduct during the war and – unlike the Protestant Churches – by its resistance to the Communists after 1945 for which it paid a heavy price. In contrast to the regime the Church offered young people constant values and a real community. In 1987, at the suggestion of lay Catholics like the Chartist Vaclav Benda and radical priests like Vaclav Maly, the Church had launched a decade of spiritual revival, an early result of which was a petition for greater religious freedom started by a stubborn employee of the Czechoslovak state railways called Augustus Navratil. By 1988 this had been signed by half a million believers: a similar but milder petition launched ten years earlier achieved no more than fifty-five signatures. Although the Communists had infiltrated the Catholic clergy and tried constantly to lame it by tampering with the selection of new priests and keeping bishoprics empty they had not been able to control its leader Cardinal Frantisek Tomasek, who celebrated his ninetieth birthday in 1989. Tomasek lived in the Rococo palace of the Archbishops of Prague just across from the residence of President Husak in Prague Castle, and as the latter's star waned so the old Cardinal's grew until he had acquired a popularity that, allowing for the considerable difference in national histories, almost approached that once enjoyed by Cardinal Wyszynski in Poland.

In 1989 a new element was added to these movements of discontent. Havel's arrest after a demonstration in January on the anniversary of the suicide of Jan Palach provoked an unprecedented protest by 360 actors, musicians and other artists, most of whom were in good standing with the regime and had never risked this sort of gesture before. The appearance of actors as leaders of intellectual protest was quite new – the Czech tradition was for writers to speak for the nation – and had its origins partly in the recent growth of numerous small theatres in Bohemia and Moravia which had developed into the sort of cultural communities dear to the heart of

Vaclav Havel the playwright. A similar protest by over six hundred scholars and scientists followed soon after. Havel was sentenced to nine months in jail but the regime, unsettled both by the restless atmosphere at home and strong disapproval abroad, paroled him in May. Havel at once set about organising another petition. Called *Just a Few Sentences*, it demanded the release of political prisoners, the legalisation of independent groups, freedom of assembly, the abolition of censorship, and public discussion of both Stalinism and the Prague Spring. The day after the petition's publication abroad on 29 June Miroslav Stepan proclaimed it to be 'counter-revolutionary' and *Rude Pravo* hurled mixed metaphors at those who signed it. 'Those who sow the wind will reap a storm. It is time for everyone who wants to play with fire to realise this.' No one was deterred. The ever inventive Havel arranged for new groups of signatories to be announced at regular intervals: among the first were people not previously known as dissenters but who would have colourful roles in November, including the popular actor Josef Kemr and the rock musician Michael Kocab.

In the late summer of 1988 Petr Uhl was saying of the opposition 'we are still very marginal'. Less than a year later callers at the flat on Anglicka Street where he and his wife Anna Sabatova operated their unofficial news agency found a notice on the front door warning 'We practically speak no English and we have no time.' A more precise message in German followed: 'No visits before 1400 and after 2100 (except for those arranged in advance).' There could not have been a clearer sign that the opposition was picking up speed. But where, precisely, was it heading? Havel and his friends did not put much faith in demonstrations. Although encouraged by the young people's fearlessness, Petr Pithart thought that waiting for an anniversary to take to the streets was 'the most modest form of political action imaginable'. Charter 77 was in a difficult position for it was plain that, given the new atmosphere, some young people would demonstrate whenever the opportunity arose regardless of their elders' advice. Just before the August anniversary Havel nevertheless warned that the regime was waiting for the chance 'to strike hard and, in so doing, to paralyse efforts at democratisation for a long time to come'. He suggested that less confrontational forms of protest were available, for example signing *Just a Few Sentences*, and said he was sure a reassessment of the Prague Spring and all the dramatic consequences that must follow from it were not far away. There were moments in history 'when great risks and sacrifices are necessary', but this moment had not yet arrived in Czechoslovakia. Nevertheless a demonstration did take place in August and two months later, on the anniversary of Czechoslovak independence, over 10,000 people took to the streets of Prague. It was the biggest public protest the capital had seen in twenty years. The police reacted violently and made many arrests.

At the beginning of November the regime still had the physical means to crush an opposition that was still nowhere near a mass movement, but the Communists were already fatally weakened from within. They had at last lost control of the cultural establishment. In a pattern familiar from East Germany and Poland they were on the verge of losing control over the satellite parties whose survival would soon depend on breaking lose from their old Communist masters. There was no help to be expected from abroad. With East Germany crippled first by the crisis brought on by its citizens' flight to the West and then by Honecker's fall, the Czechoslovak Communists had not one reputable ally left. Only danger was to be expected from Moscow. A leadership already divided between those too frightened to budge and those scared enough to risk reform was unlikely to unite and cope with sudden, dramatic crisis. By contrast the opposition had a potential for unity, largely thanks to the emergence of Vaclav Havel as its leader. Havel's old friends and associates in Charter 77 had never recognised him as their leader nor had Havel, a modest man, claimed to be this. He earned the right, or perhaps one should say duty, by a subtle, ineluctable process in which he proved himself by his steadfastness and became – almost regardless of this own wishes in the matter – the modern hero his country needed. One of the artists who had broken years of silence to protest against Havel's arrest at the beginning of the year was the well-known film director, Jiri Menzel. Explaining why he had at last spoken out he also hinted at the source of Havel's authority.

You see, I cannot stand living comfortably any more while [Havel] who deserves more respect than I do has to be in prison. Havel is not acting against the state. He is . . . more useful to the republic than all those who, deep in their hearts, are opposed to the regime but accept . . . the situation. Havel knows how to express his opinions and how to live with the consequences. Why should I make myself [out to be] better than I am? I let myself be discouraged; I am an opportunist; I don't like conflicts. This is why he deserves more respect than I do.

Fate gave Havel characteristics and qualities useful to a man about to be called on to lead his countrymen out of Communism. Unlike some Chartists he had never been a Party member, had not even been carried away by the socialist-reformist aims of the Prague Spring, and so could never be accused by the suspicious-minded (as Geremek and Kuron were in Poland, or Dubcek in Prague) of being a late and possibly suspect convert to democracy. Although he had neither studied nor practised politics he was nevertheless, in the philosopher Ladislav Hejdanek's words, an 'enormously clever political practitioner', the one among the most active Charter members who could be counted on to come up with the best ideas. Conscious, not to say guilty, that he had enjoyed a privileged bourgeois childhood (he remembered his young self as a 'well-fed piglet'), he not only struggled against cutting himself off from ordinary life and the common man but was blessed with a nature that allowed him to get on well with everyone. In one of his early plays a working man, a brewer, says to the writer who is the main character, 'I'm just the manure that makes your fancy principles grow.' The writer accepts that he cannot act on behalf of ordinary people but must act as one of them. It was necessary wisdom for any leader of the democratically inclined Czechs with their scorn of those who set themselves above the ordinary. People appreciated his lack of pride or pomposity, like the elderly Czech lady who remarked approvingly that even after Havel became President he would finish his speeches with the polite little bow a schoolchild makes after reciting a poem.

Hejdanek called Havel a 'morally integrated character' and certainly the strongest impression he made on those who met him in the 1980s was one of strength and reliability. It was not superhuman strength – that might have been too much for those many Czechs who, like Jiri Menzel, were aware of their own weakness – but strength acquired with difficulty after a period of almost biblical temptation, trial and redemption. Havel had first been sent to prison in 1977 – an experience he later admitted had frightened him out of his wits – but was let out within four months after he had written to the public prosecutor requesting his release. Although he made no concession to the authorities the letter was used by the regime to suggest he had betrayed both his own principles and Charter 77. While this was not true, Havel could not forgive himself for his imprudence; for acting so that others might think him weak. Already inclined to suspect that others saw him as a lightweight he was plunged into a dark night of the soul. He believed that he had come

> out of prison discredited, to confront a world that seemed to me one enormous, supremely justified rebuke. No one knows what I went through in that darkest period of my life . . . There were weeks, months, years, in fact, of silent desperation, self-castigation, shame, inner humiliation, reproach and uncomprehending questioning.

He escaped first into 'gloomy isolation, taking masochistic delight in endless orgies of self-blame' and then, in an effort to escape 'this inner hell', into frantic activity to 'drown out my anguish and, at the same time, to "rehabilitate" myself'. Full rehabilitation only came with his third and longest jail sentence from 1979 to 1983. Partly because of the uncertainty and inaccurate gossip about what had happened in 1977, partly because he had never been physically very hardy, some friends and supporters in the opposition wondered whether it might be too much for him. In fact those years proved a time of extraordinary self-consolidation, of which he left an imposing record in letters to his wife Olga. At last he was able to welcome what he believed was the shaming experience of 1977 as his first chance to stand 'directly in the study of the Lord God himself', to look into His face and hear His 'reproachful' voice at shattering proximity. This moment of self-abasement does not seem to have been a conventional religious experience. A man with more than his share of inborn guilt had managed to define his responsibility against an absolute that was denied by the political order under which he lived. How many Czechoslovaks understood by the beginning of November 1989 anything of Havel's private pilgrimage? Very few, for most can have had only a vague idea of who he was. But what those who did know him could recognise, without necessarily understanding its roots, was the moral authority that he had acquired not in spite, but because, of the secret policemen, judges and jailers of the Communist regime.

Havel had a further price to pay in neglect of his writer's craft. Since their national revival in the nineteenth century Czechs had demanded much from their writers and artists, and nagged them whenever they seemed to neglect the nation's cause in favour of their art. Smetana, who might have written much more fine chamber music, was forced by his public to write opera after opera in the folk-national vein. Havel's literary friends believed his best plays were his earliest; the strain of a life spent increasingly in opposition activities showed through in the later ones. But he was trapped by his own sense of duty, by his irreplaceable qualities as both political thinker and tactician, and by a steadily growing popularity particularly among the independent-minded young. By 1988 if he turned up at rock festivals the crowds received him almost like a pop star, cheering and forcing him to give countless autographs. Attitudes towards him were changing in less likely places too. During his short spell in prison at the beginning of 1989 the warders treated him as a privileged prisoner, and some even let him know they were on his side.

If the Czechs accepted Havel as a hero it was because he was both unlike and like them. His unusual strength was awesome; but his familiar habits inspired affection. Like so many of his countrymen he had a small country house: set in the pretty hills of north Bohemia it featured often in his letters to his wife from prison, for he worried terribly about its proper upkeep. With sparkling white-washed walls and doors and drainpipes painted a terracotta red, it represented both a dream and a temptation. The dream was a life of writing supported by an ordered daily existence necessarily enlivened for this sociable man by friends, food and drink, and parties. The living room with its wooden chairs and settee covered in mellow red velvet, Mucha posters and huddle of condiments within reach of a large dining table spoke of an agreeable routine. The nearby study with its papers in neat piles, one of which in the summer of 1989 was marked 'New Play', had a desk waiting for the word processor foreign friends had promised him and looked onto a little orchard. It was an invitation to work. A room under the roof reached by a ladder had space for half a dozen party guests to sleep. Havel kept a visitors' book for them and anyone else who called, the names entered in different coloured inks chosen by him. This was Havel's version of the private world into which so many Czechoslovaks had withdrawn to escape a public life they disliked and yet which, by their withdrawal, they were passively helping to support. They had succumbed to temptation; he could not, and as events gathered speed in 1989 he accepted that the little house at Hradecek was a vanishing dream. One day that busy summer he said to Zdenek Urbanek, 'I shall give up all this the moment we have decent politicians.' Before that could happen he would first have to give by his own example a lesson in decent politics.

SOME REVOLUTIONS ARE GOOD FOR YOU

In the early evening of Friday 17 November some 15,000 people gathered outside the Pathological Institute in Prague. Their purpose was to commemorate the funeral fifty years earlier of Jan Opletal, a student killed by the Nazis, although official approval for their march had been given on the pretext that it was to go to the same cemetery in Vysehrad where the Czech Romantic poet Karel Macha was buried. The procession reached its destination without incident. Speeches were made at the graveside, some of them criticising the Government, after which the unofficial student organisers led a large part of the mainly young crowd with banners calling for democratic freedoms down the embankment of the Vltava past applauding onlookers. When they came to the corner where the vast National Theatre stands the marchers turned right down Narodni Street. Actors leaned from windows and waved as did customers who came out of the Slavie Café where the spokesmen of Charter 77 sometimes tried to hold press conferences. The demonstration had swollen to perhaps double its original size by the time it poured like treacle down Narodni and there was an atmosphere of excitement and growing self-confidence. A reporter from the official Czech news agency CTK heard a girl say hopefully to her friend that it seemed like a revolution. Before the marchers could reach the bottom of Wenceslas Square which was their destination riot police appeared as if from nowhere to block their way, while more came down another side street to prevent a retreat backwards. At first the marchers did not realise what had happened. Many sat down and placed lighted candles on the ground before the policemen at the front of the column. Girls tried to decorate their riot shields with flowers. Panic broke out only when they realised that the two police lines had begun to move forward to squeeze the crowd. The young people's terror increased when men in khaki uniforms and red berets never seen on the Prague streets before materialised as if by magic, some of them jumping down from hoardings that protected buildings under repair. As members of the Ministry of

Interior's Division for Special Purposes, a highly-trained anti-terrorist unit, some of whom had protected the Czechoslovak embassy in Kabul, their participation suggested this was a very special police operation indeed. Over a hundred demonstrators were arrested and 561 people aged between thirteen and eighty-three were hurt, half of them students. Most of the wounded did not go to hospitals for fear of being tracked down by the police. One young man was reported to have died. Petr Uhl's unofficial news agency gave his name as Martin Smid, a student of the Faculty of Mathematics and Physics at Charles University. This last piece of news reached the world only the following day.

A medical student was among the lucky ones who found a place to hide. A woman in a block of apartments let him and a dozen others in and led them into an unlit inner room where they sat on the floor listening to policemen and their dogs running up and down the staircase outside. That was bad enough but he had another memory that was far worse. Before finding a door that would open for him he had knocked on several others without getting any response. He was sure there had been people behind those doors and certain they knew what was going on. Yet they had been too frightened to help. It made him sick to think of it. He could not understand it – and yet, of course, he could. Apart from the exceptional drama and violence of that evening on Narodni Street, it was how people had behaved for years. It was how the student and his friends had behaved, for what risks, till then, had they taken to challenge a regime they despised? The events of 17 November had something of this shock effect on many Czechoslovaks, particularly older ones. Within days of the Friday 'massacre' a hand-written poster had appeared on the side of the statue of St Wenceslas in front of the National Museum. 'Parents,' it read. 'Come with us. We are your children.' The guilty knowledge that over many years they had done so little that might have prevented this evening when their children were cold-bloodedly trapped and beaten, and the equally guilt-tinged admiration at the students' refusal to be cowed, awoke the nation's sense of shame. 'It was the children who helped us raise our heads,' a speaker would say in one of the huge demonstrations of the days ahead. 'It is now our duty to hold them high.'

For fifty years it had not been easy to hold heads high in Czechoslovakia. Alexander Dubcek would say that he had felt like Jan Hus before the Council of Constance when his Soviet-bloc colleagues hurled angry accusations at him during a Warsaw Pact meeting in Dresden in early August 1968. Dubcek, however, did not share Hus's fate. Condemned to death by the Council Hus resisted till the end, writing in his farewell to Prague University,

> I, Master Jan Hus, in chains and in prison, now standing on the shore of this present life and expecting on the morrow a dreadful death, which I hope will purge away my sins, find no heresy in myself.

Hus was burned at the stake and his ashes scattered so that not even the smallest relic of him should reach Bohemia. Dubcek did not recant either, but he did sign, as did almost all his colleagues in the Czechoslovak Party leadership, the document drafted by Moscow to justify the Soviet invasion. Their signatures perhaps followed logically from their refusal to contemplate resistance to the Soviet-led troops. It was the Czechoslovak leaders' instinct to protect the nation by not resisting, for they supposed resistance would not only cause bloodshed but also be pointless. Was that necessarily so? The resistance of the Hungarians in 1956 was pointless in the sense that it cost lives and yet was certain to be overcome by the Soviet army, but few Hungarians today would say it was not worthwhile. In the end it was Hungarian Communism, not Hungary, that was mortally wounded by 1956, as the reburial of Imre Nagy in June 1989 had shown. Moscow always had to take into account the possibility of resistance to any Soviet intervention in Poland. This fear encouraged the Russians to get General Jaruzelski to do their dirty work for them in 1981. Martial law artificially restored Polish Communism to life, but in the end proved fatal to it. The lack of Czechoslovak resistance in 1968 echoed an earlier failure to fight a foreign invader: Hitler's 1938 occupation of the Czech Sudetenland and his seizure of the entire country the following year. Czechoslovak Communists had always used this disaster as proof of the unreliability of the West. Czechoslovaks were encouraged to think of themselves as a helpless little nation betrayed by selfish great powers. But was Czechoslovakia so helpless or Germany, at that time, so all-powerful? The Czechoslovak army was excellently equipped (Skoda in Plzen and Zbrojovka in Brno were two of the world's best arms factories). It had powerful fortifications at its disposal. And though smaller than the German army, with only 1.35 million men compared to Hitler's 1.86 million, its size was certainly adequate to prevent a rapid German victory even if its action had not shamed the Western democracies to come to Czechoslovakia's assistance.

Should a nation fight when it knows it will be defeated? Are there times when the sacrifice of lives is a necessary investment in future national self-respect? Is a nation that submits without resisting to a foreign master and then, grumbling and cynical and not much liking itself, waits for history to remove him, in some way worse than the nation that fights but still in the end has to submit? Unanswerable questions to those who have never faced such choices, they weighed all the more heavily on Czechoslovaks because, apart from the dashing exploits of the Czech Legions in the Russian Civil War, they had not had to go to battle in the course of their struggle for independence. In a letter to his wife from prison Havel had called 'indifference and resignation . . . the most serious forms of human decline into nothingness'. The resignation of individuals translated into 'social resignation' which Havel believed had infected the country for the past twenty years as it had in other periods of its history.

The question was whether 17 November would shock the Czechoslovaks out of the resignation of which they were not proud. Some at first doubted it until the next few days proved them wrong. 'I'm so glad we have shown we can do it,' said an actress who herself had been caught up almost at once in the resistance of the Prague theatres. 'I was worried we couldn't; that we didn't have the charac-ter.' Opposition leaders were more hopeful for they understood almost at once that the situation had been completely changed by the unprecedented police brutality. They believed that the Czechs, usually 'such quiet people' who did their best to avoid bloodshed 'because blood is so precious here', as one of them put it, would change now that blood had been spilt. People recalled that Masaryk had reproached the Czechs for their fondness for martyrs, for their need to have someone to shed his blood before they were ready to take action. Friday's police action against people who had been remembering the funeral of a Czech martyred by the Nazis had touched the nation's rawest nerve. People also saw a parallel with a less dramatic but no less significant event that had taken place at the end of 1967. Prague students had then protested against the lack of electricity in their hostels by taking to the streets with banners demanding 'Give us Light'. The Central Committee, which hap-pened to be meeting at the time, was misled by their guilty conscience and, taking Light to mean Liberty, sent in the police against them. Horror at the unnecessary violence paved the way for the replacement of the hardline Party leader Antonin Novotny by Dubcek and the reforms that followed.

Events in Prague moved fast over the weekend after 17 November. On Saturday students from Damu, the drama section of the Prague Academy of Performing Arts, set up the first student strike committee. Later the same day representatives of all Prague's theatres agreed to cancel their scheduled evening performance but to remain open for what they called public dialogue. These evenings of dialogue became immensely popular and developed into a lively form of agitprop, this time for democracy, not socialism. The Civic Forum, soon to become the general staff of a peaceful revolution, was born on Sunday in the basement of an avant-garde theatre called the Cinoherni Klub. Havel, who had hurried back from his private world at Hradecek, was there and so were many of the other 'usual suspects' from Charter 77. But there were significant new faces too, among them representatives of both the People's and Socialist Parties, previously subservient allies of the Communists. Their presence was a sign that the old system of make-believe politics was crumbling. The Forum's first statement called for the resignation of Stepan and the Interior Minister, both held responsible for 17 November; an investigation into the police action; the release of prisoners of conscience; and the resignation of those Communist leaders who supported the Soviet invasion of 1968 and all that happened afterwards, starting with President Husak and Milos Jakes. The Forum also supported the idea of a general strike that actors and students had already called for 27 November; and it urged towns and cities throughout the country to set up local Forums if they agreed with its objectives. The Forum was an urgent improvisation, a 'self-defence task force', one of its creators said later, with the aim of getting rid of Jakes and when that happened with such unexpected speed the opposition had to scratch its head over what to do next. More precisely it was needed because, as another leader put it, 'we had to create something for [Prime Minister] Adamec to talk to. We had to be ready for the first contact.' Adamec was the only member of the top leadership who, though himself no Dubcek supporter at the time, was uncontaminated by any part in the repressive measures that followed August 1968. Adamec had only learned what really happened on Narodni Street when two students went to his apartment on Saturday, the following day. He seemed shocked, and when the young men asked him whose fault the crisis was he paused a moment before answering 'ours'. Havel had for some time been trying to convince the regime that if it would not talk with the experienced Chartists it would one day find itself faced by much less reasonable 'fundamentalists'. The creation of the Forum and the acceptability of Adamec as spokesman for the regime meant that there was now the chance of a dialogue as well as a framework for the peaceful resolution of the crisis.

If the situation was not to get out of control there was also a need for leadership on both sides. The people of Prague, excited, confused and nervous, were already taking to the streets in a disorganised way. Candles and flowers had been arranged at the places on Narodni Street where the worst police beatings had occurred (moving though these little shrines were, to anyone who had seen the memorials to dead wartime martyrs that marked the streets of Warsaw, and would soon appear in Bucharest, they seemed evidence of enviable Czech innocence). Ribbons of white, red and blue – the national colours – appeared on overcoats as suddenly as spring flowers, and within a few days the chef at the Palace Hotel would be making tricolour dumplings. Over a hundred thousand people had gone to Wenceslas Square on Monday afternoon and some of them afterwards marched down Narodni Street to find their way blocked by police when they tried to cross the bridges that led to Castle Hill and the Presidential palace. These aimless rambles had to be controlled. It was also necessary to guide the students, potentially a powerful force, for there were 80,000 of them in the capital. A Prague student strike-coordinating committee was in place by Monday but many students were apprehensive, particularly those who had been through the horror of Friday evening. What, usefully, were they to do? What, actually, was their aim? At that stage few really knew, and certainly fewer still believed, that they had taken the first steps to the removal of the Communist regime.

There was the chance of dangerous disorder on the Government side too. The regime quickly justified the police action against Friday's demonstration. On Sunday two students, both called Martin Smid, were shown live on television and Petr Uhl was arrested for spreading false information about a death that had not taken place. Yet the same day the Communist youth leader Vasil Mohorita met members of the Prague branch of the Socialist Youth Union and issued a statement attacking the police action and demanding a Parliamentary enquiry. Mohorita, a well-built man who had not yet quite exchanged his youthful handsomeness for the apparatchik's mask, was to be one of the most visible Communist leaders in the days ahead. Trapped between common sense and – who knows? – perhaps decency on one hand and the inflexible rules of a system he had chosen to serve on the other, he seemed to be suffering more than most of his colleagues. Mohorita's heavy face, at times sweating, at others plainly terrified, came to symbolise the agony of a Communist regime that was on the point of collapse. The Party rank and file, however, were scarcely to be seen and Stepan would soon complain that Communists were the only members of Czechoslovak society whom the crisis had failed to politicise. Certainly some apparatchiks seemed not to understand the danger of the moment. 'They don't realise how discredited they are,' was the explanation of a Prague journalist. 'They're so stupid they think they are bullet proof.' But what of those Communist leaders who were neither complacent nor inclined to self-criticism? The police had stayed away from the crowds after Friday, only blocking them if they tried to move across the river, but on Tuesday there were reports of tanks in the city suburbs and of busloads of Workers' Militia (the Party's paramilitary force made up of trusted factory workers) arriving from Moravia. Other reports said that hospitals had sent home their less seriously ill patients and were taking in new supplies of blood. This was enough for students to tell schoolchildren who had also declared an occupation strike in their classrooms not to go to the demonstration planned for that afternoon in Wenceslas Square. (Stepan would later say that he learned of plans to use the Workers' Militia against the Wenceslas Square demonstration on Thursday, though neither Civic Forum nor the public seemed aware of that and the atmosphere was less tense by then.)

The uncertainty would have been all the greater if people had known certain details about events on 17 November that became public knowledge only several months later. What emerged, after the Communists had been swept away and Havel was safely in the Presidential palace, was that one of the unofficial student leaders who organised the Jan Opletal demonstration was a State Security agent, and that he led the marchers into the trap that had been set for them by the police on Narodni Street. This same man later pretended to be a corpse in order to start rumours that someone had been killed by the police. Not long after that a second State Security agent, a girl called Drahomira Drazska, went to Petr Uhl to tell him that her boyfriend, the mathematics student Martin Smid, was dead. No one knew better than the Security Service that leaking this *canard* to Uhl was the surest and most convincing way to spread the news through Czechoslovakia and the world. But having helped bring about the 'massacre' and publicise it to maximum effect, State Security then seemed to withdraw from the scene. The men of the Division for Special Purposes vanished, and so did the riot police, except when needed to block off the bridges across the river. As demonstrations began to build up in the capital even ordinary uniformed police were scarce, though some soon appeared among the crowd at the meetings in Wenceslas Square applauding the speakers like everyone else. As for the plainclothes men who watched Havel and his friends for as many hours in the day and night as necessary, they made not the slightest attempt to hamper their movements over the days ahead though preventive detention, so often used in the past, would have been a simple way to stop the creation of Civic Forum. The Parliamentary commission that examined this murky affair and reported on it in the spring of 1990 said it had no doubt that the State Security was well informed about everything that was going on and found its inactivity after 17 November 'completely illogical'. The commission was also inclined to believe that the Party leadership was not in control of State Security, though that went against all known practice in the Soviet bloc and was partly contradicted by the later finding of the Prosecutor General that Miroslav Stepan had instructed police commanders to use all available means against the demonstrators, even though he knew the police's orders were only to block their way to the centre of the city. Milos Jakes later said he had told the Minister of the Interior on the morning of 17 November to take no action against the marchers because he understood the sensitive nature of the anniversary. The Minister of the Interior assured him the police would only close the entrance into Wenceslas Square. The Minister then went off to Ostrava to see his family, leaving his deputy in charge. This was Lieutenant-General Lorenc, the man who that evening would be having dinner with the deputy Chairman of the KGB. The Czechoslovak Parliamentary commission was baffled, not least because if the events of 17 November had been planned, no one seemed to try to take advantage of them, for example to use the outcry as a lever to oust Jakes and bring in speedily and to popular applause a more reform-minded leadership, which seemed the most plausible theory. Or did they try, and find it harder than they bargained for? Was Mohorita's Saturday statement part of such a plan? Possibly, but it soon lost any significance it might have had because as events elsewhere in East Europe had shown it was far too late to reform the system if indeed it ever had been possible. It was a student who said that 17 November had 'acted like a bomb'. It exploded the old cast of mind in which the students and everyone else were trapped. Whoever the plotters were their plans went miserably awry unless their unlikely intention was to speed up the system's collapse.

With the security forces keeping their heads down and the Party ineffectively preoccupied with its own survival the stage was left to the Civic Forum, to its pupils and students, and to its ultimate audience, the Czechoslovak people. Informal contacts between opposition intellectuals (particularly a group called the Circle of Independent Intelligentsia) and a small minority of students had existed for some time, but once the Prague faculties had gone on strike, a professional taskforce including key members of the Forum's leadership was dispatched to talk to the young strikers. 'Sometimes there are days that are more important than years,' said a middle-aged Chartist who had not been allowed to speak to academic audiences for twenty years. 'That is what it is like now for the students.' He sounded envious, for he had been seduced by the 'gentle, witty and generous' atmosphere he found in the faculties where he had spoken. Not all the students were equally ready to learn from their unexpected new teachers. Faculties where students were picked with an eye to ideological soundness, such as Pedagogy and Philosophy, had problems getting the strike going, partly because the teaching staff was obstructive. The pace was set by the Pure and Applied Sciences. At one of the three strike committees set up at the Medical Faculty someone had written on the blackboard of a lecture hall, 'If not us, who? If not now, when?' It suggested the earnestness of young people who against all their expectations found themselves at the centre of a political storm. They had no acknowledged leaders for there had been no real political activity till now. Most of them had never even talked about politics among themselves before because, as one student said, 'it was so obvious and there was nothing to discuss'. Few had read *Samizdat* papers like *Lidove Noviny*, readily admitting – because they knew it was their generation's norm – that this was because they had not wanted to get into trouble with the police. If any of them knew much of Vaclav Havel and liked him it was, as one said, 'because he is a playwright and not a politician'. Hardly any knew who a Charter stalwart like Petr Uhl was and a huge poster that went up in a subway demanding his release from prison must have puzzled most students and almost every other ordinary citizen of Prague who saw it. Suddenly these young men and women found themselves not only setting up security systems to prevent troublemakers getting into the faculties but also organising their own illegal printing shops. At the Medical Faculty they dug out an old Roneo machine from the basement. Treated as an object of the highest secrecy its black-fingered masters delivered rebukes of truly revolutionary severity to any stranger rash enough to try to take a look at it. A student apologising on their behalf said, 'You have to remember that people keep their characters even at times like this.'

He was wrong. Revolutions change people, at least for a little while. They become nicer to each other, more thoughtful, more imaginative, for these are moments of collective creation. The students and other young people helped set the mood in Prague not least by the posters that covered the subway stations and walls all over the centre of the city. Poster after poster warned against violence: that particular Czech gene had certainly been passed on to this new generation. Some posters were sentimental, in the vein of 'Freedom is beautiful, sweet as a strawberry.' Others tried to fix this rare moment when a nation seemed to have a chance to settle its own destiny: 'If we have learned to fly like birds and swim like fish, then we can learn to live like people.' There was a pedantry and tidiness about all this activity that would have puzzled young Poles or Hungarians. Signs warned people not to write difficult-to-erase slogans with aerosol cans. Many handbills and stickers were produced on Faculty word processors (most though not all Deans tolerated this, and also allowed access to Xerox machines that had previously been kept under strictest guard). This allowed them to give up-to-the-hour comments on the latest events. Posters that were out of date were taken down and the wall from which they had been removed cleaned. No one should have been surprised that in this atmosphere even the Prague Punks put up their own flyers denying that they wanted violence and giving their full support to the students. When Punks appeared at the demonstrations on Wenceslas Square they reassured their nervous neighbours with cries of 'We'll be good! We'll be good!' After a few days Civic Forum distributed a poster with 'Eight Rules of Dialogue' that summed up the atmosphere of the reasonable revolution that the students did so much to create. Rule one was to treat one's opponent not as an enemy but as a 'a partner in the search for truth'; rule four, don't stray from the point; rule five, don't try to have the last word at any price; rule six, don't offend the other. In Prague, though, gravity could not entirely replace humour. The Journalism Faculty founded a Committee for a more Joyous General Strike. Other students, thinking the Civic Forum leaders had begun to look too serious, sent them pocket mirrors and asked them to look into them from time to time and smile. But there was in general not much frivolity and certainly none of the self-indulgence of the Japanese student who during the great strikes at Tokyo University in the 1970s wrote on a lecture-room wall, *Femmes du monde! Aimez-moi, aimez-moi passionnément!* Might not people get tired of demonstrating every day in chillingly cold weather? a student leader was asked. The response was a frown and a lecture about freedom being 'too serious a matter' to be looked at like that.

Armed with high-minded advice and their own newly awoken political idealism the students set off into Bohemia and Moravia on what was perhaps their most important work, carrying news of the revolution to the factories and preparing the working class for the general strike that had been called for the following Monday, 27 November. Until television began to give decent coverage of events, which was not until the end of the first week, there was no other reliable way to reach them. 'Workers! Help your children!', 'Workers! Support the students!' appealed the posters in Prague with true revolutionary pathos but talking to the working class could be a nerve-wracking business. Police and units of the Workers' Militia guarded some factories and at the beginning of the week students were arrested as they tried to enter them. Factory managers stopped others. But some did get in, marvelled to find themselves talking to workers with oily hands and survived to tell the story. Actors shared this work too, among them the elderly Josef Kemr, a wisp of a man with the hair of an unkempt Abbé Liszt who drove himself from factory to factory to tell the workers that a new age was dawning.

Nothing was more remarkable than the revolution's speed. It took all the participants by surprise and speed for that reason became a player in its own right. This is how developments unfolded from Tuesday 21 November, the day when Civic Forum held its first organised afternoon meeting in Wenceslas Square.

Tuesday 21 November. Havel speaks for the first time from the balcony of the Socialist Party's publishing house in the square, in itself a politically significant use of real estate. Loudspeakers are provided by pop groups (if there is a pop group in the country that supports the regime it is keeping very quiet). The meeting ends with the deep-voiced Marta Kubisova, a much loved singer banned from performing since 1968, leading the singing of the national anthem, the world's only federal anthem, for its Czech part is slow and sad while the Slovak conclusion has a cheerful lilt. In the evening Jakes goes on television to say reforms are necessary but does not offer to resign as the Forum has demanded. The Party's true instincts seem to have come out at a meeting of the Parliament's foreign relations committee in the afternoon attended by Vasil Bilak and other leaders. Disturbed by noises coming from the demonstration in Wenceslas Square someone asks for the blinds to be pulled down 'so that we don't have to look at it and be disturbed'.

Wednesday 22 November. Leaders of Civic Forum's Slovak sister, Public Against Violence, speak to 100,000 people in Slovakia's capital Bratislava. At the same time the Slovak opposition leader, Jan Carnogursky, is standing trial for producing *Samizdat*. There are demonstrations in Brno and other big towns, and these, too, will continue over the days to come.

Thursday 23 November. The first snow of winter fell in the night and it is extremely cold, but 300,000 gather in Wenceslas Square to hear the Forum's new demand for free elections and for the article conferring a 'leading role' on the Communist Party to be removed from the Constitution. Representatives of the Socialist Party make their first speeches. That same afternoon Alexander Dubcek, himself a Slovak, returns to public politics at a mass meeting in Bratislava. Miroslav Stepan mounts a balcony at the CKD engineering works to talk to workers. He is heavy set, with close-cut dark hair and a fleshy, slightly yellow face. He keeps glancing to the men standing next to him, as though asking for support. The workers listen in silence, but then start to shout and whistle. Stepan does not know what to do. He is like an animal that is powerful in its underground lair but cannot defend itself once it is dragged into the fresh air and the light. Almost all Czech Television's 5,000 employees vote for full coverage of the meetings at Wenceslas Square and all other political events. TV that day shows five minutes from the square, a breakthrough of immense importance, as someone is stopping delivery of the few newspapers that are beginning to report accurately. *Lidove Noviny* has this advice for its (rather few) readers: talk to your neighbours, talk to the students, and don't be misled by the mass media.

Friday 24 November. The Central Committee meets, not at its headquarters but at the Party's Political College out near the airport. How many members are present? 'We don't know,' says a Party journalist. 'They are so old that we think some are already dead.' The debate reveals understandable confusion. Only a month before, says a miner, the leadership said the people were with us but now a 'dam has broken. How are we to get that straight in our heads?' Stepan says the state is paralysed and the Party's power limited. He defends himself against people who say he should speak to the crowds in Wenceslas Square and concludes 'the very essence of socialism is in danger'. In blind-pulling mood, the Committee decides to replace Jakes with the Moravian Karel Urbanek – which at least means the Party leader speaks good, musical Czech – but apart from removing Husak and two others from the Presidium leaves the leadership untouched. Afterwards the Party spokesman pretends not to know of Civic Forum's existence. Prime Minister Adamec, isolated in a Presidium which has virtually put him on trial for putting out feelers to Civic Forum, resigns from the Party leadership. This is also the day that Dubcek makes an emotional debut in Wenceslas Square. He somehow projects his charm over the vast square and the crowd opens its heart to him. But he talks of a 'revival of socialism' and people do not respond to him as the leader they have been waiting for.

Saturday 25 November. The Prague Party organisation gathers for an angry, tearful meeting and decides 'the people are wiser than the Communists'. Stepan resists, but then resigns as Prague's leader. Husak, who is still President, stops the Carnogursky trial and pardons seven other oppositionists against whom the police have brought actions. On a freezing afternoon a giant crowd of half a million, some say more, gather on Letna Field, an open space on a bluff above the river where Stalin's giant statue, with buttons as big as loaves of bread, once stood and that till now has been used for the regime's most pompous ceremonies. Students have decorated what was the base of the Stalin statue with a dark blue canvas covered with gold stars and placed a large bell on top of it. The conclusion of many Czech fairy stories is ' . . . And the bell rang and that's the end of the story.' Everyone knows for whom this bell is ringing. In his speech Havel attacks the new-old Party Presidium and says Monday's general strike will be a referendum on whether the Party should keep its self-proclaimed leading role. The same day Roman Catholics have a chance to unite politics with religion at a mass presided over by Cardinal Tomasek in St Vitus Cathedral to celebrate the canonisation of Agnes of Bohemia, a much-beloved national heroine whose recognition as a saint must surely bring miracles.

Sunday 26 November. After contacts with Adamec through an unofficial group called BRIDGE – the rock musician Michael Kocab is one of its members – Adamec and Havel at last meet face to face. In the afternoon Adamec appears with Forum leaders for another giant rally on Letna Field. Applauded at first, the Prime Minister then loses his touch, starts to sound like the old Party politician he is, and is booed. Another surprise speaker is Lieutenant Ludvik Pinc, a young police officer who took part in the 17 November operation. He says he is sorry. There are grumbles of 'Why did he become a cop? He didn't have to', but others seem to think Pinc has done the decent thing. The Central Committee meets again and this time does better. Only nine of the twenty-four-man Presidium keep their jobs. The youth leader, Vasil Mohorita, is promoted to Central Committee secretary. In the evening Civic Forum puts out its programme over which the Charter's best brains have been sweating in their stuffy headquarters in the bowels of the Magic Lantern Theatre. Called *What We Want* it no longer messes around with calling for this or that head to roll. Communism is to go, and Czechoslovakia to become what it once was, a European democracy with a market economy.

Monday 27 November. Four out of five Czechoslovaks take part in the general strike between 12 noon and 2pm but the impression is not that of a nation on a revolutionary rampage. Crowds in Prague and elsewhere appear on the streets at noon to make plain their support for the Forum but as one Czech points out a two-hour strike at midday is rather shorter than the lunch break and rest afterwards that many people take on normal days. A Party reform group called Democratic Forum of Communists is set up. Its organisers talk of returning to the democratic roots of Czechoslovak Communism, a sure sign that the Party is breaking up.

Tuesday 28 November. Havel and Adamec meet and agree that the Premier will announce a new federal Government by 3 December. The new Party leader Urbanek makes a conciliatory speech but is still having problems coming to grips with reality – he says demands for the abolition of the Party's army, the Workers' Militia, and of Party branches in factories are 'unacceptable'.

Wednesday 29 November. Even though two-thirds of the Federal Assembly's members are Communists, 242 of them bow to reality and meet Civic Forum's demand by voting to remove the leading role of the Party from the Constitution and end the provision that all culture and education be based on Marxism-Leninism. They also set up a commission to examine the 17 November affair. Alois Indra, a hardliner who played an infamous part in justifying the Soviet invasion, resigns as the Assembly's chairman. There is no clock in the chamber, a lack Havel comments on later, for he will also find none in his office-to-be in the Presidential Palace. He considers this appropriate, believing that time has stood still in a country that the Communists have deprived of real history. Perhaps a clock will be the symbol of his presidency. After a meeting Party activists Mohorita appears before the press as spokesman no longer of 'the Party', but of an ordinary political party. Asked if the Communists will surrender power if they lose the election planned for the coming year, he gets a laugh with his counter-question 'What power?' A Soviet journalist asks if the new Central Committee is really capable of change, or if it will 'drown proudly with the Party statutes in its hand'. 'It's good we can still laugh,' says Mohorita, adding that for at least two years some Party members have been discussing the same demands that Civic Forum is now making. Adamec says on TV that there must be a reassessment of 1968. In two days' time the Party Presidium will call the Soviet invasion wrong, an admission as inevitable as it is necessary, but tantamount to suicide.

Thursday 30 November. Forum leaders meet for the first time with a Party delegation. It is led by Mohorita who talks sense. They agree to watch out for 'provocations' from either side – some wild and demagogic leaflets have appeared, and Forum has displayed specimens of them at its information centre in the Manes gallery – and to set up a permanent telephone link. One of the Forum team reveals the depth of feelings built up over the years in opposition when he calls Mohorita 'a sincere man not of the highest intellectual quality, but not unbearable physically'.

Saturday 2 December. Havel, long a favourite devil of *Rude Pravo*, tells the paper in an interview that it is 'not the time for recriminations'. He advises the Communists to become an ordinary democratic political party. Adamec dismays the country with his new Government, fifteen of whose twenty members are still Communists. '15:5' posters appear within hours in the centre of Prague. Havel will later say Adamec was 'inscrutable and secretive' during their negotiations. The first 'Havel for President' badges appear.

Monday 4 December. In protest against Adamec's proposed Government Wenceslas Square fills up for its first afternoon demonstration for a week. This show of determination quickly brings results. Within two days Havel secures his first meeting with Urbanek. Adamec resigns to be replaced as Premier by his deputy the Slovak Marian Calfa who, though a Party member, turns out to be a sensible patriot who quickly sees eye to eye with Havel. On 9 December Husak says he will resign as President. No tears are shed for the old man who satisfied his desire for power by humiliating a nation. The following day Calfa announces his Government. Of twenty-one members ten are Communists; two each are from the Socialist and People's Parties; and all but one of the other seven are nominees of the Forum. They include Jan Carnogursky, who ten days earlier was standing trial; Vladimir Dlouhy and Vaclav Klaus, both of whom burnished their free-market theories under cover of the Forecasting Institute; and Havel's old companion in jail, Jiri Dienstbier, who is to be Foreign Minister, an appointment that gives particular pleasure to foreigners who have had dealings with the suspicious dumpling-diplomats in the Ministry's huge offices in the Cernin Palace. By this time the revolution is well won and is crowned by Havel's unanimous election as President by the Federal Assembly on 29 December.

Once the contest began it seemed an almost cruelly uneven affair. Members of one of the most effectively harried dissenting communities in the Soviet bloc became giants overnight while the Party did not so much shrink as disappear. This somersault in the balance of power was inevitable once the regime decided not to use force. Deprived of the threat of force the Party lost not only its hands of steel but its tongue. Stepan, at the Central Committee meeting on Friday 24 November, had suggested Government ministers should tour factories to talk to the workers, but what were they to say? Just how discredited the Party's messages were may be judged by the journalist at *Rude Pravo* who complained that throughout the first week of the crisis the Party paper had only been allowed to print 'bad, late information from the top leadership, most of it lies'. Journalists calling at the Central Committee on the day before the general strike found burly men loading a van with stacks of posters printed with messages like 'Communists are Realists' and 'The Czechoslovak Communist Party keeps its word' but where the posters went was a mystery, for none were ever spotted on a wall in Prague. A young official with clammy hands offered the automatic greeting of 'Honour to Labour!' and admitted the staff at the Central Committee would not take part in Monday's strike. 'Frankly, we need every minute we can get. An hour counts like a week now.' He had nothing more to say and vanished up the staircase over which a large gold-coloured statue of a Soviet soldier protecting a Czechoslovak girl stood guard.

When the Central Committee did organise press conferences they were unenlightening, and took place only after hours of delay. Civic Forum, whose Chartist members had long experience of the international press, understood the importance of winning the information war and news conferences soon became a regular evening feature in the Magic Lantern. The theatre's stage was set for a production of Dürenmatt's *Minotaurus*, and Havel and friends would emerge from what looked like the back of an old-fashioned loudspeaker to take chairs ranged in a straight line at the front of the boards. To see this little ritual performed each evening was to be reminded of the end of *Don Giovanni* when the Don has been dragged down to hell and Mozart has his characters come in front of the curtains for a cheerful finale. Proceedings were conducted by the boyish Father Maly. There were usually one or two of the young student leaders, as well as actors, a pop singer perhaps, and unexpected stars like the economist Vaclav Klaus, whose gentle wit and high-pitched voice disguised a steely commitment to the rigours of the market. Havel was his usual bohemian self, untidily dressed and unassuming, but sometimes showing his stern side; he was too serious to give an easy answer even to the most lightweight question.

From the first great meeting in Wenceslas Square the crowds had treated him as a hero, though his speaking style was little more than a hoarse shout into the microphone, a painful contrast to Havel in quiet conversation. No one knew for certain how popular he was in the country at large. When it came to discussing how to choose the country's new President, Civic Forum insisted it be left to the Federal Assembly rather than be settled by a nationwide vote, although opinion polls suggested that was what most people wanted. Havel very likely was the most popular of the possible candidates but the Forum was not inclined to take a chance on it. The November days showed how fickle the crowd could be. An appearance on television had made the economist Valtr Komarek an instant star, and almost at once posters and handbills appeared in Prague saying he should become Prime Minister. Speaking on Wenceslas Square the day after the general strike the Doctor had shown himself a skilful flatterer ('Nations get the governments they deserve but this nation has shown it deserves a better government') and another crop of enthusiastic posters at once appeared. 'After forty years of the dark ages Komarek has brought us light.' 'With Komarek the Crown will be as good as the Deutschmark.' 'He's nothing but a witch-doctor,' said a disapproving Chartist, but when people started choosing names for the underground station that was named after the unloved old Communist Gottwald the most popular suggestions were Masaryk and Komarek. The Komarek craze soon faded. He made the mistake of publishing an egotistic little autobiography which told of how, when an adviser in Castro's Cuba, he had worked with Che Guevara: 'Their amazing, complex friendship and their open discussions turned into the stuff of legends.' Legends involving Che Guevara were scarcely a recommendation to Czechoslovaks in 1989. Havel, by contrast, was solid; he had shown he was all of a piece. He did not flatter anyone, least of all the crowd. As President he would often tell his people what they did not want to hear. It seemed they accepted his right to do that, recognising themselves that they stood in need of correction.

From the moment Civic Forum was set up, its biggest worry was the working class. When Havel wrote in the dark days of 1978 that 'the issue is the rehabilitation of values like trust, openness, responsibility, solidarity and love', he knew that most of his country-men were in no condition to appreciate such a message. He understood better than anyone that 'post-totalitarianism' thrived on a mixture of fear and consumer comforts, and had himself written 'we are all being publicly bribed'. Unlike the Polish opposition, Charter 77 had not developed contacts with workers, and a couple of days after the Forum's founding, one of its leaders was to be found wringing his hands over the omission. The Forum and its supporters would have to 'pay for their negligence, for this traditional Czech weakness in links between intelligentsia and workers'. He recalled it had been much the same in 1968, and blamed it on the atomisation of society that Communism brought about, the barriers erected by the system with precisely the intention of preventing social solidarity. The Forum's propaganda teams of students and actors could not be expected to overcome this work of years in a few short days. Apprehension about what the working class would do explained why the crowd at the meeting on Wenceslas Square on Thursday 23 December cheered the arrival of 10,000 workers from the CKD engineering plant as though they were the Foreign Legion. That same evening Father Maly was eager to announce that first-division football teams had cancelled all their matches out of solidarity with Civic Forum. 'This,' he explained, 'ought to have an influence on ordinary people.' Soon there were other encouraging signs. Workers began to arrive with messages of support at the offices of those Prague newspapers that seemed likely to print them. Petr Miller, a worker from CKD who was eventually to become Minister of Labour, joined the Civic Forum ensemble for the nightly performance in the Magic Lantern. He proved a good adviser, but as a symbol he was priceless. Resistance in the factories to the Forum and its student emissaries came chiefly from the middle-aged Communists, the men and women who had bettered themselves through Party membership. Older workers tended to be for the Forum, the young ones even more so, for they felt ashamed they had let the students begin the battle against the regime on their own. When Stepan tried to tell the CKD workers that the demonstrators whom the police attacked on 17 November were hooligan children they shouted back 'they're our children'.

There was a lot of shame in Prague that November. The regime began to be ashamed at the way it had ruled; the people were ashamed at the way they had allowed themselves to be ruled. Shame lay behind the malicious pleasure with which people took out their keys and rattled them to tell the Communists the game was up. This was the revenge of the humiliated. The air crackled with the same cheerful malice when the crowds responded quickly to whoever was speaking, roaring 'Give him a shovel' when a speaker mentioned the name of Jakes or Stepan, and sometimes following it with a further chant of 'No, don't. He'll steal it.' When Petr Uhl, fresh out of prison, appeared on Letna Field to say he had left a half-eaten dinner behind in his cell, there was a roar of 'Let Stepan finish it!' The crowds did shout out other things: Masaryk's old slogan 'Let Truth Prevail' was popular. But what people wanted most was to put the boot in. 'Do you hear me?' Maly asked the half million on Letna and the answer came rolling back: 'It's only the Party that doesn't hear you.'

Searching one afternoon for a better view of the rally in Wenceslas Square, I was guided by Jan, a medical student, to the Rostov Café that sits on top of a department store half-way down the square. He had a bag of leaflets printed by his faculty strike committee that he was supposed to distribute outside Prague and, nervous a policeman might ask what he was carrying (in fact a non-existent risk), was only too happy to get off the street. A lift delivered us into an unexpected world. A trio wearing red Cossack shirts were playing Latin-American music. When they began a rumba two very plain middle-aged couples got up from tables next to the dance floor and swept into practised action, oblivious to the multitude below, to its chants, to Havel's voice, and even to the national anthem though it was easily heard through the Cossack trio's rhythms. There was an open terrace, exposed to a bone-chilling wind, from which people were looking into the square that lay like a long plank thrown across the centre of the city. On the opposite side some men had climbed onto neon signs and hung there like spiders in their webs (one was to become the revolution's Ikarus, falling and injuring himself mortally). In the distance, beyond the river, floodlights shone on the castle and the spire of the cathedral that rose like a Gothic cactus above its walls. It was an odd group on the terrace. A large red-faced man in an expensive overcoat had his arms round two smart women. They seemed the sort more likely to lose than gain by the coming revolution. The old city across the river glowed as though it were an illuminated manuscript, something one might dream of but never quite attain. The crowd in the square was not dreaming. It was enjoying itself at the expense of its old rulers. By rumba-ing away the revolution the drab couples were saying that private pleasures outlast revolutionary enthusiasm. Even Jan, experiencing for the first time the intoxication of political commitment, could not forget the approach of a dreaded exam in microbiology. It was in the acceptance of such human imperfections that Prague's perfection lay. The revolution's makers did not claim they would bring the immaculate. They neither saw themselves as angels, nor did they wish to turn other people into angels. Their aim was only to allow them to take responsibility for their own lives.

I came across Jan one evening several weeks later sitting at a table in the Slavie Café that had a view across the river to Castle Hill. He had passed the microbiology exam. He had almost abandoned his pre-revolution plan of emigrating. 'The one thing all this has changed for me,' he said, 'is that now I know everything is up to me.' The new President in the Palace within the walls of the illuminated castle would have been proud of him.

11

Romania's Bitter Revolution

NARCISSUS AND THE NATION

When a dictator is at last swept from power the reasons for his fall are usually so numerous that the world wonders why it did not happen long before. So it was when Nicolae Ceausescu was overthrown in December 1989. No one had a good word for him, while his mistakes and crimes seemed as numerous as the knick-knacks, *objets*, and plain junk that crowded the Villa Primavera where he had lived with his wife Elena throughout the years of power. What better place to reflect on the nature of his rule, for surely this terrifying couple must have left some clue there to the origins and nature of their megalomania. Set among fir trees the Villa Primavera is a handsome white building. Romanians are good architects – Ceausescu's monstrous House of the Republic notwithstanding – and the outside is a pleasant mixture of classical and Romanian styles often found in Bucharest's well-off districts, though fussy gilt lamps along the short drive to the front door hint that something may be amiss inside.

The house was opened to a few visitors shortly after Ceausescu's overthrow when Bucharest was in the grip of an unusually prolonged cold spell. Preoccupied by the revolution the city had forgotten to clear away a heavy fall of snow, leaving streets and pavements sown with patches of thick ice that shone like polished metal, and to the unwary were almost as dangerous as the bullets of the Securitate during the December days of fighting. The new Government had released food stocks but the crowded shops were still pathetic places, pervaded by the smell of stale and rotten provisions and cave-like in their gloom. The only full shelves bore dusty cans and bottles whose contents even hungry Romanians considered too dangerous to eat. But now at least there was the chance of getting staples like rice and perhaps even greater delicacies too. People struggled to get close to counters with butter and chocolate, and went away happy just to have seen such things again. It was natural to suppose the Ceausescus had gorged themselves while their people starved, and newspapers were quick to publish stories about the extravagance of the banquet arranged for Elena's last birthday. Gluttony, though, was not one of the couple's sins. The menus preserved in the kitchens at the Villa Primavera recorded the calorie count of each of their five daily meals. In Elena Ceausescu's pink and gold bathroom there were four sets of scales, one of them the large kind that hospitals use. The Ceausescus were weight-watchers and food freaks. They were natural converts to organic food, as much on their guard against poisoning by impurities as by their enemies. Their vegetables were grown under glass, and the gardeners instructed never to use chemicals. Tropical fruits came from a special greenhouse in the once royal palace of Snagov. When Ceausescu said Romanians would do better to eat less it was not just the remark of a cynical dictator. He was offering a piece of royal wisdom. The ruling pair set an example by their own leanness.

A writer from Transylvania, a Hungarian who eventually fled to Budapest, wrote of Ceausescu that 'the person who can have everything does not have to obey the laws of fate'. Nicolae and Elena Ceausescu's greed was for life and power. They dieted in order to be immortal and to keep power for ever. That the Romanians understood this was suggested by the rumours that the *Conducator* had his blood changed every month. It was possible to find even educated people who were half-inclined to believe these treatments sometimes used the blood of young babies to give Ceausescu a special boost. The interior of the Villa Primavera served to assert the couple's immortality by showing they could have whatever they wanted. It was like being in an auction house. Tables were crowded with silver, crystal and porcelain, much of it expensive kitsch. There were pictures not just on the walls but also stacked against them, including works by Romania's best nineteenth- and early twentieth-century painters – the couple's taste, as might be expected, was conservative. A small Rubens portrait in what had been the study of their son Nicu was at least done the honour of being properly hung. All the many chandeliers were crystal. Furniture was either gilded or elaborately carved and inlaid. Wallpapers were of silk. The only books to be seen were in Nicu's study and they were mainly school and university texts. Educated Romanians who had a chance to see inside the house reacted with a patronising shrug. 'What did you expect? Give a peasant money and he stays a peasant no matter what.' But the lack of taste was less interesting than the passion to accumulate that the house revealed, not least in its elaborate built-in wardrobes. The one in Nicu's old bedroom was still full of his clothes, though he had not lived there for several years: a drawer full of underwear, another of caps, another belts, yet another with white handkerchiefs bearing a large monogrammed 'N'. Elena Ceausescu's wardrobe had racks for shoes, each of the many pairs kept in shape by old-fashioned padded shoetrees. Grey silk covers protected each of her dozens of dresses. The Villa Neptune where the Ceausescus went to relax or entertain guests by the Black Sea revealed the same passion for hoarding large numbers of quite ordinary things. There were the inevitable bathroom scales; showers that gave water massages, a sauna, and a swimming-pool inlaid with handsome mosaics, but it was the wardrobes and cupboards that were most memorable. They contained boxes of clothes, including a good deal of decorous beachwear for gentlemen of a certain age; rows of shampoo bottles and packets of soap; safety razors; sets of instruments for pedicure. It is the custom in some Asian countries for peasants to fill their larders at the New Year to ensure that the coming months will be bountiful. The Ceausescus observed their version of the same superstition. How could death carry them off when they were so well provisioned for the future?

The Ceausescus' hopes also rested on something that Romanians were less eager to talk about than the couple's cruelty and extravagance. In none of the countries of East Europe were the Communists able to obliterate completely the nation with its passions and often questionable memories. They could, however, tame the nation; and their later attempts to gain popularity by flirting with those very national feelings they had done their best to suppress were either half-hearted or cynical. Romania was different. When Ceausescu became leader in 1965 at the age of only forty-seven he inherited from his predecessor Gheorgiu-Dej a Party that already seemed to some Romanians a genuine national movement. Within a few years of coming to power Ceausescu had made himself an undisputed Romanian hero. It was his good luck to be well-equipped to play this role. It was Romania's misfortune to have a history and set of national neuroses that pushed her into the hands of such a leader. Communism offered Ceausescu the chance of unmatched power and, in Romanian colours, brought the rare chance of genuine popular support.

Ceausescu's origins recommended him to Gheorghiu-Dej who, after being put in power by the Soviet Union at the end of the war, manoeuvred to get rid of other leading Party members who were under Moscow's influence, the majority of them of Jewish or Hungarian origin. The young Romanian peasant from the impoverished Olt valley who had become a Communist while still a teenager made a perfect acolyte; he was quick and shrewd, and had no tiresome pretensions to being an intellectual. Gheorghiu-Dej was as ruthless a Stalinist ruler as any in East Europe and after Ceausescu's death the elderly men who emerged to reconstitute the old Romanian political parties cursed Dej rather than Ceausescu, never forgiving the former for sending them to years of brutal forced labour and imprisonment. After Stalin's death Gheorghiu-Dej brought the country into head-on collision with Moscow (though memories of the short years of Soviet-Romanian friendship were to remain in unexpected places, like the streets named after Gorky, Tolstoy, Pushkin and Chekhov that to this day encircle the Villa Primavera). The Russians saw Romania with its rich farmlands as one of the bloc's natural food suppliers. Dej insisted on its right to be a modern industrial power. Romanian vanity and Russophobia (Stalin had annexed the predominantly Romanian-populated Bessarabia in 1945) made this an attractive policy, but having defied their Soviet ally Romanians fell victim to paranoid fears of Soviet plots of revenge. This, too, suited Ceausescu. It helped ensure his victory over rivals to succeed Dej in 1965 because the Romanian leadership was determined not to give Moscow a chance to exploit divisions in its ranks. The Prime Minister of the day, Ion Gheorghe Maurer, had feared a power struggle and therefore proposed Ceausescu who struck him as a man who 'sits, listens and tries to understand'. The argument of unity at all costs gained strength when Ceausescu became the only leader in the bloc to criticise the Soviet invasion of Czechoslovakia. Dej's achievement in persuading the Soviet Union to withdraw its troops from Romania after the 1956 Hungarian uprising was taken further when Romania's Grand National Assembly voted in 1968 to forbid the transit of foreign troops across Romanian territory without its permission. Outrageous in Moscow's eyes it was immensely popular in Bucharest. Ion Caramitru, Romania's best known actor and a leading participant in the December 1989 uprising, remembers the first years after 1968 as a time of 'wonderful spiritual life', for it was a period of liberalisation as well as national self-congratulation. Liberalisation did not long survive the Ceausescus' 1971 visit to China and North Korea. Nationalism and the personality cult – both thriving under Asian Communism – did.

Sophisticated Romanians defended the cult of Ceausescu that developed in the 1970s by referring to the Russian threat. 'Whenever Romania has not had a strong leader we have been exploited by others,' said one of the brains behind Bucharest's nimble policy of playing the great powers off against each other. Anyone who criticised Ceausescu, like the pre-war Party veteran Constantin Pirvulescu, whose unique outspokenness at the Party congress in 1979 reduced Ceausescu to incoherent rage, was dismissed as a dangerous Muscovite. 'There may be ceremonies here you do not understand,' advised another senior official at the end of the 1970s, 'but no words can express what Nicolae Ceausescu has done for this country. For us socialism is only another means for promoting Romania's perennial interests.' The 'ceremonies' of Romanian public life were indeed remarkable. On certain occasions the ingenious Securitate transformed Gheorgiu-Dej Square between the old royal palace and the Central Committee building into an operetta stage across which the Ceausescus would walk to the applause of their people, their progress every now and then interrupted by impromptu folk dances or a rush of young men and women anxious to present the couple with flowers and kisses. When the Ceausescus honoured the National Theatre with their presence everyone turned to see them enter the royal box around which the auditorium, on Ceausescu's advice, was built. No one showed surprise when the *Conducator* had his portrait painted with the regalia of old Romanian royalty. The phenomenon was not new to Romanians who had almost no experience of power exercised under constitutional restraints. There was a traditional language of court flattery – a Romanian writer described it as 'the sort of stuff you can write with both hands at once' – which sounded more outrageous to foreign ears than it did to Romanian. Many gifted members of the creative intelligentsia were enthusiastic courtiers. No one was more skilful than the young poet Adrian Paunescu who also toured the country with a music show for young people that was a brilliant mix of peace propaganda (Romania's 'peace policy' was subtly anti-Soviet) and sentimental patriotism. Standing up to applaud Ceausescu when he spoke was accepted by Romanians as a custom of the court, though it horrified even Soviet officials long accustomed to the boring rituals of Communism. When the Soviet Politburo member Vitali Vorotnikov returned to Moscow after attending Ceausescu's last Party congress in November 1989 he complained of exhaustion after having to rise to his feet seventy-five times during just one speech by the *Conducator*.

Romanians had reason to be wary of Moscow but they exaggerated the danger of purposeful intrigue against them, for Bucharest was never more than a minor irritant to Soviet policy. In Transylvania, however, Ceausescu had an issue even better suited to bring his own growing paranoia into tune with the fears of the Romanian people. Transylvania had been Romanian since the end of the First World War but Romanians still behaved as though their title to it was not secure, as though – as a Romanian historian put it after Ceausescu's fall – 'we still feel we are not the masters there' and unable to compete with the two million-strong Hungarian minority. If, as Hungarians said, the problem lay in a deep Romanian inferiority complex it was not without reason. Romanians had always had to struggle in Transylvania. The Habsburg administration recognised neither their Romanian identity nor their Orthodox religion although Romanians, most of them serfs, were in the majority since at least the eighteenth century. 1848, the year of Hungary's glorious revolt against the Habsburgs, saw a Romanian Transylvanian uprising against the Hungarians who had no intention of giving independence to their own subject peoples. Avram Iancu, one of the uprising's leaders, became an enduring Romanian hero and was an avowed model for Marian Munteanu, the first student leader of post-Ceausescu Romania. Ironically it was foreign subversion in the shape of the Habsburg-supported Uniate Church (following Rome but observing Eastern rites and making many converts among the Romanian Orthodox in Transylvania) that produced the first leaders of Romania's national revival. And it was a clever Romanian Uniate bishop who mapped out a theory of the historical origins of the Romanian people upon which, with modifications, Romanians would base their country's claims to

Transylvania and much else besides. The bishop argued that the Transylvanian Romanians were the descendants of Roman legionaries and had therefore occupied the area long before the arrival of the Hungarians and Saxons who were the region's other chief inhabitants. Ceausescu played a clever hand over Transylvania. He kept fear of Hungary alive by exaggerating the iniquities of past Hungarian rule, above all its attempt to 'magyarise' the Romanians, though in fact very few Romanian Transylvanians could speak Hungarian by the time the region came under Bucharest's control. He also played on more recent and equally unpleasant memories of the Hungarian occupation of northern Transylvania in the Second World War. The result was that most Romanians believed that whatever Hungarian Transylvanians said about only wanting cultural rights their true aim was to return Transylvania to Hungary.

Ceausescu was too clever just to frighten Romanians with the old Hungarian enemy. It was also necessary to flatter them with stories of their superior antiquity and proven historical greatness, because Hungarians in their turn used Transylvania to support their claims to superiority. Hungarians saw Transylvania as the most advanced part of Romania, and for them it was obvious that the West, the world of Rome, ended at Transylvania's border while the rest of Romania belonged in Byzantium. Transylvanian peasants, whether of Hungarian or Romanian origin, seemed more like yeomen farmers, less like the descendants of serfs that other Romanian peasants often obviously were. Pre-war bourgeois families in Bucharest had tried to engage Hungarian housekeepers because of their cleanliness and efficiency, qualities encouraged in Transylvania's Hungarian Protestant communities. Hungarian Transylvanians were the descendants of a ruling class. They had a long history. They were proud, and like their compatriots in the motherland, found it easy to feel superior at one moment, self-pitying over their fallen fortunes at the next. The history of Romanian Transylvanians was quite different. They were the children of the anonymous 'people' whose very existence had for centuries scarcely been recognised. Those Romanians who did rise to noble rank most likely forgot their origins and became 'magyarised'. Few Romanian Transylvanians moved to the towns, and when the First World War broke out almost all were still living in the countryside. Was it surprising that when provoked by Hungarian arrogance Romanians surrendered to the rage of people who lack self-assurance?

Ceausescu flattered both himself and his people when he told them they had every reason to be sure of themselves. Continuing the nationalist academic traditions of pre-war Romania the regime's historians, among them one of Ceausescu's brothers, elaborated a 2,500-year Romanian history, stretching back to the Dacians who were said to have occupied the entire territory of modern Romania and who, in a phrase of Herodotus that the *Conducator* often quoted, were 'the fairest and bravest of the Thracians'. Ceausescu would speak proudly of the 'centralised state' ruled over by King Burebista at a time when the Magyars were still nomads waiting beyond the Ural Mountains to make their entrance into recorded history. True, he would say, the Romans eventually defeated the Dacians but they had resisted for hundreds of years, and to have been defeated by Rome put them (but not the Hungarians) in the company of the greatest nations of Europe.

Some believe the Romanian Communist regime almost from the start meant to turn Romania into a homogeneous national state. The regime certainly encouraged – for a price – emigration to Israel and West Germany by the Jews and Saxon Germans. By the time of the December revolution the Jewish community had shrunk from its pre-war size of three-quarters of a million to less than 20,000. There were only 200,000 Germans left, and many of them were anxious to leave. (The Romanians, in this at least no different from the Hungarians, preferred not to mention their gypsies, of whom there were perhaps a million.) But the Hungarians and the closely-related Szeklers neither wanted to leave Transylvania nor would Budapest's Communists have cooperated in their resettlement. Romanian policy was instead to chip away at their separate Hungarian identity. Over forty years the Hungarian Transylvanians lost all trace of regional autonomy. Romanians were moved in large numbers into Transylvania until by the 1980s they were replacing many Hungarian officials and factory managers. At the time of Ceausescu's fall there were only two counties that still had overwhelming Hungarian or Szekler majorities. A Romanian held the post of Party first secretary of Hargita County, though four out of five inhabitants were Szeklers. In Covasna the first secretary was a Hungarian married to a Romanian, but he refused to speak Hungarian and gave his son a Romanian name that could not even be translated into Hungarian. It is by such minor but poisonous pinpricks that communities are driven first to hate, and then to kill, each other. Nothing maddened Hungarians more than attacks on their language and the culture that depended on it. The Hungarian-language Bolyai University in Cluj was first merged with a Romanian university and then steadily weakened until by the end of the 1980s only courses in Hungarian language and literature were taught in Hungarian. Of the ninety Hungarian secondary schools that existed in 1956 not one was left in 1989. Ceausescu was as secretive as he was dishonest about statistics but figures for 1980 suggested that under three per cent of Romanian university students came from the Hungarian minority, though the latter made up eight per cent of the country's population. Shortly before Ceausescu fled from Bucharest on 22 December a helicopter dropped leaflets warning that Romanian disunity would mean the loss of Transylvania. It was too late even for that old fear to save the *Conducator*, but he was probably right to believe that most Romanians supported his treatment of the Hungarian minority.

The Hungarian Transylvanian writer Pal Bodor suggested that Ceausescu practised a blend of Stalinism and narcissism. But Ceausescu also encouraged in his people a brand of national narcissism that is always waiting to trap countries that believe their innate greatness has been obscured by the unfair hand dealt them by fate and foreigners. Romanian Communists had made an early ally of the Romanian Orthodox Church by abolishing the latter's old enemy, the 'foreign' Uniates, and handing it their property. Although there were important doctrinal differences between the two Churches even those few saintly priests who had dared to resist Ceausescu became virulent on the subject of the Uniates' crime in dividing the Romanian people. Let there be Uniates – but at no price among Romanians or on Romanian territory. Small wonder the Orthodox hierarchy remained loyal to Ceausescu until the very end. Ceausescu and his wife of course shared their countrymen's instincts, and he never lost the knack of playing on their fears by reciting the most xenophobic passages from the nineteenth-century Romantic poet Mihai Eminescu such as

> He who takes strangers to his heart
> May dogs devour his parts
> May waste devour his home
> May ill-fame devour his name!

But in the end the couple's attitude to Romania was little different from that of Communists who think they speak on behalf of the true interests of the working class, and to that extent replace it. Believing they represented the best of the nation the couple put their own interests above everything else, and their chief interest was to keep the power for which they had developed such a passion. National narcissism was subsumed in their personal narcissism, a process perhaps no less sincere for being sinister. Was there not real indignation in Elena Ceausescu's voice when she protested to the soldiers who bound her wrists before execution, 'You have not the right to tie the hands of a mother. I have raised you like a mother'? Ceausescu flattered Romanian national pride because it suited him. There was a moment towards the end of his rule when he showed signs of distancing himself from Marxism-Leninism, for what need did he have of it as long as he was uncontested national leader? But when other Communist regimes began to crumble he brought back the old Stalinist dogma of class struggle and ordered new editions of the Marxist classics to be printed. By 1989 he was ready to protect his power even by reviving the same Brezhnev doctrine that had crushed Czechoslovakia and in the process made him a Romanian hero because of his fiery protest against it.

GETTING THEIR DESERTS

Jan Masaryk believed that governments get the revolutions they deserve and East Europe in 1989 did its best to prove him right. The revolutions humiliated regimes that had already lost their claim to dignity, but in so doing they inflicted scarcely a bruise, for it was not necessary to rise up violently against governments which, for all their last-minute hesitations, lacked the self-confidence to use violence to stay in power. The bloodshed of the Romanian revolution was real, but it was nonetheless deceptive. It was not so much the violence of a brutal regime determined to stay in power as of a criminal, cornered at last, and exacting his final victims. The game was up long before those sacrilegious boos that interrupted Ceausescu while he was speaking from the balcony of the Central Committee building on 21 December and marked the beginning of the revolution in Bucharest.

The other East European leaders had at first treated Ceausescu the nationalist with suspicion. In the latter years he simply embarrassed them and when they did have to meet him at gatherings of the

Warsaw Pact they did their best to cold-shoulder him. It was unfair, for his rule was in some respects only a caricature of theirs and nowhere more so than in economic policy. At the root of Ceausescu's problems was Bucharest's victory over Moscow in the 1960s in the matter of Romania's economic direction. The old-fashioned structure of steel mills, petrochemical plants, ship-building and other accoutrements of heavy industry that Romania insisted on acquiring, and for which a third of the national income was being reinvested each year at the start of the 1980s, had gradually impoverished Romania as surely it did the rest of the bloc. Like most of his Soviet-bloc colleagues Ceausescu had gone into debt to the West, though by 1980 only to the tune of eleven billion dollars. In 1984, however, he broke with the East European pattern by rebelling against rising interest payments. Declaring them no better than the tribute the Romanian principalities had once paid to the Ottoman Empire he announced that the country's entire foreign debt would be repaid at speed in order to achieve what he called true independence. The decision reflected a grievance common among debtor countries throughout the world, but Ceausescu was driven to act by his understanding of national dignity and also, some Romanians believed, by a latent peasant dislike of owing money. Debt repayment demanded maximum exports and minimum imports. The latter meant that Romanian industry fell even further behind world levels, for little new foreign equipment could be bought. The former meant taking from the Romanian consumer whatever could be sold abroad, above all food. There had been difficulties with food supplies at the start of the 1980s, when fresh meat, cooking oil and rice were scarce even in Bucharest, but eventually food rationing was introduced for many staples, though the ration cards could often not be met. The bread ration in the provinces (where rations were half the level allowed Bucharest) was ten ounces a day. When Gorbachev visited Bucharest in the spring of 1987 the Ceausescus took him to a new market to see stalls piled with fruit and vegetables and a butcher's shop as abundantly hung with pork carcases as Elena Ceausescu's cupboards were with dresses. As soon as the visitors left the real butchers opened up: a plastic bucket on a chair in the doorway – it was wiser not to let customers into the shop – from which a woman scooped out hard to identify bloody bits and pieces, and dropped them into the customers' plastic bags.

Ceausescu had done what none of his Soviet-bloc colleagues

dared: break the unwritten contract between Communists and the working class. Fearful of the consequences of admitting economic failure and the need for sacrifices, the other leaders had gone on borrowing in the West largely to keep living standards artificially high. Even Stalin, in the harsh post-war years when he was driving the Soviet people hard to rebuild the Soviet economy and military machine, had understood the need to humour people by lowering the price of vodka a little every year, for which some older Russians still remember him with fondness. Ceausescu had the nerve to do what the other East European leaders were often tempted to but never dared: treat his working class as harshly as he thought they deserved. It was typical that when building the Bucharest underground he had wanted the stations to be far apart, for he saw the service merely as a way to transport workers from home to factory or workplace and back. He was persuaded with difficulty to allow an extra station in the middle of the city as an obvious convenience of urban life. Four out of every five Romanians lived in the countryside when the Romanian Communists came to power. By 1981 more than half the population was in the towns. It was a pattern familiar through much of the bloc, and encouraged among Party leaders everywhere feelings that the Polish Prime Minister Mieczyslaw Rakowski was unwise enough to put into words when speaking to hostile shipyard workers in Gdansk on the eve of the 1989 election: 'if it weren't for Communism, you lot would still be raising cows'. The regimes quartered their forces among the working class as an occupying army deploys itself in a hostile country. Party cells, union officials and if need be the security service ensured for most of the time a subservient workforce. When during one of Poland's bouts of labour unrest a supervisor at the Ursus factory in Warsaw called his men 'cattle' and warned 'if we can't make you understand then the militia will', he was only putting into words what had always been the Party's unspoken policy: that East Europe's working class was largely a new working class which had not yet acquired what a leading East European ideologist called 'the habits of a true working man', indeed were still little better than a lumpenproletariat, encouraged the Party in its arrogance. The roots of the arrogance that reached its peak in Ceausescu lay in Marxist-Leninist doctrine which made it so easy for Communists to believe that they, not the working class, embodied true proletarian class consciousness.

Ceausescu's most dramatic encounter with his workers came

during the strike of 20,000 miners in the Jiu Valley in 1977 and he remained faithful to the tactics he used then. The miners were angry over the loss of previously established rights concerning working hours, retirement age and disability awards. They also demanded an end to corruption in the health-care system. Ilie Verdet, one of the leaders closest to Ceausescu who was responsible for the valley's important collieries, flew to the scene and was promptly taken prisoner by the strikers, even though the area had been flooded with Securitate men. Ceausescu was in the Villa Neptune by the seaside when he heard the news but quickly set off for the scene of the strike. The miners, supposing Ceausescu would support them once he understood their wrongs, cheered him but their mood changed when he began to prevaricate. In the end he promised them everything they demanded, not least a guarantee that no reprisals would be taken against the strike's leaders. The miners believed him, agreed to return to work the next day, and cheered him as he flew off in his helicopter. Later Ceausescu broke every single promise he had made. It was a tactic regularly used, though on a less spectacular scale, throughout the Soviet bloc. The 1980s saw more strikes in Romania, including an epidemic of labour unrest in Transylvania in 1986 and a minor uprising in Brasov the following year when demonstrators sacked the local Party headquarters and attacked Communist officials. All were dealt with by a combination of temporary concessions followed by reprisals. Fifteen Brasov workers died while being held in custody. Yet Ceausescu till the end believed he could pacify his people with promises. After the first hostile shouts that interrupted his speech on 21 December his wife could be heard urging him to 'promise them something'. He at once proposed an increase in both minimum wages and pensions; bigger child allowances and social security payments; and new maternity allowances.

Had he lost touch with reality? All the Communist leaders of East Europe were tempted by their political beliefs to suppose they could mould reality to fit their wishes. Ceausescu was not unusual in his disregard of economic common sense, though his extreme narcissism made him more wayward than most in this respect. His style of governing did not encourage subordinates to pass on criticism or unfavourable news for he had early on adopted the habits of an Oriental despot who constantly replaces his officials in order to create a chastening mood of insecurity. He was equally careful not to let any officers in the armed forces or *Securitate* (which he played against each other) become too powerful. Long before the regime began to crumble diplomats in Bucharest were calling his reluctance to hear bad news his Achilles' Heel. If people were afraid to keep him properly informed, or if he would not listen to what he did not want to hear, how could the country be properly governed since he took the decisions about every matter of importance?

The grain harvest of sixty million tons predicted for 1989 would in reality amount to little more than eighteen million; milk and egg production in his last years of rule had fallen below the level reached twenty years before. He must have known, because it was his published policy, that supplies of heat and energy had been cut back for seven winters in a row. In the winter of 1988–89 this meant four hours of heating and hot water a day for city apartment houses, and an extra half hour on Sunday. But he had faulty understanding of the effect this and the many other hardships of daily life would have on other policies that he apparently put great store by. Almost as soon as he came to power he banned abortions for women who were under forty-five and had less than five children. Romanians, heirs to the Dacians and Roman legionnaries, were to prove their greatness by multiplying. Yet the increasing hardship of daily life meant there were four times as many abortions as births in 1989, even though most of the abortions were illegal and punishable by jail sentences both for the mother and the doctor or midwife involved. These figures explain why the population of Bucharest decreased that year, for the city recorded more deaths than births. When Ceausescu was dead and Romanians began to open the locked cupboards of their country's shameful secrets one of the most pitiful were the hospital maternity wards. Young women recovering from abortions that had gone wrong said they would happily have died rather than bring another child into the world Ceausescu had made for them. Yet there were signs that the Ceausescus knew the policy was not working, for the anti-abortion laws were tightened in the mid-1980s when the rapid debt repayment began to make itself felt in the growing difficulties of daily life and an unwanted child could easily seem an intolerable new burden. The medical instruments a hospital needed to perform an abortion were locked up and the keys held by the Securitate. Doctors had to make monthly visits to factories to carry out compulsory urine tests on women, sometimes in the presence of *Securitate* agents who stood over them to see the samples were not switched.

During his brief trial Ceausescu was asked why he had humiliated and starved the Romanian nation. In reply he quoted figures to show that Romanians were well fed. 'We have built schools, ensured that there are doctors, ensured that there is everything for a dignified life.' At the very end of the hearing he objected to being called 'the accused'. It was impermissible to call him that, he said, for he was only answerable to the Romanian people, and added, 'Have you not seen how the people cheered when I went to factories?' Is any dictator so entirely calculating and cynical that he can avoid falling victim to the system he creates, and himself remain undazzled by the flattery it so efficiently produces? Ceausescu, after all, had known genuine popularity and until the mid-1980s many Romanians still treated him with awe as the possessor of supreme power and the defender of Romanian independence. Ion Pacepa, Ceausescu's personal head of security who defected to America in 1978, wrote a book whose questionable style weakens its credibility but among its many lurid stories there is one about two of Ceausescu's senior colleagues consoling each other after a tongue lashing. One produces a little box for pills and tells the other he should get one, fill it with shit, and eat some whenever he is on the verge of saying something the Ceausescus do not want to hear. It is possible to despise a courtier and at the same time believe his compliments. Yet when Gorbachev visited Bucharest in 1987 Romanian officials, and presumably Ceausescu too, were worried that the Soviet leader might get more cheers from the crowds than him, and they took care that only reliable citizens saw the two leaders together. Silviu Brucan, the veteran Party member who played a key role in organising the hesitant opposition to Ceausescu, insisted that the dictator knew very well that his position was becoming precarious and for that reason had drawn up plans for what Brucan called 'a war against his own people'. This, he said, was the plan that went into operation when Ceausescu fled from Bucharest, and included the use of snipers armed with telescopic rifles whose task was to decapitate any new government that tried to replace the *Conducator* (the revolution's leaders certainly acted as though they believed this in the days after Ceausescu's overthrow, for they moved around Bucharest in armoured cars and made very few public appearances).

If Ceausescu misjudged the effect of his increasingly harsh policies on the Romanian people, above all of the danger of ignoring the social contract on which East European Communism had come to depend, a large share of the blame must go to his wife. Her role was the most exotic, and to other Communists, most shocking feature of Romanian life. The Russians pretended she did not exist – the Soviet media tried not to show pictures of her – and Moscow was the one foreign capital where she did not invariably accompany her husband. By 1989 she was a member of the Party's seven-strong Permanent Bureau of the Political Executive Committee through which the Ceausescus controlled the country. She was also one of three first deputy Prime Ministers and through other chairwomanships controlled science, technology, education and culture. No other European Communist wife ever acquired such power, though Todor Zhivkov's daughter enjoyed a brief and controversial prominence before dying an untimely death in an accident. The only model was China's Chiang Ching whom Elena Ceausescu had met and one must assume admired during the couple's fateful journey to the Far East in 1971. Elena, believed to be a little older than her husband, belonged to the generation when wives were Communists in their own right, though mystery surrounded the revolutionary credentials of both of them. Officially Ceausescu started his Communist career at fifteen but there was a suspicion that he transferred to himself the pre-1945 underground feats of his elder brother Marin which may have explained why he later kept the latter out of the way in diplomatic posts in Buenos Aires and Vienna (though, true to the rule that few Romanian stories are uncontested, other versions say Marin used Austria for his base as head of the Securitate's European operations). Although Party historians did their best none managed to come up with a flattering record of illegal political activity for Elena. (For what it is worth Ceausescu's brother Nicolae Andruta, head of the Securitate school on the outskirts of Bucharest, claimed at his trial to have surprised Elena during the war naked with her sister-in-law and two German officers.) The Ceausescus had first met in 1939, the year Elena was elected Queen of Labour at the Jacquard textile factory in Bucharest though, if the Ceausescu-era records are correct, she was already a member of the Communist youth organisation at the time. She is said to have been waiting for Ceausescu at the prison gate when he was released in 1944 and they were married soon after.

He was a quite handsome young man, slender, with lively eyes that a journalist who reported on his trial thought ressembled 'two peppercorns'. Those restless, and increasingly distrustful, eyes would remain his most striking feature. She was long-faced, but not unhandsome, though in later years she became the personification of sour suspicion. Both were pure-blooded Romanians and both were poorly educated, two characteristics that distinguished them from many Communist cadres with seniority in the post-war Party. Ceausescu's dislike of intellectuals seems to have begun as a result of encounters in jail with Communists who had enjoyed the education denied to him. He had only four years' primary schooling in his native village of Scornicesti where he first learned the patriotic verse of Eminescu. A few months at the Higher Party School in Moscow after the war, obligatory at the time for any rising East European apparatchik, added little except acquaintance with some of Lenin's pamphlets and Stalin's *Problems of Leninism* which Silviu Brucan believed remained the main source of ideas for the rest of his life. The brilliant and Jewish Brucan was exactly the sort of person Ceausescu disliked. The two men had an early encounter when Gheorghiu-Dej, in the course of grooming Ceausescu, asked Brucan as editor of *Scinteia* to help his protégé prepare two articles for the Party newspaper. Ceausescu's ungrammatical first drafts stunned Brucan and while working together to improve them Ceausescu revealed the depths of his lack of culture, and he never forgave the older man for acquiring the insight. But there was an important difference between Ceausescu and his wife. He, in Brucan's words, was 'shrewd and smart' while she was 'shrewd but stupid'. She was also distrustful, vindictive and cruel, qualities emphasised by her insecurity and the obvious falseness of her own scientific pretensions. Following Stalin's pattern all the East European regimes were anti-intellectual to greater or lesser degree, for the Party leaders knew that Communism had failed to establish a natural hegemony over the best minds of their nations. The system also discriminated economically against all but the most favoured members of the professions. The Romanian regime was no different but Elena Ceausescu added a special poison, and it may be said that her bequest to the country was a traumatised intelligentsia. Asked after the revolution to explain her, a young writer could only mutter that it was impossible to understand how such a woman had existed in the twentieth century.

A member of the Romanian Academy once whispered to a

foreigner that it would be one of the wonders of the world to find someone who had been at university with Elena Ceausescu. The truth was that in the 1950s she took an evening course in chemistry at the Polytechnic, Bucharest's university for the sciences, though all record of this modest achievement was later removed from the Polytechnic's files. She later won her doctorate with a paper on polymers written for her by the Central Institute of Chemistry. Her later scientific works included the names of 'assistants' who were in fact the real authors. Yet these texts were displayed in Romanian bookshops next to her husband's many volumes of speeches and were the basis for her insistent demands for honorary degrees (as well as presents like fur coats) from foreign countries she visited, and which to the shame of Great Britain, among others, she often got. Even the most grudging of these tributes – like the title of 'honorary visiting scientist' from the Society of Polymer Science in New Jersey – were displayed together with the presents and honours given her husband in a special collection at Bucharest's National Museum (an idea probably inspired by the visit to Pyongyang where Kim Il Sung had a museum built to show off the tributes offered to him).

One can only guess at the insecurity induced by deception carried to such extremes. Insecurity of one kind or another was something most Romanian rulers had known: the Phanariot princes who ruled the principalities in the eighteenth and early nineteenth centuries had always lived with their money and treasure packed in trunks ready for a quick getaway. Elena Ceausescu, determined to dominate the world of Romanian science and culture, overcame her insecurity by crippling the work of real scientists, behaving with particular sadism towards the Romanian Academy whose members were supposed to be the finest flower of the country's intellectual and scientific achievement. Ceausescu was the Academy's honorary president and although everyone knew the truth about Elena's scientific achievements she was accepted as a member for fear of the revenge she might take if rejected. It did not help. During the Ceausescu years the Academy lost control of all the fifty institutes that were originally under its direction. Its 230 members dwindled to ninety-three in 1989, with an average age of over seventy, because for fifteen years Elena Ceausescu had refused to allow the election of new members. She humiliated the Academy by refusing it foreign currency to pay either membership dues in corresponding organisations abroad or subscriptions to foreign scientific journals. Its members were not allowed to travel to receive honorary foreign degrees, or to go to embassies in Bucharest to receive them from ambassadors. She ordered the Academy to close 'a modest little restaurant' it maintained (the description of the Academy's last Ceausescu-era President, who clearly felt its loss) saying it would only be used for anti-Party gossip.

By trying to pacify the Ceausescus rather than stand up to them the Academy was following a common Romanian pattern. It was all too easy to imagine the President of the Academy, a sympathetic old man with the ears of a baby elephant and soft brown eyes, doing his vain best to please the implacable Elena. What else but pacify had the Orthodox Church done? The Patriarch continued in this way to the very end, managing even to justify the massacre of Timisoara that led to the uprising in Bucharest. His excuse was that Ceausescu's men had drafted the text and ordered him to sign it. 'We considered,' a regretful Metropolitan said when the Ceausescus were safely dead, 'that our *pièce de resistance* was our sermon about God's existence . . . We did not have the courage to be martyrs. [We thought] you could only be a martyr once, which was useless because the believers needed the life-giving water of God's word.' If very few Orthodox priests criticised the regime openly intellectuals were no more daring. When the writer Paul Goma came into conflict with Ceausescu in the late 1970s the only well-known colleague to support him later recanted under pressure. After the revolution a foreign journalist asked the poet Mircea Dinescu, who had spoken out bravely against the regime, why the Writers' Union did not organise a tribunal to judge those members who had fulsomely praised the Ceausescus. 'But Madam,' Dinescu replied, 'that is half the entire Union and there are some very good writers among them.' The intelligentsia was at first seduced by Ceausescu's nationalism, and now were ready to accept sacrifices it believed necessary to industrialise the country. At the same time there was often little objection to such things as the forced emigration of Romanian Jews or the anti-Hungarian campaign in Transylvania. Much of the intelligentsia treated the Party as a convenient club where membership brought valuable privileges, not the least being the chance to travel. Many had joined in 1968 when, as a literary critic put it, 'the Communists were patriots'. Once in the Party, however, it was difficult to leave because existence was so much harder outside. The attitude that power was there to be asked favours was engrained. Soon after the National Salvation Front had taken power a queue of petitioners formed each day outside its headquarters, some of them hoping to win confirmation of favours already obtained from the Ceausescus. What really hurt the intellectuals who had joined the Party was that the regime nevertheless scorned them. '*Un mépris total!*' exclaimed one writer, still overcome with the horror of losing access to the men with power to grant them a better house or decent medical treatment. In the 1980s Party membership lost whatever meaning it originally had, for it then became almost impossible for any university student of ability to refuse to join. An alternative intelligentsia, almost an alternative establishment, outside the Party, so important in developing the challenge to the Communist regimes and then in smoothly replacing them in Poland, Czechoslovakia and Hungary, simply did not exist in Romania. Instead when Ceausescu went the professional classes moved their tents *en masse* into the camp of the new regime.

There were stubborn men who paid only the necessary minimum tribute. There were groups of actors and artists who tried to keep 'the spirit of culture' alive in private gatherings in their homes. Some Bucharest theatres would submit a plan of politically acceptable productions to the Ministry of Culture but change the programme when they were sure no important Party functionary was in the audience. Others conformed in order to avoid official attention, like the university lecturer who always attended his faculty's political education meetings that consisted only of speeches praising the *Conducator*. He called these his 'monthly crucifixion', was bored and humiliated by it, yet this one act of comformity allowed him to conduct unofficial classes with a group of student friends. The lecturer became a member of the Group for Social Dialogue which was hurriedly created after the revolution by thirty-one of the most stalwart of the country's intellectuals, but it was the sort of organisation that in other East European countries had over years prepared the way for revolution, not followed after it.

When the intelligentsia realised how wrong it had been about Ceausescu it was too late to do anything, and the last half of the 1980s became a nightmare. There was a feeling of complete isolation from the outside world, for people did not dare see even foreign friends who came to Bucharest. These were the years when Ceausescu pushed ahead with his rebuilding of the capital, ringing areas to be demolished with soldiers and often visiting the building sites to direct operations himself. A friend who was born in that part of the city had played as a child on the wooded hill where the Mihai-Voda monastery stood before Ceausescu ordered the building moved and the ground beneath it levelled. He and his friends had called it Arcadia – 'You know – *Et in Arcadia ego*'. For him its disappearance symbolised the end of his dreams for Romania. At first people joked about the Ceausescu family as though they were the creation of some Balkan Charles Addams. The spoilt son Nicu, who was known as 'the little prince', seemed the typical potentate's heir, worshipped by an indulgent mother who kept a large photograph of him in his empty study in the Villa Primavera. Unused packets of Alka-Seltzer in the drawers of daughter Zoia's room in the family house were an accurate indication of the chaotic life she led after setting up in her own apartment. But in the end they were amusing no more, reminding people too much of their terrifying parents. Ceausescu himself, Silviu Brucan believed, had become like Captain Queeg in *The Caine Mutiny*, appearing normal most of the time but showing his instability once he came under pressure. Yet what could be done about it? The Securitate were too efficient to allow intellectuals to form anything like a coherent opposition group as had been done in the rest of East Europe. In 1988 Andre Plesu, the country's foremost literary scholar, met with some of his writer friends to prepare a protest. The following day they were all taken in for interrogation. A brave man (and another future member of the Group for Social Dialogue), Plesu did not believe opposition was possible under such conditions. In the universities students were too wary of informers to talk openly to any but their closest friends, though a few university teachers were ready to risk an informer's report, like the Bucharest professor who told his psychology class, 'I don't need to explain to you what paranoia is. Just switch on your television and you'll see a perfect example.' People waited for something to happen. 'It was like waiting for a train,' Plesu thought. 'You knew it would come, but you didn't know when.' 'We all thought something would happen,' said a friend, 'because the burdens had become too great for everyone.' In such an atmosphere small pleasures like smoking acquired huge importance. A cigarette, my friend explained, gave you the illusion of a few minutes' freedom from the world that Ceausescu had trapped you in. Or you could dream. Eugene Ionesco, waiting to escape from pre-war Romania, had dreamt of getting on a Bucharest tram that dropped him at the entrance to a long passage. He would walk down it and find himself in Paris. A well-known Bucharest journalist also experienced a recurring dream of escape from Ceausesu's Romania, though it was different from Ionesco's in one sinister respect. He would walk to Bucharest's Cosmonaut Square and get on an underground train whose first stop was always Leicester Square. He got out, walked round the square, went to a cinema, reboarded the train at Leicester Square and returned to Bucharest. Once home, however, he was seized with horror. How had he been able to travel to London without a passport? How had he left the country and come back without *them* knowing? Perhaps it was not a good idea even to dream.

THE PEOPLE AND THE PLOTTERS

The young British diplomat had lived for some time in Ceausesu's Romania; he had observed the violent revolution against him at close hand and shared in the exhilaration of his overthrow; but what exercised him most was the problem of truth. You mustn't believe anyone here, he insisted. All Romanians tell lies.

What Anglo-Saxon would not have been exasperated by the storm of claims and counter-claims that soon enveloped the newly liberated country? It is hard to see that it could have been otherwise. Romanians were long used to truth being decided by the powerful. Now that something like democracy seemed to have been established contradictory versions of the truth were legitimate weapons in the struggle to acquire power. And when people had begun to re-establish a sense of dignity after years of humiliation at the hand of Ceausescu someone else's conflicting truth could seem as insulting as a slap in the face. Almost from the moment of Ceausescu's death rival versions of the revolution were used to justify, or contest, the National Salvation Front's claim to be the country's new ruler. One held that it was an elemental, unplanned uprising by a people pushed too far, a popular revolution made glorious by the blood of innocent martyrs. The other interpreted it as essentially the work of plotters who had either controlled the revolution's apparently spontaneous flow, or joined the uprising only in order to hijack it. The most plausible explanation of the events of December 1989 is that they were a combination of the two. There was an uprising of people goaded at last into violence, but there were plotters too. Had there been one without the other the Ceausescus might not have been swept away in December but survived to plague their country for some time longer.

Let us begin with the plotters. For several years a palace coup had seemed the best bet for getting rid of Ceausescu. With the working class pinned down, the intelligentsia thoroughly subdued and the Party no more than the glove on Ceausescu's ruling hand the only people with the power to overthrow him were officers in the Army or *Securitate*. Ceausescu's care to cut all subordinates down to size had not endeared him to either group. Although he developed special units within the Securitate's Fifth Guard and Order Directorate for his personal protection he had not always had good relations with the secret police. Army generals, starved of modern equipment, had no reason to love him. The regime's leading officials knew how bad the economic situation was, and how isolated the country. The West had abandoned it. All the Western ambassadors boycotted the Party congress in November 1989, something they had never done before. No help was to be expected from a Communist world whose members were themselves either on the point of collapse or openly disapproving of Ceausescu. If Silviu Brucan is to be believed some generals had been playing with the idea of a plot at least since 1976. The first had been General Ion Ionita, Minister of National Defence from 1966–76, whose fellow plotters included Brucan, by then in deep disfavour with Ceausescu, and General Nicolae Militaru, another key figure in the events of December 1989 and Minister of Defence in the first post-Ceausescu Government. In 1978 Militaru was dismissed as commander of the Second Army and the Bucharest garrison, apparently because of his contacts with members of the Soviet embassy, though he remained a Government minister until 1984 (Ceausescu expected the Russians to conspire to remove him, and the pre-Gorbachev Kremlin might well have taken the opportunity if it came its way). A coup was tentatively planned when Ceausescu was abroad that year but was spoilt when one of the army units involved was unexpectedly moved away from the capital. Militaru's breakthrough, according to Brucan, came the following year when the retired general, after 'tireless conspiratorial activity in the Army managed to create a breach inside the troops guarding the headquarters of the Central Committee . . . and . . . the presidential palace'. Brucan had been sidelined by Ceausescu since the latter came to power and earned his keep mostly as a university lecturer but it seems there were also other senior officials aware of these early plots. One of them was the physicist Ion Ursu, in 1989 a member of the Political Executive Commitee and Elena Ceausescu's deputy at the National Council of Science and Construction, who had provided the plotters with information about the dates of the *Conducator*'s foreign journeys. It was Ursu who, in spite of diabetes and deteriorating eyesight, helped the Romanian Academy survive by slipping it funds when Elena Ceausescu was not looking. Radu Voinea, the Academy's bruised old President, spoke of Ursu as a hero and had a story to tell about going to see him in his office just two weeks before the December revolution that suggests something of the atmosphere when a feared regime reproaches the edge of the precipice. Leading Voinea out of his office, which both men knew to be bugged, Ursu whispered, 'You know, I believe they are cuckoo.' Voinea, startled, asked whether he meant Nicolae or Elena. 'Both,' said Ursu. 'Both have gone cuckoo.' The two men grinned at each other and, without another word, parted.

But if there were brave men like Ursu, Brucan was by far the most persistent of the few civilian conspirators. His own account of what happened on 22 December and afterwards varied according to the political need of the moment, and was itself a fine example of Bucharest's utiltarian approach to truth. To begin with Brucan denied there had been any plot. If anyone had been plotting, he asked disingenuously in January 1990, 'why be so modest and not claim such a great historical achievement?' At that time the new Government was keen to show it was not simply the old regime minus Ceausescu, but on the contrary was the result of a popular revolutionary act, and therefore possessed a sort of spontaneous democratic authority. A few months later, however, Brucan and Militaru, neither any longer at the centre of power, were happy to show themselves as coup-planners of long standing.

In the first days after Ceausescu's fall Brucan's office, in the Ministry of Foreign Affairs that the Front had taken over as its headquarters, was a rare place of calm and clarity. The city had not yet overcome its dread of the dictator, and was still apprehensive of revenge at the hands of Securitate men on the loose. The Ministry building was ringed with armoured cars and young soldiers, by the look of them country boys ill-prepared to deal with the enemy of snipers with telescopic lenses, and its entrance was invariably thick with desperate petitioners and tobacco smoke. Brucan's handsomely furnished office, long as a cricket pitch, reflected the confidence of its occupant. It signalled that he, at least, had fully grasped the nature of the disorderly events by which he was surrounded. Though seventy-three years old he was sturdy, pink in the face and with almost a boxer's head. In his comfortable sweater and open-necked shirt he might have been taken for a successful New York Jewish businessman dressed for leisure. What he wanted to be seen as was a cool guide to the Byzantine corridors of Romanian life, the hard stone of intellect at the heart of the emotional rhetoric to which both revolutions and Romanians are prone.

Brucan claimed that his years from 1956–62 as Romanian ambassador to the United States and then at the United Nations opened his eyes to the flaws in Communism. Later Ceausescu helped radicalise him further. 'He made me ask how is it that such a criminal and insane man can lead a Communist Party and a country for twenty years.' The answer, Brucan decided, lay in the Party, in Lenin's idea of a monolithic political organisation that was bound to repress both its own members and those outside its ranks. Where that left him politically was not easy to say. He was more moderniser than democrat, putting his hopes in a trained technocracy and fearing the obstructive potential of the traditional working class. He saw little in Romanian history to encourage the belief that the country could quickly take to parliamentary democracy. Having decided Communism was a dangerous dead end Brucan had the guts to do something about it. Apart from his secret contacts with Militaru and other discreet preparatory work he publicly attacked the persecution of the Brasov rioters of 1987. In the spring of 1989 he drafted a letter attacking Ceausescu signed by himself and five of the Party's most celebrated veterans, among them Gheorghe Apostol, a former Party First Secretary; Corneliu Manescu, a former Foreign Minister and one of the architects of Romania's break with Moscow; and the ninety-four-year-old Constantin Pirvulescu who had dared criticise Ceausescu at the Party congress in 1979. It was an unprecedented challenge to the *Conducator*, but all six were protected in some measure as veterans of the pre-war Party, for Ceausescu never went down Stalin's path of murdering venerable Party rivals. Brucan was nevertheless banished to house arrest in a wretched cottage on the city outskirts, and was still there when

Ceausescu fled from the capital on 22 December. Brucan had a high opinion of himself – he thought it natural to bring foreign-language editions of his books to the office, and suggest his visitors take a look at them – but he never supposed he could be the new leader that the conspiracy would bring to power. For one thing he was a Jew, and in Romania as elsewhere in East Europe too many people still thought Jew and Communist were the same thing. Even a less arrogant man could scarcely expect to be loved by the Romanian establishment for having openly criticised the regime when everyone else was silent. And public politics had never been his forte.

Brucan had met some formidable politicians. As an aide to Gheorghiu-Dej he had twice taken part in negotiations with Stalin. He had watched Zhdanov organise the excommunication of Tito at the Comintern's meeting in Snagov. He claimed to be the only Communist ambassador to have had more than a formal acquaintanceship with John Foster Dulles. All this experience was little use when it came to spotting a likely new leader of Romania. Though there were a few dissidents outside the Party, like the plucky Doina Cornea, they were neither well known inside the country nor real political animals. Poetry, the national muse, had done its duty by producing independent spirits like Mircea Dinescu and Anna Blandiana – Dinescu would be among the first to get to the television centre to broadcast news of Ceausescu's overthrow to the nation – but they never had any illusions that they could cope with the devious practicalities of politics. When political parties were established after Ceausescu's fall the two most substantial, the Peasants and the Liberals (both revivals of pre-war parties), were obliged by lack of domestic talent to choose emigrés as their presidential candidates. The experience of the rest of East Europe was that an opposition leadership needed years to mature. It needed time not only to consolidate itself against the Communist regime, but to prepare for the problems involved in replacing it. By 1989 Walesa, Havel and their Polish and Czechoslovak colleagues had been practising and reflecting on politics for twenty years. The relative mildness of the Hungarian regime allowed an alternative establishment to develop outside the Party, and the benign process by which Hungarian Communism collapsed gave its members time to test their strength before taking power. In Romania Ceausescu had kept the grass cut far too low for any significant independent life to exist. If there were traces of the alternative *polis* that the philosophers of the East European opposition had hoped to build beneath the Communist sky it was in the Hungarian and German minorities, or among small religious sects, but they were outside the general life of the country and under constant scrutiny by the authorities. Ordinary Romanians had nowhere to turn, unless it was to the occasional Orthodox priest or monk like the elderly Ilarion Argatu whose spiritual powers drew many people to the monastery on the edge of Bucharest where he had been banished by the Patriarch. For Argatu, a lifelong opponent of Communism, the system was manifest in the evil spirits and magic spells from which he had to free so many of his adherents using the traditional prayers of St Basil. This was politics reduced to superstition. The old monk's explanation of Ceausescu's crimes against his people was that he was not Romanian at all. He was convinced Ceausescu was a gypsy, Elena a Jew.

Small wonder that Brucan and his contacts among the generals never wavered from their belief of the mid-1970s that Ion Iliescu was the only realistic candidate to replace Ceausescu, and in 1989 Iliescu was still the hope of many Romanians who wanted change. Andrei Plesu was among the most distinguished of those who looked to Iliescu. 'For the past ten years,' he recalled after the revolution, 'people were always asking who could come after Ceausescu, and we always all said, let's hope it's Iliescu.' For others, like a young economist who detested Communism, Iliescu was simply 'our last hope'. When Brucan and General Ionita began conspiring in the 1970s Iliescu was the obvious candidate of disaffected Party members. Everyone knew he had broken with Ceausescu in 1971, the year the *Conducator* had begun to go seriously wrong. Iliescu, as the newly appointed Party Secretary for Ideology, accompanied the Ceausescus on their Far Eastern trip that year and he is supposed to have infuriated the couple on the flight home by challenging their newly acquired enthusiasm for Mao's Cultural Revolution and the style and methods of Kim Il Sung. Romania, he pointed out, was not an Asian country. Within months Ceausescu organised an attack on him at a Central Committee plenum and Iliescu was out. There is a story that the Ceausescus wanted to send him to the Romanian embassy in the Central African Republic, ruled at the time by the notorious President Bokassa. Sending people 'to Bokassa' was one of Ceausescu's most feared punishments. It was the fate of a young journalist rash enough to have an affair with Zoia Ceausescu.

Bucharest gossip said he came back little better than a zombie.

Iliescu avoided that fate, probably without too much difficulty. He had the advantage of a railwayman father who had been a founder member of the Romanian Communist Party and, though only forty-one at the time of his fall, was already being talked about as a possible successor to Ceausescu. He had a proper education, albeit in the ill-fated Soviet profession of hydroelectric engineering, and had studied in Moscow as well as Bucharest. Though neither physically striking nor a remarkable speaker (his hand movements were unhappily similar to Ceausescu's) people liked him for his informal, open manner and he continued to win admirers in the provincial Party posts to which Ceausescu banished him. Later he was shifted to running the National Water Council, where he quarrelled with Ceausescu over the latter's desire for a canal linking Bucharest with the Danube, and eventually to the obscurity of a technical publishing house.

If Iliescu was seen by many as a prince in exile he was an entirely silent prince. Not once did he make any public criticism of the regime. He seems to have discouraged the first efforts by Ionita, Brucan and the others to organise a coup, for at that time he still had no interest in changing the Communist system, however much he disliked Ceausescu. Nor is it clear how closely involved he was with Brucan's later schemes. Accused by the Romanian opposition of being a crypto-Communist who tricked his way to the Presidency (that he won overwhelmingly in the May 1990 elections made no difference to this argument) he was unlikely to admit membership of Brucan's conspiracy even if it were true. Not surprisingly he brushed aside Brucan's later revelations, insisting that the Romanian revolution was a 'genuine social explosion'. By the 1980s Iliescu was coming to understand – or so he told people – that the socialist dream had turned into a 'nightmare'. Nevertheless in December 1989 he still seemed a reform Communist at heart, and Brucan admitted that Iliescu was only 'gradually and painfully' coming to accept his assessment of the Leninist Party as the root of all evil. Brucan claimed that he did not ask Iliescu to sign the March 1989 letter of the six Party veterans in order to protect him, and that during the last months he had even avoided chance encounters with him on the streets (though Iliescu seems to have met General Militaru in the summer of 1989, and been questioned by the Securitate as a result). The truth was that Iliescu did not have to do anything to be the obvious replacement for Ceausescu, for there was no other candidate. Only he was opposed to Ceausescu yet acceptable to the Romanian establishment which, whatever formally happened to the Communist Party, would in one shape or another have to go on governing the country for there was no other group capable of doing so.

Here were the makings of the misunderstanding that would poison the revolution. A little group containing experienced political operators and soldiers (with or without the active participation of Iliescu) found their plans for a coup given unexpected life by romantic revolutionaries, though that may not be the right name for men and women who took to the streets with the suddenness of Romanian peasants rising up against their landlords. People who never expected to be revolutionaries found themselves being used to power a plot that someone else had, at least in part, master-minded. These are the threads that pull the apparently chaotic events of the December revolution into meaningful shape, and explain the bitterness and suspicion that haunted the country after the revolution was over.

On the night of 15 December Hungarians in Timisoara, in the south-west corner of Transylvania, surrounded the house of their pastor Laszlo Toekes to prevent police evicting him. Toekes was a courageous critic of the regime, under attack even from his own Hungarian bishop, but no one expected that hundreds of Romanians would the next day join the demonstration to support him. Slogans of 'Down with ration cards!' developed into shouts of 'Down with Ceausescu!' There was a march to the town centre which soldiers and police dispersed but without firing any shots. Timisoara belonged to that part of Transylvania that had not been returned to Hungary during the war. Relations between the two communities were better than in northern Transylvania where Romanians claimed (and this had nothing to do with Ceausescu) that the Hungarians, briefly masters once more, had 'massacred' both Romanians and Jews. Ceausescu reacted predictably to the trouble in Timisoara. He took the involvement of Hungarians as proof that a foreign plot had been launched to topple him, and told the Political Executive Committee that the Timisoara incident was organised by Moscow and Washington with the aim of adding Romania to the list of East Europe's Communist casualties. Scolding the Defence Minister Vasile Milea and Colonel General Iulian Vlad, commander of the Securitate, for failing to use live ammunition at once against the protesters he demanded their dismissal, and threw in the suggestion that they be sent before a firing squad. Sensing opposition to this proposal Ceausescu flew into a rage and threatened to resign, but was calmed by his wife and the tears of colleagues who dropped to their knees to beg him to remain. On 17 December the Timisoara demonstrators were met with bullets. Almost a hundred died, and many more were wounded. Forty of the corpses were brought secretly to Bucharest and cremated.

In spite of rumours that put the number of the Timisoara dead at thousands (the number of those who died in the course of the entire revolution was probably about one thousand) the regime might nevertheless have remained in control of the country for some time longer. Ceausescu himself was confident enough to fly to Iran on 18 December for a two-day visit. But on his return home from Tehran he made two mistakes characteristic of a man out of touch with reality. The first was his address to the nation on television on the evening of his return. Standing stiff as a board in front of a table, his wife, senior ministers and generals ranged on each side as though posing for an Edwardian photograph, he denounced the Timisoara protesters as hooligans, Fascists and foreign agents. And he repeated his theory of a super-power conspiracy to rob Romania of its independence, adding that the country was in even greater danger than it had been in 1968. He may foolishly have believed he could revive the emotions that had brought him real popularity after the Soviet invasion of Czechoslovakia. He was also unwise enough to call a mass meeting on Republic Square outside the Central Committee for the following day, Thursday. It was his second mistake, but perhaps an understandable one, for what danger could there be in it? Most of the crowd that gathered there that morning on the order of their factories and officers expected to take part in another piece of political theatre stage-managed by the Securitate. Although perhaps many in the crowd were angered by Ceausescu's attack on the Timisoara protesters, they still had no idea they were about to become participants in an uprising. A car mechanic went into a restaurant near the square when the meeting began to cheer himself up with a glass of wine. How many more years, he asked himself, would they have to wait before someone had the nerve to shout 'Down with Ceausescu!'? As for the coup-makers, they were no more prescient and were themselves not in the square. It is not clear what stage their own plan had reached. Originally it seems to have involved the use of pistols equipped with silencers firing bullets that stunned but did not kill (for Ceausescu? for his guards? We do not yet know). Militaru apparently tried to get the weapons from a Soviet diplomat, but was told that while Moscow watched developments in Romania with interest it would not intervene itself. Militaru then persuaded the Romanian ambassador in Ankara to obtain them. The necessary guns were found but the ambassador did not have the dollars to buy them: such are the problems of making a coup in a country that has destroyed its own currency. Nevertheless Brucan and Militaru claim to have created by December 1989 a 'military committee of resistance' consisting of some twenty generals in the army, navy and air force, as well as a number of other senior officers. They had made vital further conquests of the officers commanding the 20,000 men of the battalion guarding the Central Committee itself. (These men seem to have been quickly rewarded, for one of the first acts of the National Salvation Front was to promote over thirty senior Army and Interior Ministry officers.) The plotters, however, had not managed to win over any of the commanders of the other troops in Bucharest who remained, as far as the plotters knew, loyal to Ceausescu. What they could not know was that the Defence Minister General Milea, having refused to issue ammunition to the troops in Timisoara on 16 December, would refuse to order the army to fire on the crowds outside the Central Committee on 21 December. Ceausescu had him shot – perhaps even shot him himself – that afternoon, and when the still pro-Ceausescu radio announced early on Friday 22 December that Milea had committed suicide after being unmasked as a traitor many soldiers sensed there was something wrong and gave up any thought of fighting the demonstrators. Milea's behaviour suggests that considerably more members of the military brass were ready, or almost ready, to defy Ceausescu than were known to Militaru. This would explain why the generals commanding troops in the capital so quickly switched to the revolution. They were doing neither more nor less than the rest of the Ceausescu establishment which, apart from part of the Securitate, did not lift a finger to defend their old master. (This rapid and almost total shift of loyalties contributed powerfully to the feeling of the young people who were on the streets that they had been fooled.)

No one was more astonished than Ceausescu when shortly after he had begun to speak there was a loud scream and a commotion, possibly caused by students exploding fireworks. This was the point at which his wife urged him to 'promise something'. Ceausescu continued his speech to a counterpoint of cheers and jeers, referring to the glorious demonstration in the same square in 1968 and warning that 'some people' wanted to bring back unemployment to Romania. Ending with the cry, 'Let us all act to serve the people, independence, and socialism', he retreated, peppercorn eyes darting from side to side, back inside the Central Committee building. No one on the square seemed to know what to do. Riot police formed up in front of the Central Committee. There were shots. Army tanks moved forward, but most of the soldiers seemed reluctant to shoot. Eventually the crowd was driven off the square with water cannon and tear-gas. It was from this moment that the stresses that were to weaken the Romanian revolution became visible, and that all its participants became unwitting accomplices in its partial failure. No revolutions live up to their promise. No revolutionaries are as united as they seem at the glorious moment of storming the barricades of the old regime. Solidarity had to learn this. In Hungary the opposition was a tactical alliance between quite different political currents almost from the start. Even in Czechoslovakia tension between Czechs and Slovaks as well as the usual political differences of opinion that exist in any sophisticated society meant that Civic Forum was never the monolith it seemed during the intoxicating moments of revolutionary theatre in Wenceslas Square and Letna Field. If Romanians reacted with such passionate disenchantment to this reality it was because they were so unprepared for the events of December. Romanian intellectuals and young people were fatally drawn to the idea of purity. Its attraction was understandable to a country that had known only arbitrary and corrupt governments; and some might say it suited the inflammable temperament of the nation. Certainly the neo-Fascist right wing had before the war exploited it with considerable success. The young students and workers who took part in the revolution in Bucharest and other towns like Timisoara and Sibiu where there was also violence were to be forgiven if they believed it an enterprise of sacrificial purity. There were no opposition sages like Vaclav Havel or Adam Michnik from whom they could learn that morality in politics depended on self-restraint rather than passionate pursuit of one's own version of the truth. A notice pinned up in one of the university buildings in

Bucharest suggested both the pathos and myth of the revolution.

> The most beautiful and the most kind of us have died. Let us in their
> memory be true human beings.

Convinced they had taken part in an enterprise of unparalleled
purity, it was all too easy for the young to see betrayal in the return
to reality after Ceausescu's overthrow.

What it felt like to take part in the revolution, believing it was
indeed a people's uprising and knowing nothing of the preparations
of Brucan, Militaru and others, may be judged by this account of
the next few hours by the young Bucharest actor Mircea Diaconu
who, though not as famous as Ion Caramitru, was well known both
from his film and theatre work. A lithe, compact man, Diaconu was
rehearsing a play in his Notara Theatre, five minutes from Republic
Square, when Ceausescu began his speech. Fearing that people
would be scared by the regime's show of force in the square Diaconu
decided something had to be done to 'keep the flame alive' until the
following day. He hoped that by then foreign radio broadcasts would
have informed the whole city of what had happened, but to make
sure he and colleagues set about organising students to go to the
Bucharest factories to urge them to call an immediate strike, and to
gather in the city centre early the next day, Saturday. 'Resistance
points' for students and others to spend the night were set up near
the Intercontinental Hotel, a flashy concrete molar by University
Square that epitomised the false prosperity of the 1970s, and a little
further away at Romana Square.

Diaconu and other self-appointed leaders, among them the young
Rector of the Polytechnic Petre Roman who was soon to become
Prime Minister, spent the night with them. The actors' role was
vital, Diaconu believed, because having no established leaders
people did not know whom they could trust while at least they
recognised the actors' faces. That night brought the worst terror.
The Securitate marksmen shooting from prepared apartments
throughout the city centre made their first assault under cover of
darkness. In the morning Diaconu discovered that other agents had
gone through the crowd killing people noiselessly by striking them
in the back with spiked knuckle-dusters. Soon after dawn, though,
Diaconu saw that the boulevards leading to the centre were full of
workers advancing from the suburbs and that tanks were trapped

in the middle of this human sea. The Government had by then ordered a state of emergency but no one seemed to have paid it any attention. This was the moment the actor and his friends realised they were making a revolution. They moved in the direction of the Central Committee in time to see the helicopter that rescued the Ceausescus flying away from the roof. Army tanks put their guns in the air and the crowd cheered. Diaconu took one tank up to the Central Committee, Caramitru another to the television centre. What Diaconu did not know was that the general in charge of the troops in the square had become the first of the Bucharest commanders to join the uprising, though it is not clear if this was the result of Militaru's lobbying. Diaconu was with Roman and others who entered the Central Committee building, again unaware that the plotters had made that easier for them by nobbling the guard. By two o'clock in the afternoon he was making a speech from the balcony to calm the crowds – there had been talk of burning the building down – 'so that no one should spoil the beauty of the revolution'. Other speakers had messages that were no more precise. The novelist Stelian Tanase, shortly to help found the Group for Social Dialogue, remembers that he talked to the crowd about 'the need for purification by truth, for moral purity and liberty'. At this point Tanase broke down and could only repeat 'liberty' again and again until the people in the square took it up and echoed him so that the word, Tanase believed, must have been heard even at the outskirts of the city (Tanase became one of the Front's earliest critics, calling it 'an authority imposed on the country in a moment of chaos', a remark that makes it plain how people like he failed to grasp that the moment had not been equally chaotic for all).

The two threads of the revolution's story were now mischievously entangled. Brucan, Iliescu, Militaru and some of the others who had arrived at the Central Committee (Brucan on leaving his house in the distant suburbs had first gone to the television centre) were now setting about the creation of the National Salvation Front. If not prepared for precisely this turn of events, they were certainly better placed that others to exploit it. An old member of the pre-war Peasants' Party, long banned by the Communists, was also in the Central Committee that afternoon and though he, too, was unaware of the links that bound some of the Front's founders, he realised that 'power was on the table', and that Iliescu was 'about to steal it from under my eyes'. But while the old plotters re-assembled the actor was still on the balcony coping with Ceausescu's Prime Minister Constantin Dascalescu who had got the idea that he could rehabilitate himself if he spoke to the crowd, and only retreating when he was met by roars of anger. Later Diaconu became preoccupied with people who had got into the building and were stealing food until a soldier shot a gypsy. The body, covered with a sheet, remained on the floor forcing the leaders of the new Romania to jump over it whenever they needed to pass by. When Diaconu and Caramitru were entrusted with the mission of persuading the commanders of the paratroops and armoured units to join the revolution they supposed they were entering virgin territory. It was not quite like that, for the army seemed well on the way to sliding over to the side of the Front. The old plotter Militaru, who was to be appointed the Front's Defence Minister the following day, appeared in the afternoon on television to call on army commanders not to be drawn into Ceausescu's 'crime'. He was followed by a senior officer of the Militia who told his men to use no force and wear a tricolour on their sleeves. One leading soldier, Lieutenant General Victor Stanculescu, who ran the Romanian defence industry, when summoned by the Ceausescu regime to Bucharest on 22 December faked sickness by having his leg put in a plaster cast. That afternoon he had the cast removed and joined the Front. It is not hard to imagine the anxiety of the actor, who knew none of this, when together with his wife and a young student armed with a stick who had offered to guard them he set off for the paratroops' barracks. The commanding general recognised Diaconu and invited them to have coffee. When the cups were brought the suspicious student must have remembered the many stories about Ceausescu's use of poison for he at once got up and said the general should drink first. The general meekly agreed. Paratoops were later despatched to the Central Committee and to the television station, as were tanks from the units contacted by Caramitru. These troops played an important role in beating back the rogue Securitate men's final assaults, though it is unclear whether the actors' role in getting them there was essential.

Was it surprising that young men and women with experiences of this kind treated as a personal insult suggestions that the revolution they thought was theirs had in some way been planned? 'You had to be there to feel the strength of the crowd,' Diaconu said. 'Why, even the snowmen that children had made wore helmets and

carried wooden guns, because they too were fighting for liberty.'
He was overcome by the memory of how good people had been. He
and his wife lived for two days on food provided by others. 'The
country was famished yet people put out tables with food for anyone
who needed it. Shop windows were broken in the fighting but
nothing was stolen and someone wrote up a notice that said "We
aren't thieves".' Diaconu was soon coopted onto the Front's council
but he resigned before long, like many others unable to link the
exhilaration and innocence of what he believed he had seen in
December with the political struggle that followed.

The pictures transmitted from the television centre that afternoon
suggested a nation on the brink of civil war. Corneliu Manescu, the
ex-Foreign Minister who signed Brucan's March letter, incongru-
ously elegant with his beautiful white hair among the crowd of
anorak-coated younger men, begged the soldiers not to open fire on
the people. Look, he said, opening his jacket to reveal a well-
laundered white shirt, we are unarmed. Other speakers sounded as
vague and ill-prepared as those who had spoken earlier from the
Central Committee. 'Be happy, be free, be calm,' one of them urged
the viewers. Another promised that Romania would become 'the
most correct nation in the world'. But when later that afternoon
General Gusa, the Army Chief of Staff, appeared on television with
Iliescu to declare that the soldiers were on the side of the people
there was no doubt the balance of power had turned against Ceausescu. The Patriotic Guard and the Youth Homeland Defence, almost
a million men who were supposed to be trained in Swiss-style
citizens' defence, might never have existed. Not a sound was heard
from them. The revolution took place without violence in the
majority of provincial centres. Sometimes it was as simple as the
old Party bosses slipping out of one door while the Front's men
entered by another. With the Interior Ministry's troops already won
over by Militaru the Securitate was left alone to defend the old
dictator. Its total strength, excluding communications and technical
personnel, was under nine thousand, but if Brucan and Militaru are
correct, some four thousand of these, trained for urban guerrilla
warfare, held the country at bay until the Ceausescus' death on
Christmas Day. According to others, notably Iliescu, even this
figure is too high, for it assumes that all the personnel of the training
school commanded by Ceausescu's brother, the special anti-terrorist
units, the Fifth Directorate and the Securitate's Bucharest City

office took part. By any reckoning they were grotesquely outnumbered, but that did nothing to diminish the terror of those caught up in the fighting. The secret police's evil reputation had been confirmed by the tricky behaviour of their commander General Vlad during the most critical hours of the revolution. He made an ambiguous broadcast in the early morning of Saturday 23 saying that the Interior Ministry had 'rid itself of elements loyal to the Ceausescu clan'. Brucan had met Vlad after his arrest in March when he was taken to the Securitate headquarters on Rahovei Street, and considered him a 'diabolical man' who was not to be trusted. He decided that Vlad was hiding the existence of the secret police's emergency plan and the army quickly put him under arrest.

In Bucharest the fighting took place mainly in the square bounded by the Central Committee, the old royal palace, and the once glamorous Athénée Palace Hotel. Considerable damage was done to the nation's best collections of books and paintings, for which the army's heavier weapons were partly responsible. The area around the Defence Ministry and the television centre to the north of the city in the direction of the Villa Primavera were the other main battlefields. They were well chosen from the Securitate's point of view and the army was on one night at least hard-pressed to defend the TV building. Fear was magnified by uncertainty and rumour. No one knew if the army would fight well, for it was well known that Ceausescu had kept it indifferently equipped and trained. The realisation that the Securitate marksmen were moving around out of sight in underground tunnels between prepared hideouts increased the sense of still being in the grip of a much feared monster. That Ceausescu had escaped alive compounded the panic for it was not until the evening of 23 December that Iliescu went on radio to announce that the couple had been captured. Their helicopter had dropped them seventy miles north-west of the capital. Trapped almost at once, they were taken to a military base that soon came under attack from secret-police rebels who were trying to release him. Nothing better suggests the uncertainty of the new Romanian leaders than their decision to have the couple speedily tried and executed. They, too, were not sure of the army's capability as a fighting force. Some of the Front leaders did want to wait and to hold a proper civil trial under calmer conditions. Brucan and a majority of the others, arguing there was too great a risk that Ceausescu might be rescued, voted for speed. One may suppose another reason was fear that people who had been so quick to abandon Ceausescu would rally again to his side if they thought he was about to make a comeback. The trial and execution took place on Christmas Day. It was a sordid business, with the faces of the prosecutor and judges not shown on the video film broadcast on Boxing Day, but the couple were not without dignity. Till the very end Ceausescu treated his accusers as coupmakers in the pay of foreign powers. The people's tribunal, as the court described itself, mixed the grave with the trivial in its accusations. The Ceausescus were taken to task for their daughter Zoia weighing meat for her dogs on 'golden scales' (in fact they were gold-coloured). The prosecutor's nervousness was obvious in the often insulting tone: 'Elena Ceausescu, doctor, engineer, Academician, you usually have a lot to say, why are you silent now?' The sentence described them as 'two snobbish tyrants' and contained a battery of charges. They had starved the people in the name of scientific nutrition; built 'Pharaonic edifices'; exhausted the country's riches; neglected the army; and for twenty years carried out 'genocide' against the Romanian people (it was later alleged that the Ceausescus had killed 60,000 people during their rule, but it was unclear who they were, and how and when they died). The court did not mention the words Communism, Marxism-Leninism, or the Party. The defence lawyer was scarcely heard.

Their death had the result the country's new leaders hoped for. The terrifying marksmen began to surrender, though one group of seventeen held out in tunnels under the centre of the city until 18 January when hunger forced them to emerge through a manhole cover on the Boulevard Magheru. When the first of them climbed out and put his gun down on the pavement terrified passers-by forced the cover on again and stood on it until the police arrived. The evil forces were exhausted but they left behind a divided, apprehensive nation, as ill-prepared for life after Ceausescu as it had been for the revolution that removed him.

Survivors

One morning in the early spring of 1988 I found myself in Belgrade waiting for Mikhail Gorbachev to pay his respects at the tomb of Marshal Tito. The creator of the post-war Yugoslav state chose to be buried in the office he kept on the grounds of his house. Though lying under a marble slab and surrounded by municipal garden plants, the Marshal evidently remained at his post, an impression sustained by his collection of peacocks and rare fowl which still roamed the garden. Watching them scratch and preen, a learned colleague remembered another unusual bird. While studying in Prague in the 1960s he met an old Czech lady who, as a little girl, had seen a parrot that once belonged to Emanuel Schikaneder, the librettist of Mozart's *Magic Flute*. Was that really possible? A quick calculation suggested it was. Parrots have been known to live in captivity for as long as eighty years. Schikaneder died in 1812. The old lady could have seen the creature when she was five, or even ten. Had Schikaneder taught the parrot to say anything? And would it have made sense to a small Bohemian child who heard it over half a century later?

I feel sympathy for that venerable polly. Anyone who knew East Europe during its forty years of Communism is in danger of becoming a Schikaneder's parrot, a survivor whose words may be too strange to be properly understood. In one way it is good that the things we learned will, with luck, make little sense to those who did not experience them directly. I have books filled with notes taken in planning offices and foreign ministries, the record growing sketchier as the conversation wandered deeper into familiar deserts of statistics and platitudes. So much of what both foreign visitor and local inhabitant lived through was sham, though it was sham sustained by force and grounded in a powerful will. It was ridiculous but at the same time stifling. It overwhelmed. The pleasure of escaping from it is like coming out of a dark, chill forest into a meadow lit by sunshine, and knowing you will never have to retrace your steps. Travelling to Prague or Bucharest it is no longer necessary to carry telephone numbers and addresses of acquaintances on those slips of paper that, in the old days, could never be parted with. Today you can telephone whom you like without fearing that the call might get them into trouble. The feeling has gone of visiting people suffering from what seemed almost certainly an incurable disease. They described symptoms you knew you would never observe in yourself. You asked sympathetic questions. 'Where does it hurt most? There? And there? And there, too?' The answers also went into the notebook. Perhaps seeing them written down gave comfort, though one knew the visit could also cause annoyance. In one of his *Samizdat* essays Ludvik Vaculik complained of Western journalists' 'nonchalant, offensive compassion,' their 'cheap arrogance born of safety and well-being.' Like so much else in the Communist world, the relationship of lucky Westerner and unfortunate East European was irremediably poisoned. To be free of it is an immense relief.

Work began quickly to get rid of the litter left by four decades of Party rule, with the new capitalism sometimes acting as demolition man. Eighteen firms submitted bids to take down the five-ton red star from the top of the parliament building in Budapest. Uniforms of the once so alarming Hungarian Workers' Militia were sold in the West for $700. A Romanian soldier's uniform marked with powder burns from the December revolution fetched three times as much. Factories and farms named after Lenin, Red Star, or November 7 (the three most popular in Communist Hungary) were rechristened. Streets recovered their pre-war names. The worn-out equipment of the factories and the cities' long-neglected houses were another matter. What could be done with antique industries, like those of Budapest's Csepel district, created by the Jewish entrepreneur Baron Manfred Weiss and largely preserved by the smokestack-loving Communists? The Hungarian scholar-politician Gaspar Miklos Tamas proposed turning them into 'an industrial museum of the nineteenth century' and leaving them 'for our grandchildren as a monument of human stupidity.'

There was, though, a great deal of the past that could not be so easily disposed of. Nostalgia, incurably perverse, embraced some of the remnants of Communism. Soon after the November revolution *Lidove Noviny*, the Czechoslovak *Samizdat* paper, moved into a building in Wenceslas Square that had long served as newpaper offices and was linked by a system of pneumatic tubes to the nearby offices of CTK, the government news agency. Installed one hundred and fifty years before, the apparatus still worked, which pleased the new occupants who would have found such sturdy old technology useful in their days of illegality. They also discovered a painting, life size and in socialist realist style, of a uniformed member of the People's Militia guarding a factory. They joked that if one of their staff misbehaved it would be enough to stand him in front of the Militiaman and take his photograph.

In this case a detested past was tamed by making it endearingly ridiculous. But that past also held the attention because so much had been invested in it. The experiment that was forced on East Europe was a terrifying mismatch of means and ends. That it was a mismatch – that it contained old human dreams turned by arrogance and lethal lack of charity into their opposite – was the clue to why it was still possible to look back on it with compassion. The tragedy of East Europe was that there were decent men among those who imposed Communism, and that it took so long for them to understand that they had taken the wrong turning to the promised land. Some of the new leaders, Vaclav Havel and Lech Walesa prominent among them, had never joined the Party, but many members of the old opposition had once believed in the Communist experiment. There was always an element of family feud in their struggles. Sometimes sons and daughters battled against fathers and mothers. Often it was a struggle against one's earlier or other self. The enemy was not always an anonymous apparatchik. At *Lidove Noviny,* when they brought out a postcard with their new address, they chose a drawing of two men shaking hands, one saying to the other, 'Good-bye, self-censorship. I shall miss you sometimes.'

There was also guilt, which could not be renamed, or pulled down, or displayed in a museum. Not long after Ceausescu's fall, Romanian television showed the Stanley Kramer movie *Judgement at Nuremberg.* The next day I met an old acquaintance recently retired from his job as a journalist. Had I seen the film? he asked, adding with an embarrassed grin that it 'posed some tricky questions.' He did not compare himself to the Germans whose complicity in Hitler's crimes the Kramer movie probes. He had done nothing more than write about foreign affairs. 'I only had to praise Ceausescu's disarmament policy. I did not have to praise *him*.' He smiled again, for he knew it was not a satisfactory answer. Dressed in an overcoat of cheap rough cloth that was no protection against the deep winter frosts, unable to get medicine for his chronically ill mother, what had he got from his small concessions to the regime? Yet guilt had sapped his self-assurance. He had been in the centre of Bucharest on 21 and 22 December and had still not quite recovered from his amazement. 'Frankly, I was surprised. I did not know we Romanians had it in us.'

The sense of having been accomplices, the feeling – as another Romanian said – that 'we are all guilty,' undermined self-confidence throughout East Europe. In his first speech as the new Prime Minister of East Germany, Lothar de Maizière said that 'the unending entanglement of many men and women in guilt and expiation . . . has left its mark on the face of our people.' Sometimes the awareness of guilt was precise. An official of the Bulgarian Interior Ministry, commenting on a decision by the Writers' Union not to declassify the Ministry's archives concerning its members, explained that the writers had taken it 'so as not to fall out with each other when they learn who informed on whom.' After Ceausescu's overthrow an indignant Western visitor asked why Romanian writers did not throw out of their union those members who had sung the dictator's praises. 'There were too many, madam,' replied a distinguished poet who had dared criticise the regime, 'and some of the country's greatest talents among them.' The failure of Romania's intellectual elite to produce coherent opposition to the dictator was something of a special case, but in all the countries of East Europe there were hundreds of thousands who had been informers for the secret police, or who used their Party membership to make careers at the expense of rivals. The net of complicity, however, reached far wider than that.

The Czechoslovak Chartist and Catholic Vaclav Benda, writing during the days of Communist rule, has supposed that

> The regime sees loyalty not as consensus, but as 'collective guilt', decently rewarded. The degrees of collective guilt and its rewards are graduated, but everyone has a share in it, from the most insignificant worker right up to the prime minister.

The German de Maizière agreed:

> We must all share the responsibility. It was only a few who ever dared
> to vote in opposition in the elections or to abstain altogether. Everyone
> should ask himself if he always did everything correctly and what
> lessons he has to learn from this.

This process of interrogation produced some spectacular casualties among men and women who had hoped to make a career in
the new democracies, and de Maizière was prominent among
them. Within months of guiding East Germany to unification with
the West in 1990 and becoming minister without portfolio in the
new government of the united Germany, he was forced to resign in
the face of allegations that he had worked as an agent for East
Berlin's Ministry for State Security.

Equally worrying was the realization of many less well-known
people that they, too, had not entirely preserved their honour
under the old regimes. Vaclav Benda had pointed to the danger of
what could happen if this huge body of accomplices was ever
aroused: they might want to 'exact revenge for their squandered
lives' and 'wash away their guilt in a bloodbath.' If the new
governments avoided witch-hunts it was partly because they were
so well aware of the danger. By identifying the stern angels of
Communist revolution as the bringers of past evil, the philosophers of East European opposition seemed to have inoculated at
least the new political class against the impulse to take revenge.
Vaclav Havel typically advised Czechoslovaks during the 1990
election to vote for 'decent, modest, matter-of-fact' people, and
avoid those 'whose eyes shine with fanaticism.' He suggested the
new zealots would most likely be those who were the old regime's
meekest accomplices.

> The longer someone is humiliated, the longer he serves against his
> conscience, the longer he allows himself to be pushed to breaking
> point, the more a kind of anger accumulates within him – anger not
> only toward the one who humiliated him but anger toward himself.

Havel was not afraid to remind the Czechoslovaks that 'a
relatively great part' of them had succumbed to 'the fanatical spell'
of Communism in 1948. He pointed out that the Czechs who had
sometimes taken violent revenge on the Sudeten Germans after

World War II were often those who collaborated most closely with the Nazis during it. As if to rub that home, one of his first acts as President was to apologise to those Germans who, regardless of what they had or had not done, were driven out of Czechoslovakia after the war. By mentioning the Germans Havel was enlarging the problem of guilt and revenge to include East Europeans' relations with their neighbours.

It was here that the Communist legacy passed from being a weight on the private conscience to burdening the body politic. The contours of the three main burdens of the Communist past have been hinted at throughout this account of the decline and fall of the Soviet Union's European empire. They were the dead weight of centrally planned economies guided by political whim and dogma rather than economic reason, a dead weight that included the unsuitable attitudes and skills of workers and managers as much as out-of-date plant and machinery; the threat to new democracies from the stress and pain that could not be avoided if Communism's economic mistakes were to be corrected; and national passions, suppressed by the old regimes but now released and vulnerable to exploitation by any manipulator of popular moods.

The latter was perhaps the most obvious danger. What was it the Hungarian journalist Pal Bodor said? 'In East Europe we all feel guilty, and we all point the finger at someone else.' He had been thinking chiefly of the Hungarian dispute with Romania over Transylvania in which, though each side was convinced of the justice of its cause, neither was guiltless in its behaviour towards the other. Almost as soon as new governments were settled in Budapest and Bucharest, the Transylvanian question re-emerged as an issue around which national passions could be mobilised on both sides. A supposed Hungarian 'threat' to Transylvania gave fuel to the emerging Romanian right wing led by the Vatra Romaneasca, a nationalist organization founded in January 1990 to oppose granting full rights to the Hungarian minority. It was not long before voices were heard in Budapest demanding the reconstruction of the Trianon memorial, built seventy years earlier as a reminder of the 1920 treaty that took Transylvania from Hungary and gave it to Romania. Removed by the Communists in 1945, the monument's base had been inscribed with Mussolini's dictum that 'peace treaties are not eternal.'

There was a long list of other disputes and grudges that had been avoided or bowdlerised in Communist texts but were vividly remembered. In these quarrels, some actual, some historical (though scarcely less explosive for that), the moderation of men like Havel, Michnik, and the Hungarian Janos Kis had less effect. Old wounds had not healed; old blood-stirring rhetoric was not forgotten. Among these points of guilt and anger were: Poland's grab for Teschen (to Poles, Cieszyn) when Czechoslovakia was at Hitler's mercy; the Slovaks' treatment of their Hungarian minority (and of course the Hungarians' treatment of the Slovaks when they were the masters); Slovaks' resentment at what they saw as their second-class status in the pre-war Czechoslovak republic turning rapidly, after 1989, into demands for Slovak sovereignty if not outright independence; everyone's uneasiness about their behaviour towards the Jews combined, paradoxically, with a persistent anti-Semitism that showed itself in East Europe's first free elections; everyone's preference for keeping silent about Gypsies; Poland's uneasiness about how it treated its pre-war Ukrainian minority, more than a matter of historical justice now that an independent Ukraine was no longer a fantasy; the reluctance of Poles as well as Czechs to address the justice, or lack of it, in the post-war expulsion of Germans, and in Czechoslovakia's case Hungarians, too; Romania's readiness to join in the suppression of the Hungarian uprising in 1956; Poland and Hungary's acceptance of the Soviet invasion of Czechoslovakia in 1968.

Although there was a network of compulsory economic links, most of them routed through Moscow, four decades of Soviet domination had created few new natural ties between the countries of East Europe. If anything connected them it was still these old grievances which, forced below the surface, had put down deeper roots and trapped the half-continent in a tangle of claims and counter-claims far more vital than the formal structures of Soviet empire. It was not a propitious background against which to tackle Communism's economic legacy. The chief problem for the new governments was how to introduce the market disciplines to which they were committed without lowering the living standards of the majority of the population (that a minority might be seen to do spectacularly well out of the changeover threatened to make it even more unpopular). The answer was it could not be done. The old regimes had either, like Poland's, lived beyond their means or, like the more cautious Czechoslovaks, off the fast-dwindling investments of earlier generations. Only in this way could the Communists keep full employment and prevent a rapid collapse in living standards. They left the bills for their successors to pay. Poland was the first to try to restore economic sanity when, at the start of 1990, the Mazowiecki government stabilised and made convertible the Polish currency, thereby slowing inflation, putting goods back in the shops, and balancing the budget. The price was a collapse in production, a fall in real incomes, and unemployment. This was the future facing all the countries of the region as they prepared for economic reform.

Just how difficult it would be to bring these economies into the modern world was shown by the former East Germany's experience after unification and the introduction of the Deutschmark. Although Erich Honecker's Germany was the most efficient of the Communist economies, its labour productivity turned out to be only a third of West Germany's. One result was that by the end of 1991 only four and a half million East Germans had full-time jobs, half the number of two years before. Social peace was assured only by huge transfers from the government in Bonn, amounting to $88 billion in 1991 alone.

East Germany was unique in having this life-support machine while it conducted the dangerous switch to the market. It also had in the West German business community an unrivalled pool of potential buyers for its state industries. But in the rest of East Europe change proceeded less quickly than had first been hoped. Privatization, in early discussions, had sometimes seemed only a matter of selling off state industries to the citizens at large. Realization came slowly that some state enterprises were worthless; that much of the population lacked either the resources or inclination to become capitalists overnight; and that there was a severe lack both of the necessary legal infrastructure and of trained personnel to carry out the transformation.

Economic problems put a huge strain on new systems of parliamentary democracy that would have been difficult to set up and operate even under much more favourable conditions. The temptations of nationalism added to that strain. Only Poland and Czechoslovakia had produced opposition organizations that could claim to link intellectuals and working people. Polish Solidarity had an honourable ancestry stretching back to the mid-1970s, when intellectuals first rallied to support striking workers and their families victimised by the regime. Czechoslovakia's Civic Forum had only taken shape during the very last days of the old regime. Hungary, Romania, and Bulgaria produced nothing similar. It was obvious that the new democracies would have difficulty building the nationally based political parties that were needed to support governments committed to vexatious but essential reforms.

East Germany, once again, was odd man out, for West German political parties were on hand with programs, organization, and money, all of which were much in evidence in the Christian Democrats' victory in the East German elections in 1990. In Poland, Solidarity's unity cracked, leading to presidential elections at the end of 1990 in which Lech Walesa ran against Premier Mazowiecki, his adviser since Solidarity's birth in the Lenin shipyard in Gdansk. This contest, unthinkable even only a year before, symbolised the separation of two strains in Solidarity, the Prime Minister representing above all the liberal, democratic intelligentsia who had masterminded the anti-Communist opposition, while Walesa was the hero of patriotic, Catholic, working Poland. Adam Michnik and other celebrated ex-colleagues of the new president had never been sure of Walesa's attachment to democracy, and they now attacked him as a populist with dictatorial tendencies. In the event, Walesa was himself almost outflanked in the election's final round by a hitherto unknown Polish-Canadian businessman called Stan Tyminski.

The latter's twenty-five-per-cent share of the vote underlined the moral of Walesa's own victory over the conscientious but scarcely colourful Mazowiecki. It was a moral with meaning for the whole of East Europe. The demagogue Tyminski played on the fears of ordinary Poles who did not understand the economic and social revolution into which they had been plunged – and not without reason, for no one had warned them that these were inevitable side-effects of democracy and independence. Tyminski's success was all the more alarming because he was at the very least exploited by survivors of the old Communist regime. When Havel, re-elected for a second term as president in July 1990, spoke at the end of that year of the 'dissatisfaction, nervousness, insecurity and disillusionment' in his country, he might have been describing the whole region. In Czechoslovakia one result was a flare-up of Slovak resentment against Prague, partly because the economic reform threatened to have particularly harsh consequences in Slovakia, partly because nationalism seemed to offer security at a time of growing uncertainty. Hungary's dissidents had never had extensive roots in the nation at large. The Hungarian Democratic Forum, led by Premier Jozsef Antall, and the Association of Free Democrats, though the two biggest parties in the parliament elected in the spring of 1990, failed to develop proper memberships. By the end of 1991 both had lost their earlier lead in opinion polls – the consequence of parties that were fragile in the first place trying to edge towards painful policies.

Romania offered a novel variation on the same theme. The ruling National Salvation Front of President Ion Iliescu was in some respects little more than the old Romanian establishment freed of the Ceausescus and their extreme narcissism and paranoia. From the beginning the Front used populist techniques to keep a grip on the working class and to force opposition parties to the sidelines. In June 1990 it summoned miners from the Jiu Valley to Bucharest to beat up opposition demonstrators (in effect, anyone who looked like a student or intellectual).

The roots of the difficulties facing East Europe lay in the Communist past. East Europeans had emerged from a grinding, demoralising experience but, as is often the fate of survivors, they were ill-suited to the world they could now enter by virtue of their survival. The result was a state of mind not easily understood by outsiders. East European countries often pointed an accusing finger at the Western world they were now so keen to join. Western irresolution had delivered them into Hitler's hands. After the defeat of Nazi Germany the West had surrendered them to the Soviet Union. The belief that the East had suffered so that the West might flourish was even older than that. East Europe had shielded the West from Ottoman Turks and Russian tsars, and paid the price in its own relative backwardness. According to this view of the past, the damage done by forty years of Soviet domination was only the latest chapter in the history of Eastern sacrifice.

The ending of the isolation of the last forty years was a cause for anguish as well as joy, for it revived all the old East European doubts about their ability to match the Western world that had drawn advantage from their misfortune. A young Romanian academic suggested that the almost complete isolation imposed on his country by Ceausescu was the worst of his crimes. With no one to compare themselves to, their lively imagination turned Romanians into far more remarkable people than they really were. 'We thought we were the best husbands, the best fathers, the best sportsmen: simply the best.' In the weeks following the revolution Romanians had a chance to look at themselves in the world's mirror; the result was a loss of confidence that was almost total. Romania was an extreme case, for it was more completely cut off from the outside world than any other country in the Soviet bloc, but the same tension existed between national pride and national uncertainty throughout East Europe.

The emigré Poles from whom I learned Russian could have taught me some of this had I known how to listen to them. They could have explained why, to this day, the briefest mention of Yalta in a newspaper will provoke letters to the editor, often several pages long and in none too certain handwriting, that rehearse the old arguments of the West's betrayal of Poland to Stalin at the end of the war. Those Poles could have taught me much more besides, but it is a necessary mechanism of survival that human beings do not easily overcome the gaps of age, origin, and experience that separate them. To be aware of everything would be unbearable. In the end, survivors must live with the burden of knowing that their words may make little more sense to others than the shriek of a parrot that has outlived its master by almost a hundred years. But it is our duty to try to understand them. The future of the Western democratic world depends on whether we accept that duty or merely offer, in Ludvik Vaculik's cutting words, the 'offensive compassion' that has always been good fortune's sop to the unfortunate.

Index

A NOTE ON THE AUTHOR

Mark Frankland was born in London and studied at Cambridge University and at Brown University in the United States. After a brief time in the British Foreign Office, he joined the staff of the *London Observer* in 1962 as correspondent from Moscow. He has been with the *Observer* since then, writing from Washington, Tokyo, and Saigon as well as locales in Eastern Europe and the Soviet Union. He has twice received the British Press Award for foreign reporting and is also the author of *The Sixth Continent*, a study of the Soviet Union at the start of the Gorbachev era, and of a biography of Khrushchev.